Praise for *Black Mass*

"A parable of what happens when law enforcement officers get too close to their informers. It is a story that the FBI almost succeeded in suppressing. *Black Mass* should prompt a re-evaluation of the uses and misuses of informers by law enforcement officials throughout the country."
—Alan Dershowitz, author of *Reversal of Fortune: Inside the Claus Von Bulow Case, The New York Times Book Review*

"This is a heartbreaking and enraging story of corruption and crime, but it has its heroes, especially Dick Lehr and Gerard O'Neill. These reporters were among the first to shine light on the shadowy collusion of heinous murderers and an FBI cut loose from its moral center. Now, with this powerful book, Lehr and O'Neill bring the whole story into the open. *Black Mass* is a work of rare lucidity, high drama, journalistic integrity, and plain courage."
—James Carroll, author of *An American Requiem* and *Boston Globe* columnist

"More than an exposé on the abuses of power, *Black Mass* tells of the shameful betrayal of all things decent.... Lehr and O'Neill give us all the details with a journalistic precision that does not sacrifice the power of the story. After reading *Black Mass*, you might wonder if any of us really knows who are the good guys and who are the bad guys."
—Michael Patrick MacDonald, author of *All Souls: A Family Story from Southie*

"What a marvelous read *Black Mass* is."
—Dominick Dunne, author of *Justice: Crimes, Trials and Punishments*

"A jaw-dropping, true life tale of how two thugs corrupted the FBI ... a disturbing account of corruption, blind ambition, and official complicity in dark deeds."
—*The Baltimore Sun*

"You don't have to be a Mafia buff to enjoy and appreciate the story as told in *Black Mass*.... *Black Mass* is all about the nation's premier law enforcement agency gone bad, with two or more of their own leading the way.... What makes *Black Mass* simply great is not the fantastic reporting and writing of the sordid story, but the way the two authors bring readers into the world of South Boston. The story reveals the parochial 'clan' attitude that prevails in the neighborhood where one's word is higher measure of a man than his life's accomplishments.... It is a great story, a great book, and a rare look at how deadly boyhood friendships in a neighborhood like 'Southie' can be."
—*The Providence Journal*

"The book is a great read—it reels you in and holds you. O'Neill and Lehr have the remarkable ability to put you in the room and on the street where the action takes place. The dialogue is vital, gutsy, down and dirty."
—William Bratton, author of *Turnaround: How America's Top Cop Reversed the Crime Epidemic* (with Peter Knobler), *The Boston Globe*

"[Lehr and O'Neill] vividly capture the turbulent culture and conflicting loyalties of the Boston underworld."
—*Library Journal*

"*Black Mass* is the hair-raising true story of the cozy and corrupt relationship between the FBI, Bulger, and his sidekick Steven the 'Rifleman' Flemmi ... an unholy alliance that shifted the balance of criminal power in Boston from the Italians to the Irish and left Bulger and Flemmi shielded from prosecution for two decades.... Lehr and O'Neill assemble a breathtaking account of corruption, crime, and gross legal negligence."
—*The Legal Times*

"A triumph of investigative reporting, this full-bodied true-crime saga by two *Boston Globe* reporters is a cautionary tale about FBI corruption and the abuse of power."
—*Publishers Weekly*

"An eye-opening true-crimer.... The authors offer a pile of evidence that (in South Boston at least) politics is all too local."
—*Kirkus Reviews*

"*Black Mass* tells a story of abuse of power and betrayal by those sworn to protect the public and uphold the law. It leaves me wondering whether standard operating procedures and agent-informant relationships throughout the country should be reviewed."
—*The Federal Lawyer*

"The corruption laid out by Lehr and O'Neill is pervasive and horrifying enough to make even the most inveterate cynic gag."
—*The Boston Phoenix*

BLACK MASS

THE IRISH MOB, THE FBI, AND A DEVIL'S DEAL

DICK LEHR AND **GERARD O'NEILL**

PUBLICAFFAIRS LTD

Oxford

Originally published in the United States by PublicAffairs™, a member of the Perseus Books Group, 2000.

Photo credits: *James J. "Whitey" Bulger Jr.* / Richard Bergeron, Quincy, Massachusetts police department; *Former FBI agent John Connolly* / *Boston Globe* staff photo by George Rizer; *Stephen J. "the Rifleman" Flemmi* / police surveillance photo; *Donato "Danny" Angiulo . . .* / FBI photo; *An early arrest photo of Bulger* / *Boston Globe*; *Frank Salemme . . .* / *Boston Globe* staff photo by John Tlumacki; *Flemmi* / FBI photo; *Gennaro J. Angiulo . . .* / *Boston Globe* staff photo by Jim Wilson; *John Connolly Jr., . . .* / *Boston Globe* staff photo by Ted Dully; *Boston FBI supervisor . . .* / FBI photo; *John M. Morris . . .* / *Boston Globe* staff photo by Tom Herde; *Millionaire Roger Wheeler . . .* / FBI photo; *Edward Brian Halloran* / Boston police photo; *By 1984, Bulger . . .* / *Boston Globe* staff photos by John Tlumacki; *FBI wanted poster . . .* / FBI web site; *Catherine Greig and Bulger, 1988* / *Boston Globe* staff photo by John Tlumacki; *James J. "Whitey" Bulger* / FBI photo.

For information, address PublicAffairs, PO Box 317, Oxford OX2 9RU, UK.

Book Design by Mark McGarry, Texas Type & Book Works, Inc.

A CIP catalogue record for this book is available from the British Library.

1–903985–29–3 (pbk)

First PublicAffairs Ltd Edition

10 9 8 7 6 5 4 3 2 1

For my sons, Nick and Christian Lehr

.

For my even keel wife Janet and my sons, Brian and Shane O'Neill

Contents

PART THREE

Prologue

ONE SUMMER DAY in 1948, a shy kid in short pants named John Connolly wandered into a corner drugstore with a couple of his pals. The boys were looking to check out the candy at the store on the outskirts of the Old Harbor housing project in South Boston, where they all lived.

"There's Whitey Bulger," one of the boys whispered.

The legendary Whitey Bulger: skinny, taut, and tough-looking, with the full head of lightning-blond hair that inspired cops to nickname him Whitey, even if he hated the name and preferred his real name, Jimmy. He was the phantom tough-guy teen who ran with the Shamrocks gang.

Bulger caught the boys staring and impulsively offered to set up the bar with ice cream cones all around. Two boys eagerly named their flavors. But little John Connolly hesitated, heeding his mother's instructions not to take anything from strangers. When Bulger asked him about his abstinence, the other boys giggled about his mother's rule. Bulger then took charge. "Hey, kid, I'm no stranger," he told Connolly. "Your mother and father are from Ireland. My mother and father are from Ireland. I'm no stranger."

Whitey asked again: What kind of cone you want?

In a soft voice Connolly said vanilla. Bulger gladly hoisted the boy onto the counter to receive his treat.

It was the first time John ever met Whitey. Many years later he would say the thrill of meeting Bulger by chance that day was "like meeting Ted Williams."

Introduction

In the spring of 1988 we set out to write for the *Boston Globe* the story of two brothers, Jim "Whitey" Bulger and his younger brother, Billy. In a city with a history as long and rich as Boston's, brimming with historical figures of all kinds, the Bulgers were living legends. Each was at the top of his game. Whitey, fifty-eight, was the city's most powerful gangster, a reputed killer. Billy Bulger, fifty-four, was the most powerful politician in Massachusetts, the longest-serving president in the state senate's 208-year history. Each possessed a reputation for cunning and ruthlessness, shared traits they exercised in their respective worlds.

It was a quintessential Boston saga, a tale of two brothers who'd grown up in a housing project in the most insular of Irish neighborhoods, South Boston—"Southie," as it was often known. In their early years Whitey, the unruly firstborn, was frequently in court and never in high school. There were street fights and wild car chases, all of which had a kind of Hollywood flair. During the 1940s he'd driven a car onto the streetcar tracks and raced through the old Broadway station as shocked passengers stared from the crowded platform. With a scally cap on his head and a blonde seated next to him, he waved and honked to the crowd. Then he was gone. His brother Billy set off in the opposite direction. He studied— history, the classics, and, lastly, the law. He entered politics.

Both made news, but their life stories had never been assembled. So that spring we set out with two other *Globe* reporters to change all that. Christine Chinlund, whose interests lay in politics, focused on Billy Bulger. Kevin Cullen, the city's best police reporter at that time, looked into Whitey. We swung between the two, with Lehr eventually working mostly with Cullen and O'Neill overseeing the whole affair. Even though we usually did investigative work, this project was seen as an in-depth biographical study of two of the city's most colorful and beguiling brothers.

We'd all decided that central to Whitey Bulger's story was his so-called charmed life. To be sure, Whitey had once served nine years of hard time in federal prison, including a few years at Alcatraz, for a series of armed bank robberies back in the 1950s. But ever since his return to Boston in 1965 he'd never been arrested once, not even for a traffic infraction. Meanwhile, his climb through the ranks of the Boston underworld was relentless. From feared foot soldier in the Winter Hill gang, he'd risen to star status as the city's most famous underworld boss. He had teamed up along the way with the killer Stevie "The Rifleman" Flemmi, and the conventional wisdom was that they were taking an uninterrupted underworld ride to fame and riches because of their ability to outfox investigators who tried to build cases against them.

But by the late 1980s the cops, state troopers, and federal drug agents had a new theory about Bulger's unblemished record. Sure, they said, the man is wily and extremely careful, but his Houdini-like elusiveness went beyond nature. To them, the fix was in. Bulger, they argued, was connected to the FBI, and the FBI had secretly provided him cover all these years. How else to explain the complete and utter failure of all their attempts to target him? But there was a catch to this theory: not one of these theorists could show us proof beyond a doubt.

■ ■ ■

TO US, the idea seemed far-fetched, even self-serving.

For Cullen, who lived in South Boston, it cut against everything then known about a gangster with a reputation as the ultimate stand-up guy, a crime boss who demanded total loyalty from his associates. It defied the culture of Bulger's world, South Boston, and his heritage, Ireland. The Irish have long had a special hatred for informants. We'd seen, some of us more than once, the famous John Ford 1934 movie *The Informer,* with its timeless and unmatched portrayal of the horror and hate the Irish have for a snitch. More local was a South Boston wiretap that became a classic in the city's annals of wiseguy patter. The secret recording captured one of Bulger's own underlings talking to his girlfriend.

"I hate fuckin' rats," John "Red" Shea complained. "They're just as bad as rapists and fuckin' child molesters." And what would he do if he found an informant? "I'd tie him to a chair, okay? Then I'd take a baseball bat, and I'd take my best swing across his fuckin' head. I'd watch his head come off his shoulders. Then I'd take a chainsaw and cut his fuckin' toes off.

"I'll talk to you later, sweetheart."

This was Whitey's world, where feelings about informants cut wide and deep, from the lowbrow to the high. Even brother Billy voiced a more refined version of Red Shea's sentiments. In his 1996 memoir, he recalled the time when he and some boyhood chums were playing baseball and broke a streetlight. The kids were told they'd get the ball back once they identified the offender. None broke rank. "We loathed informers," wrote Billy Bulger. "Our folklore bled with the names of informers who had sold out their brethren to hangmen and worse in the lands of our ancestors."

Since this was Whitey's folklore too, the four of us back in 1988 were flat-out incredulous about the informant theory. We turned the idea over and inside out and decided, no way. The claim had to amount to nothing more than the wild and reckless flailings of embittered investigators who'd failed in their bid to bust Whitey Bulger. The idea of Bulger as informant seemed preposterous.

But the notion nagged, an irresistible itch that stayed close to the surface. What if it were really true?

The big news in Boston in 1988 was the presidential candidacy of Massachusetts Governor Michael Dukakis, but all during these months of presidential politics we grew more intrigued and committed to the Whitey story. So Cullen went back out. Lehr joined in. There were more interviews with the investigators who'd stalked Bulger and tried to build cases against him. The investigators painstakingly reviewed their case-work, all of which ended the same way: Bulger walked away, uncharged and unscathed, laughing over his shoulder. They talked about a certain FBI agent, John Connolly, who, like the Bulgers, had grown up in Southie. Connolly had been seen with Whitey.

We wrote to the FBI in Boston and requested, under the Freedom of Information Act, intelligence files and material on Bulger. It was a formal-ity; that the request was stonewalled came as no surprise. But we certain-ly could not write a story reporting that Bulger was an FBI informant. We had only the strong suspicions—but with no proof—of others in law en-forcement. No confirmation was forthcoming from inside the FBI. The best we had, we decided, was a story about how Bulger had divided local law enforcement. It would be a piece about cop culture, with troopers and drug agents always coming up short and then hinting at their dark suspi-cions of the FBI. In a way, Bulger had divided and conquered; he'd won.

■ ■ ■

THE BOSTON underworld and the interplay between investigators in-volved ghost stories, smoke and mirrors; the idea of Bulger as an infor-mant still seemed unlikely to us. Nonetheless, we launched a final round of reporting to test what we'd learned on our FBI sources. The gist of that reporting is described in chapter 16 of this book. In the end we were in-deed able to confirm, from within the FBI, that the unthinkable was true: Bulger was an informant for the FBI and had been so for years.

The story in September 1988 was published to heated denials from local FBI officials. In Boston, FBI agents were used to playing the press, feeding information to reporters thankful for a scoop that, of course, made the FBI look good. In this context, it came as no surprise that the Boston FBI acted offended, betrayed. And many people accepted their de-nials; after all, who was more believable? The FBI, the stand-tall G-men who'd been getting good ink for taking down the Italian mob? Or a group of reporters whom the FBI portrayed as having an ax to grind? With the utter unlikeliness of Bulger being an informant and the sheer vehemence of the FBI denials, the story was seen as speculation, not the dark truth.

Nearly a decade would pass before the FBI was required by court order to confirm what it had steadfastly denied for so long: that Bulger and Flemmi had in fact been informants, Bulger since 1975 and Flemmi since before that. The disclosures were made in 1997 at the outset of an unprecedented federal court examination of the corrupt ties between the FBI and Bulger and Flemmi. In 1998 ten months of sworn testimony and stacks of previously secret FBI files revealed a breathtaking pattern of wrongdoing: money passing hands between informants and agents; obstruction of justice and multiple leaks by the FBI to protect Bulger and Flemmi from investigations by other agencies; gift exchanges and extravagant dinners between agents and informants. Many of the agents' remarks featured an unmistakable arrogance—as if they owned the city. It was easy to imagine the FBI and Bulger and Flemmi celebrating their secret, holding their wineglasses high and toasting their success in outwitting the state troopers, cops, and federal drug agents who'd tried to build a case against them, never realizing the fix was in.

■ ■ ■

OF COURSE, the Bulger case does not mark the first time trouble involving agents and their informants has exploded publicly for the FBI. In the mid-1980s a veteran agent in Miami admitted to taking $850,000 in bribes from his informant during a drug trafficking case. Better known is the affair involving Jackie Presser, the former Teamsters Union president, who served as an FBI informant for a decade before his death in July 1988. Presser's handlers at the FBI were accused of lying to protect him from a 1986 indictment, and one FBI supervisor was eventually fired.

But the Bulger scandal is worse than any other, a cautionary tale that is, most fundamentally, about the abuse of power that goes unchecked. The arrangement might have made sense in the beginning, as part of the FBI's war cry against La Cosa Nostra (LCN). Partly with help from Bulger and, especially, from Flemmi, the top Mafia bosses were long gone by the

1990s, replaced by a lineup of forgettable benchwarmers with memorable nicknames. In sharp contrast, Bulger was the crime boss who, throughout the years, was the constant fixture in the underworld. Whitey was the household name, and he and Flemmi the varsity players.

"Top echelon informant" means an informant who provides the FBI with firsthand secrets about high-level organized crime figures. FBI guidelines require that informants be closely monitored by FBI handlers. But what if the informant begins to "handle" the FBI agents? What if, instead of the FBI, the informant is mainly in charge, and the FBI calls him their "bad good guy"?

What if the FBI takes down the informant's enemies and the informant rises to the top of the underworld? What if the FBI protects the informant by tipping him off to investigations conducted by other police agencies?

What if murders pile up, unsolved? If working folks are threatened and extorted, with no recourse? If a large-scale cocaine ring, time and again, eludes investigators? If elaborate government bugging operations, costing taxpayers millions, are leaked and ruined?

This could never happen, right, a deal between the FBI and a top echelon informant going this bad?

But it did.

Today we know that the deal between Bulger and the FBI was deeper, dirtier, and more personal than anyone had imagined, and it was a deal that was sealed one moonlit night in 1975 between two sons of Southie, Bulger and a young FBI agent named John Connolly.

DICK LEHR AND GERARD O'NEILL
Boston, April 2000

BLACK MASS

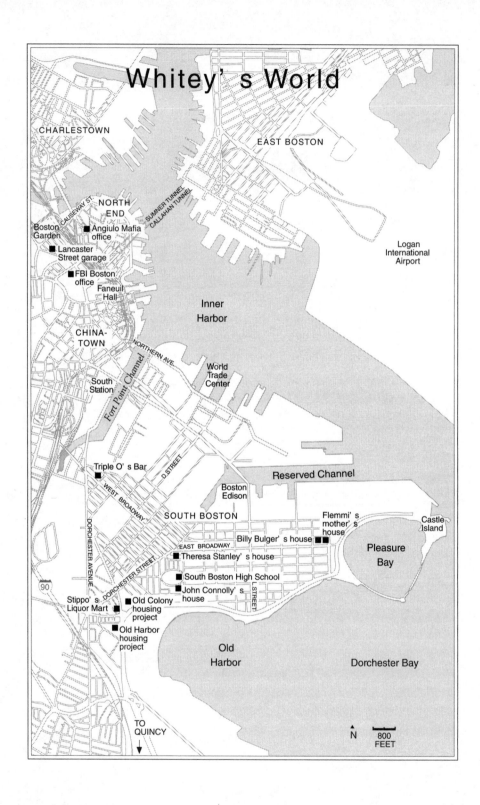

PART ONE

The Prince of Darkness is a gentleman.

WILLIAM SHAKESPEARE (ACT III, SCENE 4),
KING LEAR

CHAPTER ONE

1975

Under a harvest moon, FBI agent John Connolly eased his beat-up Plymouth into a parking space along Wollaston Beach. Behind him the water stirred and, further off, the Boston skyline sparkled. The ship-building city of Quincy, bordering Boston to the south, was a perfect location for the kind of meeting the agent had in mind. The roadway along the beach, Quincy Shore Drive, ran right into the Southeast Expressway. Heading north, any of the expressway's next few exits led smack into South Boston, the neighborhood where Connolly and his "contact" had both grown up. Using these roads, the drive to and from Southie took just a few minutes. But convenience alone was not the main reason the location made a lot of sense. Most of all, neither Connolly nor the man he was scheduled to meet wanted to be spotted together in the old neighborhood.

Backing the Plymouth into the space along the beach, Connolly settled in and began his wait. In the years to come Connolly and the man he was expecting would never stray too far from one another. They shared

Southie, always living and working within a radius of a mile of each other in an underworld populated by investigators and gangsters.

But that came later. For now Connolly waited eagerly along Wollaston Beach, the thrum of the engine a drag to the buzz inside the car that was like an electric charge. Having won a transfer back to his hometown a year earlier, he was poised to make his mark in the Boston office of the nation's elite law enforcement agency. He was only thirty-five years old, and this was going to be his chance. His big moment in the FBI had arrived.

The nervy agent was coming of age in an FBI struggling with a rare public relations setback. In Congress inquiries into FBI abuses had confirmed that the late FBI director J. Edgar Hoover had for years been stockpiling information on the private lives of politicians and public figures in secret files. The FBI's main target, the Mafia, was also in the news. Swirling around were sensational disclosures involving a bizarre partnership between the CIA and the Mafia, also unearthed during congressional investigations. There was talk of a CIA deal with mafiosi to assassinate Cuba's Fidel Castro, and of murder plots that involved poisoned pens and poisoned cigars.

Indeed, it suddenly seemed like the Mafia was everywhere and everyone wanted a piece of the mysterious and somehow glamorous organization, including Hollywood. Francis Ford Coppola's movie masterpiece, *The Godfather, Part II,* had played to huge audiences when it opened the year before. A few months earlier the picture had won a slew of Oscars. Connolly's FBI was now deeply into its own highly publicized assault on La Cosa Nostra (LCN). It was the FBI's number-one national priority, a war to counter the bad press, and Connolly had a plan, a work-in-progress to advance the cause.

Connolly surveyed the beachfront, which at this late hour was empty. Occasionally a car drove past him along Quincy Shore Drive. The bureau wanted the Mafia, and to build cases against the Mafia, agents needed intelligence. To get intelligence, agents needed insiders. In the FBI the measure of a man was his ability to cultivate informants. Connolly, now seven years on the job, knew this much was true, and he was determined to become one of the bureau's top agents—an agent with the right touch. His plan? Cut the deal that others in the Boston office had attempted, but without success. John Connolly was going to land Whitey Bulger, the elusive, cunning, and extremely smart gangster already a legend in Southie. The stylish FBI arriviste wasn't the type to take the stairs. He was an elevator man, and Whitey Bulger was the top floor.

The bureau had had its eye on Bulger for some time. Previously, a veteran agent named Dennis Condon had taken a run at him. The two would meet and talk, but Whitey was wary. In May 1971 Condon managed to elicit extensive inside information from Whitey on an Irish gang war that was dominating the city's underworld—who was allied with whom, who was targeting whom. It was a thorough, detailed account of the landscape with an accompanying lineup of key characters. Condon even opened an informant file for Whitey. But just as quickly, Whitey went cold. They met several times through the summer, but the talks didn't go well. In August, reported Condon, Whitey was "still reluctant to furnish info." By September Condon had thrown up his hands. "Contacts with captioned individual have been unproductive," he wrote in his FBI files on September 10, 1971. "Accordingly, this matter is being closed." Exactly why Whitey ran hot then cold was a mystery. Maybe the all-Irish nature of the intelligence he'd provided had proved discomforting. Maybe there was a question of trust: why should Whitey Bulger trust Dennis Condon of the FBI? In any event, the Whitey file was closed.

Now, in 1975, Condon was on the way out, his eye on his upcoming retirement. But he'd brought Connolly along, and the younger agent was hungry to reopen the Whitey file. After all, Connolly brought something to the table no one else could. He knew Whitey Bulger. He'd grown up in a brick tenement near the Bulgers' in the Old Harbor housing project in South Boston. Whitey was eleven years older than Connolly, but Connolly was oozing with confidence. The old neighborhood ties gave him the juice others in the Boston office didn't have.

Then, in an instant, the waiting was over. Without any warning, the passenger side door swung open, and into the Plymouth slipped Whitey Bulger. Connolly jumped, surprised by the suddenness of the entry, surprised he was caught unaware. He, a trained federal agent, had left his car doors unlocked.

"What the hell did you do, parachute in?" he asked as the gangster settled into the front seat. Connolly had been expecting his visitor to pull up in a car alongside him. Bulger explained that he had parked on one of the side streets and then walked along the beach. He'd waited until he was sure no one else was around, and then he'd come up behind from the water.

Connolly, one of the younger agents on the prestigious Organized Crime Squad, tried to calm himself. Whitey, who'd just turned forty-six on September 3, sat in the front seat, larger than life, even if he just barely hit five-feet-eight and weighed an ordinary 165 pounds. He was hard-bodied and fit, with penetrating blue eyes and that signature blond hair, swept back. Under the cover of darkness, the two men began to talk, and then Connolly, properly obsequious to a neighborhood elder who was also an icon, made his offer: "You should think about using your friends in law enforcement."

■ ■ ■

THIS was Connolly's pitch to Whitey: you need a friend. But why?

In the fall of 1975 life in the city was tumultuous and changing unpredictably. From where they sat along the vacant beach, the two men could see the Boston skyline across the water. At the time the citizens of Boston were electrified by the unexpected good fortunes of their Red Sox. Yaz, Luis Tiant, Bill Lee, Carlton Fisk, Jim Rice, and Fred Lynn—who, after the season, would be honored as both the rookie of the year and the American League's most valuable player—were in the midst of a glorious run for the World Series title against the powerful Reds of Cincinnati.

But closer to home the world was dark and unstable.

The nightmare of busing had begun its second year. In 1974 a federal court order to bus black students from Roxbury to South Boston High School in order to achieve racial balance in the city's segregated public schools had turned the neighborhood into a war zone. The rest of the country tuned in, and people were getting to know Southie through televised images and front-page newspaper photographs featuring riot police, state troopers patrolling school corridors, rooftop police snipers, and legions of blacks and whites screaming racist chants at one another. The Pulitzer Prize in photography was awarded for a jaw-dropping 1976 pic-

ture of a black man being rammed with an American flag during a distur-
bance outside of city hall. Nationwide the neighborhood was seen
through a prism of broken glass—a bloodied first impression that was
searing and horrific.

Whitey's younger brother, Billy, was in the middle of it all. Like all the
neighborhood's political leaders, Billy Bulger, a state senator, was an im-
placable foe of the court-ordered busing. He never challenged the court's
findings that the city's schools were egregiously segregated. He did, however, strongly oppose any remedy that forced students to travel out of
their home school districts. He'd gone to Washington, D.C., to complain
and present their case to the state's congressional delegation, and once
there, he delivered a speech to a group of anti-busing parents in the pour-
ing rain. He hated the view outsiders were getting of his neighborhood,
and he denounced the "unremitting, calculated, unconscionable portrayal
of each of us, in local and national press, radio and television, as unrecon-
structed racists." To him the issue was his neighbors' legitimate worry for
the welfare and education of their children. Back home Billy Bulger spoke
out regularly against the unwanted federal intervention.

But busing would not go away, and the summer just ended had not
gone well. In July six young black men had driven to Carson Beach in
South Boston and ended up in a fight with a gang of white youth that left
one black hospitalized. In his younger days John Connolly had been a lifeguard along the beaches of South Boston, just as Billy Bulger had been before him, and now the sandy beaches had become another battleground.
On a Sunday in August police helicopters circled over Carson Beach and
Coast Guard boats patroled offshore while more than one thousand black
citizens drove to the beach in a motorcade of several hundred cars. They
were accompanied on their "wade-in" to the beach by more than eight
hundred uniformed police officers. The cameras rolled.

By the time Connolly had arranged to meet Whitey along Wollaston
Beach, the schools had reopened. Student boycotts and fights between
blacks and whites were regular events. Thinking it might help ease the
racial tension, officials for the first time tried to integrate the football team
at South Boston High School. But the four black players who reported to
the first practice had to do so under police protection.

The neighborhood was torn apart, and Connolly knew that, could feel that pain, because it was his neighborhood as well, and he had played off this bond in lining up his meeting with Bulger. But while the bond might have gotten him an audience with Whitey, he now had to pitch a deal to his boyhood hero. Connolly most of all wanted to exploit the wider underworld troubles brewing between the Boston Mafia and a gang Bulger had signed on with in neighboring Somerville. Bulger, in charge now of the rackets in Southie, had hooked on with the Somerville crime boss Howie Winter. The gang operated out of a garage in the Winter Hill section of the small city just across the Charles River to the west. In the past year Whitey had paired off with another member of the gang, Stevie "The Rifleman" Flemmi. They got along, found they had certain things in common, and had begun to hang out.

By the time Connolly and Bulger met, the young FBI agent had done his homework. He knew Bulger and the Winter Hill gang were facing a two-pronged threat from a local Mafia that for decades was controlled by the powerful underboss Gennaro J. Angiulo and his four brothers. Pending at that moment was a dispute between the two organizations over the placement of vending machines throughout the region. There had been wiseguy bluster about shoot-outs as a way to settle the matter. With all this instability, Connolly argued, a wiseguy could use a friend.

Besides, Angiulo was wily and inscrutable. He had a knack for setting up for arrest those he no longer had any use for. For example, a few years earlier a mob enforcer had veered out of his control. Angiulo, the story went, had reached out to his contacts inside the Boston Police Department, and the mob renegade was soon picked up on phony gun charges after crooked cops planted weapons in his car. No one knew for certain whether Angiulo in fact had the kind of access to manipulate an arrest like that. But this was the story making the rounds, and Whitey Bulger and the rest of Howie Winter's gang believed it. As Connolly well knew, perception was all that actually mattered.

Bulger was clearly concerned about Angiulo setting him up. "What if three cops stop me at night and say there was a machine gun in my car," Whitey had complained. "Who is the judge gonna believe? Me or the

three cops?" Connolly had positioned himself to play off such crosscur-
rents of underworld paranoia.

The two men sat in the Plymouth, the city lights rippling on the water.
You should use your friends, Connolly stressed, a line that caused Bulger
to consider the agent intently, sensing an opening for the upper hand.

"Who?" Whitey said at last. "You?"

"Yeah," replied Connolly to a ruthless man who used up people and
threw them away. "Me."

■ ■ ■

CONNOLLY'S proposal was simple: inform on La Cosa Nostra and let the
FBI do the rest. Bulger knew, Connolly recalled, "that if we were chewing
on the Mafia, it was very difficult for the Mafia to be chewing on them."

In fact, the moment Connolly had indicated he wanted a meeting
Bulger knew what the FBI wanted. For weeks Bulger had already been
working the proposition over in his mind, weighing the pros and cons,
figuring the angles and potential benefits. He'd even gone and consulted
with Stevie Flemmi. Bulger brought up the subject one day when the two
of them were in Somerville at Marshall Motors, the auto repair shop
owned by Howie Winter. The one-story garage was a faceless building
made of cinder blocks. It resembled a concrete bunker and served as a business front for the gang's wide-ranging illegal enterprises, which since 1973
had expanded to include fixing horse races up and down the East Coast.

Bulger told Flemmi that the FBI agent John Connolly was making a
bid for his services. "What do you think?" Bulger asked Flemmi when the
two were alone. "Should I meet him?"

The question hung in the air. Flemmi later decided that, if Whitey
Bulger was confiding in him about an FBI overture, he was signaling that
he already knew something about Flemmi's own secret "status." Flemmi
had a history with the Boston FBI, and what a history it was. He was first
enlisted as an FBI informant in the mid-1960s. Flemmi adopted the code
name "Jack from South Boston" for his dealings with his FBI handler, an
agent named H. Paul Rico (who was Dennis Condon's partner).

Rico, a dashing senior agent who favored a Chesterfield topcoat and French cuffs, cultivated Flemmi because of his access to the New England Mafia. Flemmi was not a made Mafia member, but he knew all the leading players and was frequently in their company. The Mafia liked Flemmi, a former army paratrooper who went from a juvenile detention center at age seventeen to serve two tours of duty in Korea with the 187th Airborne Regimental Combat Team. He had a reputation as a tough killer, even if he was only average in height, five-feet-eight, and in weight about 140 pounds. Flemmi worked on his own, out of his Marconi Club in Roxbury, a combination bookie joint, massage parlor, and brothel, where he got messages, took calls, and held meetings. A popular guy with his curly chestnut hair and brown eyes, a guy who enjoyed cars and the late-night company of young women, Flemmi got around.

Even the New England godfather, Raymond L. S. Patriarca, revealed a fondness for him. In the winter of 1967 Flemmi was summoned to Providence. He dined with Patriarca and Patriarca's brother Joe, a lunch that lingered long into the afternoon. They talked about family. Patriarca asked Flemmi where his parents were from in Italy. They talked about business. Patriarca promised to steer cars to the new auto body shop Flemmi had opened. They talked a bit about Flemmi's brother, Jimmy the Bear, who was in prison serving time on an attempted murder rap. In a gesture of goodwill, Patriarca gave Flemmi $5,000 in cash to put into the auto shop.

Back in Boston, Flemmi mostly moved around with a boyhood pal, Frank Salemme, whose nickname was "Cadillac Frank." The two had grown up in Roxbury, where Flemmi's family lived in the Orchard Park housing project. His father, Giovanni, an immigrant from Italy, had worked as a bricklayer. Flemmi and Salemme worked the streets together as enforcers, bookmakers, and loan sharks. They frequented the North End, the tight-knit Italian neighborhood where underboss Gennaro Angiulo had his office, and they often ended up at late-night blowouts in the company of hard-drinking Larry Zannino.

Zannino was the brutal and bloodless mafioso whom Angiulo relied on to bring muscle to the Boston LCN enterprise. In turn Zannino relied on Flemmi and Salemme to put some of his loan-sharking money out on the street. But while everyone liked Stevie, the feeling was not mutual. Flemmi didn't trust the North End, not Angiulo and especially not Zannino. When drinking with Zannino, Flemmi would pace himself, careful not to let down his guard. But Zannino and the others didn't notice, and they took Flemmi further in. There was the night, for example, in the summer of 1967 at Giro's Restaurant on Hanover Street, a night spent with a lineup of local wiseguys. Zannino, Peter Limone, Joe Lombardi. Flemmi was with Salemme. They ate, drank, and then Zannino insisted they retire to a near-by bar, the Bat Cave.

Over more drinks a slobbering Zannino and Limone indicated that they'd all decided to sponsor Flemmi and Salemme "for membership in our organization."

Peter Limone, swaggering, then put his arms around Flemmi and Salemme. "Ordinarily, before you're a member you'd have to make a hit," confided the senior mobster, "and I'd have to be with you as your sponsor to verify that you made a hit and report how you handled yourself. But with the reputation you two have, this may not be necessary."

Flemmi wanted no part of joining the Mafia, however, and resisted the recruitment drive. For one thing, he didn't like the brutal Zannino, who was capable of hugging you one moment and blowing your brains out the next. The same could be said for Angiulo. Besides, Flemmi had Rico, and Rico had Flemmi.

Given the gang war and all the shifting alliances, Flemmi's life was always up for grabs. More than once he'd told Rico he "was a prime target for an execution," and in other reports Rico noted that Flemmi had no permanent address because if "the residence becomes known, an attempt will probably be made on his life." Flemmi grew to rely on Rico to alert him to any trouble the FBI might have picked up from other informants.

More than that, Flemmi came to expect that Rico would not push him about his own criminal activities—not his gaming or his loan-sharking, or even the killings. In the spring of 1967, following the disappearance of gang-ster Walter Bennett, Flemmi told Rico, "The FBI should not waste any time looking for Walter Bennett in Florida, nor anyplace else, because Bennett is not going to be found." Rico then asked what actually happened to Bennett. Flemmi shrugged off the inquiry, telling Rico there wasn't any "point in going into what happened to Walter, and that Walter's going was all for the best." Rico simply let the matter go at that. By the late 1960s Flemmi was a suspect in several gangland slayings, but the FBI never pressed him hard to talk about the murders.

In early September 1969 Flemmi was finally indicted by secret grand juries in two counties. He was charged in Suffolk County for the murder of Walter Bennett's brother William, shot to death in late 1967 and dumped from a moving car in the Mattapan section of Boston. Then in Middlesex County, Flemmi, along with Salemme, was charged in a car bombing that had blown off a lawyer's leg.

Just before the indictments were handed down, Flemmi received a phone call.

It was early in the morning, and Paul Rico was on the line. "It was a very short, brief conversation," Flemmi recalled. "He told me that the indictments were coming down, and he suggested that me and my friend leave Boston—leave immediately—or words to that effect."

Flemmi did just that. He fled Boston and spent the next four and a half years on the lam, first in New York City and then mostly in Montreal, where he worked as a printer at a newspaper. During that time Flemmi often called Rico, and Rico kept him posted about the status of the cases. Rico did not pass along any information about Flemmi's whereabouts to the Massachusetts investigators who were trying to track him down.

Even though Rico had instructed Flemmi that he was not to consider himself an employee of the FBI and had gone over with Flemmi some of the FBI's other ground rules for informants, the agent and Flemmi regarded most of those instructions as an annoying formality. What was important was that Rico had promised Flemmi he would keep confidential the fact that Flemmi was his informant, and this was the key to their alliance. It was a pledge most agents customarily gave to their informants, a pledge viewed as "sacred." But in Rico's hands the promise was sacred above all else, even if it required that he commit the crime of aiding and abetting a fugitive. Rico promised that as long as Flemmi worked as his informant he would see to it that Flemmi wasn't prosecuted for his criminal activities.

For obvious reasons, such a deal had proven advantageous for Flemmi. He also liked how Rico did not treat him like some kind of lowlife gangster. Rico wasn't the pompous G-man ready to spray the room with disinfectant immediately after he'd left. He was more like a friend and an equal. "It was a partnership, I believe," said Flemmi.

Eventually the criminal charges against Flemmi were dropped, after key witnesses recanted, and in May 1974 Flemmi was able to end his fugitive life and return to Boston. With the help of the FBI, he'd survived the gang wars and outlasted the murder and car bombing charges. But Flemmi had no intention of going straight. Once back in Boston he'd hooked up with Howie Winter and gone back to what he knew best. And now he was standing alongside Whitey Bulger at Marshall Motors. "Should I meet him?" Bulger had asked. Flemmi thought for a moment. He had been back less than a year, and it was obvious to him that things were in flux. It was clear that some new arrangement was in the works. He'd even met on his own with Dennis Condon, a short meeting at a coffee shop where he was introduced to John Connolly. Flemmi regarded all the huddling as a kind of "transition," with Connolly being set up to take over now that Paul Rico was transferred to Miami and nearing retirement. Over time, of course, Flemmi had experienced a strong upside to his FBI deal. But he was just Stevie Flemmi, not the already legendary Whitey Bulger.

Flemmi cautiously opted for a short answer. It was an answer soaking in subtext, but short nonetheless.

"It's probably a good idea," he told Bulger. "Go and talk to him."

■ ■ ■

CONNOLLY wasn't in any rush to make his pitch. "I just want you to hear me out," he told Bulger in the car along Wollaston Beach. Connolly carefully played up the double-barreled threat that Bulger and his Winter Hill gang presently faced from Gennaro Angiulo's Mafia. "I hear Jerry is feeding information to law enforcement to get you pinched," he told Bulger. They talked about how Jerry Angiulo definitely had an advantage over the rest of the field, able to call on a crooked cop to do him a favor. "The Mafia has all the contacts," Connolly said.

Then Connolly moved along and stoked the vending machine dispute. Word on the street, observed Connolly, was that Zannino was ready to take arms against Bulger and his friends in the Winter Hill gang. "I'm aware that you're aware that the outfit is going to make a move on you."

This last remark especially caught Bulger's attention. In fact, the LCN and Winter Hill had always found a way to coexist. Not that there weren't disputes to work out, but the two groups were closer to being wary partners than enemies on the verge of a war. Even the vitriolic and unpredictable Zannino, the Mafia's Jekyll and Hyde, could one moment angrily denounce Winter Hill and promise to mow them down in a hail of bullets and then suddenly turn operatic and proclaim lovingly, "The Hill is us!" Truth be told, Gennaro Angiulo was at this time more concerned about threats he was receiving from a runaway Italian hothead known as "Bobby the Greaser" than he was about imminent war with Winter Hill. But for Connolly's purposes, it was better to play up the beef percolating between the LCN and Winter Hill over the vending machines, and Connolly could tell right away he'd hit a hot button with the fearless Bulger when he mentioned the potential for violence. Bulger was clearly angered.

"You don't think we'd win?" Bulger shot back.

Connolly actually did think Bulger could prevail. He fully believed Whitey and Flemmi were much tougher than Angiulo and his boys—"stone killers" he called Bulger and Flemmi. But that wasn't the point.

"I have a proposal: why don't you use us to do what they're doing to you? Fight fire with fire."

The deal was that simple: Bulger should use the FBI to eliminate his Mafia rivals. And if that alone wasn't reason enough, the FBI wouldn't be looking to take Bulger himself down if he were cooperating. In fact, at that moment other FBI agents were sniffing around and making inquiries into Bulger's loan-sharking operations. Come aboard, Connolly said. We'll protect you, he promised. Just as Rico had promised Flemmi before him.

Bulger was clearly intrigued. "You can't survive without friends in law enforcement," he admitted at night's end. But he left without committing.

Two weeks later Connolly and Bulger met again in Quincy, this time to cement the deal.

"All right," he informed Connolly, "deal me in. If they want to play checkers, we'll play chess. Fuck them."

This was music to John Connolly's ears. Incredibly, he'd just brought

Whitey Bulger into the FBI. If developing informants was considered the pinnacle of investigative work, Connolly was now, he proudly concluded, in the big leagues. In a single bold stroke he'd put FBI gruntwork behind him and now belonged to an upper crust occupied by the likes of the retiring Paul Rico. If, in Connolly's mind, Rico was the agent a slew of the new young turks in the office wanted to model themselves after, Bulger was the neighborhood legend all the kids in Southie were in awe of. Connolly had to sense that the moment marked the slick merger of both worlds.

Moreover, this particular deal had a certain élan to it. The last gangster anyone in Boston would suspect of being an FBI informant was Whitey Bulger of South Boston. Indeed, Connolly was always sensitive to this seeming incongruity. Among his FBI colleagues Connolly rarely, if ever, called Bulger an informant, a rat, a snitch, or a stoolie. He would still grate when he later heard other people use those labels. To him Bulger was always a "source." Or he used the terms that Bulger requested: "strategist" or "liaison." It was as if even the man who convinced Whitey to become an informant couldn't believe it himself. Or maybe it was just that the deal from the beginning was less a formal understanding with the FBI than a renewed friendship between Johnny and Whitey from Old Harbor. And though John Connolly was surely thinking about his career, the deal wasn't about what might come—it was about where he had come from. A circle, a loop, the shape of a noose. All roads led to Southie.

Connolly always remained deferential to the older Bulger, calling him by the birth name he preferred, Jim, rather than the street name that the media preferred. Such things might have seemed like petty details, but they were details that made the deal palatable. Bulger, for example, insisted that he would provide information only on the Italian Mafia, not on the Irish. Moreover, he insisted that Connolly not tell his brother Billy, then a state senator, about this new "business deal."

There was a certain charged and inescapable irony to this deal between Bulger and the FBI, coming as it did during the second year of court-ordered busing in South Boston. The tableau, in its entirety, was bizarre. The people of Southie, including leaders like Billy Bulger, had been helpless in their efforts to repel the federal government, which was plowing through the neighborhood to enforce busing. The federal authority was mighty and despised and would not go away. This was the harsh reality of the neighborhood's public life. But in a different part of Southie, Whitey Bulger had cut a deal that would freeze the feds. The FBI needed Whitey and would not be looking to do him in. The rest of the world might belong to the feds, but at least the underworld did not. Whitey had found a way to keep them out of his Southie. In an odd way he'd succeeded where his brother had not.

Immediately the information highway was up and running. More meetings were held. Bulger blended in Flemmi, and a package deal was forged. For his part, Bulger clearly recognized the value of teaming up with Flemmi, given Flemmi's rich access to mafiosi and the kind of information Connolly so badly wanted. Flemmi, meanwhile, had to recognize the value of teaming up with Bulger, not just for his cunning mind but also for his marquee status, particularly with Connolly. He could see something special pass between them right from the beginning. "They had a relationship."

For Connolly, Flemmi was a hand-me-down, but Bulger was his own, a coup for the FBI in Boston. It was a beast of a deal, a high-five achievement, with Connolly in charge of two midlevel gangsters positioned to assist the FBI in its stated campaign to cripple the Mafia enterprise. But the new deal hardly meant Whitey would curb his style. In fact, just five weeks after the Whitey Bulger informant file was opened officially on September 30, 1975, Whitey chalked up his first murder while on FBI time. He and Flemmi took out a longshoreman from Southie named Tommy King. The hit was part power grab, part revenge, and mostly Bulger hubris. Bulger and King, never friends, had gotten into an argument one night in a Southie bar. Fists began flying. King had Bulger down and was pounding away on him when others finally pulled him off. Payback for Bulger came November 5, 1975. No doubt buoyed by the secret knowledge the FBI would always be looking to curry favor with him, Bulger, Flemmi, and an associate jumped King. The longshoreman vanished from Southie and the world. Not surprisingly, Bulger mentioned none of this in his meetings with Connolly; instead, one of Bulger's first reports was that the Irish gang unrest and bloodshed supposedly pending between Winter Hill and the Mafia had fizzled—much ado about nothing. The streets were calm, reported Bulger.

So it began.

CHAPTER TWO

South Boston

In order to wait for Whitey at Wollaston Beach, John Connolly had to first get himself home from New York. Flemmi's boyhood pal "Cadillac Frank" Salemme would be his ticket.

Salemme's arrest happened on a cold bright New York afternoon in December 1972 when the good guys and the bad guys floated past each other on Third Avenue. A face in the crowd suddenly clicked with Connolly, who told his FBI companions to unbutton their winter coats and draw their guns. A slow, almost comical footrace on snow ended with jewelry salesman Jules Sellick of Philadelphia protesting that he was not Frank Salemme of Boston, wanted for the attempted murder of a mobster's lawyer. But indeed he was.

The young agent had no handcuffs with him and had to stuff Salemme into a taxi at gunpoint and bark at the bewildered cabbie to drive to the nearby FBI headquarters at East Sixty-ninth and Third. His boss chided him good-naturedly about the handcuffs, but there were envious smiles and back slaps all around for bagging one of Boston's most wanted mobsters. Some were amazed that Connolly had been able to recognize Salemme, but in fact it wasn't quite as lucky as it first appeared. An old pro in the Boston FBI office had taken a shine to Connolly and earlier had sent him photographs and likely locations for spotting Salemme, gleaned from informant reports. It was a perfect example of how valuable informants could be. Connolly's apprehension of Cadillac Frank resulted in a transfer back home, an unusually quick return for an agent with only four years of duty under his belt.

By 1974 Salemme was off to fifteen years in prison and Connolly was back to the streets of his boyhood. By this time Bulger was the preeminent Irish gangster in the flagrantly Irish neighborhood of South Boston. When Connolly returned, Bulger had just solidified his hold on Southie's gambling and loan-sharking network, the culmination of a slow steady climb that began in 1965 with his release from the country's toughest prisons.

The two men spoke the same language and shared deep roots in the same tribal place. They came together as book ends on the narrow spectrum of careers available to Irish Catholics who lived in splendid isolation on the spit of land jutting into the Atlantic Ocean. Their cohesive neighborhood was separated from downtown Boston by the Fort Point Channel and a singular state of mind. For decades Southie had been immigrant Irish against the world, fighting first a losing battle against shameful discrimination by the Yankee merchants who had run Boston for centuries, and then another one against mindless bureaucrats and an obdurate federal judge who imposed school busing on the "town" that hated outsiders to begin with. Both clashes were the kind of righteous fight that left residents the way they liked to be: bloodied but unbowed. The shared battles reaffirmed a view of life—never trust outsiders and never forget where you come from.

A retired cop once recalled the constricted choices a young man had coming of age in the South Boston of the 1940s and 1950s. Armed services. City hall. Utility companies. Factory work. Crime. "It was gas, electric, Gillette, city, cop, crook," he said. The decades of travail made Southie residents quick to fight for limited opportunities.

Bulger and Connolly, crook and cop, grew up in the first public project in Boston, a spartan village of thirty-four tightly spaced brick tenement buildings. It was built by a contractor friend of the legendary Mayor James

Michael Curley with money from the Public Works Administration of Franklin Delano Roosevelt. Both men were revered in the Bulger home on Logan Way—Curley for his roguish repartee and Roosevelt for saving the workingman from the ravages of capitalism.

Connolly's parents—John J. Connolly, a Gillette employee for fifty years, and his stay-in-the-background mother, Bridget T. Kelly—lived in the project until John was twelve years old. In 1952 the family moved "up" to City Point, which was Southie's best address because it looked out to sea from the far end of the promontory. Connolly's father was known as "Galway John," after the Irish county of his birth. He made the church, South Boston, and his family the center of his life. Somehow the father of three children pulled the money together to send John to the Catholic school in the Italian North End, Columbus High. It was like traveling to a foreign country, and John Jr. joked about a commute that required "cars, buses, trains." The Southie instinct for patriotic duty and a public payroll also led Connolly's younger brother James into law enforcement. He became a respected agent with the U.S. Drug Enforcement Administration, a subdued version of his swaggering older brother.

The Connollys and Bulgers reached adolescence in a clean, well-lit place by the sea surrounded by acres of parks and football and baseball fields and basketball courts. Sports were king. Old Harbor had intact families, free ice cream on the Fourth of July, and stairwells that were clubhouses, about thirty kids to a building. The twenty-seven-acre project was the middle ground between City Point, with its ocean breezes and lace curtains, and the more ethnically diverse Lower End, with its small box-shaped houses that sat on the edge of truck routes leading to the factories and garages and taverns along the Fort Point Channel. To this day the neighborhood consistently maintains the highest percentage of long-term residents in the city, reflecting a historic emphasis on staying put rather than getting ahead that engenders fierce pride. As South Boston bowed slightly to gentrification along its untapped waterfront in the late 1990s, its city councilor sought to reaffirm traditional values by outlawing French doors on cafés and roof decks on condos facing the sea.

■ ■ ■

THE us-versus-them mentality at the core of Southie life goes even deeper than its Irish roots. Before the first major wave of Irish immigrants washed over the peninsula after the Civil War, an angry petition to the "central" government had arrived at city hall in 1847 complaining about the lack of municipal services. It would be a couple of decades before the famine immigrants, who stumbled ashore in Boston as the potato blight wracked Ireland from 1845 to 1850, made their way to the rolling grass knolls of what was then called Dorchester Heights. The famine had reduced Ireland's population by one-third, with one million dying of starvation and two million fleeing for their lives. Many of them headed to Boston as the shortest distance between two points and spilled into the fetid waterfront tenements of the North End. By the 1870s they were grateful to leave a slum where three of every ten children died before their first birthday.

The newly arrived Irish Catholics took immediately to Southie's grievance list with outside forces. Indeed, it became holy writ as the community coalesced around church and family, forming a solid phalanx against those who did not understand their ways. Over the decades since then, nothing has galvanized Southie more than a perceived slight by an outsider who would change The Way Things Are. In the Irish Catholic hegemony that came to be, a mixed marriage was not just Catholic and Protestant. It could also be an Italian man and an Irish woman.

Although Boston had been an established city for two centuries by the time the bedraggled famine immigrants arrived, South Boston did not become a tight-knit Irish community until after the Civil War, when newly created businesses brought steady employment to neighborhood residents. In the war's aftermath the peninsula's population increased by one-third to its present level of thirty thousand. Irish workers began to settle in the Lower End to take jobs in shipbuilding and the railroad that spoke to the era. Soon local banks and Catholic churches opened their doors, including St. Monica's, the Sunday destination of Whitey Bulger's younger brother Billy and his tag-along pal John Connolly.

In the latter part of the nineteenth century most men worked on Atlantic Avenue unloading freight ships. Women trekked across the Broadway Bridge after supper to the city's financial district, where they scrubbed floors and emptied wastebaskets, returning home over the same bridge around midnight. By the end of the century the Irish Catholic foothold was such that residents congregated by the Irish county of origin —Galway was A and B Streets, Cork people settled on D Street, and so on. The clannishness was part of the salt air. It was why John Connolly of the FBI could quickly resume an easy relationship with an archcriminal like Whitey Bulger. Certain things mattered.

Beyond common ethnic roots, the magnet of daily life was the Catholic Church. Everything revolved around it. Baptism. First Communion. Confirmation. Marriage. Last rites. Wakes. On Sundays, a day apart, parents went to early mass and sons and daughters attended the children's mass at nine-thirty. There was a natural cross-fertilization with politics, with one of the first steps toward public office sometimes being the high-visibility job of passing the hat along the pews.

Like Ireland itself, Southie was a grand place—as long as you had a job. The Depression swung like a wrecking ball through South Boston's latticed phalanx of family and church. The network that had worked so well collapsed when the father in the house was out of work. A relentless unemployment rate of 30 percent badly damaged the Southie worldview that the future could be ensured by working hard and keeping your nose clean. It changed the mood in a breezy place, and ebullience gave way to despair. It wasn't just Southie. Boston's economy had calcified, and well into the 1940s, the formative years for the Bulger boys and John Connolly, the city was a hapless backwater down on its luck. Its office buildings were short and dreary and its prospects dim. Income was down, taxes were up, and business was lethargic. The city was afflicted by the legacy of a ruling oligarchy of Brahmins who lost their verve. The dynamic Yankees of the nineteenth century had given way to suburban bankers indifferent to downtown, a generation of cautious coupon clippers who nurtured trust funds instead of forging new businesses. In tandem, hopeful immigrants became doleful bureaucrats. Nothing much changed until the urban renewal of the 1960s.

It was to this hard time and place that James and Jean Bulger arrived in 1938, looking for a third bedroom for their growing family in the first public housing project in Boston. Whitey was nine, Billy four. The Bulgers

would raise three boys in one bedroom and three girls in another. While
the Old Harbor project was a massive playground for the children, parents
had to be nearly broke to get into it. The Bulgers easily met this criterion.
As a young man, James Joseph Bulger had lost much of his arm when it
was caught between two railroad cars. Although he worked occasionally
as a clerk at the Charlestown Navy Yard, doing the late shift on holidays as
a fill-in, he never held a full-time job again.

A short man who wore glasses and combed his white hair straight
back, James Bulger walked the beaches and parks of South Boston, smoking a cigar, a coat hanging over the shoulder of his amputated arm. His
hard life had begun in the North End tenements, just as the Irish neighborhood of the famine era was giving way to another immigrant wave,
this one from southern Italy in the 1880s. He had a strong interest in the issues of the day; one of Billy's boyhood friends remembered bumping into
him on a walk and being waylaid by a long discussion of "politics, philos-
ophy, all this stuff." But the father was a loner who stayed inside the apartment most of the time, especially when the Red Sox were on the radio. In
contrast, the loquacious Jean was usually found on the back stoop at
Logan Way, chatting with neighbors, even after a hard day of work. Many
of the neighbors recalled Jean Bulger as a sunny, savvy woman who was
easy to like and hard to fool. They say Billy was like her, friendly and out-
going, running off to the library with a book bag or to the church for a
wedding or funeral, his altar boy cassock flying over his shoulder.

But Billy also shared his father's concerns for privacy and his solitary
ways. In a rare interview about his family, Bulger talked wistfully about
his father, his stoic manner and hard-luck fate, wishing that they had
talked more and that there had been more shared moments. He recalled
the day he went off to the army toward the end of the Korean War, his
parents tight-lipped with worry because their son-in-law had been killed
in action two years earlier. James and Jean took Billy to South Station for
the train to Fort Dix, New Jersey. His father, then nearly seventy years
old, walked behind him down the aisle, following him to his seat. "I
thought, 'What's this?' You know how kids are. My father, and this was
unusual for him, he took my hand and said, 'Well, God bless you, Bill.'

I remember it because it was quite a bit more than my father was inclined to say."

. . .

BILLY BULGER ran for public office in 1960 because he needed a job as he neared graduation from Boston College Law School and married his childhood sweetheart Mary Foley. John Connolly was one of his campaign workers. Originally, Bulger was going to stay a few terms in the House of Representatives and then leave for private practice as a criminal defense lawyer. But he stayed on, juggling a small law practice, the legislature, and a booming family. The Bulgers would have nine children, about one a year during the 1960s. Billy moved up to the senate in 1970 and went on to be president of the chamber longer than any man in Massachusetts history.

As he progressed through the legislature, Billy came to epitomize South Boston, with his jutting jaw and conservative agenda. He became a provocative statewide figure who delighted in tweaking suburban liberals who thought busing was a good idea for his neighborhood but not for their own. He had a passion for refighting old lost battles, none more emblematic than the statewide referenda he forced on an indifferent electorate in the 1980s to right an ancient wrong he found in the state constitution. An anti-Catholic 1855 provision banned aid to parochial schools and, while Bulger readily admitted it had done no lasting harm, he wanted it smitten because of the original intent. That the correcting amendment was overwhelmingly rejected twice at the polls made no matter. The fight was the thing.

It was all part of what made him one of the dominating politicians of his time, a paradoxical figure who drew on a rare mixture of scholarship and mean streets. At once he was a petty despot and masterful conciliator, a reserved man who loved an audience, a puckish public performer who had a dark side and took all slights personally. His bad side remains a precarious place to be.

Though Billy Bulger was well-known for his scholastic and high-minded style, he could show another side as well. In 1974, when anti-busing protesters were arrested outside a neighborhood school, Bulger was on the scene and denounced the police for overreacting. He went nose to nose with the city's police commissioner, Robert diGrazia, jabbing his finger at him about his "Gestapo" troopers and angrily walking away. DiGrazia yelled a retort about politicians lacking "the balls" to deal with desegregation earlier when things could have been different. Bulger spun around for more, working his way up to the much taller diGrazia. "Go fuck yourself," the senator hissed into diGrazia's face.

As busing turned Southie on its ear, even Whitey Bulger got into the act, but in the incongruous role of peacemaker. He worked behind the scenes to try to bring some calm to the streets among his followers. His exhortations were hardly the stuff of civic altruism. By raising the prospect of a protracted police presence in South Boston, busing was simply bad for business. So Whitey spread the word to his associates not to exacerbate the tensions boiling over in the schools.

Despite the fractious 1970s, Billy rose quickly in the senate and ruled it with an iron hand by decade's end. But he would struggle with an image steeped in Southie lore, the good and the bad. It made him a hero in the town and anathema in a liberal Democratic state. His dilemma was captured in the late 1980s when he was fighting off the latest reform movement to bring debate and democracy to the senate. A colleague tried to convince him he could be a hero if he loosened his grip on the chamber ever so slightly. But Bulger just shook his head. No, not guys like me, he said. "I'll always be a redneck mick from South Boston."

■ ■ ■

AS A project kid, Connolly got to know both Bulger brothers. He became good friends with Billy, drawn to the maturity and humor that made Billy as distinctive as Whitey was notorious. It was Billy who Connolly tagged along after on the way home from mass at St. Monica's and Billy who got him into books, though Connolly and his friends generally thought it was a crazy notion in such a sports-mad environment.

Connolly also came to know the infamous Whitey as the hellion of Old Harbor who kept the project in an uproar with his street fights and audacious antics. Indeed, everyone knew Whitey, even eight-year-old kids like Connolly. Once Connolly was in a ball game that turned ugly. An older boy decided Connolly was taking too much time retrieving a ball and fired another one into the middle of his back. His back stinging, Connolly instinctively picked up the ball and fired a high hard one into the kid's nose. The older boy was all over the smaller Connolly, pounding away, beating him up pretty good. Then, from the margins of the playground, Whitey swooped in to break up the one-sided fight. Bloodied, Connolly staggered to his feet, forever grateful. At some level, Connolly would stay a poor city kid looking for acceptance in a hardscrabble world, permanently susceptible to the macho mystique of Whitey Bulger.

■ ■ ■

WHEN John Connolly was a toddler on O'Callahan Way, Whitey Bulger was already tailgating merchandise off the back of delivery trucks in Boston's minority neighborhoods. He was thirteen years old when first charged with larceny and moved on quickly to assault and battery and robbery, somehow avoiding reform school. But he was nevertheless targeted by the Boston police, who frequently sent him and his fresh mouth home more battered than they'd found him. His parents worried that the bruising encounters would only make him worse, and indeed, the stubborn teenager exulted in his confrontations at the police station, swaggering around the tenement and daring younger kids to punch his washboard stomach so he could laugh at them. In a few short years he became a dangerous delinquent with a Jimmy Cagney flair, known for vicious fights and wild car chases. His probation files reveal him to have been an indifferent student who was lazy in school, the polar opposite of his brother Bill. He never graduated from high school, but he always had a car when everyone else took the bus.

One Bulger contemporary, who grew up in Southie before going into the marines and law enforcement, played in the ferocious no-pads football games on Sundays and recalls Bulger as an average athlete but a fierce competitor. "He wasn't a bully, but he was looking for trouble. You could sense him hoping someone would start something. There was some admiration for the way he handled himself. At least back then, there was a sense he would be loyal to his friends. That was the culture of the time. It was incredibly tribal, and the gang affiliation meant so much to poor city kids."

Bulger did most of his tailgating with the Shamrocks, one of the successor gangs to the mighty Gustins. The Gustins had had a chance to be Boston's dominant crime organization during Prohibition. But its leaders reached too far in 1931 when they sought citywide control over bootlegging along Boston's wide-open waterfront. Two South Boston men were murdered when they went to the Italian North End to dictate terms to the Mafia and guns roared out at them from behind the door of C&F Importing. Law enforcement still views the Gustin gang's fate as a demarcation point in Boston's crime history. Boston's stunted Mafia would survive in Italian sections of the city, and the more entrenched Irish gangs would retreat to South Boston, ensuring a balkanized underworld in which factions stayed in ethnic enclaves. Sometimes, for the sake of high profits, the two groups collaborated. But Boston, along with Philadelphia and New York, would be one of the few cities where persistent Irish gangs would coexist by putting the Mafia loan-shark money out on the streets of their neighborhoods.

The Gustin gang's stand-off with the Mafia also gave Whitey Bulger the freedom to move around South Boston's freewheeling crime circuit, graduating from tailgating trucks in Boston to robbing banks and, at age twenty-seven, doing hard time in the country's toughest federal prisons. His prison file portrays a hard case who was fighting all the time and doing long stretches in solitary. He was viewed as a security risk and once did three months in the hole in Atlanta before being moved to the ultimate maximum-security prison, Alcatraz, because he was suspected of planning an escape. He wound up in solitary there too, over a work stoppage, but finally settled down to do his time, moving east to Leavenworth in Kansas and then to his last stop before returning to Boston—Lewisburg, Pennsylvania. Bulger went to prison when Eisenhower was still in his first term in 1956 and returned home in 1965 when Lyndon Johnson was firing up the Vietnam War. His father, who had lived long enough to see Billy elected, had died before Whitey's release.

Bulger came home as a hard-nosed ex-con who nevertheless moved back in with his mother in the projects. For a while he took a custodian's job, arranged by Billy, at Boston's Suffolk County Courthouse. The job reflected the politics of South Boston—a magnified version of Boston's old-style ward system in which bosses built fiefdoms by controlling public jobs. In the old days this system had been a lifeline for unskilled immigrants with large families, but in the 1960s, it could result in a janitor's job for an ex-con. After a few years of keeping his nose clean on parole, Whitey took a deep breath and jumped back into the underworld, quickly becoming a widely feared enforcer. The Southie barroom patrons from whom he collected gaming and shylock debts were seldom late again.

The disciplined, taciturn Bulger was clearly a cut above in the brutal world he so readily reentered. For one thing, he was well read, having used his decade in prison to focus on World War II military history, searching for the flaws that had brought down generals. It was part of an instinctive plan to do it smart the second time around. This time he would be a cagey survivor, mixing patience with selective brutality. He would no longer provoke police with flip remarks but present himself as someone who had learned the ropes in prison, someone who would assure detectives during routine pat-downs that they were all good guys in their small gathering and he was just a "good bad guy."

A couple of years after being released from prison in 1965, Whitey Bulger did much of his work with Donald Killeen, then the dominant bookmaker in South Boston. But after a few years Bulger developed misgivings about Killeen's faltering leadership and incessant gangland entanglements. More important, Bulger began to fear that he and Killeen would be killed by their main rivals in South Boston—the Mullin gang of Paul McGonagle and Patrick Nee. One of Bulger's closest associates had been gunned down in a desperate run for his front door in the Savin Hill section of Boston. It seemed a matter of time before Killeen or Bulger himself met the same fate.

In May 1972 Whitey's dilemma about standing with the beleaguered Killeen was resolved when he ruthlessly chose survival over loyalty: even though he was Killeen's bodyguard, Bulger entered into a secret alliance with his enemies. In order to survive, Bulger had to make a hard choice about business partners in Boston's bifurcated underworld: subordinate himself to the Italian Mafia, which he detested, or forge a deal with the Winter Hill gang, which he distrusted. There would simply be no patching up the Mullin rift with Killeen, what with Paul McGonagle's murdered brother and the nose that got bitten off Mickey McGuire's face. Howard "Howie" Winter, who ran the dominant Irish gang out of a garage in nearby Somerville, was friendly with Mullin gang members and mediated its dispute with Bulger. Once the fiercely independent Bulger had taken hat in hand and gone to see Howie, it was the end of Donald Killeen.

Shortly afterward, Killeen was called away from his son's fourth birthday party. As he was starting his car, he saw a lone gunman racing at him from the nearby woods. As Killeen went for his gun under the seat, the gunman pulled open the driver's door and jammed the machine gun near his face. He then fired off a fifteen-bullet burst. The gunman fled down the driveway to a revving getaway car. No one was ever charged with the shooting, but it became part of Southie lore that it was Bulger. The finishing flourish occurred a few weeks later when Kenneth, the youngest brother in the Killeen family, jogged past a car parked near City Point with four men in it. A voice called out "Kenny." He turned to see Bulger's face filling the open window, a gun tucked under his chin. "It's over," the last Killeen bookmaker standing was told. "You're out of business. No other warnings."

The fast, bloody "Godfather" takeover was the stuff of legends. It was the kind of dramatic, decisive move that would be known throughout Southie by nightfall, a formal notice to the underworld that Bulger was soon to manipulate and control. And it was just the beginning. Within months of Donald Killeen's death, Bulger joined forces with Winter Hill assassins and, to consolidate Bulger's power, mowed down South Boston rivals at a breakneck pace. In two days in March 1973, they killed six mobsters. By the end of 1975, the Bulger body count was up to sixteen, including prime movers in the archrival Mullins Gang—Paul McGonagle and Tommy King. Both were buried in Quincy in sandy beaches in view of the busy Southeast Expressway.

It was a new era awash in blood as Bulger eliminated the Killeens and then showed up for work at the Marshall Motors garage in Somerville that served as Howie Winter's base of operations. Bulger spoke for all the

South Boston rackets and was looking for bigger opportunities. Whitey had Southie and, for a short time, Howie had Whitey.

While his wealth grew exponentially, Bulger's lifestyle would never change. He was the antithesis of the gaudy mafiosi of the North End. No Cadillacs. No yachts. No oceanfront homes. Bulger seldom drank, never smoked, and worked out daily. His one weakness was for a Jaguar that he kept garaged in City Point most of the time. Overall, he lived a quiet life with his mother in the Old Harbor project, staying with her until her death in 1980.

His new agenda was to stay disciplined and not give in to the anger of his youth, when he had been charged with rapes in Boston and in Montana while in the air force. He would indulge neither the restlessness that had led him as a fourteen-year-old to bound impulsively out the door in Old Harbor and join Barnum & Bailey's circus as a roustabout, nor the recklessness of the young gangster who walked into a bank with a silver gun and other amateurs to take away $42,112 in deposits from an Indiana bank. Gone were his days as a crook on the run who dyed his hair black to go into hiding from the FBI, only to be arrested at a nightclub surrounded by agents. No, the second time around he would stay in control and behind the scenes. Those years of reading in prison libraries had sharpened his instincts, and his mind had become an encyclopedia of law enforcement tactics and past mobster mistakes. Like a chessmaster, Bulger was confident that he knew the moves, that he could watch your opening and lead you straight to checkmate. He vowed to friends that he would never, ever go back to jail.

Like all mobsters, Bulger worked the underworld's night shift, starting out in early afternoon and ending in the wee hours. He presented a studied, icy detachment for those in his world, but a small smile for his mother's aging friends at the project, where he would hold doors for them and tip his hat. For a time he delivered holiday turkeys to families in need at Old Harbor. In his own way he remained devoted to his family and was fiercely protective of Billy. When their mother died in 1980, Whitey kept a low profile for his brother's sake, fearing that a news photographer would put him and the new president of the Massachusetts State Senate in the same frame on page 1. His furtive and alienated life was such that he sat up in the balcony behind the organist during the services and then watched as his five siblings slowly walked the casket out of the church below. As a parish priest summed it up, blood is blood.

But Bulger had a fearsome mystique about him that terrified Southie's rank and file. When a resident accidentally bumped into him coming around a corner in Bulger's liquor store, the cold hard glare he got was enough to make him soil his pants. As John Connolly conceded, "You cannot have a problem with him."

Ellen Brogna, wife of the usually incarcerated Howie Winter, had been around gangsters most of her life but was chilled by Whitey Bulger. Not long after Bulger began working out of the garage in Somerville, they were all having dinner one night. For some reason Bulger had to move Brogna's Mustang. She flipped him the keys, but he came raging back in when he was unable to turn the car over, not realizing there was a button to press before the key would turn. She tried joking with him that he should be an expert now that he was hanging around Marshall Motors. Bulger just stared daggers at her and then stormed off. Later that night she told Howie that dealing with Bulger was like looking at Dracula. Howie just thought it was funny.

■ ■ ■

THE post-Alcatraz Bulger was still a volatile man, but one who had learned the value of controlling himself. He was a poster boy for stoic, stand-up Southie, with a chiseled macho look that gave him an instant presence. His ice-cold manner cut like a cleaver to the heart of the matter. This trait, of course, made him the perfect informant, which is why Dennis Condon, the wily FBI agent who worked organized crime for decades, had kept after Bulger in the early 1970s. But though he came from a similar background across the harbor in Charlestown, Condon didn't come from the unique place at issue—South Boston. Condon closed out the Whitey Bulger informant file with great reluctance, sensing it might work for the bureau if he could just put Bulger with a "handler" from "the town." The young agent John Connolly was from central casting—streetwise, fast-talking, and, best of all, born and raised in the Old Harbor project.

Condon had first met Connolly through a Boston detective who knew them both. Connolly, finishing up a stint as a high school teacher, was attending law school at night but eager to join the bureau.

After Connolly signed on with the FBI in 1968, Condon kept in touch with him during his tours of duty through Baltimore, San Francisco, and New York. They talked when Connolly came home to marry a local woman, Marianne Lockary, in 1970. While Bulger bobbed and weaved for survival, Condon took steps that would help Connolly get transferred back to Boston. It was believed that the precise details on Frank Salemme's whereabouts, given to Connolly by Condon, came from Stevie Flemmi, who had had a falling out with his boyhood buddy.

Connolly returned to the smaller, more intimate scale of Boston, readily swapping Brooklyn for Southie, Yankee Stadium for Fenway Park. He left an office with 950 agents focusing on New York's five crime families for one with 250 agents who were barely up to speed on Gennaro Angiulo. He could see the playing field better, and he knew the people by their nicknames. He was a Boston boy and he was back home, raring to fill out the G-man's suit with style. But Connolly was also an empty vessel who got filled up by those around him. As a teenager, he was seen as a "shaper," a wanna-be who looked good in a baseball hat but was never much of a player. As an agent, he was more about playing the role than doing the work. He was always more glib salesman than hard-eyed cop. When he returned home from New York, he was an impressionable young agent suddenly plunged into a movie script life. His dream assignment became getting close to a bad guy he had long admired. John Connolly fell in love.

It was a fatal attraction to the seductive personality of Whitey Bulger. Bulger was magnetic in the reverse glamour way of elite gangsters who break all the rules and revel in it. For Connolly, it was an enthralling prospect, a future assured. Working with Whitey. What could be better? What could be easier? It sure beat being one of 250 selfless agents riding around in a government car. Whitey would be the head on Connolly's glass of beer.

In the first few years of his renewed relationship with Whitey Bulger, Connolly's "209" informant reports were split between accounts of disenchantment within the ranks of Gennaro Angiulo's chronically unhappy

Mafia family and more concrete tips about Bulger's rivals within South
Boston. Connolly did not remind Bulger that he had originally pledged to
inform only about the Italians. And while the Mafia information was
mostly generic gossip about problems in the House of Angiulo, the rat file
on South Boston came with addresses, license plates, and phone numbers.
For instance, Tommy Nee, one of a handful of homicidal maniacs who
were regularly committing mayhem out of South Boston barrooms in the
1970s, was arrested for murder by Boston police, with an assist from the
FBI, in New Hampshire—just where Whitey said he would be.

But the FBI priority was the Mafia, not sociopaths like Tommy Nee.
Through Flemmi, Bulger found out that Angiulo had removed his office
phone for fear of wiretaps. Angiulo and his brothers, Bulger told
Connolly, were talking only on walkie-talkies. Gennaro was "Silver Fox"
and Donato Angiulo was "Smiling Fox." Bulger even recommended a
Bearcat 210 automatic scanner to monitor conversations.

In the button-down FBI office in Boston, such reports were impressing
the top bosses, even as Connolly's increasingly brash ways were irritating
his colleagues, who began to jokingly call him "Canolli" because he
dressed and acted like a slick mob dude. Jewelry. Chains. Pointed shoes.
Black suits. But for his part, Connolly was unconcerned. He knew what he
had in Bulger and what it was worth to his career. Bulger's 209 files were a
coup for him and a coup for the bureau, a synergy possible only because of
who he was and where he came from. South Boston Irish. "Whitey only
talked to me," Connolly bragged, "because he knew me from when I was
a kid. He knew I'd never hurt him. He knew I'd never help him, but he
knew I'd never hurt him."

But sometimes in Whitey's world, not hurting could be very helpful.

CHAPTER THREE

Hard Ball

As District Attorney William Delahunt was getting into his car to drive to a restaurant near his Dedham office, Whitey Bulger and two associates were barreling down the Southeast Expressway toward the same destination just outside Boston's city limits. Delahunt was meeting another prosecutor for dinner. The mobsters were planning to terrorize the restaurant's owner, who had stiffed them on a $175,000 debt. In one of life's strange split screens, each party would do its business on a different side of the same big room in the Back Side Restaurant.

It was 1976, and the thirty-five-year-old Delahunt had been Norfolk County district attorney for only a year—just a little longer than Whitey Bulger had been teamed up with John Connolly and the Boston office of the FBI. But the chance encounter was not the only thing the DA and the gangsters had in common. One of the mobsters in Bulger's crew, Johnny Martorano, had been a grammar school classmate and schoolyard rival of Delahunt's. They had even been altar boys together.

When Delahunt looked up from a table near the bar, he recognized the Winter Hill hitman immediately. Martorano ambled over and sat down, while the other two gangsters hung back. The former school chums shared a drink and got to jiving each other about their opposite lots in life. Johnny Martorano jabbed Billy Delahunt about there being more honor in his world than in the one populated by bankers and lawyers. Delahunt just chortled and did not argue the point with him. But when it was Delahunt's turn to dish it out, he touched a nerve. Delahunt urged his old classmate turned gangster to stay out of Norfolk County. Stick to Boston, "for both our sakes," Delahunt cautioned.

Martorano told Delahunt to pound sand, and the repartee got animated enough that one of Martorano's companions joined them at the table to see what was going on. Bulger hung back, waiting by the entrance and out of sight, but Delahunt certainly recognized Martorano's companion, Stevie Flemmi. Then the odd encounter ended suddenly, and amicably enough, when Delahunt's dinner companion, federal prosecutor Martin Boudreau, arrived at the table. When they were alone, Delahunt rolled his eyes and said, "You'll never guess who I was talking to."

Meanwhile, Bulger joined Martorano and Flemmi, and the threesome picked a cocktail table against the back wall and set up there. Arms folded, they sat waiting for the owner to appear. They had come to see Francis Green because Francis Green had some explaining to do.

About a year earlier Green had borrowed $175,000 from a high-interest Boston finance company for a real estate investment. The problem was that Green had not paid back a dime and, while he didn't know it, was stiffing a friend of Winter Hill's. Whitey knew a way to solve such bad debts. It was not genteel.

Green came into the large central room, spotted the three gangsters, and slid into an empty seat. As was his wont, Bulger skipped the small talk. "Where's our money?" he asked. Green, a glib salesman with a checkered past, tried a salesman's tap dance. His finances were in shambles. His business deals had gone bad. He was in bad shape. This had to count for something.

But Bulger would have none of it. No money is no answer. It didn't matter that two prosecutors were seated across the way. Bulger leaned into Green's face, his eyes cold marbles. Understand this, Bulger told him, "if you don't pay, I will absolutely kill you. I will cut off your ears and stuff them in your mouth. I will gouge your eyes out."

Then Bulger leaned back. He told Green he really should make an appointment with his loan officer to arrange a schedule for repayment. And Flemmi, playing the good cop to Bulger's tough cop, advised Green to pay something real soon. That way, comforted Flemmi, no one would get hurt. Then it went back to Bulger, who made one final chilly comment: make it $25,000 within a few days.

An ashen Green said he would see what he could do. The brisk business meeting was over. An FBI report afterward recorded in leaden government prose that the conversation "greatly upset" Green. It was an understatement. Green was in fear for his life, and it was fear mixed with bewilderment. He was aware that Martorano and Delahunt had earlier been mingling at the bar, and the entire scene that night left him confused about what exactly he was up against.

It was all pretty bizarre, the kind of odd occurrence that comes with life in and around a big small city like Boston. For their part, the two prosecutors were oblivious to the extortion nearby. Over at their table, Delahunt and Boudreau joked during dinner about winding up at the same restaurant with Martorano and Flemmi of the Winter Hill gang. They hadn't realized that the third man in the entrance shadows was the notorious Whitey Bulger. But Delahunt had no idea at the time that the business activity at the cocktail table was actually a prelude to the bad relations to come between the rest of law enforcement and the Boston office of the FBI. In the future it would seem like the world was divided between the FBI and Bulger, on the one hand, and all the other police agencies on the other. At the moment, though, the chance meeting just seemed to be one of those crazy things that happen but don't really mean anything.

The Bulger ultimatum—pay or die—quickly sent Green scrambling to seek out his own contacts in Boston's law enforcement community. He started with Edward Harrington, who was the former chief prosecutor at the federal Organized Crime Strike Force for New England. Green not only had had some dealings with the strike force over the years but had raised money for Harrington's unsuccessful run for state attorney general in 1974. Harrington was about to rejoin the ranks of government service as the new U.S. attorney in Massachusetts, but he was in private practice at a law firm when Francis Green came calling in full panic.

Green wanted Harrington's counsel. What should he do? Harrington, according to an FBI report, was blunt. He told Green he had three options: Pay the money. Get out of town. Or testify against Bulger.

Green took stock of the situation. Repayment was out of the question. He had squandered the money. Relocation was not appealing. Testifying against the reputed killer seemed even worse. But it was this last option, the one that perhaps carried the highest risk, at least to life and limb, that Green began to contemplate.

In the weeks that followed Green asked Harrington more questions about cooperating, and Harrington decided that because the extortion occurred in Norfolk County, the matter could best be pursued through a state investigation. He told Green that the case should be developed out of District Attorney Delahunt's office. But what about Delahunt? Green was worried about Delahunt's ties to Martorano. He had seen the two men sitting there at the Back Side Restaurant sharing a drink and having a laugh.

Harrington phoned Delahunt and briefed him about Green and Bulger's threat. Then he mentioned Green's concern about the county prosecutor bantering with Martorano. Delahunt assured Harrington that it was only a chance meeting, that there was nothing between the two men beyond faded boyhood memories. Arrangements were made for Green to take his evidence to Norfolk County prosecutors.

Soon afterward Green met with Delahunt and his top staff. In gripping detail, Green re-created the dramatic night at the Back Side. The story stunned Delahunt. He'd had no idea that this conversation was happening just out of earshot of his dinner with Boudreau.

Later Delahunt huddled with his staff. Green's story was explosive, and Delahunt was personally involved. He had, after all, been in the restaurant that same night and could provide eyewitness corroboration that Martorano and Flemmi were present. Could he be both witness and prosecutor? Unlikely. Plus, the county prosecutors wondered if Harrington had been wrong to conclude that this kind of case should be pursued at the state level. They knew that federal extortion laws carried stiffer penalties than they could ever hope to win under Massachusetts law. So Delahunt consulted with Boudreau, the federal strike force prosecutor and law school classmate he'd dined with that night at the Back Side, who agreed with Delahunt's analysis. He even offered to personally walk the case over to the FBI office to get the ball rolling. With Delahunt's approval, the case was forwarded to the FBI.

■　■　■

JOHN CONNOLLY was worried. Green was the first big bend in the Whitey Bulger highway. But priorities were priorities, so Connolly quickly set out to ensure that the case would never leave the Organized Crime Squad where he worked.

Two agents from the squad did some perfunctory poking around. The agents, both of whom worked side by side with Connolly in the close-knit squad, interviewed Francis Green. They even visited Delahunt and wrote down what he knew.

Then they wrote up a report and put it in the FBI files. And that was the end of it. In about a year the agents asked their boss for permission to officially close the case against Bulger, noting that Green was reluctant to testify against him. Local prosecutors had heard that Connolly had conducted an interview in the case and asked for a copy of his report, but the FBI denied it had taken place and said there was no paperwork.

In the years to come a similar pattern would emerge about witness "reluctance." Time and again John Connolly and his colleagues would talk to a potential witness against Bulger and come back to the office and throw up their hands—the once promising person was now reluctant to cooperate. Or reluctant to testify. Or reluctant to wear a wire. And what was an agent supposed to do if the witness was so reluctant? Time and again leads went nowhere, and it was a pattern that began with Francis Green's "reluctance." Eventually Green would testify for federal prosecutors in an unrelated public corruption case, but no one ever contrasted his willingness in that case to his reluctance in the Bulger matter. Instead, once inside the FBI the extortion case had found its way to the back of a file cabinet. It would be the first of many.

■ ■ ■

GIVEN the fast pace and short memory of law enforcement, the Green case drifted unnoticed into limbo. Bulger backed off Green because of the heat, while Delahunt assumed that the FBI was pursuing the issue. It would be months before the district attorney realized that nothing had been done on an easily made case.

About a year after the initial contact, Delahunt ran into the top federal prosecutor, Jeremiah T. O'Sullivan, at a social function. Whatever happened with that Green thing? Delahunt asked him. "We checked it out, but there was nothing there," he told Delahunt.

Delahunt shrugged and thought, Okay, that happens. "And I meant it," Delahunt said later. "Cases don't work out."

But this one gnawed at him because, every time he thought about it, things didn't compute. A district attorney as a witness who could put notorious gangsters at the scene. An owner's compelling testimony. Why hadn't the FBI picked up the ball and run hard with it against the infamous Bulger and Flemmi?

Five years would go by before some answers began to crystallize for Delahunt. Over time his office's relations with the Boston FBI would sour. Tensions between different police agencies and different prosecutors' offices were not uncommon. It came with the turf, in Boston or in any jurisdiction. But this was different.

First came a sensational murder case that Delahunt's office got involved with not long after the Green matter was turned over to the FBI in early 1977. To solve the murder case and locate the bodies of two eighteen-year-old women from Quincy, Delahunt and his state police investigators cut a deal with an informant by the name of Myles Connor. Connor was a vicious con man who had a high IQ and a long history of trouble. He was a rock musician and an accomplished art thief and drug dealer. His past included a 1966 shoot-out with a state trooper who was badly injured. Even in the venal world of informants, Connor was a mixed bag of trouble. But he knew where the bodies were buried.

Nonetheless, cutting a deal with Connor was controversial, both inside Delahunt's office and beyond. The FBI was enraged because Delahunt, to win Connor's help, had negotiated his early release from prison. Even though with Connor's help Delahunt would find the bodies of the missing women and then convict the murderer at a trial in 1978, the FBI angrily challenged the district attorney's unholy alliance. It was the FBI that had put Connor behind bars on a stolen art conviction. FBI agent John Connolly himself began urging the U.S. attorney to investigate what role, if any, Connor had in the grisly murders. Eventually Connor was charged with planning the killings. He went to trial and was convicted, an outcome that was overturned on appeal. During the subsequent retrial Connor was acquitted.

Delahunt had known that cutting a deal with Connor would prove controversial. Key staff in his own office, whose judgment he relied on daily, had told him as much. But he'd had no idea the situation would explode into the open warfare that followed, with angry exchanges in courtrooms, in the newspapers and on television, and in more sinister ways that would have seemed unimaginable at the start.

Some of the warfare got personal. One day John Connolly contacted one of Delahunt's top assistants, John Kivlan. The young prosecutor was known to have had reservations about using Connor as an informant. Connolly called Kivlan and set up a lunch date. Kivlan showed up thinking the FBI agent wanted to discuss another murder investigation. But quickly Connolly began asking a lot of questions about Delahunt and the deal he'd cut with Connor. The FBI agent was especially curious to know if Delahunt and the state police had believed that Connor was guilty of the murders but had given him a pass anyway to bask in the glory and publicity that came with recovering the bodies.

"It wasn't long," Kivlan said later, "before I realized the lunch was about getting some dirt on Bill."

Kivlan was taken aback by Connolly's overture. "I thought to myself,

'He must think everyone is an informer,'" Kivlan recalled. "I guess he thought my concerns would amount to trading information with him. It was a short lunch."

Looking back, and long after telling Delahunt about the bizarre encounter with Connolly, Kivlan would wonder if the rabid battle between Delahunt's office and Connolly's FBI was less about Connor and more about Bulger. In any case, when Connolly could have been busy fighting crime, he was spending much of his time in a down-and-dirty public relations battle. In fact, crime fighting was becoming less of a clear-cut priority for the young agent from South Boston.

■　■　■

DELAHUNT had limped away from the bruising encounter with the FBI over using Myles Connor as an informant, chewed up in the FBI public relations maw. He was publicly chided by federal officials for using an informant who was involved in the kinds of crimes he was giving information about. By and large, the media sided with the FBI, mostly on the strength of John Connolly's personal ties with reporters at the *Boston Globe* and the *Boston Herald* and with some television reporters. Indeed, Connolly was fast becoming a public relations maven and a talented improviser with the truth. Garrulous and engaging, he was breaking free of the grim, button-down G-man persona, a welcome change from the aloof, stone-faced demeanor of most federal agents. Connolly not only occasionally talked to reporters but regularly courted them.

But this was early on, and there were only a few within law enforcement who suspected the FBI was tilting Bulger's way. Delahunt was one of them, but he had learned there was a price to pay for confronting the Boston FBI. It was hardball. And being Boston, it was personal.

In 1980 a rumor took hold that Delahunt had had an affair with a waitress from Quincy that ended badly, with a door broken at her apartment and raised voices overheard by neighbors. The media heard about it, and one television reporter began calling the woman. The calls continued for the next two years, and each time the woman was urged to take Delahunt to court and go on air for an interview. But each time the woman said there was no case, that there was nothing to the rumor, "not a speck of truth." If any of it were true, she said, "Delahunt would not be DA today, believe me."

But the media weren't the only parties interested in the rumors. Two FBI agents showed up at the restaurant in Quincy one day in late 1982 asking for the waitress. The chef told the agents she didn't work there anymore. The agents took down some notes, thanked the chef, and left. They never called again.

Then there was the call the woman got in January 1983. It was from a man in her past. She later described the old friend to local police as "someone on the other side."

The two met for a drink in a Quincy lounge. The friend, Stevie Flemmi, shocked the woman by knowing about the Delahunt rumor. Flemmi really just wanted to know one thing—was it true?

No, it wasn't, the woman said one more time. Stevie never called again either.

CHAPTER FOUR

Bob 'n' Weave

The Boston FBI was convinced it needed Bulger and Flemmi, and Paul Rico, Dennis Condon, and John Connolly were going to make the match work, even if it meant dispensing with the Frank Greens of the world, and even if it meant juggling three regulatory hot potatoes—the FBI manual of operations, the attorney general's guidelines for handling criminal informants, and federal criminal statutes. Luckily for them, Rico had fashioned a "unique" style in his approach to the messy business of managing informants and had set the tone for other handlers in Boston: rules were made to be broken.

It was all worth it, they believed, to get at the Mafia. Throughout the United States the FBI's field offices were under great pressure to develop informants of a certain kind—top echelon informants—to wage war against the mob. Much of the pressure was fallout from how embarrassingly late the FBI had been in acknowledging the Mafia. The problem had been J. Edgar Hoover's intransigence. He preferred piling up statistics on bank robberies and hunting down Communists to taking a hard look at evidence of the Mafia's existence.

For instance, in November 1957 Mafia leaders convening in the upstate New York town of Apalachin became front-page news after a New York State Police sergeant stumbled upon the invitation-only event. Troopers set up a roadblock, and the Mafia delegates arriving from around the country were sent scurrying, some jumping from their cars and running into the woods. Others took refuge inside the hilltop mansion of their host, beer distributor Joseph Barbara. More than sixty mobsters were eventually rounded up and identified, many flush with wads of cash. The roster included figures from the Mafia's hall of fame: Joseph Bonanno, Joseph Profaci, and Vito Genovese. The FBI did nothing.

Two years later, on December 8, 1959, a larger group gathered closer to Boston, in Worcester, Massachusetts. The estimated 150 Mafia figures sneaked into the city, assembled at a downtown hotel, held all-night meetings, and then slipped away at dawn before any significant detection could occur. The news media and many experts in crime called these assemblies proof of a national criminal enterprise, an "invisible government," that was meeting to set policy and solve disputes. But Hoover dismissed it as hype and media sensationalism.

Only after Robert F. Kennedy became U.S. attorney general in 1960 did the FBI, slowly but steadily, move to take on the so-called enemy within. By the time of the historic public testimony of Mafia informant Joseph Valachi, during congressional hearings in 1963, the FBI was officially catching up. In cities around the country special FBI units were created to focus on La Cosa Nostra. In Boston, Dennis Condon and Paul Rico were among the handful of agents picked to staff the city's first-ever Organized Crime Squad.

The agents hit the street trying to figure out the scope and the power of the New England Mafia underboss Gennaro J. Angiulo, while Kennedy's Justice Department in Washington, D.C., worked to beef up the legal tools available in the new national war.

In 1961 Congress had passed legislation, at Kennedy's behest, that elevated much of the Mafia's criminal activity to federal status. Interstate travel in aid of racketeering, known as ITAR, now came under federal jurisdiction, meaning that the previously local crimes of extortion, bribery, gambling, and the interstate movement of gambling paraphernalia were within federal reach.

Later on, in 1968, Congress passed the Omnibus Crime Control and Safe Streets Act. The act's Title III set up procedures to obtain court approval for the use of electronic surveillance against mobsters. The new legislation signaled a relaxation in privacy rights, but the government viewed it as necessary, as the kind of trade-off between personal liberty and state power that had to be allowed, it was argued, if police agencies were to have a fighting chance in their efforts to break open conspiracies like the Mafia's. Eventually the so-called Title III bugs were put to stunningly good use by the FBI in a series of major cases that toppled Mafia leaders in many cities in the United States, including Boston.

In 1970 Congress passed a law that eventually became the government's most powerful weapon against organized crime. The Racketeering Influenced and Corrupt Organizations Act, known simply as RICO, would be used in nearly every major prosecution against the Mafia during the 1980s. RICO made operating a criminal racket, for the first time, a major federal criminal offense carrying huge prison sentences. If the government could prove a pattern of racketeering—that is, show that the mobster was involved in several existing state and federal offenses—then the heavy RICO sanctions kicked in. The RICO penalties were not something mobsters took lightly. Instead of the softer sentencing that often accompanied a separate conviction for gambling or loan-sharking, the government began to win terms of twenty years and more.

Finally, the organized crime strike forces created during the 1970s quickly assumed command in the anti-Mafia crusade. The commonsense idea behind the regional strike forces was to pool the resources of the various law enforcement agencies, such as the FBI, the Internal Revenue Service, and the Drug Enforcement Administration, along with local police agencies. The representatives from the different agencies then joined with federal prosecutors as a team in an organized, multipronged attack against their specific target, the Mafia.

But for all the statutory enhancements, the anti-Mafia crusade was still going to be won or lost in the streets, and the best tool FBI agents possessed on that front was the criminal informant. "The way you solve crime, 99 percent of it is when people tell you what happened," John

Connolly once explained in a Boston radio interview. "I mean, every director of the FBI has said that informants are our most important resource."

Indeed.

"Without informants, we're nothing," Clarence M. Kelley said after being named the new FBI director following J. Edgar Hoover's death in 1972. The reason was simple: the police cannot be everywhere, and when investigators look to solve crimes they do not possess unchecked power to search and interrogate suspects and citizens. In a bid to fill in intelligence gaps, a police agency finds that informants are the essential tool—the eyes and ears of the police. Police agencies' reliance on informants developed as a partial solution to limitations on police power in the United States.

Like every FBI agent back in the 1970s, John Connolly knew full well the enormous value the bureau placed on cultivating informants. The message was drummed into rookie agents training at the FBI Academy in Quantico, Virginia: develop informants and win prestige. Later on, agents at work in the field saw that informant handlers were regarded as rainmakers. The FBI's own manual reinforced in no uncertain terms a handler's high-class status: working informants was the ultimate—a "source of great satisfaction because of the accomplishments which are obtained as a result of their successful operation." In fact, compared to the numbingly dry prose of the rest of the FBI's lengthy *Manual of Investigative Operations and Guidelines (MIOG)*, the dramatic language used to cheer on agents regarding informants borders on the breathless. Operating informants, the manual proclaimed, "demands more of an agent than almost any other investigative activity. An agent's judgment, skill, resourcefulness, and patience are tested constantly." The work required "dedication and ingenuity. The success each agent enjoys normally depends on the strength of the agent's personality and resourcefulness." Not every agent had the knack for it. But an agent who established a reputation as a handler could achieve several aims simultaneously: advance an FBI investigation, impress the bosses, and dramatically shift upward the trajectory of his own status. In training agents and in fieldwork, the FBI culture made it clear that the working of informants was center stage.

Just about the only cautionary note amid the froth in the manual reflects longtime director J. Edgar Hoover's obsession with the bureau's public image. FBI agents, above all else, were never to shame the FBI, a commandment that covered their work with criminal informants. FBI handlers were not to sponsor an informant until they were "convinced that the potential informant [could] be operated without danger of embarrassment."

In early 1976 Bulger reported to Connolly about business meetings between the Winter Hill gang and the Mafia's Larry Zannino and Joe Russo. In March 1976 Bulger reported that underboss Angiulo had sent an emissary to Winter Hill in Somerville "in an attempt to establish contact with Stevie Flemmi." The continued Mafia courtship of Flemmi was good for relations between the two criminal outfits—and good for the FBI. Bulger added that there was word that gang leader Howie Winter was going to meet with Angiulo, and then godfather Patriarca, "to create a better relationship." Later in 1976 Bulger told Connolly about the betting lines his gang and the Mafia had agreed to so that bookmakers for the respective organizations were working in sync.

Flemmi served a key role in all of the Bulger-Connolly meetings, given his easy access to Angiulo, Zannino, and the rest of the Mafia crew. Flemmi passed along what he picked up to Bulger, who would pass it along to Connolly. Bulger's reports were flavored with underworld tidbits —who was meeting with whom, who was mad at whom, who wanted to whack whom. For example, he told Connolly that a senior Mafia associate had faked a heart attack to avoid a federal grand jury subpoena. In April 1976 Bulger passed along a tip about a murder in an attempt to direct attention away from an enforcer who worked for him, Nick Femia. Bulger told Connolly: "Nick Femia had nothing to do with the hit of Patsy Fabiano." Despite his earlier insistence that he would never inform about the Irish, Bulger regularly reported to Connolly about the jockeying of various Irish gangsters in his own South Boston.

All of this information was helpful, though it wasn't as if Bulger's inside track was going to topple the House of Angiulo. Most of it amounted to underworld gossip, and it was often flat-out self-serving. Often the reliability was questionable, but Connolly did not challenge it. Instead, just as

Rico had before him, he filed reports that served to divert suspicion away from Bulger and his gang.

■ ■ ■

THE OLDER agents Paul Rico and Dennis Condon belonged to the city's first generation of FBI Mafia fighters, and they, along with their counterparts in every major U.S. city, had worked feverishly in the late 1960s to turn around the bureau's ignorance about all things Mafia. These agents had been instructed to get information, and to get it fast. One of the best techniques had proved to be electronic surveillance—even if the use of "gypsy wires" had required agents to bend the rules of law, or even break them.

In cities around the country, agents had burglarized the offices of local mobsters to install microphones, often crude devices planted behind a desk or a radiator with the wires, hidden as best they could, snaking out to a nearby location where agents secretly recorded the mobsters' conversations. In Chicago the bug secretly installed by agents in a tailor's shop used by mobster Sam Giancana operated for five years, from 1959 to 1964. In Providence, Rhode Island, agents made secret recordings of the New England godfather Raymond Patriarca. In Boston agents Condon and Rico were part of a crew that secretly bugged the basement office of Jay's Lounge, a Tremont Street nightclub where underboss Gennaro Angiulo often conducted Mafia business.

The FBI was not above engaging in dirty tricks—some silly, some far worse—in those hectic days of catch-up. In New York City agents one night grew tired of following a mob figure who'd picked up two women and was seen heading for a motel. The agents, wanting to go home, let the air out of the subject's tires, hoping that would keep him in place for a while. There were also stories about agents who rattled suspected mobsters by visiting and questioning their friends and family; the aggressive, full-court press may have been designed to gather information, but it was also used to harass the targets.

Far more serious was an incident in Youngstown, Ohio: FBI agents monitoring their makeshift bug picked up Mafia talk about a plan to kill the one FBI agent the mobsters most disliked. In short order, and with Hoover's approval, about twenty FBI agents, the toughest batch that could be assembled from nearby offices, were sent to Youngstown for a private audience with the Mafia boss. The agents crashed into the mafioso's penthouse, trashed the place, and issued a warning that considering harm to an agent was truly unwise.

These were some of the FBI tactics of the time—before the 1968 passage of federal legislation authorizing court-approved electronic surveillance. None of the information obtained during these warrantless break-ins and bug installations could be used against the mobsters in court, but the bugs provided a windfall of intelligence that put the FBI on a fast track to closing its information gap. Eventually the FBI drew up a list of twenty-six U.S. cities that were identified from then on as "LCN cities." Among those cities was Boston.

The whole premise of the top echelon informant program rested on the bureau's understanding, even acceptance, that its informants were active in crime. It was what made them top echelon informants: they were criminals with access to the LCN. Bulger's gambling and loan-sharking constituted the threshold crimes that the FBI was generally aware of going into the deal, eyes wide open. The challenge was, what about other crimes? Then what?

In the late 1950s the FBI had developed a set of regulations for the development and handling of informants. Over the years the regulations were revised and refined, most notably in the late 1970s when U.S. Attorney General Edward H. Levi crafted for the Justice Department a series of informant guidelines that the FBI incorporated into its manual of operations. By decade's end the FBI was reporting that it had 2,847 active informants on board in its 59 field offices, an unknown number of them serving in the hot-ticket top echelon category.

For handlers the guidelines were the bureau's soup-to-nuts primer. For example, when developing an informant, an agent was required to conduct a *suitability review* to assess the informant's reliability and motive. Motivation could vary: money or revenge or the competitive edge against other gangsters. If the FBI succeeded in taking down the underworld competition, an informant obviously stood to gain.

There was also a section on the *admonishments* an FBI handler was re-quired to convey regularly to his informants—warnings intended to pre-vent an informant's deal from softening into a cozy, protective cover. The informant was not to consider himself an employee of the FBI or to expect the FBI to protect him from arrest or prosecution for crimes he committed on his own time. Furthermore, the informant was warned against com-mitting any acts of violence and was not to plan or initiate a crime.

The regulations also outlined *controls* intended to keep the agent from being compromised or, worse, corrupted. The safety checks were an ac-knowledgment of the danger and temptations inherent in having agents team up with criminals. Provisions emphasized the "special care" that had to be exercised "to carefully evaluate and closely supervise" the use of in-formants, in large measure to ensure that "the government itself does not become a violator of the law." In an effort to keep the deal on track, an al-ternate FBI agent was to be assigned to work alongside the primary handler in managing the informant. To ensure that the FBI was keeping the upper hand, the handler's squad supervisor was required to meet with the informant periodically to assess the bump and grind going on between the informant and his FBI handler. The informant's reports were to be test-ed constantly for accuracy and quality. Meanwhile, agents were barred from socializing with their informants or having any business ties with them. The exchange of gifts between agents and informants was prohibited.

Taken as a whole, the regulations on paper seemed fairly airtight, but they also provided plenty of wiggle room. Even though the regulations stipulated that FBI informants could not commit any crimes, another sec-tion allowed for the "authorization" of an informant to break the law when "the FBI determines that such participation is necessary to obtain information needed for purposes of federal prosecution." Though the guidelines discouraged use of this escape clause, the discretion to permit criminal activity rested with FBI agents in the field, agents like John Connolly, Paul Rico, and Dennis Condon. There was little oversight from FBI headquarters in Washington and no requirement that the bureau consult with anyone outside the FBI—namely, Justice Department lawyers—to review the wisdom of authorizing a particular crime. It was the FBI's private business, an in-house matter. Deferring to the FBI, Levi and other Justice Department officials had agreed there was no other way if the FBI was going to fulfill its "sacred promise" of protecting an informant's confidentiality. To seek outside review was to risk exposing an informant's identity, and informants, according to the guidelines, were told right from the start "that the FBI will take all possible steps to maintain the full confidentiality of the informant's relationship with the FBI."

It was a pledge right down John Connolly's alley, an institutional version of the loyalty oath taken on the streets of Southie: you never turn your back on a friend, and you always keep your word. But Southie was not the FBI. Even if field agents possessed the power to give informants room to move in the underworld, the guidelines nonetheless required that agents consult the Justice Department if they learned that their informants were committing unauthorized crimes that had nothing to do with their deal with the FBI—particularly crimes of violence. "Under no circumstance shall the FBI take any action to conceal a crime by one of its informants." This commandment was regarded as one of the guidelines' core principles. Getting word of a crime, the FBI had some choices. It could report the criminal activity to another police agency for possible investigation. Or it could consult with federal prosecutors and together consider whether the extracurricular criminal activity was worth tolerating given the informant's high value. But something had to be done; some assessment of the informant's status had to be made, a review that required outside ventilation of the FBI's usually exclusive and secret domain.

But the rules were only as good as the agents abiding by them, and in Boston, Paul Rico had already shown how the rules could be exploited, or even ignored. It was as if the Boston agents focused on another section tailored to their personal styles: "The success of the Top Echelon Criminal Program depends on a dynamic and imaginative approach." If need be, the Boston agents concluded, the rest of the guidelines could be treated as a nuisance.

■ ■ ■

BOSTON, of course, wasn't alone. Street agents everywhere learned to bob and weave their way through the thicket of rules, at once trying to honor them and cut their informants as much slack as possible, all in the name of keeping the flow of intelligence uninterrupted. Given law enforcement's own laws of gravity, gaps opened up between theory and real-world application. During the 1970s the FBI botched the handling of an informant inside the Ku Klux Klan. The klansman, Gary Thomas Rowe, was said to have committed a number of crimes, including a murder, while working as an FBI informant—crimes the FBI knew about but had covered up to preserve Rowe's status. The peril was always out there.

Stevie Flemmi was a good example of some of the problems inherent in the system. In 1966 Flemmi had described to the FBI in detail the severe beating he gave an underworld flunkie in a dispute over a loan-shark debt. The victim required "a hundred stitches" to his head and face, according to the FBI report that Rico wrote up about the incident. But beyond the report, no action was taken. In 1967 Flemmi regularly told Rico about his illegal football lottery card operation—the ups and downs, when the money was good, when it was slow. In 1968 Flemmi described his loan-sharking business, and how he'd put money on the street that he'd borrowed from Larry Zannino. Flemmi got the money from Zannino at an interest rate of 1 percent a week; in turn, Flemmi loaned out the money at a rate of 5 percent a week, which translated into a usurious annual rate of 260 percent. He'd even hinted strongly that he killed the Bennett brothers, but it was as if Rico covered his ears: hear no evil. After all, Rico had, on his own, not only promised Flemmi that the FBI was not going to use information about his illegal gambling and loan-sharking against him but also pledged to protect Flemmi from other investigators, even if it meant breaking all the rules. It left Flemmi feeling pretty special.

Now it was John Connolly's turn.

Connolly had finally managed to get the Green matter pushed aside, in order to keep Bulger and Flemmi going, when another brushfire broke out. This time two businessmen from a local vending machine company named National Melotone were complaining to the FBI about Bulger and Flemmi's competitive business practices. In a predatory and expansive move, Bulger and Flemmi were intimidating bar and store owners in the greater Boston area, demanding that they replace Melotone's vending machines with those from a company controlled by the two gangsters. Melotone went to the FBI for help.

Melotone was right to seek an investigation. During 1976 and 1977 Flemmi, Bulger, and two associates from the Winter Hill gang had scouted locations—bars and restaurants—where their vending machines could be installed. "In South Boston, Jim was looking for locations," Flemmi said. "And I was looking for locations in Roxbury and Dorchester."

Bulger and Flemmi had notified "salesmen" from their company about potential sites, and the salesmen had then paid visits to the bars and restaurants to explain why each establishment ought to install their company's vending machines. It was a fairly persuasive pitch that included the muscle of a certain kind of underworld name recognition. "They would use our names," Flemmi said.

The Melotone matter found its way to handler John Connolly.

After huddling with Bulger, Connolly set up a meeting with the executives from Melotone to outline for the company officials the hard-core truths about pursuing a criminal case. The agent told them they could certainly go after Bulger and Flemmi; that was their legal right. But he asked them if they'd really thought the whole thing through. Did they understand what it meant to testify against the mobsters? The disruption to their lives, even the risk to their families' safety? "He painted a very bleak picture to them," Flemmi recalled.

Connolly also told the company men their lives might be in danger. "If they wanted to prosecute, he was willing to, you know, to prosecute us," Flemmi recalled. "But he said that they'd have to go into the witness protection program because of who we were."

John Connolly's grim forecast had its desired effect. Soon, said Flemmi, "they backed off." Connolly even worked out a compromise. He promised the executives he'd arrange for Bulger and Flemmi to concede a bit. "One location was in question," said Flemmi. "The machine came out of the place. Their machine stayed in place. . . . There wasn't any problem after that."

No harm, no foul.

It was unorthodox, but, to Connolly, why not? He'd negotiated something akin to an out-of-court settlement. No one had gotten hurt. And if the complaint evaporated into thin air, there was nothing for the FBI to investigate. Just as important, there was no reason to conduct any kind of internal review at the Boston office of Bulger and Flemmi. And certainly no reason to bring headquarters into it. The requirement in the guidelines that an informant's crimes be reported was not even triggered. Connolly had found a way to protect the deal.

"He didn't want to see us get indicted," Flemmi explained, and the FBI culture provided Connolly with the room he needed to improvise; he could talk the talk of the manual but also make up his own lines along the way.

Five months after Whitey Bulger was opened up as an FBI informant, Connolly succeeded, on February 2, 1976, in having him elevated to top echelon status. The Boston-bred agent now had two "TEs" in hand, Bulger and Flemmi. Flemmi, once "Jack from South Boston," became known as "Shogun." Bulger was "Charlie."

But cracks—small fissures, but cracks nonetheless—began to show. "Connolly fashioned himself as a very important guy," recalled Robert Fitzpatrick, a seasoned agent who became an assistant special agent in charge (ASAC) of the Boston office in the early 1980s. He always seemed to be moving around the city working people in the media, in politics, and at the office. He became the go-to guy for Red Sox tickets. On occasion Connolly failed to make the mandatory morning sign-in. His manner began to change, and his style became more charged. He began to operate like a salesman—skilled at feigning sincerity but uninterested in the real thing. It was the consummate skill of a great pretender, a skill that became his hallmark.

And he'd apparently outgrown his marriage. John and Marianne Connolly separated in early 1978. He promptly relocated to an apartment in Quincy just a few blocks from the beach road where he'd met with Bulger that moonlit night. The apartment was also practically across the street from the Louisburg Square condo complex where Bulger bunked with Catherine Greig, the younger of his two girlfriends. But for Connolly, Quincy was part of a journey, not a destination. He began thinking about moving back into Southie.

Fitzpatrick was one FBI manager who began having reservations. He and Bulger and Connolly had a secret meeting, a rendezvous that was part of a required, periodic supervisory check of an FBI handler and informant.

"I let him bullshit," recalled Fitzpatrick, about how Bulger immediately took control of the session. Bulger talked about his weight lifting, the good shape he kept himself in.

"He did a lot of talking. He did a lot of bragging—what I would consider bragging—about how strong he was, what he was doing in prison. He told me about his background. We talked about Southie. And generally speaking, it was my impression that he was trying to impress me."

After the meeting, Connolly told his FBI boss, "Isn't he a great fuckin' guy?" Fitzpatrick never forgot agent Connolly's line. Bulger, the reputed killer, loan shark, and drug trafficker—a great fuckin' guy? Fitzpatrick blanched.

■ ■ ■

IN AN office where some agents had their doubts, managers took comfort in the December 1977 promotion of another agent to oversee Connolly. The new supervisor of the Organized Crime Squad, veteran agent John Morris, was viewed as a good match for the savvy street agent, a straight-arrow supervisor who could serve as counterpoint.

The two paired off like an odd couple. Connolly was gregarious, tall, and dashing. Morris, a man of midwestern origins, was quiet and plain-looking. Connolly was a free man moving about the town. Morris was married, with a family. He lived in the suburbs, often commuted to work with Dennis Condon, and was considered a smart, capable manager whose paperwork was thorough and of high quality.

But over time Morris would himself turn out to be the polar opposite of a role model. The FBI brass had made a horrible mistake. The intense, thin-lipped Morris was no match for all that was brewing inside the Boston office of the FBI. The deal between Connolly and Bulger and Flemmi was going to turn out to be bigger than Morris could handle—bigger than any subsequent supervisor, or even the FBI itself, could handle.

CHAPTER FIVE

Win, Place, and Show

The third race at the Suffolk Downs racetrack was set to go according to script. The Winter Hill gangsters were standing by in Somerville in eager anticipation. Led by Howie Winter, and including associates Whitey Bulger and Stevie Flemmi, they had placed thousands of dollars in bets at both the track in East Boston and with bookmakers.

Time to sit back and smell the roses.

But something was wrong. One jockey, who'd been paid $800 to do his part, had decided to improvise. Instead of holding his horse out of the running, he'd raced hard to the end. Bets had been made, and now money had been lost. Howie Winter was not happy.

In the back room of a restaurant in Somerville, the jockey dutifully showed up for a postrace secret meeting. Winter was there waiting, along with one of his henchmen and the fixer himself, Anthony "Fat Tony" Ciulla. Howie Winter had gone into business with Ciulla in order to make big money off horse races up and down the East Coast. Known as the "master fixer," Fat Tony was a hulking beer keg of a man: six-feet-four and 230 pounds.

The menacing Winter got right to the point.

"You realize you took my money and allowed your horse to run?"

The jockey was nervous. He tried responding with a light touch, but his remark came off as flip. Before he could finish, Winter's sidekick, Billy Barnoski, whipped out a blackjack and whacked the jockey on the head. For good measure, Winter stepped up and slapped the jockey's face.

The jockey decided to adjust his attitude. Profusely apologizing, he offered to hold back horses in upcoming races for nothing. Winter wasn't sure. There had been talk about killing the jockey and dumping his body in the back stretch of Suffolk Downs. Nothing like a cold corpse to send a message.

But Winter decided the beating itself would suffice. The mangled race result in mid-October 1975 probably signified nothing more than a rare bad day. Federal prosecutors estimated that the gang's race-fixing enterprise with Ciulla had amassed more than $8 million in profits while operating in eight states. It could afford to lose one race.

. . .

IT WOULD always be Connolly's position that the extent of the Boston FBI's knowledge of Bulger and Flemmi's criminal activities was narrow— restricted to the gambling and loan-sharking the two had going in order to maintain their underworld credibility. But the truth was that Bulger and Flemmi had all kinds of rackets going, including the racetrack plot.

The scheme was straightforward. Using bribes and intimidation, Ciulla made sure that certain horses, usually the favorites, lost. Depending on the jockey and the horse, the bribes ran from eight hundred to several thousand dollars. Meanwhile, Winter's associates were putting down bets on the long shots, either to win, place, or show or in various high-paying combinations; in a trifecta, for instance, a winning bettor picked, in sequence, the first three winners. The gangsters spread their bets around, at the track, with bookies in the Boston area and with bookies out of Las Vegas. In some races handicapping the outcome of the race was a cinch. For instance, the field at Pocono Downs in New Jersey was often small. Ciulla bribed three of the five jockeys, and then watched the money roll in.

For his part, Ciulla really had no other choice but to hook up with Winter's gang. The son of a fish merchant, Ciulla grew up in the Boston area tagging along with his father to the track. He began fixing races in his twenties at tracks in Massachusetts and Rhode Island, sometimes bribing jockeys, sometimes drugging the horses. By late 1973 the thirty-year-old hustler had made the mistake of hoodwinking bookmakers controlled by Howie Winter. The crime boss discovered he was being "victimized" by young Ciulla. Winter decided to pay Fat Tony a visit.

Ciulla recalled meeting Winter at Chandler's Restaurant, a restaurant in the South End of Boston that Winter controlled. "He told me he knew I had bet with his bookmaker, Mario, on a fixed race." The amount was $6,000. "He told me I was responsible for beating him out of X amount of dollars and that I would have to make this money good or otherwise I would be in trouble."

But by the time they were finished talking the beef had evolved into a new business opportunity. Soon afterward the two met again in Somerville. They talked some more. Then, near the end of 1973, they convened at Winter's Marshall Motors. This time Winter had his inner circle present, including Bulger. Terms were negotiated; techniques were discussed. For each party there was a strong upside. Ciulla had the racing expertise. He knew the tracks, the jockeys, and the horses. Winter had the access to bookies. He and his associates also had the deep pockets to finance the substantial betting action they all had in mind. Just as important, Winter Hill brought along its muscle to ensure that the bookmakers they exploited would not think about retaliation if and when they realized they'd been cheated.

Starting in July 1974, Ciulla and Winter's gang began fixing horse races along the East Coast—in East Boston (Suffolk Downs), in Salem, New Hampshire (Rockingham), Lincoln, Rhode Island (Lincoln Downs), Plains Township, Pennsylvania (Pocono), Hamilton Township, New Jersey (Atlantic City), Cherry Hill, New Jersey (Garden State), and at other racetracks as well.

Then things went wrong. A jockey in New Jersey began cooperating with state police. Ciulla was busted, convicted at trial, and sentenced to serve four to six years in New Jersey state prison. But Fat Tony did not cotton to prison life. By late 1976 he'd begun talking too. The New Jersey State Police brought in the FBI, and suddenly, in early 1977, Ciulla was plucked out of prison and deposited into the federal witness protection program. In return for leniency, Ciulla was going to reinvent himself as a star government witness, and in the early days of 1977 he began talking to agents about his venture with Howie Winter's gang, about the regular meetings at Marshall Motors with Winter's crew, about Bulger, and about Flemmi, who in 1974 had returned to Boston from Montreal.

■ ■ ■

BACK in Boston during the early part of 1977, word about Ciulla's career change was not widespread. Though FBI agents in Boston were assigned to the case, Connolly was not one of them. John Morris had yet to take over as supervisor of the Boston office's Organized Crime Squad. None of the controls were in place that in the future would help snuff out inquiries into the prized informants. The race-fix probe had gotten under way out of state and only then looped back into Boston. It was all happening beyond Connolly's control. No chance for Melotone-redux.

The FBI case agent was Tom Daly, who worked out of Lowell, Massachusetts. Daly later grew close to Connolly but for now was discreetly developing Ciulla as a major trial witness to take down Howie Winter and his gang. Things got even more complicated not long after John Morris stepped into the picture as Connolly's new supervisor. The FBI could not be running informants who were simultaneously targets of a major FBI case. Thus, Morris ordered the top echelon informant shut down. Bulger, wrote Morris in a memo, was being "placed in a closed status at the present time as subject could possibly become involved in legal difficulties in the near future." Connolly himself had no choice but to sign off on the report of January 27, 1978, that was placed in Bulger's administrative file and sent to FBI headquarters in Washington, D.C. The bureau's guidelines and regulations for handling informants required no less.

Had the dance ended so abruptly?

Hardly. Morris and Connolly had something else in mind.

The January memo actually marked the start of an era of creative record-keeping that Morris and Connolly would adopt when it came to the FBI's files on Bulger and Flemmi. It was nothing short of cooking the books. Morris may have appeared to be the no-nonsense career agent—his guarded manner, thin-lipped face, and small size combined to give him the look of a pencil-pushing stickler for the rules—but all this concealed another side. Looking around the office at the likes of the flashy Connolly and, before him, the silver-haired Paul Rico, Morris was like the team manager jealous of the jocks who started and starred in the big game. And not long after transferring to Boston in 1972 he'd even sought to show that he too had the right stuff.

He was toiling on a stubborn loan-sharking investigation and had made little headway trying to persuade a wiseguy named Eddie Miani to become a cooperating witness. Having failed one on one, Morris and two other agents one night went to Miani's house and crawled around under his car. "It was a wire and a blasting cap," Morris said later, "as if you were going to rig an explosive device on it." Then they left and hurriedly placed an anonymous call to the local police reporting unknown persons monkeying with a car outside Miani's house. The police went to the scene, roused Miani, and showed him the mangled bombing device. The very next day Morris was back in Miani's face: See, I told you. Your "friends" are trying to kill you. Get smart. Come with us. The FBI is your only hope.

Miani told Morris to get lost, and the dirty car bomb trick remained the agents' secret. But the bit of law-breaking had given Morris a taste for the wild side, so that by the time he assumed command of the Organized Crime Squad he'd already developed the flexibility that made him a fitting match with Connolly. Next to faking bombs, fooling with the FBI's paperwork was lightweight; starting with the race-fixing case, the lies they wrote seemed to come easy.

For example, Morris's 1978 memo might have reported that Bulger was out of the informant business, but Bulger was never told about his putative change in status, and Connolly continued to see him as if nothing had changed. Moreover, Morris flat-out lied in a later document saying that during the race-fixing probe Connolly had "discontinued contacts." It was just not true. Then, in the 1980s, there would be a three-year period when Flemmi was closed down as an informant. But no one ever told Flemmi, and during those three years Connolly would file forty-six FBI reports of contacts he and other agents had with Flemmi during the supposed shutdown. No FBI manager would ever ask Connolly to explain the large number of contacts he and other agents were having with a closed informant. As long as the paperwork appeared in order, all was well.

For his part, Morris at the time had other, more pressing concerns than someone else's race-fixing case. The ambitious supervisor was determined to have his Organized Crime Squad devise a plan to do what no police agency had yet been able to accomplish—put a bug in Gennaro Angiulo's North End office. More immediately, Morris was up to his eyeballs overseeing another investigation already under way.

This one involved the widespread hijacking of trucks in New England. The joint probe between the Boston FBI and the Massachusetts State Police was given the code name Operation Lobster. Dozens of agents and troopers had been assigned to the case, which was built around an undercover FBI agent, Nick Gianturco, who had become Nick Giarro. He'd been brought in for the job from the FBI office in New York to minimize the chances of detection by the local hijackers. In fact, John Connolly was the one who'd nominated Gianturco. The two agents had worked on the same squad together when Connolly was stationed in the Big Apple, and they had remained friends ever since.

Gianturco was set up in a ten-thousand-square-foot warehouse in the Hyde Park section of Boston that was wired for sound and closed-circuit television. Just a few doors down the FBI and state police had rented another site, a "monitoring plant," to work the videocameras and microphones. Just a few more blocks away investigators had rented an apartment to use as a command post.

Midway through 1977 Gianturco opened for business, posing as a fence to an expanding lineup of hijackers, many of whom operated out of Boston's Charlestown neighborhood. The stolen merchandise Gianturco recovered ran the gamut—flour, liquor, shaving products, furniture, tool boxes, beer, ski jackets, sports coats and other clothing, heavy construction equipment, cigarettes, coffee, and microwave ovens. Fifteen months later, in the fall of 1978, Gianturco's field supervisors were writing FBI headquarters that "Boston now has a date of 10/31/78 as a possible date of cessation of the operation phase." By then more than $2.6 million in stolen goods had been recovered.

While Morris was busy with Operation Lobster, Connolly was meeting with Flemmi, and at one of the meetings the separate investigations suddenly came together. "It was an accidental statement made to me by a friend of mine," Flemmi recalled. "He had said to me that there was a fence, that this guy was wide open, and he was buying trailer loads of stolen goods. They were eyeing him as a potential [robbery] target because of the money he was handling, but the reason they were reluctant to do anything was that they didn't know if he was connected to anyone. So my friend asked me about it. He says: 'Can you find out if he's connected with anyone?' Because people wanted to do something, and they didn't want to take the chance of doing something and have repercussions."

Flemmi later insisted he had no idea at the time that Connolly's FBI pal was working undercover as the fence in question. But Connolly was immediately concerned for Gianturco's safety. He picked up the telephone to give his friend a heads-up.

"I got a call from Mr. Connolly at home," Gianturco said later, "and he asked me if I was going, if I had a meeting set up with the Charlestown people."

Nick Gianturco told Connolly that, yeah, he actually did have a meeting scheduled for later that night at the warehouse.

"He told me not to go," recalled Gianturco. "Because, he said, they were going to kill me." Gianturco, weary from the long months of living an undercover life, was shaken to the core. He was tired of looking over his shoulder all the time, commuting between Hyde Park and his role as Nick Giarro to his home and real life as a husband and father. Right after talking to Connolly, he bailed out of the meeting, and in the years to come he would say how grateful he was to Connolly for watching his back.

In the days following the incident Connolly did not document the episode in any FBI report. He did not notify the two FBI and state police field managers of Operation Lobster who were responsible for the safety of "Nick Giarro." Connolly told Morris about it, and the Flemmi tip was

transformed as it was passed along, just as in the child's game of telephone, deepening in seriousness from a possible shakedown to a threat of
murder. The more they talked about it, the more they dramatized the idea
of a heart-pounding, midnight scramble that resulted in saving an agent's
life, the more they now had in hand a profound illustration of the importance of the deal they had with Bulger and Flemmi. The "accidental tip"
that began with Flemmi seemed suddenly to capture the essence of why
Connolly and Morris had to do what they could to keep Bulger and
Flemmi for the FBI.

■ ■ ■

AS 1978 came to a close, the FBI handler and the FBI supervisor had a big
problem looming on the horizon: the gathering storm of the race-fixing
case. Instead of fizzling, the case building around Fat Tony Ciulla had
taken off. For Howie Winter, Ciulla was turning out to be the biggest in-
sult to a string of injuries he and his gang had suffered. In a state prosecution, Winter had been convicted of extortion and was sitting in a
Massachusetts state prison as Ciulla was unloading before the federal
grand jury in Boston. Hit by a run of huge losses in his New England
sports-betting operations, Winter had actually gone to see the Mafia's
Gennaro Angiulo before his incarceration and borrowed more than
$200,000.

The November 6, 1978, issue of *Sports Illustrated* featured a cover story
about Ciulla and his life in crime as the "master race fixer." The newly
minted government witness was paid $10,000 by the magazine for the long
piece, which mentioned the ongoing Boston probe. Down in Mt. Holly,
New Jersey, Ciulla was busy walking through a dress rehearsal of sorts for
the upcoming Boston case, testifying as the key witness at a local trial
against nine jockeys and trainers.

It all worried John Connolly. He didn't care about Howie Winter, but
he cared about Bulger and Flemmi. In a sense, the New Jersey trial was not
the immediate threat. That trial involved only the jockeys. But Ciulla's
role in the New Jersey trial was nonetheless making life in Boston miserable. Testifying against the jockeys, Ciulla was talking publicly for the first

time about how the race-fixing scheme worked. During the same weeks when Connolly was scrambling with information he'd gotten from Bulger and Flemmi that might affect undercover agent Nick Gianturco's safety, Fat Tony was providing a blow-by-blow account of who had done what to fix horse races that netted millions of dollars for the gangsters back in Boston. At one point Ciulla had been asked to identify his partners in Boston. Ciulla at first hesitated, like an actor setting up his best lines.

"Your honor, I have been in front of federal grand juries with these names. I don't know if I am allowed to say these names here in open court."

The local judge was unimpressed with Ciulla's dilemma. "You are here now," the judge replied from the bench. He ordered Ciulla to identify the key partners in Boston.

There was to be no holding back, and Ciulla didn't.

"Fellows that were partners of mine," he began.

"One's name is Howie Winter.

"One name is John Martorano. M-a-r-t-o-r-a-n-o.

"Whitey Bulger.

"Stephen Flemmi."

It was the end of 1978, and the much-anticipated Boston indictments in the federal race-fixing probe were being assembled. John Connolly and John Morris both decided they had to do something, even if Ciulla's sworn testimony in another state had made any backstage maneuverings to guard Bulger and Flemmi all the more difficult to pull off.

■ ■ ■

FIRST OFF, Connolly and Morris huddled secretly with Bulger. The meeting was "off the books." No report or memo was ever written up describing the January 1979 session. Connolly and Morris rendezvoused with Bulger at his apartment in South Boston, and the three talked through the case that had been constructed around Ciulla. "We thought we were going to get indicted," Flemmi said about those tense days of early 1979.

To Bulger, his position was pretty simple. He told the two agents that he and Flemmi were not part of their gang's race-fixing scheme. The government was in bed with a liar.

Bulger's claim hardly came as a surprise to the FBI agents—a criminal target's assertion of innocence was neither unique nor unusual. To cover his bases, Morris could have played hardball with Bulger. He could have insisted that Bulger and Flemmi execute a sworn affidavit attesting to their innocence. Doing so would have made the FBI look more responsible. If evidence ever surfaced showing Bulger to be the liar, the informants could have been prosecuted, at a minimum, for making a false statement to the FBI.

But Morris was not about to put Bulger and Flemmi through that kind of meat grinder. He "never gave that any thought," he said. Bulger was a prime cut, not ground chuck. Instead, Morris and Connolly wholeheartedly adopted Bulger's position—Bulger's word against Ciulla's—and promised to pursue the cause by seeking an audience with the chief prosecutor in the case, Jeremiah T. O'Sullivan.

Bulger was heartened when the agents said they would go to bat for him. He immediately told Flemmi they were off the hook. Bulger explained that "John Connolly had told him that we would be taken out of the case and we would not be indicted." It was music to Flemmi's ears.

Within days Morris and Connolly were crossing the few city blocks separating their FBI office in downtown Boston at the John F. Kennedy Federal Building and prosecutor O'Sullivan's office on the upper floors of the John W. McCormack Courthouse in Post Office Square. O'Sullivan was not pleased to be taking up a matter like this so late in the game. The intense prosecutor, a bachelor in his midthirties, was all business, nearly all of the time. To many lawyers who went up against him he came off as a self-righteous zealot. But to his associates he was a relentless crime fighter, even if humorless and demanding. He'd grown up in a three-decker in nearby Cambridge, graduated from Boston College and Georgetown Law School, and was determined to work his way through the ranks of local organized mobs until he reached his ultimate ambition, nailing the Mafia.

By the time Morris and Connolly walked into his office, the finishing touches were being put on indictments in the race-fixing case, and at that point Bulger and Flemmi were indeed in the mix of the nearly two dozen figures facing arrest. This was hardly the right time—the final days of a two-year investigation—to come asking for favors.

Morris and Connolly had no way of knowing the extent to which Ciulla had implicated Bulger and Flemmi. But O'Sullivan knew. In debriefing sessions in Sacramento, California, with agent Tom Daly, before the grand jury and, later, at the federal trial itself, Ciulla had been consistent and convincing. He'd described exactly how Winter and his six key associates—John and James Martorano, James Bulger, Stephen Flemmi, Joseph McDonald, and James Sims—shared the proceeds. "Profits were divided from this illegal scheme as follows: 50 percent to Howard Winter and his six abovementioned associates; 25 percent for Ciulla and 25 percent for Ciulla's partner, namely William Barnoski." He'd described the various duties: "Mr. Winter said that him and his partners would finance the situation, would be responsible for placing bets outside with illegal bookmakers, also supplying runners to the racetracks and various parts of the country. He would be responsible for collecting money with bookmakers."

Most troubling, he'd put Bulger and Flemmi right in the middle of the whole scheme. "I had them dead to rights," Ciulla recalled. Bulger and Flemmi might have left before Ciulla and the gang began partying and snorting coke, but they were around when it mattered. "Did I hang out with him?" Ciulla said about Bulger. "Socialize after the day's business? Go with him to Southie? No.

"But there was always money for him and Stevie."

The visit to O'Sullivan was stealth: without permission from FBI headquarters, the agents had no business confiding in a prosecutor. In addition, the identity of an informant was considered a palace secret; disclosure, even to a prosecutor, violated FBI rules. But that didn't stop Morris and Connolly from telling O'Sullivan about their arrangement with Bulger and Flemmi.

"We went to the prosecutor," Morris recalled, "and we told him that they had represented to us that, first of all, they weren't in it, that it was not their scheme."

Just as important, the two agents brought up a matter they knew was dear to the intense prosecutor's heart—Gennaro Angiulo. Morris said they told O'Sullivan, "These guys were in a position to help us in what was our number-one priority, the Mafia, and we asked O'Sullivan to consider these facts and consider not indicting them based on this."

The prosecutor did not press the FBI agents for the basis of their trust, why they took the gangsters at their word or whether they had undertaken any investigation to corroborate the claims of innocence. But Morris knew that for O'Sullivan to go along the prosecutor was going to have to find a way around his star witness. The entire prosecution was being built around Ciulla. His credibility was paramount to winning at trial, and here were Bulger and Flemmi pitting their word against his.

Though still not happy that the agents had waited so long—it was virtually the eve of the indictments—O'Sullivan listened intently to their pitch. When they finished, he said he would get back to them. "He would consider it," Morris recalled O'Sullivan saying. "He was favorably inclined toward it, but he wanted to discuss it with Tom Daly, who was the case agent."

Morris and Connolly left the meeting feeling encouraged. It would not be the first time that informants had been held out of harm's way in a criminal case—and properly so—in order to nurture them for bigger payoffs in the future. Indeed, at this time in the history of the FBI's ties to Bulger and Flemmi, they believed they had a strong argument for cutting the informants some slack. There was, as they'd told O'Sullivan, their potential value in developing the mega-case against Gennaro Angiulo. Moreover, Bulger and Flemmi were not the primary targets in the race-fixing case. Howie Winter was the main man. Bulger and Flemmi were midlevel, not the top dogs, and as such ideally positioned to help the FBI. O'Sullivan, the FBI could argue, should go ahead and topple the Winter Hill gang, but amid the rubble, he should just let the two lieutenants stand.

Within days O'Sullivan sent word to Morris at his FBI office that Whitey Bulger and Stevie Flemmi would be dropped from the indictment. There was some talk about how, with Bulger and Flemmi, he didn't have the kind of corroborating evidence in place, like telephone records and hotel receipts, that would buttress Ciulla's account, as they did for the other defendants. But this was simply taken as prosecutorial spin to cover their tracks. Morris quickly passed along the good news to Connolly, who was pleased. Connolly later recalled his own conversation with O'Sullivan. "He hoped they [Bulger and Flemmi] appreciated this, and that the FBI appreciated this, because he felt we waited a little bit too long in telling him their identities," Connolly said. It turned out, added Connolly, that the government had the goods on Bulger and Flemmi. "Ciulla had actually buried them, apparently, in his grand jury testimony."

Nothing, however, comes without a price. Fat Tony was now beside himself. "They tried to con me," he said. O'Sullivan "tried to justify Stevie's not being in the indictment by the fact he was a little bit on the lambrooskie. Then he said they couldn't correlate certain dates.

"I said, 'Fuck that. That's not true.'" Bulger and Flemmi had rounded up bookies to unwittingly take bets on fixed races. After suffering huge losses, the bookies would be indebted to—and controlled by—Winter Hill. "And Whitey was there all the time." Ciulla fought O'Sullivan. "Things didn't add up, and I'm not a total buffoon. Why are these guys being left out? They were partners. Why leave them out when I had direct dealings with them?" O'Sullivan kept up the double-talk, but his FBI handlers finally told Ciulla the truth.

"They had to tell me because I was going fuckin' nuts." To Ciulla it was about self-preservation, not justice. "The more of them left out on the street," Ciulla said he realized, "the more likely I get killed."

After getting back to the FBI with the good news, O'Sullivan, continued Connolly, required that Bulger and Flemmi promise not to even think about taking out Ciulla. "He told me that as a condition of their being cut loose from the race-fix case they had to give their word that they would play no role in hunting down Anthony 'Fat Tony' Ciulla."

Ciulla, still dissatisfied, felt reassured. "I wasn't okay about Stevie and Whitey, but I had to swallow that load.

"That's how it was."

Several weeks later, and amid much anticipation, federal indictments in the celebrated case were handed up. It was Friday, February 2, 1979, and the news was splashed across the front pages of the city's two daily newspapers.

In all, twenty-one men were charged, led by forty-nine-year-old Howard T. Winter and including nearly all of his associates in the Winter Hill gang, along with three Las Vegas casino executives, three jockeys, and two racehorse owners. Police were unable to round up everyone. Bulger and Flemmi, knowing from Connolly that indictments were coming down, had taken a couple of preventive measures. They warned John Martorano in time so he could get out of town, and they notified Joe McDonald, who was already a fugitive, that he had new troubles. "Because Mr. Bulger and I had been told that the indictment was imminent, we were able to warn them," said Flemmi. "Martorano fled, and McDonald remained a fugitive."

The indictment itself skipped over Bulger and Flemmi. The more than fifty-page federal court filing mentioned them only in a two-page attachment in a list of sixty-four "unindicted co-conspirators": James Bulger, South Boston, and Stephen Flemmi, unknown. "The winnings," wrote O'Sullivan, "were divided by defendants Howard T. Winter, John Martorano, James Martorano, Joseph M. McDonald, James L. Sims, and others."

Bulger and Flemmi had become a couple of friendly ghosts.

■ ■ ■

COME summertime, John Morris decided to host a party at his home. He lived outside Boston in the quiet, tree-lined suburb of Lexington, Massachusetts. It was a bedroom community with a bedrock place in U.S. history. His house was not far from where, in 1775, the opening shots in the American Revolution had been fired; the modest, colonial-style home was located near streets named after giants in American history, like Hancock and Adams.

Morris had a small guest list in mind. John Connolly was invited; it was he, in fact, who had urged Morris to hold the gathering. Nick Gianturco was going to come, all finished now with life undercover and back safe at home with his family. Then there were the special guests: Whitey and Stevie.

Morris's home life was increasingly troubled—his marriage was stormy—but professionally he and the others had much to celebrate. The FBI agents were on cloud nine. They'd blocked the indictment of Bulger and Flemmi; the race-fixing trial was under way with Tony Ciulla, on the witness stand, pummeling Winter; and third, the truck hijacking case, Operation Lobster, had gone to indictments on March 15, also making front-page headlines. It was as if they'd hit a trifecta—win, place, and show.

Back at the office, Morris and Connolly had made certain to take care of some FBI paperwork. Morris sent a teletype to FBI headquarters on May 4 saying that Bulger was "being reopened inasmuch as source is now in a position to provide information of value." The storm had passed. Seven days later Morris and Connolly added a second teletype that more fully explained the basis for the move. Bulger, wrote Morris, had not been closed in January

> due to unproductivity, but due to the fact that he became a principal subject of a Bureau investigation.
>
> In view of source's status at that time, a decision was made to discontinue contacts with him until the investigative matter was resolved. Since then, the matter has been resolved resulting in numerous indictments.

Most important, the two Boston agents reported, Bulger had not been charged. "No prosecutable case developed against source in the opinion of Strike Force attorney handling matter. Accordingly, source was recontacted and continues to be willing to furnish information." It didn't matter to the agents that this information was false, and Morris made no mention to FBI headquarters of their backroom lobbying.

"Boston," concluded Morris, "is of the opinion that this source is one of the most highly placed and valuable sources of this division." Morris said later he'd puffed up Bulger at Connolly's urging, recommending he be elevated back to his top echelon rank. Morris didn't care what Bulger was called so long as he gave the FBI information it wanted. But Connolly cared. "Top echelon informant is a credit to him," Morris noted. "In other words, that's reflective of his work and the caliber of informants that he's operating." The label was mostly about an agent's ego and had no bearing on how the office worked with Bulger. "It made no difference whatsoever," said Morris about the ranking of FBI rats. But Bulger was indeed quickly restored to his top echelon status.

These were the sorts of developments the group could toast. Moreover, Bulger would soon turn fifty, on September 3. Morris turned his attention to deciding what food to serve, what wine would be on hand.

He was a wine connoisseur, an interest Bulger and Flemmi had noticed. They would bring bottles for John to subsequent soirees, and they eventually nicknamed the FBI supervisor "Vino."

Together, as a group, they could consider what a new good thing they had. Look at Nickie Gianturco. He might have been dead if not for the alliance Connolly had made with Bulger and Flemmi. In a sense, as a result of the race-fixing case, they had even enlarged the family to now include prosecutor O'Sullivan. Connolly said later that O'Sullivan's intervention provided a new layer of protective veneer to the FBI's deal. It was as if the prosecutor had sanctified the notion that Bulger and Flemmi were protected from prosecution. "The first few years I met with Flemmi and Bulger there was no understanding. The understanding didn't come until the race-fix case, and the conversations that I had with Jerry O'Sullivan," Connolly later said.

Even though no government document would ever be drafted that reflected any kind of immunity or no-prosecution clause to the deal the FBI had with the two informants, that didn't trouble Connolly. To him it was all in the secret talk, the wink, the body language, and, most important to this agent from South Boston, his word. To make the alliance seem more palatable, the FBI began portraying Bulger and Flemmi as a couple of leftovers from the now devastated Winter Hill gang. As John Connolly always liked to say, they were merely a "gang of two."

If only it were true. Bulger and Flemmi were hardly passive, sitting idly by. Instead, beyond the FBI's radar, they'd spent the better part of 1979 taking care of business, masters of their own destinies. Bulger especially was proving to be the grand puppeteer, pulling the strings of both the FBI and La Cosa Nostra.

Early in the year they'd had a sit-down with Gennaro Angiulo in a room at the Holiday Inn in Somerville. The Mafia underboss wanted to discuss the more than $200,000 debt that Bulger and Flemmi had inherited from their fallen boss, Howie Winter. Angiulo wanted to talk interest rates and timetables for repayment. Bulger put him off, pleading hard times given the race-fixing probe, and he and Flemmi even managed to leave the meeting with $50,000 in cold cash that Angiulo gave them as a token of goodwill. Bulger and Flemmi might well have snickered afterward; they knew the FBI had begun poking around surreptitiously in the North End, looking for a way in. In fact, a few months later they overheard that Angiulo had erupted angrily after discovering two surveillance cameras aimed right at his 98 Prince Street office. Bulger knew the cameras belonged to the FBI, and he knew that if the FBI eventually made good on its promise to bring down Angiulo, he and Flemmi were never going to lose any sleep over the repayment of the $200,000 debt. Bulger eagerly told Connolly about Angiulo's temper tantrum.

In more ways than one, the underworld picture was in flux. By the time of Morris's party Howie Winter was out of the way. Bulger and Flemmi were no longer anybody's sidekicks, and Bulger was making his move upward as a crime boss in his own right. He and Flemmi were moving out of Winter Hill and relocating into new quarters in Boston not far from the Boston Garden, the aged home of the Celtics and Bruins. But by far the biggest change was a whole new approach that he and Flemmi had devised to conduct their underworld affairs. Gennaro Angiulo might enjoy the day-to-day of running an illegal gambling business. Howie Winter too. But Bulger and Flemmi had come up with a new idea that would not only take them out of the daily grind but also provide them with added insulation from law enforcement. They decided to strong-arm gamblers and loan sharks into paying them for the right to do business. They would extort from them a user's fee. Like a credit card company, they would take a percentage out of every transaction, reinventing themselves as chief operating officers, as collectors of cash payments. It was a brilliant strategy that would soon have Gennaro Angiulo, with an unmistakable trace of admiration, calling the pair the new "millionaires."

In 1979 Bulger and Flemmi began making the rounds to independent bookies to explain the new deal. Bulger, for instance, cornered one of the smartest sports-betting bookies in the region, Burton L. "Chico" Krantz. The two had a prior history: Bulger had once threatened to kill Krantz over an unpaid $86,000 debt Krantz had incurred to one of Howie Winter's bookies. Krantz could offer little resistance, and soon he began paying Bulger and Flemmi $750 a month. The bookie, along with increasing numbers of other bookies, kept up those payments until well into the 1990s. By then Krantz's monthly tribute had risen to $3,000.

These activities had not gotten completely by the FBI's radar. Trickling in from other informants was word about the moves that Bulger and Flemmi were making on the bookmakers and loan sharks. In June, around the time of Morris's party, another informant told the FBI that "Whitey Bulger and Steve Flemmi have been in the Chelsea area shaking down local independent bookmakers for payment." Morris even had an informant who told him Bulger and Flemmi had expanded their collection business to include drug dealers.

But it was as if Morris and Connolly and the Boston FBI didn't want to hear any of this. Like a drug, their ties to Bulger and Flemmi had evolved into a dependency that was hardening quickly into an addiction. Coming together for dinner at Morris's Lexington home, they were all having too good a time. It was the end of a decade, and the ambitious agents stood atop a slope with their prized informants, a perch from which they took a long view over their city and saw the promise of FBI careers on the rise.

They saw only what they wanted to see. It was a moment built on a shared premise: the future belonged to them. They'd feed the Mafia to the beast that was FBI headquarters, the press, and even the public's imagination. It didn't matter how they did it, or what methods they used, so long as they got there. Glory awaited.

Morris greeted his guests. It was the first of many such gatherings to come. "It was more social than anything," Morris said. The easy tone of the evening conveyed the feeling that they all belonged to something special, that the playing field of Boston was theirs. Morris was one of many government officials who would recognize eventually that in this instant the rule book was being put aside for good. Something much stranger than the proper, arm's-length FBI informant relationship was going on in Boston. But at the time Morris went ahead, opened some wine, and filled everyone's glass. Bulger, it turned out, had indeed brought a gift, a token of affection revealing that the gangster had a sense of humor. He presented FBI agent Nick Gianturco with a little wooden toy truck, a remembrance of the agent's undercover work in the Operation Lobster hijacking case.

"It wasn't an adversarial relationship," Gianturco said afterward. Everyone was happy.

PART TWO

*"I do my best to protect you and I may break a
few rules, but I break them in your favor."*

RAYMOND CHANDLER,
THE BIG SLEEP

CHAPTER SIX

Gang of Two?

Like a curtain rising, the garage doors at the Lancaster Foreign Car Service flew open in the spring of 1980 on a new era in Boston's underworld order. Howie Winter had fallen, and a realignment was under way. It was an industry shakeout, and standing in the bays of the repair shop were Whitey Bulger and Stevie Flemmi, arms folded, ready to take center stage and exploit any and all opportunities.

The old haunt, Marshall Motors in Somerville, had been abandoned in favor of this new downtown location. Though some of the former Winter Hill gangsters were on the run, others had come along. George Kaufman, who had operated Marshall Motors as a front for Howie Winter, now operated the Lancaster Street garage for Bulger and Flemmi. In the mornings the bays might be filled with the clanging and banging of mechanics' tools, but by early afternoon the tone of the place would change markedly. Most days Bulger and Flemmi arrived around one-thirty to take over the show. Whitey pulled into an empty bay and climbed out of his shiny black 1979 Chevy Caprice. The hushed conversations, the stream of visitors—it all revolved around Bulger and Flemmi. And accompanying them was the big and beefy Nick Femia, an enforcer with a reputation as a killer hooked on shotguns and cocaine. Femia, Kaufman, and other wiseguys stood outside as lookouts as Bulger and Flemmi took up in an office inside.

The Lancaster Street site represented an upgrade, the mobster equivalent of a law firm or bank moving its base from the margins to the center of a city's business district. It was a location that came with certain frills coveted by just about any Bostonian—a couple of blocks west and across the street stood Boston Garden. The Celtics, led by a rookie named Larry Bird, had just fallen short in their surprising run at the Eastern Conference title against Philadelphia.

More important, the Lancaster Street garage was situated in close proximity to the city's Mafia heartland in the North End. In a matter of minutes you could walk from the garage to the front door of 98 Prince Street, where Gennaro Angiulo and his four brothers oversaw the region's LCN racketeering enterprise. Finally, there were Bulger's neighbors a few blocks south. The Lancaster Street garage stood practically in the shadow of the FBI's Boston field office in Government Center, where John Connolly and John Morris were stationed.

In many ways Bulger was on a roll. Even though their former Winter Hill gang had suffered a crippling blow from the government's wildly successful prosecution in the race-fixing case, Bulger and Flemmi seemed to have adopted the optimistic view that in life there were no setbacks, only new opportunities. They'd heard that an unaffiliated East Boston wiseguy named Vito was running a loan-sharking and gambling business without the blessing of either Bulger or the Mafia. Soon the gun-toting Femia paid Vito a visit and put a pistol to his head. Then Bulger and Flemmi had their own session with Vito in the back room of a downtown smoke shop and explained the meaning of life. Vito decided to retire, and Bulger, Flemmi, and Femia took control of the East Boston franchise.

No question, when the need arose, Bulger and Flemmi were hands on. If a "client" was late on a loan payment, they would take the wayward one for a ride in the black Chevy. Flemmi would drive with the recalcitrant debtor seated by his side. From the backseat Bulger would whisper in a low but unmistakably firm tone about the need to "get it up" or "face the consequences." If a second trip was necessary, Bulger and Flemmi would have someone like Femia trash the debtor's apartment while the two crime bosses talked over the problem during the ride-along.

Usually there was no call for a third ride.

Inside the FBI Connolly and Morris were stuffing the bureau's files with confidential reports about how down and out Bulger and Flemmi were in the wake of Howie Winter's fall, but out on the street the two gangsters hardly appeared to be suffering. In addition to coordinating their affairs with the Mafia, the two were busy launching their new tactic of extorting tribute, or rent, from already established rackets. The book-maker Chico Krantz was now stopping by to drop off his monthly pay-ments, at one point plunking down an extra $5,000—an additional fee Bulger had demanded for settling a dispute Krantz had had with another bookie. Krantz was only one of many bookies now paying such tributes.

There was one hardship, a personal one. On New Year's Day 1980 Bulger's mother had died at Massachusetts General Hospital after a long illness. She was seventy-three. Whitey Bulger had stayed on in the family apartment on O'Callaghan Way in the South Boston housing project where he, his brother Billy, and John Connolly had all grown up. It was where Flemmi often picked him up in the late morning in the black Chevy to start their business day.

Bulger did have two other women in his life to comfort him. One was his longtime girlfriend, Theresa Stanley, who lived in South Boston. He'd met Stanley in the late 1960s, when she was twenty-five and aimless, al-ready a single mother of four children. He taught her how to organize her life and to have dinner ready for him each night at the same time. She was always grateful for his presence in her life. He was strict with her children, and he wanted everyone to sit at the dinner table together. But these days, even if he played father to Theresa's four kids, Bulger often ended his day in the arms of a much younger woman, a dental hygienist named Catherine Greig, who lived in North Quincy.

Despite the loss of their mother at the start of the year, 1980 was a time when both Bulgers were consolidating their power and fast approaching the top of their games. Elected as president of the state senate in 1978, Billy Bulger had established himself as a charming orator and cunning powerbroker. Conservative on social issues—opposing abortion rights and supporting the death penalty—Bulger was an outspoken defender of the working class. He remained impatient with dissent, however, if not intolerant. In words that could have been ascribed to his gangster brother, politicians described having worked with "two Billy Bulgers."

"If you are going to be just his friend, he's very polite, very proper, a very nice person, a good host, all that," George Keverian, the house speaker, said about dealings with his counterpart in the state senate. But, he added, if you opposed Bulger, you faced a different and darker side: "He gets steely-eyed, he gets cold."

In a number of highly publicized disputes Billy Bulger's reputation as a vindictive autocrat was cemented. In one, Billy became enraged when a Boston housing court judge refused to fill a clerkship with his handpicked choice. The judge lashed out against Bulger's raw patronage move by calling Bulger a "corrupt midget." Payback came through legislation that cut the judge's pay, reduced the size of his staff, and ended the court's independent status by having it folded into another branch of the judiciary. Both Bulgers were used to having the last word.

Indeed, the Bulger brothers—each in his own way—seemed determined to make a struggling city theirs. It was a period of economic unrest, of high inflation, with an aging ex-movie actor, Ronald Reagan, on his way to ousting the unpopular incumbent president, Jimmy Carter. It was the dawn of what would soon become known as the high-flying 1980s, the "Me Decade," featuring yuppies, skinny ties, designer food, and leg warmers, an era of Wall Street greed and corporate takeovers led by megafinanciers like Carl Icahn and Michael Milken.

Strutting into the Lancaster Street garage each day were Bulger and Flemmi to take care of their own mergers and acquisitions. And Jane Fonda wasn't the only one exercising hard. Both Whitey and Stevie worked out, lifted weights, and stayed fit. Bulger, even at fifty, took his appearance seriously, and he showed up at the garage to flex his underworld power wearing the body-fitting shirts that were in style. There wasn't a mirror or a windshield he didn't like. He'd pause, catch his reflection, secure in the feeling that no one—at least not the Boston FBI—was watching what he was really up to.

■ ■ ■

BUT someone was watching.

Peering out from behind the shabby curtains of a second-story window in a flophouse directly across from the Lancaster Street garage was a group of hard-driving troopers from the Massachusetts State Police. Six days a week, beginning in late April and lasting into July, the troopers were hunkered down at the window in the roach-infested bedroom, chronicling the mob action across the street.

They saw the little things—Bulger and Flemmi preening on the sidewalk between appointments, sucking in their stomachs when a pretty woman walked by or making sure their shirt buttons lined up with their belt buckles. They watched Bulger's body language downshift into business gear when he was displeased—charging hard at a visitor and jabbing a finger into the man's chest, swearing at him all the while. When Bulger was done, Flemmi would take over and do the same. More significant, the troopers saw the big things—men arriving with briefcases and betting slips. They watched money change hands. They took notes, and they took pictures. In all, during the eleven weeks they watched, they counted more than sixty noted underworld figures come and go; in fact, virtually every organized crime figure in New England, at one time or another, showed up at the Lancaster Street garage for a meeting with Whitey Bulger and Stevie Flemmi.

Like a silent movie—no words and all action—the garage provided a panoramic shot of the whole of the Boston underworld. And the action filling the wide screen in living color contrasted sharply with the narrow snapshot of Bulger and Flemmi the Boston FBI was planting in the bureau's files and in the minds of anyone who asked about the two gangsters.

The state police surveillance had begun quite by accident. Trooper Rick Fraelick happened upon the garage one day while he was driving in the neighborhood on a tip about a stolen car ring. He drove down

Lancaster Street and noticed George Kaufman and some of the other mobsters standing on the sidewalk. He pulled over and, out of their view, checked out what was going on.

It was a jaw-dropping moment. He recognized other mobsters coming and going. He saw Bulger and Flemmi. Fraelick returned to headquarters and told Sergeant Bob Long, the supervisor of the Major Crime Unit. Long accompanied Fraelick on a few drive-bys to view the activity for himself. They felt the adrenaline rush that comes with the prospect of a potentially big case. The question was where to set up. Directly across from the garage was a run-down brick building, 119 Merrimac Street. The first floor was a gay bar. Upstairs rooms could be rented. It was a dump, a cheap place where winos crashed. There was little privacy: the uninsulated walls were made of thin wood paneling that a fist could pass through easily. Posing as a gay man, Fraelick rented the room looking directly on to the Lancaster Street garage and, starting in late April, he and Long and trooper Jack O'Malley began documenting Bulger's affairs.

Other troopers were involved along the way, but these three were the principal investigators who arrived early each day and took up at the window, usually in shifts of two. The men were all local. Long, in his midthirties, had grown up just outside of Boston, in nearby Newton, the fourth in a family of ten kids. His father was a lawyer, and since he was a boy he'd dreamed of becoming a state trooper. Long was a jock in high school, even won a partial basketball scholarship to a local junior college, but once he blew out his knee his sporting life was over. Less than nine months after earning a college degree in criminal justice from City College in San Francisco in 1967, he was back in Massachusetts standing at attention at the state police academy.

Now in charge of a special investigations squad, Long had handpicked Fraelick and O'Malley—both, like himself, athletic and solidly built, the brown-haired Fraelick originally from the North Shore and the reddish-blond O'Malley from Boston's Dorchester neighborhood and a family of cops. (O'Malley's dad, a Boston cop, still patrolled Roxbury.) The two troopers, both in their late twenties, were pulled off the road to work with Long. The hours were a killer, but O'Malley was single and Fraelick, though newly married, didn't have any kids yet. Long had two sons, and the youngest, ten-year-old Brian, had just been selected as the poster boy for the Massachusetts Cystic Fibrosis Foundation. The boy got to pose with Bobby Orr of the Bruins in the poster.

The room the troopers shared was small and stuffy, and as the weeks passed into June and July it got hotter. They'd come to work wearing shorts and T-shirts, carrying gym bags that concealed their cameras and logbooks. They practically had to whisper so the other occupants in the flophouse would not overhear them. Fights frequently broke out in the other rooms running down the hallway. But it was worth it, they thought.

The garage's daily rhythm quickly revealed itself: Kaufman opened up in the morning, and then Bulger and Flemmi took over in the early afternoon. Besides Bulger, Flemmi, Kaufman, and Femia, there were a number of other regulars, including established mobsters like Phil Waggenheim and Mafia associate Nicky Giso.

Then there were the heavy hitters. Bulger met with Donato Angiulo, a *capo de regime*, or captain, in his brother's crime family. Larry Zannino, Flemmi's old acquaintance who ranked second only to underboss Gennaro Angiulo in the hierarchy of the Boston Mafia, made entrances that resembled a Hollywood set piece. Zannino would pull up in a new blue Lincoln Continental or a polished brown Cadillac driven by an underling. The men at the garage would scatter like ants as Zannino made his way from the car to a meeting inside the office with Bulger and Flemmi. Sometimes the flamboyant mafioso would embrace Bulger and kiss him on the cheek. Not every visit was so lovey-dovey, though. Once Zannino emerged from the office and was met by two men who'd been waiting outside. Zannino embraced one, but when the second man moved in for a hug, Zannino slapped him violently. The man dropped to his knees, and Zannino began yelling. Bulger and Flemmi hustled out of the office to catch the show. Zannino berated the fleeing man and then stopped, composed himself, and climbed back into his cool blue Continental.

To the troopers taking notes across the street, Bulger and Flemmi and the Mafia—it all seemed like one family. The troopers developed a feel for the garage. They could tell when an associate was "in the shits" with Bulger. Bulger would make these men wait, and the troopers watched the men nervously pacing outside the garage, checking their wristwatches for the time, looking up and down the street, their faces clenched. When Bulger finally appeared, he would begin the finger jabbing. The body language spoke volumes. Bulger was in charge, no doubt about it. The other men at the garage deferred to him, including Flemmi.

Over time the troopers could detect when Bulger was in a funk. He would turn dark, refuse to talk to anyone or to be bothered, and sulk over in one corner. In keeping with his fanaticism about fitness, he'd take a hamburger and throw out the bun, eating only the meat. Long, O'Malley, and Fraelick learned that Bulger was neat as a pin, a casual but careful dresser who wouldn't let a hair fall out of place. He liked the things around him kept up and in place. One time Femia had gone down the street to the McDonald's near Boston Garden. Upon his return the hungry henchman spread out the Big Mac and french fries on the hood of the black car. Bulger came out of the office, saw the greasy display of fast food, and turned white-hot. He marched over, grabbed the french fries, and began whipping them at Femia. He whipped french fries into Femia's chest and into Femia's face. The 240-pound Femia backpedaled and stumbled, a hulking hitman cowering before Bulger's rage. It was as if, instead of hot french fries, Bulger were swinging a crowbar. The troopers would never forget the food fight, and its clear message: you did not mess with Whitey Bulger.

At times Long, Fraelick, or O'Malley followed Bulger and Flemmi in order to pick up their routine. They learned that Flemmi often kept the Chevy overnight. They saw that Whitey was not the only one with a complicated love life; Flemmi was the true underworld Lothario. In fact, his juvenile rap sheet contained a portent of the man's appetites: an early arrest at fifteen for a bizarre charge of "carnal abuse," without further explanation. Flemmi always had a slew of women. He might age, but he made sure the women on his arm were young.

Since the 1960s Flemmi had lived on and off with Marion Hussey in a house, just over the Boston city line in Milton, that once belonged to his parents. He kept Hussey as his common-law wife since he'd never divorced Jeannette A. McLaughlin, the woman he'd married in the 1950s when he was a paratrooper. Then, in the mid-1970s, Flemmi became smitten with a teenager working behind the counter at a Brookline jewelry store. Debra Davis was stunning. She had shiny blond hair, a big white smile, and long legs. Flemmi showered her with clothes, jewelry, even a car, and the two began to play house, first in a luxury apartment Flemmi kept in Brookline and later in a smaller apartment in Randolph, a suburb on the South Shore. By the late 1970s Flemmi had added another captivating blond teenager to his stable: he was fooling around with Debbie Hussey, Marion's daughter. Stevie and Debbie could sometimes be seen tooling around in Flemmi's Jaguar.

There were other women too, but these were the regulars. While the troopers were never sure where the Chevy might land for the night — Brookline, Randolph, Milton, parts unknown — like clockwork Stevie would pick up Bulger at the housing project around midday. Flemmi would slide over, and Bulger would slip in behind the steering wheel. They realized that Bulger's demeanor seemed to soften in South Boston, away from Lancaster Street. He greeted kids, waved to mothers, and stopped his car to allow elderly women to cross the street.

But even in Southie he had his moments. One day that summer O'Malley was following Bulger and Flemmi when Bulger turned down Silver Street. Bulger supposedly owned some property on the street, and his girlfriend, Theresa Stanley, lived there. Turning onto Silver, Bulger came upon a group of old men seated on the front stoop of one of the houses. The men were drinking. Bulger hit the car's brakes and jumped out. The men scrambled off, but one was too slow to react. Bulger hit him across the face, back and forth. The man fell to the ground and curled up. Bulger kicked him. Then he grabbed the man's hat and threw it down the street. Flemmi, meanwhile, looked up and down the street, keeping watch, but Bulger was done. He and Flemmi laughed hard, got back into the car, and sped away. O'Malley raced over to the bleeding man, but the man was no fool: he waved the trooper off, told him to get away. "I don't know nothin' and don't bother me." Even a drunk knew better.

While they were assembling their own intelligence about Bulger, the troopers also checked in with their criminal informants. One informant, code-named "It-1," reported that starting that year "there was a large Money Bank at the garage on Lancaster Street, where the 'Big Boys' go to deliver money collected as a result of illegal gaming operations run by the

North End. This garage is where the accounts are settled up." Another informant, named "It-3," told the troopers that "Bulger is a former lieutenant in the Howie Winter organization and is believed to be assuming control of the operation in Winter's absence." Another informant, "It-4," told them that "Whitey Bulger and Stevie Flemmi were presently overseeing the majority of the sports betting, numbers action, and loan-sharking for the Boston area and in particular the Somerville area."

The troopers tapped other informants as well, all of whom hooked Bulger and Flemmi up with the Mafia in a flourishing joint venture. By the time July rolled around, Fraelick, Long, and O'Malley felt they had enough probable cause in hand. In open view from the window was a case with the potential to stand as the hallmark of any investigator's career—nailing the entire lineup, the Mafia and the Bulger gang. The troopers had put up with the squalor of the flophouse, logged the long hours of surveillance, and even gotten a little wacky: on the walls of their room they'd mounted the largest of the cockroaches they killed during the surveillance, transforming the "room kill" into a trophy.

By early July the troopers had witnessed plenty of street action; now they wanted to know what the mobsters were actually saying. They sensed they'd stockpiled enough intelligence and were eager to take their case to the next level—installing a microphone inside the garage.

■ ■ ■

SEVERAL times that spring, Long, along with his commander, met with Jeremiah T. O'Sullivan, still the top federal prosecutor at the New England Organized Crime Strike Force. Long briefed O'Sullivan on what he and his troopers were witnessing at the Lancaster Street garage. They came up with a plan in which the feds would provide funding for the state police bugging operation. They brought in a local prosecutor, Tim Burke, an assistant district attorney in Suffolk County, to prepare the court papers to win a judge's approval.

Despite the federal funding, it would be a stand-alone state police effort. No other agency. It wasn't as if the troopers could not work with the FBI. After all, Long had served as state police commander in

Operation Lobster, the joint FBI and state police investigation that had involved Nick Gianturco. But there were the new rumors, especially after the race-fixing indictments when Bulger had eluded prosecution. The rest of law enforcement had begun wondering about Bulger and the FBI. But O'Sullivan, despite what he knew, told Long nothing. It was their case.

On July 23, 1980, Superior Court Judge Robert A. Barton approved Burke's application for a warrant to bug the Lancaster Street garage. Pumped up, Long, Fraelick, and O'Malley went to work. None of them had had much experience when it came to electronic surveillance, but they'd make up in energy what they clearly lacked in expertise. They'd actually made a trip to Radio Shack to buy the microphones they were going to use. Then, to case the garage's interior and get a sense of the layout of the office, O'Malley posed as a tourist needing to relieve himself. He wandered into the garage one day, looking lost and looking all around. Bulger confronted him, saying there was no bathroom, and sharply ordered O'Malley out.

It was all trial and error.

The troopers came to call their first attempt "the Trojan Horse." They obtained a fancy-looking, souped-up van, pulled up the floorboards, and created crawl space for O'Malley. Then they replaced the floorboards, covered them with a shag rug, and filled the van with furniture. With a state police secretary at his side, Fraelick drove up to the garage late one midsummer afternoon. He told George Kaufman that he and his bride were new to Boston and having some car trouble. He was worried about leaving the van with all their belongings overnight on the streets of Boston. What if he pulled the van inside the garage and then first thing in the morning a mechanic could take a look at it?

Kaufman gave his okay and waved the van in. The "newlyweds" thanked Kaufman, promised to return in the morning, and walked off. Kaufman eventually closed up and left too. The plan was for O'Malley to emerge from the van during the night and let a crew in to install the microphones. But none of the troopers had counted on one of the winos from the flophouse across the street setting up right by the garage. O'Malley, bathed in sweat and grime, had no idea what was going on. He was not in radio contact with the others, but he could hear the wino making noise outside. The troopers improvised. Long had one of his crew go out and buy a case of beer. The trooper plopped down next to the wino and began feeding him beers. Once the man passed out, the troopers could move in. But waiting ate up precious time, and just when the man was going down Kaufman unexpectedly reappeared. Kaufman started yelling at the two men drinking at his garage, and he chased them off. By this time it was too late to pull off a bug installation. Eventually O'Malley emerged from his suffocating hiding spot only to learn that Long had called off the effort.

Their next try met with more success.

Early one evening the troopers parked a U-Haul truck snugly next to the garage. The truck not only carried a crew but also created a wall so that no one from the flophouse could look down onto the garage. Most nights the winos and wackos were yelling and hanging out the open windows in the sweltering heat. The truck took care of the flophouse follies. Then, after Kaufman left, two troopers dropped down by the side of the truck and kicked out a bottom panel of the garage door. The troopers crawled in and, with the help of a technician they had hired for the job, installed three microphones—one in a couch, one inside a radio, and one in the ceiling of the office. They left, replacing the panel on the garage door.

Bob Long and his troopers were ecstatic. But the operation went quickly downhill from there. Testing the reception, they faced technical problems. Instead of mobster talk, they were picking up pager calls for doctors at nearby Massachusetts General Hospital. The microphone installed inside the radio didn't function at all. The one in the couch worked but wasn't of much use, producing little more than a rush of sound, like a hurricane, when one of the mobsters, especially the oversized ones like Nicky Femia, collapsed into it. But they were getting transmission from the microphone in the office, and that was the prime location; after straightening out the hospital interference, it was soon up and running.

Then the sky fell in.

Bulger, Flemmi, and Kaufman mysteriously started looking up at the windows in the flophouse. Abruptly they altered their routine. Instead of talking in the office or in the open bays, Bulger and Flemmi held meetings inside the black Chevy. The office was now off limits. The troopers were stunned. They kept monitoring their bugs, but shortly after the gangsters moved their talk to the backseat of the Chevy they had to stop coming to the Lancaster Street garage altogether. Early in August the court order permitting them to bug the garage expired. The troopers had their notes, a pile of great photographs, but nothing more. Bulger was gone.

■ ■ ■

IN THE days before Long, Fraelick, and O'Malley failed in their bugging attempt, trouble had been brewing for the FBI. It began with a chance encounter at a Friday night party. John Morris, cocktail in hand, sidled up to a hulking Boston detective. The diminutive Morris still managed to talk down to him—the federal agent lording over a local cop. "You have something going at Lancaster Street?" Morris asked with a conspiratorial smile that urged: C'mon, you can tell me.

Taken aback, the detective put on a poker face to mask his surprise. A direct question about another agency's secret investigation wasn't expected cocktail chatter at a midsummer party. The question hung in the air, unanswered.

Morris pushed on. "If you have microphones in there," he said, "*they* know about it."

After some more dead air, the police detective finally replied, "I don't know what you're talking about."

The detective moved away from Morris. But his heart was racing. The next morning he called Bob Long. The early morning phone call did not take Long completely by surprise. He had been sensing something was wrong. All that the bug inside the Lancaster Street garage's corner office was picking up was a jaunty Whitey Bulger commending state troopers for the great job they did patroling the Massachusetts Turnpike. Ballbusting or coincidence?

Long wasn't entirely sure. But the more he thought it over, a pattern became clear. He and his troopers had watched for months from the flophouse across the street as Bulger harassed anxious gamblers who owed money and bantered with visiting Mafia dignitaries. Then, exactly one day after a bug was up and running inside the garage, Bulger had been praising highway patrols and, more important, changing his routine. Business conversations had moved from inside the office to the backseat of Bulger's black Chevy parked inside the bay area.

Initially Long had figured that Bulger and Flemmi spotted the troopers across the way. But now word of Morris's overture made Long realize that the problem was much worse than a blown surveillance. To Long, the gangsters' new routine wasn't just one of those things that happened. It was treachery. The call from the police detective confirmed the shocking truth that Long saw through a red haze of fury. And he became transfixed by two questions:

How did John Morris know about the state police bug?

And how did he know Bulger and Flemmi knew?

By Monday morning, August 4, 1980, it was war. The ranking state police officer, Lieutenant Colonel John O'Donovan, was on the phone complaining about the leak to the head of the FBI's Boston office. The state police and FBI office were already accustomed to tangling over glory and credit for fighting crime in Massachusetts, but this kind of accusation marked the nadir of a strained relationship.

Faced with the angry finger-pointing, law enforcement did what it always does—it held a meeting. The summit at a Ramada Inn in Boston convened four days after Morris's party blunder. Attending was a who's who of law and order: O'Donovan and Long from the state police, county prosecutors, Boston police officials, an FBI official, and Jeremiah T. O'Sullivan.

O'Donovan presented the grievances of the state police. Looking around the room, he spiced his indignation with a small bluffing game. He claimed their bug had been "extremely productive" until it was tipped. And he said they knew Bulger and Flemmi were informants. Of course, the state police had no solid proof that Bulger and Flemmi were FBI snitches. But O'Donovan had a strong hunch about Bulger's possible ties to the FBI, going back to an encounter he'd had with the gangster a couple of years earlier. O'Donovan recalled going to see Bulger at Marshall Motors. The issue was a threat against a state trooper from one of Bulger's associates in the Winter Hill gang. Packing two guns, O'Donovan stopped by the garage to convince Bulger that any move against a trooper was a stupid idea. Bulger quickly assured the lieutenant colonel that nothing would come of the hotheaded rhetoric. Then the two chatted sociably about life along the law enforcement landscape, with one thing leading to another, and finally to the FBI. O'Donovan mentioned that he preferred the older agents in the Boston office to the younger ones, saying that newer agents like John Morris were too inexperienced in the ways of Boston. He made it clear that he was not impressed by Morris and other young turks.

About two weeks later O'Donovan took a call from a fuming John Morris, who wanted to know why he was badmouthing the FBI with Whitey Bulger. O'Donovan was brought up short and concluded that either the FBI had a bug planted inside Marshall Motors or Bulger was an FBI informant.

Morris's indiscreet call only compounded O'Donovan's mistrust for the FBI supervisor. O'Donovan saw the agent as a schemer who maneuvered behind a friendly demeanor. Another time he'd passed along a state police tip to Morris about a fugitive on the Ten Most Wanted List. The same day Morris and several agents raced to capture the terrorist bomber. There was no joint arrest, just an FBI press conference. O'Donovan and his troopers were forgotten on the sidelines.

But none of this was proof of skullduggery. It was just troubling background that an experienced policeman never forgot. And at the Ramada, O'Donovan didn't get into this kind of history. But neither did he and Sergeant Long disclose that the troopers, despite the setback at the Lancaster Street garage, were planning to take another run at Bulger and Flemmi later in August. Instead, O'Donovan focused on recapping the debacle at the garage, climaxed by his conviction that the FBI had compromised the bug. Between the lines the topic on the roundtable was nothing short of accusing FBI agents of a crime: obstruction of justice.

But the FBI men did not flinch. It was their kind of game. The bureau's representative, an agent named Weldon L. Kennedy, one of the assistant supervisors in Boston, listened politely to O'Donovan of the state police. Once O'Donovan was done, Kennedy had little to say.

We'll get back to you, he finally offered. But that was it.

After the meetings, however, the FBI in Boston went into spin cycle.

Initially the bureau insisted that Morris had learned about the bug by putting two and two together: first, his own informants from the North End Mafia had detected "new faces" in the area, and second, Morris had heard that Boston police were ordered to stay away from Lancaster Street. To a professional like Morris, there was only one conclusion to draw: something investigatory was under way. Morris even offered that his approach to the Boston cop was a well-meaning bid to use his insight as a warning to the troopers.

But O'Donovan and his troopers viewed Morris's account as disingenuous at best and, during the weeks after the Ramada Inn summit, made it clear they were not buying the FBI's explanation. In turn, the FBI moved the tense, interagency dispute up a notch. The FBI said it had learned from its informants that any leak had come from within the state police; the collapse of the bugging operation was the state police's own fault. The agent who had brought this new juicy intelligence to the table was John Connolly.

■ ■ ■

BACK at state police headquarters the troopers kept debating what went wrong, going over every move they'd made. They weren't going to give up, not yet. They'd seen too much of Bulger and Flemmi.

They let a few weeks go by to give Bulger and Flemmi some room to move. Then they hit the street again, riding around to see if they could pick up the gangsters' scent. It wasn't easy, especially after the debacle at the garage. Bulger was crafty, a difficult mark. Behind the wheel of the Chevy he employed a number of evasive driving techniques. If he was approaching a traffic light and the light was turning yellow, he accelerated and raced through the intersection. Sometimes he simply ran the red light. He drove down a street and suddenly pulled a U-turn and came back at you. Sometimes he drove the wrong way down a one-way street, and Southie seemed cursed with one-way streets. He knew South Boston cold, and he often zigzagged his way through the old neighborhood rather than take a direct route to his destination.

But soon enough the troopers picked him up. Just before Labor Day,

Long, Fraelick, and O'Malley established that Bulger and Flemmi had a new pattern, and it revolved around a bank of public pay phones outside a Howard Johnson's restaurant right off of the Southeast Expressway.

The new routine went like this. Nicky Femia drove into the HoJo's parking lot, circled around, and then parked. He'd saunter over to the pay phones, look around, stuff a few coins into the phone, and make a call. The black Chevy pulled in a few minutes later, carrying Bulger and Flemmi. Then they climbed out and looked around, and each went into a telephone booth to make some calls. They chatted away, their heads bobbing and turning, always looking out over the parking lot and studying any vehicle that might drive by. Once off the phone, they drove off. The troopers, if they could keep up, followed them to Southie or into the North End, where they met up with any one of the number of underworld figures they used to meet in the bay and office of the Lancaster Street garage.

So far the investigation had focused on loan-sharking and gambling, but the troopers now began to make out the hint of a drug connection. The troopers didn't know at first who Frank Lepere was; in fact, a number of photographed wiseguys were written up in their logs as "unknown white male." But showing one such photograph around, the troopers learned it was Lepere, a former Winter Hill associate who'd gone into the business of marijuana trafficking with Kevin Dailey of South Boston. Lepere had shown up at Lancaster Street carrying a briefcase; looking back, Long and his troopers realized "it wasn't full of candy bars, that's for sure." After Labor Day the troopers had followed Bulger and Flemmi from the pay phones to South Boston, where the two gangsters met up with Kevin Dailey. This time Flemmi was the one carrying a briefcase. They met for an hour in the parking lot of a closed-down gas station across from the Gillette Company plant along the Fort Point Channel.

The next day at HoJo's, on Friday, September 5, Femia caught the troopers' attention when he tucked a small automatic handgun in his pocket before locking up his blue Malibu. Bulger and Flemmi pulled in, and then a short while later a gray Mercedes 450SL rolled into the lot. Driving the car was Mickey Caruana, who at forty-one was reputedly the biggest drug trafficker in New England. Caruana was the Mafia's own drug kingpin, a brash high roller who answered to no one except Raymond L. S. Patriarca, the Providence-based godfather of New England. (In 1983 he would become a fugitive, fleeing a federal indictment for drug trafficking that charged him with netting $7.7 million between 1978 and 1981.) Bulger and Flemmi greeted Caruana. Femia stayed back while the three men went into the restaurant. The meeting lasted about ninety minutes. Outside, Bulger and Caruana shook hands heartily before splitting up.

It was all tantalizing stuff. There was another meeting with Kevin Dailey in Southie, and yet another encounter with the Mafia's Larry Zannino, who arrived at HoJo's in his blue Continental. Compared to the flophouse, the troopers' command post was posh. They'd set up in a fourth-floor bedroom at HoJo's overlooking the pay phones and were photographing and videotaping Bulger's comings and goings.

Pulling all their intelligence together, the troopers went back to court. On September 15, 1980, Judge Barton approved their second bid to capture Bulger's and Flemmi's incriminating words. The troopers had all five pay phones tapped. The wiring was done two nights later, on a Wednesday night.

But once again the troopers came up empty. Eager and optimistic, they took up their position in their hotel room the next afternoon, awaiting their targets' regular arrival. But one o'clock came and went. Two o'clock. Three o'clock. The hours passed. Bulger and Flemmi were no-shows. They didn't show up the next day either, or the day after, or the day after that. Once again Bulger was gone.

Inside their hotel room the sullen troopers had a lot of empty time on their hands. The court order they had lasted until October 11, but Bulger never reappeared. They could have screamed and yelled, cursed the high heavens, but they didn't. They didn't trash the room. But they did talk obsessively about their plight, talk that went in dizzying circles. What the hell was going on?

■ ■ ■

MAYBE they were crazy, or at least too stubborn for their own good, but Long and his unit reviewed the intelligence they had amassed against

Bulger and Flemmi and, despite their setbacks, decided to launch a third and final try. They all felt some pressure to produce something tangible— a prosecutable case—after investing more than six months of manpower and resources in the investigation. They also weren't naive: with each failure the chances for success narrowed. Bulger and Flemmi were on high alert. But Long and the troopers were still fired up, and they decided to take a final shot at the high-riding crime bosses. "We didn't think our chances were good," Long recalled, "but we figured what the hell—go for it. If it doesn't work out, we close the books on it and move on."

Their target would be the black Chevy—installing a bug in the car would be their "Hail Mary" pass. The troopers had chased Bulger from the Lancaster Street garage and from the pay phones outside HoJo's. From their surveillance, they now saw that Bulger was using the car as a mobile office. For a few weeks in the fall the troopers once again eased off to give Bulger and Flemmi some breathing room. Resuming their surveillance in late 1980, they saw that Bulger and Flemmi continued to conduct most of their business in the Chevy.

Bulger's new routine was to drive into the North End in the early afternoon and park outside of Giro's. The restaurant, located on one of the neighborhood's busier streets, Commercial Street, was only a few blocks from Angiulo's headquarters at 98 Prince Street. Giro's, like the garage before it, was a hub of underworld activity: wiseguys were moving in and out of the restaurant throughout the early afternoon. Sometimes Bulger or Flemmi went inside and sat at a table for a meeting with various underworld figures, but most of the time they sat in their car and hosted a stream of wiseguys who climbed into the Chevy, talked a bit of business, and then got out.

Following Bulger into the North End, it was a wonder the troopers did not bump into the FBI. The troopers, of course, didn't realize it at the time, but for most of 1980 the FBI had been putting the finishing touches on its sophisticated plan to bug 98 Prince Street. The operation, code-named "Bostar," targeted Gennaro Angiulo and the top tier of Boston's Mafia. Throughout the year FBI agents had been combing the North End, documenting the daily rhythms at 98 Prince. John Morris, as supervisor of the Organized Crime Squad, was in charge, along with case agent Edward

M. Quinn. John Connolly and a dozen or more agents were part of the top-secret team.

By the fall of 1980 strike force attorney Wendy Collins had already gone through several drafts of the Title III application to win the federal court approval the FBI needed to break into 98 Prince Street to install bugs. Even though Bulger and Flemmi were Connolly's prized informants, the two had not been used to develop the probable cause the FBI needed for Wendy Collins's Title III work-in-progress. Instead, the FBI was mostly relying on five or six other informants—all of them gamblers and loan sharks—who, unlike Bulger and Flemmi, regularly met with Angiulo inside 98 Prince Street.

Of course, it wasn't as if Bulger had not been discussing the Mafia in his surreptitious meetings with Connolly. He had, but Connolly's FBI reports for those sessions contained mostly secondhand Mafia gossip. Early in 1980, for example, Bulger described a "brawl" that had erupted at a Mafia wedding reception after a young hothead made the stupid mistake of "ridiculing Larry Zannino." Instantly some of Zannino's men attacked the young man, who "suffered multiple lacerations and a couple of broken bones." Bulger told Connolly about Nick Giso, who was Bulger's daily Mafia contact at the Lancaster Street garage and then at Giro's. The Mafia, said Bulger, "is supposed to be upset with Nick Giso...because of Nick's continual use of cocaine." To his credit, Bulger did provide some information about the activities of the drug traffickers Caruana, Lepere, and Dailey. "Mickey Caruana and Frank Lepere were behind the load that was interrupted recently in Maine," Bulger told Connolly in April. Bulger even gave Connolly Caruana's phone number. But these Bulger reports did not include any disclosures by Bulger about the extent and nature of his own growing business ties to the marijuana and cocaine traffickers.

At Giro's, Bulger and Flemmi met with a who's who of Mafia associates of Gennaro Angiulo's—Zannino, Danny Angiulo, Nicky Giso, Domenic F. Isabella, Ralph "Ralphie Chong" Lamattina, Vincent "Fat Vinnie" Roberto, and a steady stream of bookmakers and loan sharks. In March, armed with a 102-page, sworn affidavit authored by Rick Fraelick and with accompanying surveillance photographs of Bulger and his Mafia contacts, the troopers went back to court.

Superior Court Judge John T. Ronan authorized their third bid for electronic surveillance on March 19, 1981; that court order gave them five days to get their bug in the car. But five days later the troopers were back in court seeking an extension to the original court order. They hadn't been able to get near the car long enough to install their one-watt transmitting microphone along with a tracking device. Flemmi kept the Chevy at night, either in Milton or in Brookline at the apartment complex, Longwood Towers. Neither location was accessible. In Milton, each time the troopers approached the car under the cover of darkness Flemmi's dog went nuts. At Longwood Towers the state police technician actually got into the Chevy, but then a delayed car alarm went off. Fraelick threw a rag over the security camera, grabbed the technician, and fled, just ahead of a security guard and Flemmi himself.

The judge approved an extension, and the troopers, their hopes waning, devised their most ambitious plan. A trooper would stop Flemmi for a phony traffic infraction. The trooper would run Flemmi's plate, inform him the Chevy had been reported stolen, and then order the car towed away. With the car in their possession, the troopers could install a bug before Flemmi retrieved it.

The trooper, Billy Gorman, stopped Flemmi one afternoon as he drove the Chevy through an intersection in Roxbury. Hidden but nearby, Long and the other troopers watched and monitored the cruiser's radio. Gorman had been handpicked for the assignment; he was unflappable, and the mission called for a trooper who would not be drawn into an ugly exchange with the volatile gangster.

The cruiser's lights flashed, and Flemmi pulled over. The trooper got out, and so did Flemmi. They headed for each other right there in the street. The trooper spoke first: "Did you see that old lady there you almost ran over?"

The many months of only being able to study gangster body language now ended abruptly, and at long last the troopers finally heard actual noise from one of their targets. Flemmi's first words were hardly pleasant ones.

"What the fuck is this shit?" he shouted. No ordinary citizen, the gangster was not impressed by a trooper's uniform and badge. His temper raced from zero to sixty in an instant. "Do you know who I am, you fuckin' jerk? This is harassment!"

Methodically, Gorman asked Flemmi for his license and registration. "I don't got no fuckin' registration," Flemmi yelled. "These are dealer plates, can't you see?" The trooper calmly told Flemmi he should still have a registration. The trooper explained he was going to have to run the plate and that Flemmi would have to wait patiently. Gorman headed back to his cruiser, and Flemmi stormed off into a convenience store where he began making telephone calls.

In the cruiser Gorman consulted with Long. The tow truck was summoned. The installation crew was waiting in the back lot of the nearby abandoned Mattapan State Hospital. Flemmi came back out of the store, and Trooper Gorman explained that the car had been reported stolen. Gorman and Long even play-acted on the cruiser's radio, with Long telling the patrol trooper, "Please be advised that the vehicle comes back as stolen from Nassau County, New York, in July 1979." Gorman told Flemmi the Chevy was going to be towed.

Flemmi was apoplectic. Then he uttered the words that made Long's and every other state trooper's stomach turn to mush. "You tell fuckin' O'Donovan that if he wants to bug my car so bad, I'll drive it right up to fuckin' 1010." "O'Donovan" was obviously Lieutenant Colonel John O'Donovan, Long's commander, and "1010" was a reference to state police headquarters. Flemmi knew.

It was over.

Flemmi went back inside the convenience store. The car was towed away, but even before its arrival behind the hospital Flemmi's lawyer was telephoning O'Donovan screaming about the blatantly absurd seizure of the car. The state police commander kept a stiff upper lip and didn't give the lawyer anything, saying the car had come back as reported stolen. But the troopers all knew the ruse was up. Long told the troopers not to even install the bug. Don't give Bulger and Flemmi the satisfaction of taking apart the car and finding the bug, he said. Let them wonder, maybe they'll get a little paranoid.

This was the troopers' only consolation. They'd thrown the Hail Mary, and it had fallen woefully short. Despite their many months of successful surveillance, they'd lost in the streets against Bulger and Flemmi. They may have seen Bulger and Flemmi joined at the hip to the Boston Mafia, but they would not be taking them to court. They'd been outmaneuvered at every turn. But even in failure the state police had triggered, unbeknownst to them, a massive internal crisis over at the FBI, a crisis that, more than any other in the FBI's long history with Bulger and Flemmi, posed the biggest threat to the cherished deal Connolly and Morris had with the two gangsters.

CHAPTER SEVEN

Betrayal

Responsibility for the stunning breach in security in the potentially devastating state police bugging of Bulger and Flemmi fell squarely in the FBI's lap, and on one agent in particular. "It was Connolly," Flemmi later admitted. But Connolly wasn't the only FBI agent watching out for Whitey Bulger like a lifeguard monitoring shark-infested waters. Morris, Flemmi added, had also tipped them off. The supervisor, said Flemmi, had told Bulger that another agent had come to him looking for background information on the two gangsters. Morris interpreted the inquiry as groundwork for another group's plan to launch electronic surveillance.

In fact, before he heard from Connolly and Morris, Flemmi had gotten an even earlier tip about a possible bug from one of the bookies he and Bulger were in business with. The bookie claimed to have picked up his information from a state police trooper. But Flemmi was the first to acknowledge that this was second-hand, underworld hearsay that could not compare to the solid confirmation Connolly soon provided. "His job was to protect us," said Flemmi about Connolly's help.

Years later Connolly would finally admit that he warned Bulger and Flemmi, but his version came with a self-preserving twist: he claimed O'Sullivan had asked him to alert his informants. Flemmi, in court testimony, backed up Connolly. "Jeremiah O'Sullivan told John Connolly . . . [we] were being bugged down at Lancaster Street and to provide us with that information."

O'Sullivan's camp has denied Connolly's version, a strained account that did not square with the prosecutor's passion for putting gangsters behind bars or his animated enthusiasm for the state police operation in his meetings with troopers. Flemmi's testimony was simply seen as a bid to protect the agent who for years had protected him. The more likely scenario, according to state police, was that O'Sullivan may have taken Connolly into his confidence out of professional courtesy—mindful that Connolly was in fact the FBI's handler of Bulger and Flemmi—and that Connolly then betrayed that confidence. Indeed, the state police's long-held suspicions of FBI duplicity hardened into dogma when one of the troopers doing surveillance spotted Bulger sitting with Connolly in a car in South Boston. Whatever the fine details, Morris and Connolly had warned Bulger and Flemmi, and the FBI leaks had undermined another police agency's bid to target Boston's Irish gang.

But amid the Morris and Connolly cover-up, there was one potential bright spot. O'Donovan had found an earnest audience in the one agent who counted—the new FBI boss in town, special agent in charge Lawrence Sarhatt, who did not buy Morris's defensive explanations. They didn't sound credible, and the more Sarhatt thought about it, the more he began asking a question far more threatening. Sarhatt wondered whether Bulger had become more trouble than he was worth. Had this South Boston gangster grown too close to his FBI handlers? Beyond the question of the leak, Sarhatt began asking Morris and Connolly about Bulger's "suitability." This whole new line of inquiry further jeopardized the core deal established by Connolly five years earlier.

The strife landed on Morris's desk at a difficult time. At home his marriage was falling apart. His reckless party chatter and phone call to O'Donovan had almost blown everything. And work was all-consuming. He was coordinating the strategy to win federal court approval to bug

Gennaro Angiulo's office at 98 Prince Street. He was overseeing a punishing schedule for his expanding squad of agents. Now along came Sarhatt questioning the cornerstone of the Organized Crime Squad—Whitey's and Stevie's information highway. On top of all that, Morris knew he was losing control over the loose cannon on his squad, the crafty and connected Connolly.

Connolly had been livid at Morris for his foolhardy overture at the midsummer party. Morris had tried to make things better with Connolly. During the leak inquiry Morris had omitted in his reports that Connolly also knew about the bug well before Morris had shot his mouth off at the Friday night party. Morris's report kept Connolly off the FBI's internal suspect list of leakers. But Connolly was exerting his influence over Morris more than ever before, his bombastic personality overwhelming the introverted boss. "I should have said no to Connolly," Morris said. "But I didn't want to take him on." After weathering a crisis of his own making, Morris began to fear Connolly's political connections with a vindictive Billy Bulger and Connolly's South Boston brotherhood with the dangerous Whitey.

Late in 1980, as the FBI internal inquiry evolved from a look at a possible leak into a more dangerous review of Bulger, Morris began to follow Connolly's lead in converting the challenge they faced into something resembling an old South Boston us-versus-them fight against outsiders. To rebut Sarhatt's concerns, Connolly and Morris would have to prove that Bulger and Flemmi were invaluable assets that the state police were simply trying to destroy out of jealousy. Look at Bulger's potential, they would argue right up the FBI chain of command, not at his life in crime. No matter what it took, this is what they had to make Sarhatt see.

As the new FBI man in town, Sarhatt learned quickly that boisterous Boston was not at all like his last posting in sleepy Knoxville, Tennessee. Never before during his twenty-year career had he encountered such a tangled tale of treachery. But he was determined to get to the bottom of it. Almost alone at the FBI, he viewed the state police's O'Donovan as a straight shooter with a genuine problem. Prodded by O'Donovan, Sarhatt kept demanding more sensible answers from Morris and kept getting specious ones. After weeks of internal go-arounds and lame memos, Sarhatt began to turn up the volume about possibly closing Bulger down.

If the state police knew about Bulger's ties to the FBI, he worried, then everyone else at the roundtable at the Ramada knew. If all those state and police officials knew, that meant eventually the top-secret information might spill into the city's underworld. Indeed, Sarhatt worried that the word was already out about Bulger and that it would get him killed, leaving blood on everyone's hands. Besides, Sarhatt questioned whether Bulger's information was all that good. He began to entertain the heretical thought: shut Bulger down.

But Morris and Connolly had an answer: cut Bulger and Flemmi into the biggest case ever in the history of the Boston FBI office—the bugging of Angiulo headquarters. It was a brilliant plan, and John Morris sat in an extraordinary catbird seat, a traffic cop directing the players on both sides of the line to suit his own needs without any disruption in the Organized Crime Squad.

Winning a court's permission to plant a bug required jumping through a number of legal hoops, all of which had to do with providing the court with detailed information about the specific location the FBI was targeting for its proposed invasion of privacy. The FBI, working with prosecutors from Jeremiah O'Sullivan's office, had to prove to the court that it had "probable cause" to infringe on the mafiosi's otherwise constitutionally protected right to be left alone. In other words, the FBI had to show that the Angiulos used the office as their base and were likely to be committing crimes there.

To get the inside information that Gennaro Angiulo presided over his wide-ranging rackets at 98 Prince Street, Morris relied on a number of informants who often went there. These six or so informants—gamblers and bookmakers who regularly visited 98 Prince Street to do business with the Angiulos—brought the FBI squad intelligence that was ample and impressive. Many of them reported to Connolly, but one—the best informant in the lot—reported to Morris. This informant was a well-established bookmaker from the city of Chelsea, just north of Boston, and Angiulo depended on the bookie's financial acumen.

For his part, Whitey had rarely, if ever, stepped inside 98 Prince Street. The Mafia was wary of the cheeky Bulger. He was Irish and hoarded South Boston profits for himself. But Flemmi had always been a Mafia favorite.

He was Italian and had a long history of ruthlessly collecting loan-shark debts for the North End. But even Flemmi had been inside Angiulo's office only four or five times.

By the fall of 1980 one of the federal prosecutors assigned to work with the FBI was already putting the finishing touches on the government's application for electronic surveillance, known as a "T3 application." In painstaking detail, the application incorporated Morris's reports from agents and from agents' informants. They contained no mention of Bulger and Flemmi.

Morris and Connolly had to find a way to turn Prince Street to their advantage, and the T3, though in its final draft, was not yet complete. There was still time, and during the frenetic days leading up to its filing in court, Morris and Connolly went to work. The plan was to give Bulger and Flemmi credit for 98 Prince Street.

It began with Morris cleaning up some paperwork. Ever since the race-fixing investigation, Flemmi had been closed as an informant. (Morris had reopened Bulger in 1979, but Flemmi had been overlooked.) Flemmi did not know he'd been closed and still met with Connolly as often as he ever did; he had to be officially reopened in order to be tucked into the Prince Street T3. Morris arranged the reopening in a teletype to FBI headquarters in Washington, D.C. Flemmi's new code name was "Shogun," the term for the ruling military governors in ancient Japan who paid lip service to titular emperors.

Next came a meeting between Morris and Sarhatt on October 10. The top FBI agent in Boston told Morris straight out that he was thinking of closing Bulger. Sarhatt's alarming ruminations sent Morris and Connolly into overdrive. They called an emergency meeting for that very night, at Bulger's Quincy condominium. They explained the crisis at hand to their informants. And then the scheming agents explained that they wanted to add Bulger and Flemmi to the pending T3 as additional confidential informants who had provided inside information about 98 Prince Street.

To fend off Sarhatt's concern about Bulger's value, Morris and Connolly had come up with a master stroke—a cameo appearance inside 98 Prince Street. Flemmi could walk easily into 98 Prince Street. But now Bulger would tag along, and afterward the agents could convert the walk-on part into a starring role. It was a dream solution: save Bulger to sink Angiulo. And once in place, Sarhatt would not be able to oppose the two agents except by spurning the collaborators who helped the FBI find its Holy Grail: a surefire case against the Boston Mafia.

The last obstacle to the devious plan was some stage fright by Bulger and Flemmi. The savvy pair knew that a bug in Angiulo's office would inevitably produce evidence of their own gambling and loan-sharking ventures with Angiulo, maybe even some old murders by Flemmi. Later Flemmi would say that he and Bulger pressed Morris and Connolly about whether they would be prosecuted for crimes revealed in bugged conversations at 98 Prince Street. Flemmi would claim the agents "assured us we wouldn't have a problem and not to be concerned about it." The FBI, they were repeatedly told, would look the other way on everything short of murder.

Reassured, Bulger also blew off the state police contention that word about him was out and he was in danger. He said the only gangsters up to the job of "taking him out" were the ones who would never believe he was an informant in the first place—the Boston Mafia. He said his one worry was that the perceived weakness of Winter Hill, with some of its leaders in jail and on the lam, might prompt Angiulo to make "a move" on him to reclaim territory and lost authority. Law enforcement was not even a concern worth mentioning.

■ ■ ■

INSIDE the FBI, Connolly and Bulger teamed up, collaborating on an extraordinary memorandum that reduced agent Connolly to a ghostwriter for the rampaging Bulger. Recasting the whole issue as a political attack, Connolly's internal memo said that Bulger viewed the state police as part of a conspiracy to embarrass his brother Billy. It was a toned-down FBI version of a *South Boston Tribune* editorial that railed at intruders from across the Fort Point Channel. It was us-against-them.

Furthermore, the memo continued, Whitey wanted it known that the troopers were trying to make Connolly the fall guy for their own failures at the Lancaster Street garage. Look at the players, Bulger and Connolly exhorted—some of the same troopers who had worked for Norfolk County district attorney William Delahunt. They were all after revenge because of Connolly's recent success in investigating their murderous informant, Myles Connor, the one who ratted out other people for his own crimes.

Bulger/Connolly even went so far as to put the conspiracy inside the State House. The memo said that Delahunt and a political ally, Attorney General Francis Bellotti, were plotting revenge against Billy because he bottled up legislation that would have allowed Bellotti personal use of $800,000 in campaign funds. Whitey even protested that the state police were spreading rumors that Connolly passed him information through Billy.

Connolly's memo invoked the South Boston maxim: always retaliate when attacked by outsiders. But it misfired. Sarhatt suddenly had a highly spun polemic on his desk, a bizarre memo from an arrogant agent on behalf of an entitled informant, full of undocumented, even crazy inside baseball about political enemies seeking vengeance. For Sarhatt, it heightened rather than assuaged his original concerns.

■ ■ ■

HAVING vented his spleen, Bulger finally got down to the business of providing the FBI with some intelligence from Prince Street. It wasn't much, but that wasn't the point. It was something that could be dressed up and written about. Perception, not reality.

On a crisp late fall day at the end of November, the pair dropped by for a visit arranged by Flemmi. They talked with Danny Angiulo. Jerry wasn't even there. Danny beefed about the poor football betting season, and they talked about how Vincent "The Animal" Ferrara, an up-and-comer in the Mafia, had agreed to track down a $65,000 blackjack debt that Billy Settipane owed Larry Zannino.

Later memoranda extolled the mission as vital to the Angiulo effort, but nothing of the sort showed up in Connolly's initial report. He even credited Flemmi but not Bulger for information about Ferrara's mission for Zannino. But a few months later, when Connolly folded the ballyhooed Prince Street visit into larger memos listing Bulger's contributions, he claimed that Bulger provided detailed information on the momentous case, though he never explained what it was. Morris and others later testified that Bulger and Flemmi did a reconnaissance of Angiulo's security system and that Flemmi drew an office layout for agents.

In truth, the prized informants only told the FBI what it already knew —where the doors and windows were and that no alarms were visible. Morris admitted later that the foray was helpful but not necessary to get court approval for the bug. But at the time it was enough: Bulger and Flemmi made it into the massive T3 document.

Still, even with Morris and Connolly pushing the 98 Prince Street angle, Sarhatt wanted more: a face-to-face meeting with the crime boss from South Boston to satisfy himself that retaining Bulger was the right thing to do. Connolly used one of his many connections around town to get a room at the Logan Airport Hotel on short notice.

While the meeting-on-demand had an edge to it, Whitey arrived alone and with all his brash confidence. Flanked on each side by his FBI handlers, he was the most relaxed man in the small room. Sitting across from Sarhatt in one of the cheap chairs, he clasped his hands behind his head and plunked his cowboy boots on a small table. He talked for four hours about his relationship with the bureau and his life in crime.

Bulger proclaimed himself an old-fashioned, true-blue FBI man. In fact, he said, his entire family were all admirers of the bureau, dating back to the kindness shown to them in 1956 by none other than agent Paul Rico, Flemmi's onetime handler, who went to Bulger's home in Southie to mollify his stricken parents after Whitey was arrested for bank robbery. It was such a transforming experience for him, Bulger told Sarhatt with a straight face, that he no longer harbored indiscriminate "hatred for all law enforcement." He threw in kudos for his good friend from the neighborhood, saying his affinity for the FBI was cemented by his "close feelings" for Connolly.

Bulger also got in some licks at the state police, working the institutional bias against locals. He assured Sarhatt that even though the state police knew about his informant role, he was not concerned about his own safety. He recycled his standard answer that no wiseguy would ever believe he was a rat. "It would be too incredible," he told the FBI boss, stressing his desire to remain an active informant. He also roundly denigrated O'Donovan, saying that their meeting in the late 1970s was marred by the detective's derogatory comments about the FBI. Taking a page out of Connolly's book, he took "great umbrage" at the criticism, standing tall for the FBI and praising Morris and Connolly for being "nothing but the most professional in every respect."

And finally getting to the point of the meeting, Bulger denied that the FBI had leaked word of the state police bug to him. He told Sarhatt that he learned about it from a state trooper. In a stunning breach of informant protocol, Bulger refused to identify the trooper, saying only that the tip had been given as a favor and not as a "corrupt act." For the state police, Bulger's refusal to identify a mole within law enforcement was a high-risk outrage. It should have been a simple matter of standard housekeeping for Sarhatt: you plug the leak or you close the source. Otherwise, Bulger would keep his purported snitch in the state police while rank-and-file troopers such as Bob Long, Jack O'Malley, and Rick Fraelick risked their lives chasing a crook who always knew they were coming.

But Sarhatt blinked and moved on.

■ ■ ■

SARHATT was clearly troubled by the airport hotel meeting, driving back to his downtown office with serious concerns about Bulger's credibility. But he was a new man in town with no allies. His top organized crime agents clearly wanted to keep Bulger and make use of him in pending Mafia cases. Mulling what to do, Sarhatt reached out to O'Sullivan. What would be the impact of closing Bulger, he asked.

O'Sullivan jumped on him, saying it would amount to a calamity in chasing the Mafia. In his clipped, cocksure way, O'Sullivan told Sarhatt that Bulger was crucial to the mother of all Mafia cases, the imminent Prince Street bugging. "Crucial" became the watchword among all the sentinels guarding the FBI's secret deal with Bulger. Somehow, in a matter of weeks, Bulger had gone from being a troubling liability causing seismic fractures within law enforcement to the key to the future. Connolly and Morris had done well.

Of course, the relentless O'Sullivan viewed the issue through his prosecutor's tunnel vision. He was *for* just about anything that would get him closer to nailing the Angiulos, and he needed the Organized Crime Squad led by Morris and Connolly to get there. To the firebrand prosecutor, Bulger was such a means to an end that he told Sarhatt to retain him "regardless of his current activities," a recommendation that covered a lot of dirty ground. This tipped the scales for Sarhatt, who could live with unhappy agents but would have trouble making his way if the chief prosecutor in his new jurisdiction was against him.

As part of a one-two punch, Connolly quickly sent Sarhatt a long memorandum justifying the continued use of Bulger, listing all his contributions over the prior five years. Although Whitey's recent visit to Angiulo's office had produced no new information, Connolly proclaimed Prince Street the centerpiece of accomplishments that made Bulger the "highest caliber" informant in recent FBI history.

Connolly's memo was the ultimate spin document. It covered the waterfront, almost hailing Whitey Bulger as a crime fighter. Connolly gave him exaggerated and at times false credit for solving murders, saving two FBI agents' lives, and breaking news with inside information on a headline-grabbing bank heist. Morris weighed in to second the motion, saying that losing Bulger would be a "serious blow" to the bureau's Organized Crime Squad.

By the time Connolly's memo of December 2, 1980, landed on Sarhatt's desk, the boss had touched all the bases. It was decision time. He had talked to the man himself, wrangled with the key agents, and got braced by the best prosecutor in town. Any reservations Sarhatt had were reduced to a final, face-saving demand he scrawled at the bottom of Connolly's glowing memo. Sarhatt ordered that a "tickler" be placed in Bulger's file so the issue would be revisited in three months. But it was a paperwork matter now. Connolly would do the review under Morris's supervision. Whitey was home free.

Connolly would even walk away from the state police challenge with a career "stat," or commendation, in his file for Bulger's covert Prince

Street work. It was the kind of formal recognition that was a hot item within the bureau. It brought salary bonuses to agents with informants who provided material incorporated into T3s.

■ ■ ■

WHEN all was said and done, the Lancaster Street caper had a dispiriting ending out of *The French Connection,* the movie in which drug dealers walked and cops were reassigned.

The state police wound up with what one of them called "a bloody bag of nothing." The valiant effort to target the collaborating organized crime leaders of the Winter Hill gang and the Mafia was sabotaged and in ashes.

Sergeant Bob Long was transferred to the narcotics squad.

And within months an effort was made at the State House to eliminate the state police leadership that oversaw organized crime investigations, including O'Donovan and four others.

During one of the late-night sessions that became a hallmark of Billy Bulger's long reign as senate president, his chamber passed an anonymous amendment to the state budget that struck back at O'Donovan in an exquisitely simple and perversely personal way. A short provision with no fingerprints required officers fifty or older—O'Donovan, a major, and three captains—to make a choice: take a reduction in pay and rank or retire. The provision also covered the chief detective in District Attorney Delahunt's office, Major John Regan.

After several anxious days and protests from public safety officials about a ploy by organized crime, the item was vetoed by the governor. But the point was made.

CHAPTER EIGHT

Prince Street Hitman

Around midnight, long after agents had followed Gennaro Angiulo home and reported back that the Mafia boardroom was a dark office on a still street in the North End, the FBI entry team began to move out from head-quarters about a mile away in downtown Boston.

A dozen agents had whittled the night away in the big open squad room, sitting on desktops, drinking coffee, trading wisecracks. Some talked about the Celtics' tight victory over Los Angeles that afternoon, a good win despite Larry Bird's bad game. Others wondered why the boss, Larry Sarhatt, was going on the mission that night. Did it mean he lacked confidence in the game plan? Or was Sarhatt doing what most twenty-year FBI men would do—getting involved on a big night? No one was sure.

After everyone was in place in the North End, John Morris, as the Organized Crime Squad supervisor, called the shots over a two-way radio from a car on the other side of a small hill from Angiulo's office. He was now spending 98 percent of his time on the case, and 2 percent worrying

about Whitey Bulger's standing within the bureau and his own relationship with the disdainful John Connolly.

Nervous as a cat and bundled against the frigid January night, Morris
sat in the front passenger seat as he fielded reports from agents in cars
around Prince Street. At two o'clock the word from the other side of the
hill was "all's quiet." Morris turned to the backseat and dispatched agents
Ed Quinn and Deborah Richards and an FBI locksmith, sending them
down the hill to 98 Prince Street. They were to break into Angiulo's small
suite on this crisp clear night. Surveillance had revealed that early Monday
morning was the quietest time of the week in a neighborhood of double
parked cars outside restaurants, bakeries, pizza joints, and apartment
buildings. Even the wiseguys stayed in on Sunday nights. Now the usually
watchful neighborhood of narrow streets and five-story tenements had
finally turned in.

Quinn turned his collar to the night and started down Snow Hill Street
to Prince Street, linking his arm with the uninhibited Richards, who carried a bottle of scotch that Quinn brought from home so the trio could
look like revelers sharing a drink and looking for an after-hours party.
They meandered down the hill but stepped lively when they hit the street,
moving quickly to the faintly lit doorway at 98 Prince Street. Quinn and
Richards, no longer the party seekers, stood with arms folded across bulletproof vests while the third agent dropped to one knee to pick the front
door lock. Across the street, freezing in the trapped arctic cold of a parked
van, two other agents watched their back as the trio entered the foyer.
One more door to go.

Using radio code, Morris issued orders for FBI cars to shut down a section of Prince Street. Blocks apart, hoods were popped and agents stood
by "disabled" cars to make sure no traffic drove by 98 Prince while agents
were making their way into the Mafia's sanctuary. Larry Sarhatt stood
outside his blue Buick until word came that Ed Quinn was standing in the
garlic-saturated darkness of Jerry Angiulo's office. Inside, the inner sanctum came slowly into view—restaurant stoves against the back wall, a
table in the middle, and cheap vinyl chairs by the television near the front
windows.

Morris then ordered a second team of agents inside. No meandering down the hill with scotch this time. These were the "techies"—this was a military operation now. The three techies hit the ground running, lugging heavy satchels of equipment and looking like paratroopers taking a beachhead. All the paths to 98 Prince Street were now blocked by agents in vans and cars as Quinn opened the door for the reinforcements. Suddenly there were six agents inside of Jerry Angiulo's impregnable domain. They all stood still for ten minutes to make sure no hidden alarms had gone off and to acclimate themselves to the dark room.

Then the techies got out their cloth-covered flashlights and got to work. It took three hours to plant two microphones at the top of the side wall and wire them to big batteries the size of logs that were hidden on top of the ceiling. The bugs would transmit a scrambled signal to foil scanners and send Angiulo's conversations across Boston Harbor to an apartment in Charlestown that was jammed with agents. After several problematic tests of the signal, Ed Quinn was finally able to talk clearly to agent Joe Kelly from Jerry Angiulo's kitchen. The tape reels that would prove so lethal to Angiulo were mounted and ready to roll.

At first light, a drained Ed Quinn walked out of the Prince Street office. The last thing he did was make sure sawdust from drilled holes was swept up. At five in the morning, he climbed back up Snow Hill Street and clambered into the backseat of Morris's car. They pumped each other's hand, but it was a quiet jubilation. Wide grins but no loud yelps. It was the FBI, after all.

Four hours later Frankie Angiulo, the Mafia's day shift manager whose job was to stay on top of local bookies, made his short commute across Prince Street. While agents had worked in the dark office, Frankie had slept about thirty yards away in a ramshackle apartment in a vacant building that concealed wads of cash stuffed in heavy safes. As he did every morning at 9:00 A.M., Frankie started the day at 98 Prince Street by spitting in the kitchen sink and putting on the coffee.

By the time Jerry Angiulo showed up for work at 4:00 P.M.—working the night shift as he had for three decades—about the only thing on his mind was a trip to Florida to beat the unusually prolonged cold spell of a bitter January. But nasty weather would soon be the least of his problems.

■ ■ ■

AFTER more than a year of secretly gathering evidence in an edgy neighborhood, the new enemy in the FBI's pursuit of the Angiulos was the
deafening din inside 98 Prince Street. Listening in a Charlestown outpost
five miles away, agents struggled to decipher the fractured syntax of the
five Angiulo brothers and their henchmen as they all talked at once
against the background of a blaring all-talk radio station that was on
around the clock.

Some, like John Morris, never got the hang of it. John Connolly never
even tried, ducking out on the tedium of listening to mob talk, protesting
that he was needed more on the street. But the rest of the agents managed
to master the maddening argot of Prince Street, getting so they could follow staccato bursts of profane half sentences, snatches of Italian vernacu-
lar, gutter slang, and lightning changes in subject. The star in every way
was the domineering Gennaro. For one thing, he shouted and could be
heard over the incessant radio. For another, he mostly made sense. He
was self-absorbed and bloodless and opinionated, but you could follow
what he was saying. There was no mistaking his message, for example,
when he talked about some underlings who were arrested after a gambling raid. "We find that one of these individuals that we use becomes in-
tolerable, we kill the fuckin' motherfucker and that's the end. We'll find
another one."

Usually the bugging at Prince Street didn't reveal much until Jerry's
four o'clock arrival from his waterfront mansion in Nahant, north of
Boston. His red and silver AMC Pacer or his baby blue Cadillac would pull
up, Angiulo would enter the building, and the mood changed immediately. There was almost no small talk. Angiulo walked in the door barking
questions about food and gambling and money and murder, holding court
with the imperious impatience of a judge too long on the bench. At
seven-thirty he took a supper break, frequently cooked by the youngest
Angiulo brother, Mikey. The only other break was for the public television
series The Wild, Wild World of Animals. The underboss never missed an
episode and provided a running commentary on the wonders and
strength of reptiles.

Having successfully fought off conspiracy charges in long trials in state court during the 1960s, Angiulo was ever wary of law enforcement's reach and tools. His were prescient concerns: the FBI bugs captured a frustrated Angiulo shouting, "They can stick RICO." But no one else in the office knew what he was talking about. Angiulo worried out loud about the ease with which a racketeering case could be made against his long-running criminal organization. He alone saw the jeopardy.

Over the years Angiulo had come to view himself as shrewd beyond his merit, but he was right about the power and danger of the RICO statute. Reading out loud to indifferent henchmen, Angiulo dissected newspaper articles about a Massachusetts defendant's appeal of his twenty-year racketeering sentence that was before the U.S. Supreme Court. He lectured his brothers about the danger posed by federal prosecutors only having to prove the Angiulos committed two of thirty-two federal and state crimes over a ten-year period to establish a pattern of racketeering. He lamented that "if you break one of those crimes this year and within the next ten years you break the other one, they will take your fuckin' head off."

But Angiulo, whose high school ambition was to be a criminal lawyer, took delusional refuge in a mistaken belief that RICO applied only to those infiltrating legitimate business, as the Mafia in New York City frequently did. Oblivious to the finer points of RICO, Angiulo railed on, with hidden microphones picking up every word.

Then, in a fateful misstep that sealed his fate, Angiulo unwittingly outlined the racketeering case against himself in a colloquy with Zannino. The rambling recitation of his criminal endeavors was the bare bones of the indictment he would face just two years later.

"Our argument is we're *illegitimate* business," he said to Zannino.

"We're shylocks," answered Zannino, the family's *consigliere*.

"We're shylocks," echoed Angiulo, warming to the litany.

"Yeah," said Zannino.

"We're fuckin' bookmakers," Angiulo added.

"Bookmakers," confirmed Zannino.

"We're selling marijuana," said Angiulo.

"We're not infiltrating," replied Zannino.

"We're, we're, we're illegal here, illegal there. Arsonists. We're every fuckin' thing," said Angiulo, warming to his own argument.

"Pimps, prostitutes," added Zannino, bringing the discussion back to where it belonged.

"The law does not cover us," Angiulo declared. And then quizzically: "Is that right?"

Zannino again brought the discussion back to reality. "That's the argument," he said glumly.

The truth was, the argument was a big-time loser. Later that same night a talked-out Angiulo confronted the cruel reality. "The law was written for people like us," he said wearily.

■ ■ ■

AS Angiulo surveyed his ebbing domain, he noticed one small thing. Stevie and Whitey hadn't been around since they last visited Prince Street, when some of their indebtedness to the Mafia was discussed. Angiulo beefed about the pair not coming around "for two fuckin' months"—or since the time of their secret FBI reconnaissance mission in November 1980. As with nearly all mob matters, Angiulo thought their absence was about money. But it wasn't that simple. Bulger and Flemmi could have cared less about any money they owed a dead duck with microphones in his walls. They stayed away because their handlers tipped them off. Bulger and Flemmi knew their loose confederation with Angiulo would be discussed while the tapes reeled it all in. But it would only be hearsay for investigative leads if there was no talk about crimes from their own mouths.

From the beginning the agents did the best they could to cover up for Bulger and Flemmi as their misdeeds tumbled off the tapes in 1981 and, later, when the tapes were transcribed for Angiulo's racketeering trial. With Morris in charge, the agents distorted the meaning of raw information coming into headquarters about Bulger's gambling, loan-sharking, and potential use as a hitman by the Mafia. Running interference, Connolly raced headlong into the record. For example, the FBI tapes caught Zannino urging Angiulo to use Whitey and Stevie to kill a fringe mobster. The tapes also had Zannino paying homage to Winter Hill as a formidable partner in some loan-sharking and gambling enterprises. Indeed, the tapes revealed the Angiulos routinely discussing what the thwarted state police were after—a racketeering case based on a joint venture between the Mafia and Winter Hill. The Mafia leaders talked frequently about how best to divide gambling and loan-sharking territory with Winter Hill. Jerry Angiulo himself summed it all up when he referred to the millions of dollars in extorted payments by the FBI's pair of prized informants: "Whitey has all of South Boston, and Stevie has all of the South End."

But those fiefdoms were not only left alone by the FBI; they were protected. And the FBI's protection was hardly confined to nonviolent gaming crimes. The bulk of the business was from extorting drug dealers and bookies who faced ultimatums every month to either pay or die.

Zannino knew Stevie's work firsthand as a killer from the gangland wars of the 1960s. He reminisced with gusto about how Stevie murdered Dorchester loan shark William Bennett after Bennett crossed the Mafia. (Willie Bennett was one of three Bennett brothers murdered at Zannino's behest over financial and territorial disputes.) The bloodthirsty *consigliere* knew about Bulger's work only by reputation, aware of his use of selective violence from afar.

But Zannino knew a job for the pair when he saw one and immediately pushed them as the solution to Angelo Patrizzi. A dim-witted mobster on the periphery, Patrizzi had just come out of jail vowing vengeance against two Mafia soldiers who had killed his brother for holding back on loan-shark payments. It was a widely known threat that put the Mafia leaders on the spot. They decided to stop Patrizzi in his tracks. Patrizzi was a thirty-eight-year-old escaped convict with an eighth-grade education, a drug and alcohol problem, and a bullet fragment in his head. But he knew what it meant when Zannino had Freddie Simone start coming around the garage where he worked, making nice. Patrizzi went into hiding in Southie. Zannino offered Angiulo a suggestion for a threat living on Bulger's home turf: "Whitey and Stevie will clip his fuckin' head."

But Angiulo didn't want to owe Bulger a favor, especially when Bulger had his $245,000 outstanding bill due the Mafia. Angiulo, who saw the net-tlesome problem as internal housekeeping, preferred the safer course of using several Mafia soldiers to execute the foolish man making rash threats. And Angiulo was always thinking about who could testify against him if something went wrong: Bulger was not "one of us" who would au-tomatically stand up if caught. Angiulo even rejected the idea of having soldier Connie Frizzi team up with Bulger so Frizzi could identify Patrizzi and then get out of Bulger's way.

Connolly cleverly took the whole incident out of context and claimed that the internal Mafia debate debunked the law enforcement rumor that Bulger was sometimes used as a hitman. He reported to his boss that the Prince Street eavesdropping operation had established two "indisputable facts"—one that papered over Bulger's standing as a killer for hire and the other that jabbed the state police for overstating the general knowledge about Bulger's rat status. Connolly offered two bulletins from Prince Street to a boss just in from Knoxville.

"A. That source [Bulger] is not a hit man for Jerry Angiulo as has been contended.

"B. That the hierarchy of the LCN do [sic] not consider source to be an FBI informant as Col. O'Donovan of the Massachusetts State Police has stated."

Morris, as the supervisor of the Organized Crime Squad, weighed in with an addendum that also distorted the record being compiled in the Charlestown tape room and from a steady stream of FBI informant re-ports. He proclaimed that the Winter Hill gang was dead. The passé, empty shell that foundered when Howie Winter went to jail, Morris con-cluded, "does not merit further targeting at this time or anytime in the foreseeable future."

Angiulo's preference for an all-Mafia hit team on Patrizzi may not have been included in Connolly's FBI memo to Sarhatt, but the FBI tapes were still damaging to Bulger if anyone paid attention or was pointed in the right direction. Angiulo's true sentiments were recorded earlier in the bugging when he talked about all the people who would kill for him. Talking to a soldier about Bulger and Flemmi, Angiulo said, "We could use them. If I called these guys right now, they'd kill any fuckin' body we tell 'em to." Connolly had no choice but to steer people away from such damning declarations.

In the end, nine men dragged Patrizzi, nicknamed "Hole in the Head" (and proclaimed "real dumb" by the likes of Freddie Simone), out of a private club. They hog-tied his legs to his neck, put him in the trunk of a stolen car, and let him slowly strangle himself to death. His body was found months later in the far corner of a parking lot behind a little-used motel north of Boston. The listening FBI agents heard the plotting against Patrizzi and Zannino's concerns that the state police would find the parole violator before the Mafia did, but they did virtually nothing to intervene. Federal prosecutors convicted Angiulo of the murder seven years later, but nothing was ever done to stop it from happening.

■ ■ ■

THE FBI also turned a deaf ear to Angiulo's monomania about Bulger's $245,000 debt, incurred when he took over the Winter Hill gang in 1978. The money was being used for loan-sharking; Winter Hill charged 5 percent a week but was not paying Angiulo his 1 percent. Bulger claimed the debt was $195,000, and Angiulo became convinced that he was never going to be paid. Since there was nothing he hated more in his tightly controlled world, the debt could mean war. But it would put more blood on the sidewalk than the frustrated Angiulo was willing to shed.

Beyond the much discussed dispute over the loan-shark money, Angiulo and Bulger clashed over who controlled Watertown bookie Richie Brown. After Howie Winter went to jail, Bulger had begun clamping down on any bookie who strayed onto his playing field. Pay or die. Whitey told Brown that it would cost him $1,000 a week to stay in business and that his boss, Mafia bookmaker Charles Tashjian, should come see him. Following standing orders, Tashjian said to Bulger that he "belonged to Prince Street. Talk to Danny Angiulo."

Both sides had given the mobster version of a Miranda warning. A confrontation was now inevitable. Whitey and Stevie had no choice but to go see Danny, the one truly tough Angiulo, a killer who had made his bones on the street, unlike the short, voluble Jerry. The brothers were not on the best of terms. Every once in a while Danny would throw it in Jerry's face and their estrangement would result in Danny avoiding Prince Street. Then he would work out of his own office around the corner in the back of the Cafe Pompeii.

In a breach of protocol that left the sensitive Jerry fuming, Bulger and Flemmi made an unannounced visit to Danny's office, asking about Richie Brown. In a conversation related by Jerry to cohorts at Prince Street, he quoted Danny as challenging Bulger when Bulger claimed that Winter Hill was short of funds and needed Brown's money. "Don't say you're broke," Danny told Whitey. "I know of fifty guys that claim they give you one thousand a month... fifty thousand a month." In the end it was agreed that Brown would stay put with the Mafia. But Danny Angiulo's financial analysis of Bulger's extortion portfolio hardly reflected the moribund Winter Hill mob that John Morris told his boss was not worth targeting now or in the foreseeable future.

Despite the posing and preening along the underworld's borders, both sides knew that the wary collaboration between Bulger and the Mafia was the cornerstone of organized crime in Boston. Late one night a drunk Zannino chastised a subordinate when he learned that he had cheated Bulger and Flemmi out of $51,000. Jerry Matricia had been asked to do some Winter Hill business in Las Vegas. He was supposed to put the money down on a prearranged winner in one of Winter Hill's fixed horse races but lost it at the crap tables instead. Years after the fact Zannino was berating Matricia over a breach that could unravel the tenuous peace with Winter Hill. It also had the potential of a shooting war. Zannino declared, "If you fuck someone close to us, I'm going to give you a shake now. Do you know the [Winter] Hill [gang] is us?"

Zannino then sent Matricia out of his office and conferred with his top two associates, who agreed with Zannino that Bulger was "going to hit him." They called Matricia back and read him the riot act. Get some money quick to Stevie, they told him. A few hundred will do but start paying the debt down. Zannino ended his tirade with some fatherly advice about the little-understood virtues of collaboration. "These are nice people," he told the quaking Matricia. "These are the kind of fuckin' people that straighten a thing out. . . . Anything I ever asked them. What happened? They're with us. We're together. And we cannot tolerate them getting fucked. Okay?"

But the profusion of mob talk about LCN joint ventures with Winter Hill was ignored by an FBI in denial. The tapes were used exclusively to pursue mafiosi, and the FBI put a score in jail, including all the Angiulo brothers and Jerry's son Jason. The only action Connolly took after the Prince Street bugs ended was to tell Bulger it was safe to go back in the water.

■ ■ ■

DESPITE the smashing success of his Prince Street operation, supervisor John Morris was now flying blind. Even with the afterglow of the Angiulo case lighting his path, Morris's compass was broken. Within days of the bugs being turned off, he arranged a private celebration with Bulger and Flemmi at the Colonnade Hotel in Boston. Bulger brought two bottles of wine for "Vino" at the gathering in the upscale hotel. In the next two hours Bulger and Flemmi each had only a glass or so and Morris finished off the rest.

Feeling no pain, Morris played a tape from Prince Street for the two informants. They heard Angiulo and Zannino talking about the need to deal with the loose-lipped girlfriend of Nicky Giso because she'd shown bad judgment in talking openly about how one of Angiulo's henchmen had cut up a North End man.

To be sure, John Morris had coordinated a seven-days-a week bugging operation that required around-the-clock staffing by forty agents. He'd handled a crisis a day for four months. Operation Bostar wiped out the Angiulo crime family, an enduring law enforcement triumph that Morris hoped would carry him to a job as special agent in charge in a major city.

But Morris was also failing just as surely as he was succeeding. He left telling signs of his slowly unfolding destruction behind in the Colonnade room. Besides emptying more than two wine bottles, Morris had stumbled out of the hotel leaving behind the top-secret government tape recording he had so proudly played for Bulger and Flemmi. Indeed, the tape was retrieved only when Flemmi realized it was being left behind and went back for it himself.

Though the turning point had been long before, perhaps nothing so summed up just how masterfully Bulger had turned the tables on the FBI and just how corrupted the FBI had become than the end of the Colonnade night. A drunk Morris was driven home in his own car by Whitey Bulger. Flemmi followed in the black Chevy. Morris and Connolly may have once thought they were in control of the relationship, but they and the FBI were now just intoxicated passengers. It was midnight in Boston.

CHAPTER NINE

Fine Food, Fine Wine, Dirty Money

John Connolly and John Morris were now the keepers of the Bulger flame inside the FBI. And for Boston's increasingly fearsome foursome—Connolly, Morris, Bulger, and Flemmi—an era of good feeling had begun all around as the boundary lines between the good guys and bad guys blurred.

Perhaps they had always been blurred. Certainly Flemmi saw that there was something special between Connolly and Whitey Bulger. It was South Boston, for sure, and maybe part of it was a father-son thing. But Flemmi didn't mind; he'd come to like Connolly in his own way. The brash agent, Flemmi said, "had a personality." Bulger and Flemmi had grown fond of Morris as well, and Connolly made a point of telling his boss the good news. "These guys like you and will do anything for you," said Connolly, according to Morris. "If there's anything you ever need, just ask, and they will do it."

Theirs was a mutual admiration society.

Morris, in turn, continued to envy the swagger, the confident style, the influence that Connolly had around town. The local agent seemed to have friends everywhere. Inside the office he may not have been particularly close to Sarhatt, or even Sarhatt's successor, James Greenleaf, who took over in late 1982, but Connolly had strong friendships with many agents on the Organized Crime Squad as well as with other FBI managers. Nick Gianturco, for one, was enamored of Connolly. "He was by far the best informant developer I've ever seen in the bureau," Gianturco said. More important, Connolly maintained ties with key agents he'd worked with earlier in New York City who by now had been promoted to headquarters and held high-ranking positions, particularly in the criminal division. John Morris was fully aware that Connolly's FBI friends in Washington "had influence on me personally and my career."

Then there was Billy Bulger, who had emerged as the state's most powerful—and feared—politician since being elected president of the Massachusetts State Senate in 1978. Connolly had made sure to take Morris over to meet Bill Bulger, and the supervisor was impressed by Connolly's easy access. "He just seemed to know a lot of politicians."

Connolly, recalled Morris, liked to talk up his influence. The two agents might be chatting, looking ahead to life after the FBI, and Connolly, noting his cache of contacts, would say that "there would be a lot of good opportunities for jobs and so forth once we left the bureau." The friendships that Connolly had inside the FBI and in Boston were like money in the bank.

Morris carefully tracked these matters. He was ambitious too and wanted to make a name for himself. Connolly seemed to be everything, however, that he was not. The intense Morris envied Connolly's easy style, his ability to turn any problem that arose into someone else's concern. In Connolly, Morris saw a fixer, and therefore, thought Morris, "it was important to me that he liked me."

It was also a time for Connolly and Morris to count their professional blessings. Connolly had spun, Morris had covered, and together they rebuffed the suitability review of Bulger and Flemmi that began in late 1980 and lasted into 1981. They'd kept Sarhatt at bay, displaying a genius for exploiting loopholes in the FBI's oversight of informants.

FOR his part, Connolly was soaking up the good vibes.

Ordinarily an informant handler worked mostly alone, in a kind of iso-lation—all part of protecting the informant's confidentiality. And Connolly was mostly by himself when he met Bulger and Flemmi, either at one of their apartments or, in good weather, in the middle of the Old Harbor housing project where he and Bulger had both grown up, at Castle Island, a Revolutionary War fort overlooking the water at the easternmost point of South Boston, or along Savin Hill Beach.

But everyone on the Organized Crime Squad seemed to know he was handling the legendary Bulger, and Connolly seemed to like it that way. Besides Morris and Gianturco, agents Ed Quinn, Mike Buckley, and Jack Cloherty all knew. The word even spread beyond the squad. It was as if Connolly wanted others in the FBI to know about his prize. He was showing off.

"I have two guys you may want to meet," Connolly told rookie agent John Newton one day at work. Newton had been transferred to the Boston office in 1980. He'd been assigned to an entry-level squad running background checks on new government hires—a far cry from a coveted assignment like Connolly's on the Organized Crime Squad. Looking for a place to live, Newton was steered to John Connolly, and Connolly had helped Newton find an apartment, right in South Boston. They'd become friendly. Connolly learned that before Newton had become an FBI agent he'd served in the army's Special Forces Unit. "John seemed interested in that," Newton later said about his new pal.

"He said he had, you know, two informants, Jimmy Bulger and Stevie Flemmi," continued Newton, "and that they were interesting guys." Given Flemmi's army background, Connolly suggested that Newton might "have something in common with them."

You want me to hook you up with them? Connolly asked.

Newton figured, why not?

The meeting was scheduled for around midnight at Whitey's. Newton rode with Connolly, who knew his way around Southie blindfolded. Connolly might have chatted on about what a good thing the FBI had in

Bulger, maybe even replayed for the new listener the excitement of the Wollaston Beach rendezvous. Enlisting Bulger had been the stuff that FBI legends were made of, and Connolly liked to make it clear that he had the starring role.

Connolly pulled over a few blocks from the apartment Bulger had begun using after closing down his mother's place in Old Harbor following her death. Once inside, Newton just sat and kept his mouth shut for the first hour or so, as the other three talked business, mostly about the Mafia's Angiulo. Then, said Newton, "we just had a general conversation." They talked about "military topics and things." They opened a bottle of wine. They all drank, including Whitey, a sign that he was completely at ease.

This was the first of a number of times Newton tagged along for a session with the two informants. Just like that, Connolly had enlarged his circle.

By now Connolly was right back into the old neighborhood. He had bought a house at 48 Thomas Park in 1980, on a street atop one of Southie's rolling hills; more than a few notches above the Old Harbor project in status, these hills, two centuries earlier, had been a windswept pasture of rich grass with a commanding view. Like all the surrounding streets, the natural topography had long since been covered by rows and rows of double- and triple-deckers and shingled houses built right up against one another. They formed the wall of residences in the tightly woven Irish-American community. The FBI agent's new home was also situated across from South Boston High School, the battleground over forced busing just a few years earlier.

In Connolly's work, day was night; Bulger usually came around for a secret meeting after hours, while most of Boston slept. Sometimes even Connolly was asleep, dozing off on the couch with the TV on. He'd leave his door unlocked for Bulger and Flemmi, and the two mobsters would walk right in and make themselves at home.

Connolly appreciated the company. Now in his early forties, he was also officially single again. Citing an "irretrievable breakdown" after a four-year separation, his wife had filed for divorce in January 1982. Marianne, a registered nurse, was making do on her own. They'd split up their things long before, and with no children, the divorce was a routine, uncontested matter that became official a few months later. Now Connolly was out and around town, the ladies' man others in the office knew him to be. Like Bulger and Flemmi, he showed a preference for younger women. The twenty-three-year-old Elizabeth L. Moore, a stenographer at the office, had caught the flashy agent's eye, and the two were an item. They were soon off together to a getaway on Cape Cod, where Connolly, fulfilling the dream of so many who grow up in Boston, now owned his own place, an $80,000 condo in Brewster.

Morris was jealous of the new couple. His own marriage was also irretrievably broken down, and he struggled seeing Connolly free to escort a new young girlfriend in the city while he could only sneak around with his: Debbie Noseworthy, an FBI secretary who worked directly for Morris and his Organized Crime Squad. The adulterous affair was an open secret at the office, but for Morris it was a lie that began to eat away at him. There would soon be more and far worse deceptions to come.

■ ■ ■

EVEN though Morris and Connolly had dodged a bullet during the Sarhatt review, the two agents did not want to take any chances. They had to make sure no one would again second-guess their ties to Bulger and Flemmi. To carry this off they would have to play off the high-minded provisions in the agency's guidelines for monitoring informants. There was a fundamental tension in the guidelines that could be exploited. To secure intelligence, agents like Connolly and Morris were, on the one hand, encouraged to court gangsters like Bulger and Flemmi. And for the deal to work, gangsters were going to have to be given some breathing room.

The question was, how much? How much criminal activity could the FBI tolerate? In theory, no deal was without limits. FBI managers and handlers were always supposed to be evaluating their informants. The crux of oversight could be reduced to two issues: balancing the value of the informant's intelligence against the severity of his crimes. The trick in the Boston office was to manipulate those two sides of the equation, and inside the FBI no two agents were better positioned to shape the hierarchy's views than a handler and his supervisor.

Connolly and Morris were right there at ground control. To keep the flame burning bright, the two began creating the FBI paperwork that downplayed Bulger and Flemmi's dark side while inflating the value of the intelligence they provided. Connolly was the Bulger chronicler, and Morris signed off on the narrative. They possessed enormous influence up the chain of command and, between them, seemed to have every FBI angle covered. The Irish of South Boston have long been known for being great storytellers. In the Bulger file, native son John Connolly showed himself to be one of the great spinners of tall tales. John Morris would do pretty well for himself too.

■ ■ ■

THE crudest technique involved outright lying.

During the late 1970s, as the FBI's reliance on Bulger and Flemmi hardened, Morris had shown a knack for mendacity in his internal reports about Bulger in the race-fixing case. He'd reported that contacts with Bulger had ceased when, in truth, Connolly was seeing him regularly. Morris then lied in reports he'd filed to Sarhatt during the internal inquiry about leaks in the state police's bugging of Bulger and Flemmi at the Lancaster Street garage. For his part, Connolly sometimes filed reports to satisfy certain FBI rules that Morris afterward admitted were false. In one instance Connolly described a meeting he and Morris supposedly had had with Bulger and Flemmi to go over the warnings and ground rules agents were required to discuss with their informants. The report documenting the so-called annual review included a time and date, but Morris later admitted: "I do not believe such a meeting took place."

The more artful moves employed to downplay Bulger's crimes not only served to make Bulger appear less bad but, more important, provided a way around the bureau's guidelines requiring a strict evaluation of any unauthorized criminal activities. If a complaint or tip against a prized FBI informant could be rendered too vague or unreliable, then there would be nothing solid for the FBI to pursue. Morris and Connolly could then continue to pay lip service to the guidelines—offering assurances that if they ever did get a hard and fast tip against Bulger they would certainly perform their duty and run it down.

But somehow, in their hands, tips regularly turned to sand. It was a pattern Connolly established early on in the way he parried the vending machine executives who complained to the FBI that Bulger and Flemmi were shaking them down, and again, in the way the extortion of Francis Green fizzled once the matter landed in the FBI's lap.

The new challenge in the early 1980s was what to make of the information other FBI agents were gathering from their own informants about Bulger and Flemmi's widening criminal empire. The gangsters, said one informant, were taking over gambling operations in communities surrounding Boston. In early 1981 yet another informant reported that "James Bulger, aka Whitey, is a known bank robber and is trying to finance the funds from bank robberies into gambling activities."

The juiciest intelligence broke new ground. Crossing Morris's desk for the first time was information about Bulger grabbing a piece of the action in cocaine, the big-money narcotic that was red-hot in the early 1980s. South Boston, it turned out, was no different from any other part of the city: drugs were rolling down Broadway in a tidal wave, despite Bulger's glamorized reputation as the neighborhood's protector. Bulger might continue to promote himself as the anti-drug crime boss, but the kids shooting up and snorting in the alleyways of the housing projects knew otherwise. They might never deal directly with him, and they rarely, if ever, actually saw him, but they all knew that without his blessing there would be no "product." Bulger was riding the crest of the coke wave.

In February 1981 an informant told one of Morris's agents that Brian Halloran, a local Boston hood, was "dealing in cocaine with Whitey Bulger and Stevie Flemmi." Halloran had been linked to Bulger and Flemmi for years, especially Flemmi. He used to ride with Flemmi and often served as an advance man who checked out a club or meeting place prior to Flemmi's arrival, much as Nicky Femia did. The next month a different informant told one of Morris's men that "Brian Halloran is handling cocaine distribution for Whitey Bulger and Stevie Flemmi. Other individuals involved with Halloran are: Nick Femia, responsible for ripping off 30 drug dealers thus far. Word has been placed on the street that any drug dealer involved in cocaine has to give a 'piece of the action to Bulger and Flemmi' or they will be put out of business."

In June 1982 another informant told the FBI that a South Boston gangster was overseeing loan-sharking and drug-dealing out of a particular neighborhood bar. "He is reportedly making $5,000 a week from drugs and is paying Whitey Bulger a large percentage for the right to operate."

When these intelligence reports landed on Morris's desk, he'd review them, initial them, and file them away. Ordinarily FBI reports containing charges were indexed by the target's name, so that other agents could locate the intelligence in the investigative files. But Morris often sabotaged the process by not indexing the reports properly, making the negative material hard, if not impossible, to find. There was virtually no follow-up. The state police may have observed Bulger's tie-in with major drug dealers. The FBI's own informants may have begun reporting the same development. But Morris would have none of it. Not once did he initiate a probe or refer any of the tips for action.

Out of sight, out of mind.

While Morris directed traffic at the supervisory level, Connolly took care of padding the Bulger file. Following a drug bust at a South Boston warehouse in early 1983, Connolly filed a Bulger report saying the crime boss was "upset" with the drug dealers for "storing the grass in his town." In other FBI files Connolly always described Bulger as staunchly anti-drug, abetting the mythic portrayal Whitey clung to.

Not surprisingly, Connolly had emerged as the expert about Bulger and Flemmi inside the FBI office. If an agent had a question about Whitey's personal history, he was sent to John Connolly, and usually John Morris was the one making the referral. Whitey's rank in the underworld scheme? See Connolly. Whitey and drugs? See Connolly.

■ ■ ■

MANY of the FBI documents about Bulger were simply invention—and at this Connolly became the master. He repeatedly took a dull nugget of Bulger information and tumbled it into glittering gold.

There was the mention, for example, that Connolly made in a report to Sarhatt about the help Bulger gave the FBI in connection with a bank robbery over the Memorial Day weekend in 1980 at the Depositors Trust in Medford, Massachusetts. Connolly credited Bulger with being the "first source" to provide the names of the robbers. But it just wasn't so. The morning after the robbery callers to police and other informants were naming the suspects. "I'll be honest with you, I didn't get it from Whitey Bulger," said Medford police chief Jake Keating about early leads in the case. It took a few years to charge the robbers, but their identities, said Keating, were "common knowledge."

Connolly also gave Bulger credit for breaking open a murder case. Until Bulger had offered his helping hand, went a Connolly memo, the FBI had had "no positive leads" in the slaying of Joseph Barboza Baron, an underworld hitman who had turned into a valuable government witness. Baron was gunned down in San Francisco. In his memo, Connolly wrote that three months after the slaying Bulger had told him who set up Baron to be killed—a wiseguy named Jimmy Chalmas. In fact, Chalmas's role in the murder was old news by the time Bulger mentioned it to Connolly. Chalmas was a prime suspect from the start. Baron had been shot outside Chalmas's apartment. City homicide detectives had interrogated Chalmas that night. Following Bulger's chat with Connolly, the FBI may have finally gone out and confronted Chalmas, but from the moment Baron died Chalmas was a hot lead. None of this was part of Connolly's writings to Sarhatt. Nor was Sarhatt, in conducting the internal review of Bulger's viability, supposed to dig up the rest of the story. He was, in theory, supposed to be able to rely on the completeness and veracity of his own field agent in Boston. Instead, he got Connolly's angle, skewed in Bulger's favor.

Connolly knew how to hit the hot buttons as well. He told Sarhatt that Bulger had saved the lives of two FBI agents who'd worked undercover in two separate cases in the late 1970s. These may have been the most intriguing of all of Connolly's claims, in part because he had no records to back him up. Throughout his years as a handler, Connolly filed hundreds of the reports, known as "209 inserts," documenting fresh Bulger intelligence. They ranged from the sublime, such as information about important Mafia policymaking meetings, to the ridiculous, such as the scoop on

Larry Zannino's latest temper tantrum. But with agents' lives supposedly hanging in the balance, oddly, perhaps even unbelievably, Connolly had not written up contemporaneous reports about Bulger's aid. To explain the omission, Connolly insisted later that he'd had no reason to file reports, although Morris conceded that documenting help of this sort was standard FBI procedure.

One of the two supposed life-saving instances was the old truck-hijacking case, Operation Lobster. In a memo to Sarhatt, Connolly revived the exaggerated claim that back in 1978 a Bulger tip enabled the FBI to "take steps to insure the safety of Special Agent Nicholas D. Gianturco." In a follow-up report, Connolly reminded Sarhatt about the tip and added that Bulger had provided the information to protect FBI lives "at great personal risk" to his own life.

Over time too, Connolly's retelling of this Bulger moment grew more rarefied. "They saved one of my friends' life," he liked to say. Connolly could also count on Gianturco—to a point. Gianturco said Connolly had called and persuaded him not to meet with the hijackers. "He said they were going to kill me." But pushed to say whether he indeed thought Bulger and Flemmi had saved his life, Gianturco was evasive. "I was glad that Mr. Bulger and Mr. Flemmi were kind of watching out for me." He wouldn't flat-out credit Bulger with saving his life. And Flemmi himself undercut Connolly's take, later calling the information Bulger passed along an "accidental tip" about a possible shakedown, not a planned murder.

Just as important, police supervisors of Operation Lobster said they did not recall any specific death threat to Gianturco. A plot to kill an FBI agent was not something any police official would ever forget, they said. And word of a planned hit would have set off internal alarms and been documented at the time, not just in a Connolly memo two years later. If anything like what Connolly claimed had actually happened, said trooper Bob Long, who had also supervised Operation Lobster, "it's incredible that he would not have advised Gianturco's immediate supervisors, who were responsible for his safety and security.

"If you had information that someone was planning to kill an FBI agent, wouldn't you want to monitor the suspect's movements? Because if he didn't succeed that day, there would be another day, and he'd keep trying." None of the truck hijackers were ever tracked by investigators as potential assassins.

The bundle of Connolly hype rescued Bulger from internal scrutiny, and the memos were part of a blizzard of paperwork assembled by Connolly and Morris that, like a high-gloss finish, sealed the FBI's rosy view of Bulger and Flemmi. Lying and deceit were clearly on Morris's mind. In his office he kept a copy of *Lying: Moral Choice in Public and Private Life*. He'd come across the book by Sissela Bok while taking a graduate course in ethics at Northeastern University. The book was heady and philosophical, not a how-to guide to lying, but it had captured his interest. He kept it near him and had marked up certain passages and underlined others. As he supervised Connolly and together they distorted the truth about Bulger and Flemmi to FBI superiors, Morris was flipping through a book with such chapters as "Lies in a Crisis," "Lies Protecting Peers and Clients," and "Justification."

■ ■ ■

BUT the early 1980s was not just a period of pushing paper. Besides customizing the FBI's books, the agents were putting out some home cooking. The group's social life took off. The inaugural dinner held at Morris's home in Lexington in 1979, in part to celebrate the close call in the race-fixing indictment, had only broken the ice. Since then, Morris had hosted more dinners. Gianturco did too, at his suburban home in Peabody, north of Boston. Flemmi did his share, leaning on his mother to prepare an Italian spread for Bulger, Morris, Connolly, Gianturco, and other agents. The first of the Flemmi affairs was held at his parents' home in the Mattapan section of Boston, but by the early 1980s his parents had moved into South Boston right next door to none other than Billy Bulger. (The houses faced one another.) Flemmi began hosting gatherings within arm's reach of the most powerful politician in Massachusetts. Flemmi and Bulger even turned Flemmi's mother's property into a weapons depot. In an outdoor shed where most homeowners would keep a lawnmower, the gangsters accumulated what amounted to a small military arsenal. They stockpiled handguns, rifles, automatic weapons, shotguns, ammunition of all kinds and calibers, and even explosive devices, all of which were kept in a hidden compartment behind an interior wall in the shed.

Over drinks and dinner it became increasingly difficult to distinguish between business and pleasure. John Connolly took care to act as a master of ceremonies, arranging the times, places, and guest lists. ("I never arranged for any of the meetings," said Morris, even though he often hosted. "I never knew how to get in contact with them.") Connolly seemed to fuss as well. Having persuaded Morris and Gianturco to open up their homes to the gangsters, he then wanted to make sure they behaved. Connolly, recalled Morris, did not want FBI agents treating Whitey Bulger and Stevie Flemmi like run-of-the-mill snitches. They were to be shown the "special respect" they deserved.

Even though the FBI in no uncertain terms banned socializing with informants, Connolly had proposed—and Morris readily accepted—a rationale for why the rules did not apply to them. Bulger and Flemmi, said Morris, "were very, very, very well known in the crime community, and there were very few safe places that we could meet with them, and Connolly did not want to meet with them in the usual alternatives—hotel rooms and that sort of stuff. He wanted an atmosphere where it would be a little more relaxing, would be more sociable, more pleasurable, and that left very few alternatives, and I agreed to have them for dinner."

There were indeed people stalking Bulger and Flemmi—like state troopers. Years later the irony was not lost on the investigators from other police agencies: the gangsters had shaken the troopers tailing them by finding a safe haven and a hot meal in the homes of FBI agents.

The FBI dinners were off the books—the agents never filed reports about them—and over fine food and fine wine the group was already waxing nostalgic about their times together. They chatted, said Flemmi, about "things that happened in the past, like the racetrack case." The conversation was friendly and often featured, recalled Morris, "pretty strange things." If Connolly was the emcee, Bulger was the chairman of the board, "talking about life in Alcatraz, talking about life—what it's like being a fugitive, talking about family matters, talking in generalities about people." He entertained the others with descriptions of taking LSD while he was in prison during the 1950s. Said Flemmi: "He was in Alcatraz when they closed it down. Then he went to Leavenworth, and he participated in a CIA program. The name of the program was Ultra. He was a volunteer in that program, the LSD program, for eighteen months. He was one of the people selected, because he was—he had such a high IQ."

Flemmi might offer some of his own stories, about living in Canada when he was a fugitive, but Bulger clearly commanded center stage. "Jim Bulger was the talker. Anyone who knows him will attest to that," said Flemmi.

Though Connolly frequently met privately with Bulger and Flemmi—on hundreds of occasions—the FBI dinner parties unfolded as a kind of biannual banquet. The agents and the gangsters took certain precautions for their evening affairs. To meet once to chat over beers at Bulger's apartment in South Boston, Connolly and Morris parked their car several blocks away. "Connolly was familiar with the back alleys," said Morris. The supervisor, meanwhile, was lost in South Boston. "I had no idea in the world where I was. And we took a series of back alleys and entered his apartment in a back alley." Morris and Connolly both wore hats, a token stab at a disguise to conceal their faces. Bulger greeted them and served up St. Pauli Girl beer while Morris casually scanned issues of *Soldier of Fortune* magazine that Bulger had around.

Morris was less concerned about security or startling his neighbors when hosting in suburban Lexington. "My neighbors wouldn't have the slightest idea in the world who Bulger and Flemmi are." Even so, some caution was always in order. "They came after hours of darkness. Sometimes they'd pull into the garage. They were always wearing hats."

Morris did, however, startle his wife, Rebecca. She was not happy about having reputed killers as house guests. The marriage was already strained, and the couple fought. In all his FBI years Morris had never done anything like this. Maybe he'd brought work home with him, but never two actual gangsters. Bulger and Flemmi now knew where he lived, now knew his family, could wonder if Morris made a practice of hosting informants, and, to discover their identities, might consider staking out the Morris home. To Rebecca Morris, the whole setup was just plain crazy. But John Morris prevailed, arguing with his wife about the necessity of this extraordinary move, about how special Bulger and Flemmi were. He would concede to his wife they were "bad guys," but dinner was "necessary to inspire their trust."

It was all part of the inflation of Bulger and Flemmi. Morris was not surprised that his wife did not fully appreciate the unique deal he and Connolly had with Bulger and Flemmi. After all, she could not appreciate the continued blossoming of the intimacy the group had going, as it flowed from dinner parties to gifts. During the early 1980s the agents and informants began giving each other presents—at holidays, to mark special occasions, or simply because they were moved to give. Rebecca, John probably thought, was simply missing the obvious.

■ ■ ■

CONNOLLY served as gift coordinator, bearing presents to the agents from the gangsters and vice versa. Gianturco got a black leather briefcase, a glass decorative statue, and a bottle of cognac. The second time Bulger came to his house for dinner, recalled Gianturco, he "brought some wineglasses. I think the ones I had were the $1.25 Stop & Shop's. He brought a better set of wineglasses the next time. Usually Mr. Bulger would bring a bottle of wine or a bottle of champagne when he came up for dinner."

Gianturco happily reciprocated. While window-shopping during a trip to San Francisco, he spotted a belt buckle with an engraving of Alcatraz and thought of Whitey Bulger. He bought the buckle and then gave it to Connolly to give to Bulger. Bulger liked it and began wearing it. Connolly and Bulger, meanwhile, also exchanged books and wine, and Bulger once presented his handler with an engraved hunting knife.

"I received a sweatshirt from Nick Gianturco," Flemmi recalled. "I received a book from John Connolly." Morris, he said, once gave him a painting of Korea by a Korean artist. "It was a nice painting." Said Morris: "I had picked it up in the army. I had served in Korea, and he had served in Korea, and I gave him that painting."

Bulger noticed that the dinner table at Morris's home lacked a bucket to keep wine chilled, so he surprised Morris with a gift of a silver wine bucket. The ornate gift infuriated Morris's wife and sparked another round of marital grief. She didn't want Bulger's largesse and told her husband not to accept it. But Morris did, rationalizing again the need to maintain Bulger's trust. Rebecca Morris banned the bucket from their home, and eventually John Morris, without ever telling Bulger, quietly threw it out.

Bulger and Flemmi continued to ply Morris with fancy wine—here and there a $25 or $30 bottle of French bordeaux. "I don't think that I articulated a specific interest in it," said Morris. "I think that it evolved, and I believe it evolved from the standpoint where they first brought wine. I believe conversation flowed from that as to my interest in wine."

The two crime bosses even arranged once for a special delivery to Morris at the FBI office in Government Center in Boston. "Connolly gave it to me," recalled Morris. "He said that he had something for me from these guys." Morris was instructed to go to Connolly's car in the parking garage. "I went down to the basement of the federal building, opened his trunk, and there was a case of wine."

It was as if the gangsters were probing Morris's weak spot. He'd showed himself capable of losing it at the Colonnade Hotel. Indeed, Flemmi had kept the audiotape that Morris left behind that night as a souvenir. And even though Morris knew full well that the growing intimacy and gift-giving were clearly wrong, he couldn't stop himself. It was as if he got a charge out of the bizarre alliance with Bulger and Flemmi. With a little alcohol, it all went down even more smoothly. Morris liked the two gangsters. He liked Connolly. They all seemed part of an important secret.

In early June 1982 Morris left Boston to attend a two-week training session in Glynco, Georgia, at the Federal Law Enforcement Training Center. Sarhatt had approved the trip, as did the Boston office's assistant special agent in charge, Bob Fitzpatrick. Morris was enrolled in a program entitled "Narcotics Specialization Training." Even though another federal agency, the Drug Enforcement Administration (DEA), already specialized in targeting drug traffickers, the FBI during the early 1980s was looking to enhance its own drug enforcement capabilities. Immediately Morris missed his girlfriend Debbie Noseworthy, and once in Georgia he got an idea.

"I called Connolly," said Morris, and he reminded Connolly of the offer Bulger and Flemmi had made: if he ever needed anything, just let them know. "So I asked Connolly: 'Do you think they could arrange for an airline ticket?'

"He said, 'Yeah.'"

John Connolly had taken Morris's call at the Organized Crime Squad. Debbie was seated nearby at her desk right outside Morris's office. She could only wonder what Connolly and her boyfriend were discussing. Then Connolly hung up and left. He returned later, and he walked up to Debbie Noseworthy holding an envelope that he then gave to the FBI secretary.

"He said that John wanted me to have this," she recalled. "I asked what it was, and he said, 'Well, look at it.'" Debbie opened the plain white envelope and counted $1,000 in cash. She was startled and asked where the money had come from. Using a cover story that he and Morris had concocted, Connolly explained that her boyfriend had been saving up money and hiding it in his desk for an occasion just like this one. Morris, said Connolly, wanted her to take the money and fly down to see him in Georgia.

Debbie had not seen Connolly enter Morris's office and go through the squad supervisor's desk. She had been in her boss's desk many times before and had never seen the money. But she wasn't about to second-guess her good fortune. She was thrilled. Connolly, Debbie recalled, then said to her, "Isn't that nice that you're going to get to go?" Debbie arranged hastily to take a few vacation days. She rushed out and bought a ticket and then caught a departing flight from Logan Airport. Thanks to Connolly and Bulger, the couple were soon romancing in Georgia.

■ ■ ■

SIX MONTHS after Morris sought his first payoff, he turned over supervision of the Organized Crime Squad to Jim Ring. Morris was named coordinator of a new FBI drug task force. It was early in 1983, and Morris was feeling a little burned out. The public reason for the burnout was legitimate and understandable. Morris had overseen a squad of agents through the spectacular but exhausting bugging of the Mafia's Boston headquarters. The investigation was now in the hands of Ed Quinn, who was overseeing a group of agents carefully listening to and transcribing the FBI tapes. The evidence against Gennaro Angiulo and his associates was stunning, and all of it was in the Mafia's own words. But Morris's burnout had a private side to it too—he was now thoroughly compromised.

No question, he'd taken a gift too far.

Between himself and Connolly, Bulger and Flemmi now had two agents cold. Morris tried to warn his successor, Jim Ring, about Bulger. Morris, of course, did not mention the money. He talked to Ring in FBI-speak, suggesting to the new supervisor that perhaps Bulger and Flemmi had "outlived their usefulness" and should be closed down as FBI informants. It was Morris's lame wish that Ring would somehow clean up his mess. Ring later said he had no memory of Morris ever advising him to close Bulger. In the office the two agents were regarded more as rivals than as friends. Ring was eager to make his own mark, not just serve as custodian to the picked-over remains of the Angiulo case.

Connolly immediately brought Ring around to meet Bulger and Flemmi—the start of a new chapter in glad-handing. Connolly made the initial introductions at his own apartment, and the two gangsters found that Ring wasn't warm and soft like Morris. "I felt comfortable with John Morris, but Jim Ring was a different type of a person," Flemmi said. "He seemed to be more focused in on details and didn't seem to be the type of guy that wanted to maybe socialize."

Soon enough, though, Ring joined the others at the dinner table, including a memorable night spent at the house of Flemmi's mother. Billy Bulger, the senate president, walked into the Flemmi kitchen from his own home across the way. The startled FBI supervisor did a double take as Billy walked right in and gave Whitey some family photographs to look at. (Billy later denied this ever happened, but Ring testified about the cameo appearance under oath.)

But no other supervisor or fellow agent could ever replace what the group had had in John Morris. Maybe he wasn't Connolly's boss anymore, or in charge of the Organized Crime Squad, but Connolly and Bulger and Flemmi were going to stick close by. They had Morris in their grip, and he'd come cheap—a plane ticket for an illicit tryst. Morris soon sensed as much. He knew the moment Debbie Noseworthy buckled herself in for the flight out of Logan that it was over. He was finished, and it would only get worse as the 1980s continued. He'd try to rationalize as best he could, try to imitate Connolly—fluff everything up in earnest talk about the special deal and the special task they'd all undertaken to defeat the Mafia. But the protection they were providing Bulger and Flemmi was no longer just about gathering underworld intelligence, which was always good to get but never as vital and indispensable as the agents had portrayed it. The protection was now about FBI corruption.

Morris had been unable to hold his own, through the Colonnade and the dinners and the gifts, through the leaks about the state police's attempted bugging and now the cold cash. He knew full well they'd all moved far beyond crafting distortions and lies for the FBI's files, beyond the padding of the Bulger files so that their bosses thought only good thoughts about Bulger, beyond the stretching of the rules to their outermost limits.

They'd fallen completely off the game board during the eighteen months from late 1980 to mid-1982—now criminals all, FBI agents and two gangsters looking to deflect trouble of any kind, including charges of murder.

CHAPTER TEN

Murder, Inc.

Shortly after the new year arrived in 1981, Brian Halloran backed his ratty Cadillac into a space in front of the Rusty Scupper, a busy North End restaurant, and bounded upstairs to the loft apartment of his drinking buddy from the world of high finance. Accountant John Callahan had asked him to stop by to talk business, and that sounded like money to the usually strapped Halloran.

They were an odd pair that got on. Halloran, a rangy leg-breaker from the Winter Hill gang, and Callahan, a squat CPA and consultant to Boston banks, had struck up an unlikely friendship rooted in Boston's nightlife. They had first bumped into each other in the early 1970s at Chandler's, a wiseguy hangout in the South End controlled by Howie Winter. The extroverted Callahan liked to walk on the wild side, and that is where the scruffy Halloran lived, usually at loose ends, just getting by on the feast-or-famine cycle as an enforcer in the underworld's brutal collection business.

Callahan talked to bankers by day and socialized with mobsters by night. Like Halloran, he took a drink and liked a good time. The wiseguys saw him as a big spender who knew how to make money and, more important, how to launder it. After hanging out at Chandler's for a couple of years, Callahan tried connecting the corporate world with the underworld by proposing a deal that startled Halloran. One night in the mid-1970s Callahan asked Halloran if he would "rob" him as he lugged a money bag from his main place of business, a company called World Jai Alai that was a gambling cash cow. Halloran would hold him up as he walked the pouch to a Brink's truck, and then afterwards they would split the money. The phony robbery never took place, but Halloran understood that Callahan was more than a "fun" guy with a fat wallet. He was a player.

■ ■ ■

AFTER Halloran was buzzed into Callahan's apartment overlooking Boston Harbor, he was surprised to see Whitey Bulger and Stevie Flemmi sitting in the living room. Callahan gave him an effusive greeting. Stevie said hello. Bulger said nothing. Whitey didn't like Halloran much, and it showed. On the street Bulger's silent treatment was seen as the kiss of death.

But Halloran was surprised only for a moment. In recent months, Callahan had been bragging to him about Bulger and Flemmi wanting to be partners in the "World Jai Alai action" Callahan had carved out of the heavy-betting that accompanied a court game mostly resembling racquetball and played at "frontons" in Connecticut and Florida. To Halloran, the presence of Bulger and Flemmi signaled the deal was past the negotiating stage — and it was also now clear Callahan was no longer just a hot shit accountant with a party personality and banking connections. In fact, Callahan was washing money for Bulger and Flemmi and, whether Callahan realized it or not, he'd traveled a long way from the city's financial district and now belonged to Winter Hill.

There was some strained small talk all around and then, in a nervous patter, Callahan got right to the heart of the matter. He said a serious problem had come up at the World Jai Alai company in the form of a new owner from Tulsa named Roger Wheeler. The hard-driving CEO from

Oklahoma "had discovered something was not right." Wheeler, he said, had figured out someone was skimming one million dollars a year from the overflowing company coffers. Now the owner planned to fire the company's top financial officers and replace them with his own people. This Wheeler was a danger, Callahan emphasized, and Callahan feared he'd end up in jail because of the owner's plan to conduct an extensive internal audit.

But then John Callahan also had a solution. Brian Halloran, he proposed, could "take [Wheeler] out of the box," which was to say shoot him in the head. He said a "hit" was the only way to stop the paper trail short of his office door, the only way to end any possibility of an embezzlement charge against him. He added that Winter Hill's seasoned hitman, Johnny Martorano, should probably get involved. Nothing beat experience. Flemmi chimed in from the couch with some much needed skepticism: would "their friends" at World Jai Alai stand up once the police were called in? Because the prospect of co-conspirators turning against Callahan was not an acceptable business risk. And the unasked question: Would Callahan himself be able to take the heat?

During the talk, Bulger hung back, sitting there, watchful and listening hard, not saying a word. By this time, he was a long way from South Boston barroom gambling and the tense days of 1972 when he worried about being killed by the Mullin gang. He'd not only risen to the top but was living on gangland's easy street, choosing his investments from a wide variety of options. He actually had more business than he could handle, in large part because a key asset, FBI agent John Connolly, was watching his back within law enforcement.

He'd made it to the top echelon by carefully plotting his course, making full use of the extraordinary latitude he'd come to expect in running an underworld franchise that inherently had its messy moments. There'd been a number of housekeeping murders of minor figures in Southie's underworld since he'd teamed up with the FBI in 1975, but the growing body count brought not a single knock on Bulger's door. No sign of trouble even when the bloodletting extended to one of Stevie's girlfriends. Debra Davis, the voluptuous 26-year-old who'd been with Flemmi for seven years, was making plans to leave him. Vacationing in Acapulco, she'd fallen in love with a young Mexican entrepreneur in the olive oil and poultry business. Davis wanted marriage and, eventually, a family—impossible dreams in the Flemmi arrangement. But a break-up was not an option to the possessive Stevie, and Davis disappeared without a trace on September 17, 1981. Davis had started the day shopping with her mother and then, after a goodbye kiss, said she had to see Flemmi. Her mother and brothers tried going to the FBI, but the agents who came around seemed more interested in learning exactly what Debra knew about Stevie than in solving her disappearance, and soon the investigation petered out. By working carefully within their violent world, Bulger and Flemmi had learned they could do anything they wanted.

The question Whitey now had to decide was how far was too far? Would a murder in Oklahoma bring too much heat? Would the FBI, through Connolly and Morris, look the other way on an execution undertaken far beyond the boundary lines of South Boston's gritty underworld where a periodic bloodletting was as normal as a quarterly business report on profits and losses?

Then again, why not? Bulger now assumed Connolly would help him out anywhere. Roger Wheeler may have been a multi-millionaire from Tulsa with seven corporations branching into everything from oil to electronics, but as 1981 dawned over Boston, Wheeler was just another guy in Whitey Bulger's way.

■ ■ ■

IT WAS a lot for Halloran to take in. And it was a lot to ask of a minor league player who had pulled a few bank robberies before catching on with Winter Hill in 1967 toward the end of the Irish gang war, a bloodbath that began when a drunken mobster insulted somebody's girlfriend at the beach. Over the years Halloran had talked a good game but was best known for slapping around overextended sad sacks who owed shylock money. Halloran was on the second team, but Bulger still used him only to enforce loans and move cocaine. He had not killed anyone.

Halloran played a bit part, however, in the murder of one of Southie's better-known bookies, a killing that had hammered home how dangerous Bulger could be. In April 1980 Halloran had chauffered Louis Litif to the Triple O's bar, located along Southie's main thoroughfare, West Broadway.

For years Litif had been one of Bulger's most productive bookmakers, but he had recently veered into drug dealing and, in a fatal misstep, murdered another dealer without clearing it with Bulger. After Halloran dropped Litif off, he parked the Lincoln behind the bar and waited. It wasn't long before he saw Bulger and another man lugging a heavy green trash bag down the back stairs. They dumped the bag in the Lincoln's trunk. Halloran drove the car to the South End and left it there. Later Litif was found in the trunk with a bullet hole in his head.

So when the subject turned to murder at Callahan's apartment, Halloran knew it was not idle talk. But this time he would be pulling the trigger, not parking a car. He got darty-eyed, cleared his throat, and asked if there was any alternative to "hitting the guy." This brought him one of Bulger's patented cold glares. The hour long meeting broke up with Bulger saying he would think about it some more, but Halloran drove away from the North End believing Roger Wheeler was a dead man.

■ ■ ■

WHEELER had an eclectic empire that specialized in electronics through a flagship company named Telex, a manufacturer of computer terminals and tape decks. He had grown up in Massachusetts but went to school in Texas and became an electrical engineer. By the late 1970s Wheeler's high energy and ambition got him to the point where Telex earned $8.1 million on revenues of $86.5 million. But for several years he had been in the market for something with a higher profit margin, and he became mesmerized by the money in the gambling industry.

The father of five was a family man and a churchgoer, but no choirboy. He could be brusquely demanding, even imperious in the CEO kind of way. He made no bones about being drawn to gambling by its high cash flow and relatively low capital costs. He had nibbled around the edges of the industry for several years, first looking into Virginia's Shenandoah racetrack in 1976 and a Las Vegas casino in 1977. He settled on the World Jai Alai company, with its outlets for racquetball-style betting games in Connecticut and Florida, because of an irresistible $50 million financing package put together by the First National Bank of Boston.

As it turned out, the bank had its own consulting relationship with John Callahan, and its loan provisions reflected that. Although Wheeler protested, the bank would put up the money only if he retained Callahan's former business partner, Richard Donovan, as president of World Jai Alai. The other stipulation was that Wheeler keep former FBI agent Paul Rico as head of security.

With the rest of the deal too good to walk away from, Wheeler took the loan and bought the company. It was a coup for Callahan, for just two years before he had been discharged by the World Jai Alai board of directors for profligate spending and underworld ties with the likes of Brian Halloran and Johnny Martorano.

Although some of the handwriting about World Jai Alai was already on the wall, Wheeler was distracted by the opportunity to finally get a gambling business and dazzled by the $5 million profit a year, a healthy 16 percent of revenue. But behind the beguiling bottom line were some disturbing dossiers on Callahan and his longtime business partner.

Nevertheless, Wheeler thought he could have it all—gambling revenue and a clean skirt. He thought his business acumen could override the "shady characters." Gradually, however, Wheeler had second thoughts about what he had gotten into. He became fearful, according to business associates. He took some ironic solace in the large retinue of former FBI agents who worked for World Jai Alai, including the redoubtable Paul Rico.

■ ■ ■

ABOUT a week after the meeting with Bulger, Halloran ran into Callahan at one of their watering holes and asked where things stood on Wheeler. Callahan was a little evasive and said they were still "working out the details"—as if they were pondering the fine points of a merger. Callahan changed the subject, and they bent their elbows.

A couple of weeks later Callahan called Halloran, asking him to stop by his North End apartment again. This time Callahan was waiting for him alone. He had a consolation prize for his friend, who didn't make the hit squad. He handed Halloran a bag with $20,000 in cash—two stacks of hundred-dollar bills—and told him they had decided to take care of Wheeler without him. "Take the money," Callahan said. "It's best that [you] not get involved in the Wheeler deal." Slapping him on the shoulder, Callahan said the group "should not have involved [you] to begin with."

Halloran didn't need much convincing to take the cash. He would not have to murder someone he didn't know, and he had money for nothing. He viewed it as a professional courtesy from a big spender with money to burn. Halloran roared through the wad in a matter of days, spending it on furniture for his Quincy apartment, a blowout week in Fort Lauderdale, and a new car.

With Halloran on the sidelines, the Winter Hill hit team arrived in Tulsa three months later. On a bright spring afternoon Wheeler finished his weekly round of golf at an exclusive Tulsa country club and strolled from the locker room to the parking lot. Two men sat there waiting in a rented 1981 Pontiac with stolen license plates. They watched the dapper executive get into his Cadillac. Then one of the men, wearing sunglasses and a fake beard, walked briskly toward the car. He had one hand inside a brown paper bag and the determined look of a military commando on his face. As he approached the car door, the businessman looked straight at him. Johnny Martorano put the bag to the window and shot Wheeler once between the eyes with a long-barrel .38. He then walked just as briskly back to the tan sedan. The Pontiac peeled away as youngsters at a nearby swimming pool looked on and wondered what the noise was all about.

■ ■ ■

HALLORAN sensed he was standing at a Rubicon that ran through South Boston. His sour relationship with Bulger only complicated a deteriorating personal life. Cocaine consumption had become more important to him than cocaine sales. And he was alienated within the Winter Hill operation, hanging on to his job with Bulger's sufferance. He had fit better with the older guys in Winter Hill—Howie Winter and Joe McDonald and Jimmy Sims, but those veterans were in jail or on the lam.

After the Wheeler murder, Halloran, as a survivor of Boston's mean streets, was acutely aware that he and Callahan had been in on a murder plot with a ruthless executioner who didn't like him. One morning in the fall of 1981 someone took a potshot at Halloran as he emptied his trash in front of his Quincy apartment. Notice had been served.

The unraveling of Brian Halloran continued on course a few weeks later, this time by his own hand. Dealing with some fallout from the drug trade, Halloran killed dealer George Pappas at close range inside a Chinese restaurant at four in the morning after they finished their meal. Halloran fired across the table while mafioso Jackie Salemme, Frank's younger brother, looked on. It was just like the murder in the *Godfather* movie, with Michael Corleone dropping the gun on the table and running out the restaurant door to a waiting car that whisked him toward Sicily, an unlikely hero in his family. But the driver in this murder just took Halloran back home to Quincy, where his problems got worse. The Chinatown execution further alienated him from his peers, who saw him spinning out of control. The murder also meant trouble with the law.

After hiding out for a month, Halloran surrendered in November 1981 and then hit the street on bail, a frazzled coke addict facing first-degree murder charges that involved a Mafia soldier. He had made himself persona non grata with the Mafia and with Bulger—the worst place to be in Boston's underworld. Halloran had become too much trouble for just about everybody. Bulger had the opening he was looking for.

In the fall of 1981 Connolly filed reports from Bulger and Flemmi that predicted trouble in Halloran's future. Bulger told Connolly the Mafia wanted Halloran "hit in the head" to eliminate him as a false witness blaming Salemme for the murder. Two months later Flemmi piggybacked the Bulger report by saying that the Mafia was hiding Salemme until Halloran could be "taken out." The tip was a page out of Stevie Flemmi's original playbook. Flemmi had presaged problems for Boston bookie William Bennett back in 1968, presenting the information as a tidbit he had heard on the street. But Flemmi had already murdered Bennett, rolling his dead body out of a speeding car. It was a time-honored Flemmi deception to cover his tracks and send law enforcement off after someone else.

Halloran had a strategy too. In a no-man's-land at the end of the line, it was time to trade up with law enforcement. He decided to strike a deal with the FBI, asking for their help in getting a reduced sentence for the Chinatown murder in exchange for his story about the party animal accountant, the Tulsa tycoon, and the killer from South Boston.

Almost a year to the day after the North End meeting with Callahan about murdering Wheeler, Halloran talked nonstop to the FBI, from January 3 to February 19, 1982. He moved between three safe houses as the agents pressed him for corroboration that proved elusive. They had Halloran wear a wire, but that was unproductive—the wiseguys always seemed to know when he was coming. They demanded a polygraph, which Halloran refused. The Halloran debriefing became a stalemate, with agents believing his basic story but demanding more proof than Halloran could provide.

■ ■ ■

HALLORAN became part of Bulger's bitter legacy within the FBI when agent Leo Brunnick went to the ever-approachable Morris and asked him for his "take" on Halloran's tale. Morris instantly realized that Halloran's story posed a dire threat to the unholy alliance with Bulger. It was against FBI policy to retain an informant who was also under investigation by the bureau. Morris quickly disparaged Halloran's credibility.

While Halloran dangled in the breeze and shifted from one safe house to another, Morris told Connolly that Bulger had been accused of being part of the Wheeler murder. Morris fully believed Connolly would tell Bulger about the danger to him. Although Morris knew that dire consequences could follow his tip-off, he claimed he felt they were unlikely because Halloran's account probably wasn't true.

It got worse. Jeremiah O'Sullivan was the prosecutor whom pro-Halloran agents needed to get the Winter Hill snitch safely off the street. If he gave the okay, approval would become a routine matter up the line. But

O'Sullivan became obdurately against giving Halloran a new identity in a new community to protect a witness with a story to tell. To him Halloran was a problem not worth having. O'Sullivan had taken a coldhearted look at the issue and decided there was simply not enough corroboration available to make a case with Halloran. Indeed, Halloran was not an easy call. It was his word against Callahan's, and he refused to take a lie detector test. He also had little success in developing other Winter Hill cases while wearing a wire.

But it was also clear that O'Sullivan was partially blinded by the tight nexus of considerations involved in his prosecution of the Angiulos. "Was he part of the protection of Bulger?" another prosecutor asked rhetorically. "Not consciously. He refused to give Halloran a break on a fresh murder charge without some corroboration of the story. In those circumstances, a reduced charge would be a tough one to swallow. I'm not sure what he could have done differently."

Yet investigators working the Wheeler case say that O'Sullivan lost sight of the danger to an informant providing sensitive information on a major case. Several agents, according to Robert Fitzpatrick, the number-two man in the Boston FBI office at the time, became convinced Halloran could be killed if he was not enrolled in the witness protection program.

Fitzpatrick took his concerns directly to O'Sullivan but hit a brick wall. "O'Sullivan wasn't buying Halloran," Fitzpatrick recalled. "To him Halloran was a wanna-be hyping a story, a drunk not worth the bother. I went back at him and said, 'Look, my guys are coming to me and saying, 'Get him off the street. He's in danger.' He said, 'We've talked about this, and I've heard what you said, and I'll let you know.' That means no."

By May 1982 Fitzpatrick felt so strongly about the danger to Halloran that he went over O'Sullivan's head to the newly appointed U.S. attorney, William Weld. "I told him, 'Hey, this guy could get shot. Agents are telling me about it. We need to do something.'" Years later Weld confirmed the Fitzpatrick visit. "Fitzy said to me, 'You know, people always say there's danger for this snitch or that snitch. They may be killed for cooperating. I'm telling you this guy—I would not want to be standing next to this guy.'" But Weld did not intervene with O'Sullivan, who had been something of a mentor to Weld when he first took the top prosecutor's job.

Toward the end of his debriefings Halloran learned that Whitey Bulger was an FBI informant. Panicking, Halloran suddenly felt that he had nowhere to turn, that he was in danger on the street and even at the FBI office. "This really was the gang that couldn't shoot straight," said Halloran's disgusted cousin, Maureen Caton. "It just slips out one day that, 'Oh, by the way, Bulger's an informant.' Forget Waco. Just look at what happened to Brian Halloran."

The upshot was that the unfocused and terrified Halloran was left on his own to move furtively through a hostile landscape while the two FBI squads chafed against each other over his fate. The agents who developed Halloran found themselves fighting a rearguard action against Connolly, who had dismissed Halloran's lurid account as self-serving prattle from a dirtbag. Although the agents who sided with Halloran had some doubts about his precise role in the crimes and plots, they firmly believed that Bulger was in their sights and Halloran was their ticket. The fight quickly intensified. Connolly was accused by two agents of rifling their files about Halloran, and the exasperated Fitzpatrick was forced to secure the material in his office safe.

In fact, Fitzpatrick recalled, Connolly never really denied looking over the shoulders of other agents compiling information on Bulger. Connolly just stuck his jaw out, saying, "Either you trust me as an agent or you don't. He's my guy, and I need to know what he's up against."

According to Fitzpatrick, Connolly proceeded to set up an interview of Bulger and Flemmi about the Wheeler case. In a departure from standard techniques, the pair were interviewed together; as a result, investigators lost the chance to play contradictions in their accounts against each other. The interview went nowhere and was filed away.

■　■　■

BY THE spring of 1982 Halloran's life had became a daily ordeal of constantly checking the rearview mirror and looking over his shoulder. He couldn't go home to his wife and young son because he was afraid the door would be kicked in and a machine-gun burst would kill them all. His father and an uncle paid the rent and brought the weekly groceries to his wife.

After several weeks of lying low, with his wife in the hospital about to deliver their second son, Halloran got a call, according to his family, that his sister living near the South Boston waterfront wanted to see him. A friend drove him into Southie, a place he had been avoiding. Around 6:00 P.M., while Halloran and his friend were parked outside a restaurant, a car containing Bulger and Flemmi pulled alongside Halloran's Datsun. There were some shouted words and then two shots rang out. Then a fusillade. Halloran staggered free of the car and fell in the street. One of the assassins raced up to him and shot him several more times. He died with twelve bullets in him from two guns. It had all the firepower and finality of a Bulger-Flemmi execution. And it even included a telltale swerve from Stevie Flemmi. He met with agent Connolly the day after the murder, and Connolly filed a fast report saying that Charlestown gangsters may have been behind Halloran's death.

A Boston detective at the murder scene claimed that the dying Halloran was able to identify Charlestown gangster Jimmy Flynn as his killer. Flynn had the motive, according to police, because he and Halloran were two Winter Hill gang members who never got along, particularly after Flynn learned that Halloran had ratted him out on a bank robbery. Flynn went into hiding and was not captured until two years after the murder. In fact, he was not at the murder scene. Investigators concluded that Flynn was a patsy set up to send police in the wrong direction. Halloran's murder was a case of Bulger doing his own dirty work, a rare instance when he stepped out of the shadows to pull the trigger himself.

Ironically, after the Halloran murder, the discord within the FBI office abated, with agents from the two squads only occasionally glaring at each other in the back of an expansive room. It was like a dysfunctional family papering over incest. An informant had been killed, and agents began to live with the embarrassment.

At the same time the office leadership fell into a resigned torpor about Bulger. The agent in charge, Larry Sarhatt, had gone from being a new man determined to get to the bottom of Lancaster Street in 1980 to a harried boss looking forward to retirement after twenty years in the bureau.

As one by-product of the Boston office's effort to smooth over internal strife, upper management became permanently hobbled by the Bulger dilemma. For the most part, the managers didn't entirely trust Connolly. But no one wanted to deal with the institutional grief involved in taking him on. Connolly might be too close to an informant, but it wasn't worth a brawl. It happens.

"Connolly just became a force unto himself," Fitzpatrick said, "a vortex in a constantly changing system. He stayed put as new agents in charge came and went. And he could take care of other agents. He became the guy who could get you sports tickets. He could help you get a day off through the secretaries. He made no secret that he could help you get a job after re-tirement through Billy Bulger. But he just wasn't much of an agent. He couldn't write a report. He was no administrator. He was just this brassy bullshit artist. We enabled him to some extent. No one had the stomach for examining what he was up to. We just never came to grips with that guy."

But the Halloran episode lingered in Morris's mind. Although he had rationalized his passive role in Halloran's demise, he knew exactly what had happened. Later, during a back-channel tip-off to Bulger and Flemmi that one of their bookies was being targeted by other FBI agents, Morris felt compelled to warn the pair against murder. Stay away from the book-ie, Morris said. No more bloodshed.

Morris had reason to fear the worst. He knew what had happened to Wheeler and Halloran. And he had firsthand experience in the fate of an-other underworld figure who ran afoul of Bulger. Arthur "Bucky" Barrett was an expert safecracker who got caught in the no-man's-land between the bureau and Bulger. He had pulled a daring bank heist in 1980, working with five others to rifle safety deposit boxes of $1.5 million in cash. Shortly after the robbery Morris and Connolly were put on to Barrett by Bulger. The agents approached the safecracker with an off-the-books double mis-sion: they wanted to soften him up for Bulger with a friendly "warning" that Whitey would be looking for a cut from the bank job. And then they offered him the perilous haven of the FBI informant program if he would become a snitch. It was a mission of staggering corruption. Here were two seasoned FBI agents acting as Whitey Bulger's emissaries on the street.

Nevertheless, Barrett rejected the FBI overture. And even though

Barrett paid much of his bank withdrawal to placate Bulger, it did not save him from being kidnapped, tortured, and dragged into the cellar of a South Boston home in 1983, never to be seen alive again.

But Bucky Barrett was an anonymous casualty of war. He simply disappeared, and no one misses a safecracker except his wife and kids. It was Brian Halloran's dead body on Northern Avenue that left a deep mark on agents in the Boston office. Fitzpatrick looked back on it and felt "defeated by it all. I still think about it and fight off the ghosts."

■ ■ ■

TULSA homicide detective Michael Huff, the first officer on the Wheeler murder scene in 1981, had learned quickly that John Callahan and the World Jai Alai business were probably behind the killing and that the Winter Hill gang was in the picture. But he could get no hard information out of Boston. Phone calls went unreturned, and conferences were canceled or rescheduled. The Massachusetts State Police told him that Winter Hill was probably involved, but Huff could not induce the FBI to help him get background information on gang members. He never heard the name Bulger until Halloran was dead.

Callahan was the early focus for Huff and some Connecticut State Police detectives who had been chasing the accountant with the double life for several years because of the swirl of dust around the jai alai outlet in Hartford. They began looking into Callahan's finances and the company books for irregularities that could be used to pressure him to talk about Wheeler's death. Detectives had even gone to Switzerland to check his accounts and recent stay there. With investigators from two states rummaging through his books, Callahan became chillingly aware that he was now the last person alive who could implicate Bulger on the murder.

The former driving force of World Jai Alai was clearly in the crosshairs. But the pursuit of Callahan as a suspect ran into the usual detour in Boston. When Callahan first came into view as a suspect in late 1981, Huff began working with the Tulsa FBI office, which sought information about Callahan's Winter Hill associates from none other than John Morris. In response to the queries from Tulsa, Morris sent Connolly to question

Callahan. A defensive Morris later argued that Connolly was the "absolutely logical choice" to ask Callahan if Winter Hill was involved in the Oklahoma murder. Not surprisingly, Connolly reported back that Callahan had no dealings with Winter Hill and that Bulger had nothing to do with the Wheeler hit. One more time Connolly said Whitey didn't do it. Morris obligingly closed the file.

The quick action confused Huff. He could understand there being no hard information available, but case closed? It burned him up that Wheeler's death didn't strike a chord in Boston. Wheeler was a "big damn guy" in his town who hired hundreds of people and gave money to good causes. Something's wrong here, he thought. Why won't anyone talk straight to me about a broad daylight murder of a prominent businessman whose family deserved some answers?

Huff and his new colleagues in Connecticut did the only thing they could do—they pushed on, scratching their heads about what was going on with the bureau in Boston. Their focus shifted to the Miami outlet of World Jai Alai to develop incriminating information on Callahan. By July 1982 Huff and the other detectives felt they had gathered enough damaging financial material to pressure Callahan in person toward the end of July 1982. They headed down to Florida on August 1. But one of Callahan's old drinking buddies, Johnny Martorano, was already there. When Huff and Connecticut detectives landed at Miami airport, John Callahan was dead in the trunk of his rented Cadillac in a garage at the same airport. The peppery Callahan, who liked drinking with wiseguys, died like one at age forty-five.

Now there were three dead men who shared more than the grisly fate of being shot in the head and found splayed in their cars. They had all become enemies of Whitey Bulger.

Huff had seen Callahan as the key to the Wheeler murder. But Huff, a straightforward midwesterner, felt patronized every time he came to Boston. A weak smile, a pat on the shoulder, and then the door. The only time Huff felt he was talking sense about the case was when he got together with Connecticut and Florida homicide detectives. They began to entertain dark shapeless thoughts about what was happening in Boston. But in truth, they didn't even know who to be mad at.

Within the FBI Connolly hung tough against all comers on Halloran. He helped set up the long-overdue interrogation of Bulger and Flemmi about Wheeler that finally took place two years after the murder. The FBI report on the meeting records a speech by Bulger. He told agents that he was only consenting to the interview so he could put all the baseless accusations to rest. He sounded like his brother Billy talking to the State House press corps. Everything was done on Bulger's terms. He announced that he would not take a lie detector test, and it would take a court order to get his mug shot. And that was that.

CHAPTER ELEVEN

Bulgertown, USA

Julie Miskel Rakes and her husband Stephen were like a lot of other couples from the old neighborhood—family-oriented, hardworking, and determined to make their own modest way in life. They'd grown up in Southie. Julie was from the projects, just like the Bulgers and John Connolly, and her family belonged to the same parish as the Bulgers, St. Monica's, situated at the outer boundary of the Old Harbor housing project and across a rotary from another, the Old Colony housing project.

Though only two years apart, Julie and Stephen did not really know each other while at South Boston High School. They met later when Julie was twenty years old and Stephen was twenty-two and operating the first of his many business ventures—Stippo's Sub and Deli. Stippo was Stephen's nickname, and the popular corner store sold coffee, donuts, and groceries. It was open from dawn to midnight, with Stephen's brother, sister, mother, and father all working shifts. Stephen's father was a particularly loyal employee. Unable to sleep, he'd go over and turn on the lights at 3:00 A.M. "We used to make jokes because he opened up at three o'clock in the morning, but he didn't have to be open until six o'clock," Julie recalled. "But he wanted to be ready."

Julie began working at the store in 1977. Stephen was the owner and manager; he was in charge of ordering the stock, handling the banking, and pricing and shelving the inventory. Soon enough the couple began dating, and then, in 1978, the Rakeses and the Miskels gathered with their friends to celebrate the marriage of Julie and Stephen Rakes. It was a South Boston family affair.

Stephen was no stranger to trouble; in the past he and his brothers had tangled with police. But with Julie, he was going to make a go of it. Two years after marrying their first daughter, Nicole, was born, and a second daughter, Meredith, was born in November 1982. During this time Stephen sold the deli and became a partner in a liquor store, but by 1983 he and Julie had decided they were ready to go it alone again. Stephen preferred owning his own business. The work pace might be punishing, but the rewards would be theirs alone. Julie suggested a video rental store, but Stephen persuaded her that a liquor store was more profitable.

Hunting around, Stephen spotted an abandoned Texaco gas station right at the rotary near St. Monica's Church. It was a prime site on a main street, Old Colony Avenue. Traffic was always flowing down Old Colony and around the rotary out front, and the property had a rare commodity in the compact business districts of South Boston—a parking lot. Together they researched Boston property records to identify the owner. The deed belonged to a woman, Abigail A. Burns. Julie Rakes had trouble keeping the woman's name straight. "I used to call her Abigail Adams." She was confusing the owner with one of the nation's first families: the wife of John Adams, the second president of the United States. It was an amusing mix-up that became one of the couple's inside jokes.

"We were going to make it big," Julie recalled. "This was going to be our source of income that was going to give us the lifestyle that we wanted—for the rest of our lives."

But in spite of all their hopes and hard work, there was a problem. Whitey Bulger had been chased out of the Lancaster Street garage, harassed by state troopers in his black Chevy, and, most recently, hounded as a murder suspect. The time had come for him and Flemmi to quit all their running around and find a new home office. The way Bulger saw it, why not the cozy confines of the old neighborhood? There was no substitute for the familiar and insulated feel of South Boston. The Rakeses, unfortunately, knew none of this, and their modest ambition was about to collide with Whitey Bulger's desires in a town where whatever Whitey wanted, Whitey got.

■ ■ ■

THE FALL of 1983 was a mad scramble for the couple, who were trying to accomplish all that was necessary to open in time for the holiday season. In a relatively short period of time things had actually gone pretty smoothly, beginning with their successful bid for a liquor license at an auction during the summer. Watching for legal notices appearing in the newspaper, Stephen had spotted the auction of a license from a liquor store that was closing, displaced by construction. The eager couple dressed up one Saturday and went downtown to the law firm overseeing the sale.

"I was nervous," said Julie Rakes. "It was my first auction." Stephen was more used to the particulars of operating a liquor store, having been a partner in another one, but the couple decided Julie should do the actual bidding. "He was saying, 'Go ahead. You can do it,'" said Julie, "and I was saying, 'What do you do? What do you do?' It was fun. Exciting. He said, 'Go ahead. Raise your hand. Raise your hand!'" Julie did. The bidding opened at $1,000. There was other interest, but Julie kept going. Suddenly the bidding ended, and the Rakeses walked away with a liquor license for the relatively cheap price of $3,000.

It was a great start, possibly a good omen. They created a business corporation, Stippo's Inc., that consisted of an all-family lineup of corporate officers. "I was president," said Julie, "and we made jokes about it." Stephen took the title of treasurer and clerk and also director. Then came some other good news: Julie was pregnant with their third child. At the end of September the couple got in touch with a contractor, a friend from the neighborhood, Brian Burke. Burke started on the toughest part of the project—converting a gas station into a liquor store. The ground had to be dug up and the huge gas tanks removed, all in accordance with state environmental codes. Burke cleaned up the lot, replaced the roof, and applied a new look to the building's exterior. "Lots of cement," said Julie. The Rakeses were not out to break new ground in design or aesthetics. Their pockets were not deep. The goal was a basic renovation that achieved functionalism: a clean, well-lighted, cement-block building with glass windows. The couple felt a rush of excitement after the sign was hoisted into place on the front—Stippo's Liquor Mart.

But family and friends were not the only visitors to the construction site during the final days leading up to the opening. Also taking note of the progress were Bulger and Flemmi. Under the cover of darkness, the two gangsters were coming around to inspect all the remodeling. Late at night, with no one around, they slipped into the parking lot. There was usually a third man with them, Kevin Weeks, who had replaced Nicky Femia as sidekick, driver, and sometime enforcer. Bulger had discarded the coke-crazed Femia who, freelancing and spinning out of control, in early December tried to rob an auto body shop but had his brains blown out when one of the victims shot and killed him. Half Bulger's age, Weeks had the perfect résumé. The bushy-haired kid might stand a few inches shy of six feet, but his upper body was all muscle, and most important, he had quick hands. The son of a boxing trainer, he'd grown up in the rings around the city. And like John Connolly's, his boyhood was spent in thrall to the Bulger mystique. He filled up on stories about Southie's very own gangster but didn't catch his first glimpse of the man only whispered about as a young teen until he happened to spot Whitey marching through the housing project.

After graduating in 1974 from South Boston High School, Weeks's first job was the one he was made for—a bouncer, or "security aide," at his alma mater, patrolling the hallways and breaking up the fights between white and black students that were a regular feature of court-ordered busing. Then the next winter, a few days before St. Patrick's Day, the eighteen-year-old moved up to Whitey's world when he went to work at Triple O's. He started out behind the bar lugging ice. Then one night the bar's big-bodied enforcers seemed unable to handle a brawl, and Kevin leaped from behind the bar and leveled the miscreants with blazing combinations.

Whitey took notice. Weeks was promoted first to a Triple O's bouncer and then to Bulger's side. By the early 1980s Bulger was Weeks's mentor, and Weeks was Bulger's surrogate son. Weeks liked to show off his loyalty, telling people he'd rather serve hard time, even see harm come to his own family, before ever uttering a bad word about Whitey Bulger.

Inspecting the construction site, the men would get out of their car and walk around. For Bulger it was a good time to be considering a new office. He and Flemmi were doing well—indeed, better than ever. The local Mafia was rocked: Gennaro Angiulo was now in jail, along with a number of other key mafiosi. Bulger's own rackets had prospered in the aftermath of the FBI's bugging of the mob. "The more that we worked on the Mafia the less of a threat the Mafia was to them," John Morris acknowledged. The amount of rent, or tribute, Bulger charged was increasing steadily, as was the number of bookmakers and drug dealers making such payments. More than ever, Bulger and Flemmi were willing to help the FBI clear out the clutter from the city's underworld. It was great for business.

Looking for a new office, Bulger and Flemmi's priority was a location that included an actual, legitimate business. Running a real business made it possible to launder profits from their illegal gambling, loan-sharking, and drug dealing. Bulger had often used the rooms above Triple O's. Bulger even had his mail delivered there. But bars were crowded, public, and often chaotic places. The fights that broke out at Triple O's drew police scrutiny. Instead, he and Flemmi wanted a place that might fit more tidily into the palms of their hands, and this new liquor store at the rotary had caught Bulger's eye.

By year's end Julie and Stephen Rakes were in a rush. They'd missed Christmas and were not going to have time to hold a grand opening. Julie's two sisters, her mother, and Stephen's father and mother helped set up inside and stock the shelves. The Rakeses oversaw the installation of a bank of refrigerators—their biggest investment to date. To capture part of the holiday season, they hurriedly opened up just in time for New Year's.

Their families sent over plants with ribbons to display on the counter to mark the occasion, but beyond that the Rakeses simply opened their doors for business. Stephen took out a newspaper advertisement in the

South Boston Tribune announcing that the store, located at "The Rotary in South Boston," was "Now Open" and had "Parking Available." Listed were the hours: "Monday through Saturday, 9 A.M. to 11 P.M." It was pretty basic stuff. Then at the bottom of the display ad Stephen included an enticing item he hoped would catch a few South Boston readers' eyes. "Win a trip for two to Hawaii or $1,000 in a cash drawing on Wednesday, February 8, 1984, 5 P.M., at the Mart." The promotion was Stephen's idea, his brainstorm to draw customers to the store. "In the area stores never offered things like trips," said Julie Rakes, "so we thought it was kind of big. It would attract attention."

Customers came. The husband and wife worked as a tag team, moving between store and home, handing off the business and the kids. Relatives always pitched in, but they were volunteers. There were no partners, no one to answer to. It was exhausting and all-consuming, but the business was theirs and the cash register was ringing.

Before they could complete even a week's worth of business, the Rakeses would be finished. They wouldn't even be around long enough to hold the advertised raffle. Whitey and Stevie had no plans to fly anyone off to Hawaii for free.

■　■　■

JULIE threw on her coat and headed out into the winter night, a night that was beginning like so many other nights: busy and hectic. One spouse coming, the other going, a pace the couple had maintained throughout the renovation of their new store and into its opening days. It was cloudy outside, and the forecasters on the radio had talked about the possibility of snow flurries. But it seemed too mild for that, with temperatures in the forties. The talk around town was mostly about the city's new mayor, Ray Flynn, the "People's Mayor," an Irish son of Southie who was starting his new job during these first days of 1984.

Julie drove over to the store from their house on Fourth Street, a short drive that took her along routes she'd known her entire life, past the homes, stores, and bars along Old Colony Avenue. It was the only world she knew, and she was thinking good thoughts, about her family, about the new business, about Stephen. After she arrived, she chatted with the person they'd hired to work in the stock room and make deliveries. Then the telephone rang.

It was Stephen.

"How am I supposed to know when the lamb is ready?"

Stephen. He and Julie were learning to be interchangeable parts—she in business, he at home. Julie walked him through the instructions for the roast, and then she got off the phone and tended to a few customers. It was midweek and actually pretty quiet. Julie was taking a moment to catch her breath and consider how far she and Stephen had come when around nine o'clock the phone rang again. Stephen? she wondered. What this time?

"Julie?"

"Yes."

Julie did not recognize the deep and husky voice coming at her over the line.

"I know you, I like you, and I don't want to see you get hurt."

"Who is this?"

The voice ignored her question. "You should get out."

"Who *is* this?"

"The store is going to be bombed."

"Why are you doing this?" Julie's voice was rising in alarm. "If you like me, why don't you say your name?" She was shouting. "Why don't you say your name!" But she was yelling into an empty hum. The caller had hung up.

Julie was frightened. She looked around the mostly empty store, feeling like someone was watching. She was back on the telephone with her husband, upset and explaining to him about the call she had just taken, and the more she described the anonymous call the more upset she got. Stephen, for his part, tried to sound comforting. Julie could hear the television in the background, and she could hear the kids making noise. But hanging up, Julie also thought Stephen's voice sounded awfully tense.

Stephen Rakes had a good reason for sounding that way. In his kitchen at that precise moment he was entertaining three uninvited visitors. He had been cleaning up after dinner, playing around with his two girls, getting them changed for bed and letting them watch some television, when he heard a knock at the door. He hadn't been expecting anyone. He went to the door and pulled it open. In the dark stood three men, and Rakes recognized them all. He actually knew Kevin Weeks from growing up, although they were never close; in one of those Southie coincidences, one of his brothers had married one of Weeks's sisters. Stephen and Julie sometimes stopped by Triple O's for a drink, and Weeks was often there—his wife was one of the bartenders. Stephen also recognized the other men. He sometimes saw them at Triple O's too. But he didn't know them personally, he'd never had anything to do with them, and they'd never come around to his house before. It's just that everyone knew Whitey Bulger and Stevie Flemmi.

It did not look good. The men walked right in and took Stephen into the kitchen. Bulger and Flemmi sat down. Weeks stayed on his feet nearby. Bulger was in charge. "You got a problem," he told Rakes. The competition, Whitey said, some of the other liquor store owners, wanted him dead. But Bulger had an option. "Instead of killing you, we'll buy the store."

Rakes fidgeted. "It's not for sale," he said.

It was the last peep of protest Stephen Rakes would make. Bulger exploded, saying they would kill him and take the store. Bulger stormed out, Flemmi and Weeks at his heels. In a panic, Rakes called his wife and told her about the surprise visit. They didn't know what to do. Before Stephen had time to begin to think clearly, there was another rattle at the door.

Bulger was back. He pushed his way past Rakes, accompanied again by Flemmi and Weeks and squeezing a brown paper bag. Back in the family's kitchen, Bulger put the bag down and stood over Rakes at the table. Bulger had a pocket knife in his hand, which he opened and closed as if to punctuate his words. Stephen's little girl wandered into the kitchen to see what was going on. Flemmi pulled out a handgun from his waist, put it on the table, and lifted the girl up onto his lap. "Isn't she cute," Flemmi said. The gangster tousled her blond hair. The gun's hard metal caught the girl's attention, and she reached for it. Flemmi let her touch it, and the girl even put part of the gun in her mouth. "It would be a sin for her not to see you."

Stephen Rakes watched in horror. Bulger continued: either we kill you or we buy the store. Rakes sat still and listened. Bulger explained that inside the paper bag, packed in neatly folded bunches, was $67,000 in cash. Never mind that Stephen and Julie actually had put about $100,000 into their new business—between the cost of the lease, the renovation, the refrigerators, and the stock—all of which they fully expected to make back and more. Bulger had set his own price, and this was Bulgertown.

"You're lucky you're getting what you put into it," Bulger told Rakes. Lucky? Bulger said offhandedly that they would give him another $25,000 if all went well. "Now go away," he told Rakes. The three visitors moved to leave.

"It's ours," said Flemmi.

Rakes sat transfixed. He certainly didn't look lucky. Instead of seeming as if he'd just been made whole, he was falling apart. It was now approaching eleven o'clock, and back at the liquor mart Julie Rakes, struggling to keep her wits, was anxious to close for the night. The telephone rang. She grabbed the phone.

It was Stephen again, and this time he was beyond tense. His voice sounded strange and far away, and then Julie Rakes realized her husband was crying. Stephen explained the sudden turn of events, about a new deal that had fallen into their laps, and Julie just listened in cold silence, a numbness washing over her. This was what shock must be like, a suspended, out-of-body feeling: Stephen, whimpering, muttering things beyond belief, explaining what would happen next, what she had to do.

Julie Rakes looked up and saw an oversized man—well over six feet and heavily built—walk into the liquor mart. It was Jamie Flannery, someone she'd known from high school. They'd been friends. Flannery was also a regular at Triple O's. He had a drinking problem and sometimes worked as a bouncer at the bar. Julie had seen him at the bar with Whitey Bulger. Things suddenly were making terrible sense.

Julie put down the telephone. Flannery was abrupt. He told her to gather up her things, that he'd come to take her home. He told her not to ask any questions, and Julie Rakes complied. Hurriedly, she collected some money from the cash register. She picked up the plants her family had sent to mark the opening of the store. Flannery carried out some wine Julie and Stephen had stocked for a friend who'd made it and was looking for their help in distributing it. They put these things in the car and then Julie, fumbling, turned out the lights and locked up. They quickly drove away.

She never went back to their liquor store again. In the car Julie was shaken, but Flannery said little, just drove, and as he made his way down Fourth Street and began to slow down Julie saw that up ahead in the dark three strangers were standing outside her door. She wanted to know, who were they? Flannery identified the three—the one at the front steps (Bulger), the one just off the stairs (Flemmi), and the one nearing the car parked at the curb (Weeks)—and as Flannery got closer Julie could recognize for herself two of the men, Bulger and Weeks. Behind them Julie saw her husband frozen in the doorway.

"Keep driving, keep driving," she shouted. Frightened, she didn't want to meet these people, and Flannery did cruise on past the house. It was the least he could do. He circled around the block. By the time they returned the three men were gone, but now Stephen Rakes was standing at the curb, waiting for his wife to pull up. He wouldn't even let his wife get out of the car. He handed her the paper bag and told her to go to her mother's house. Right away, he said, and he was talking through clenched teeth.

"I am going to my mother's house at this hour of the night?" Julie yelled, all upset. Stephen told her about the cash in the paper bag and repeated his demand. Just get out of here and take it to your mother's.

"What is going on here? Why is this happening?"

Stephen could not help her with the existential.

Julie was confused, crazy. "I can't go to my mother's. It's almost midnight. What are you talking about?"

Holding it together as best he could, he told Julie he'd already called her mother. She was expecting her. Get going. His voice and his body were rigid. His eyes were still wet from crying earlier. "Your mother is waiting for you." He wore an expression that said, Do as you're told.

The money, he said, was from Whitey Bulger. "It represents our investment," he said, parroting Bulger's angle. "We're lucky to have got it," he added, hypnotically.

Julie was off to her parents' house on Old Colony Avenue. Her mother and father were waiting at the door, a stone-cold look in their eyes. They'd heard enough from Stephen to know that the couple were entangled in business with Bulger—new territory for Julie's family, ground none of them wanted to occupy. Inside the bag was more cash than any of them had ever seen. Julie handed the bag to her mother. "Hide it." Her mother took the bag and padded into her bedroom and tucked it away inside a hope chest. Hysterical and now inside her parents' home, Julie broke down to her father.

"I don't believe it," she said, and she cried.

■ ■ ■

IT TOOK a few days for the Rakes family to fathom what actually had happened, to grasp fully that a bomb indeed had exploded in their midst. Part of the delay was likely due to certain stories, or myths, about Bulger. It was often spread around town that Bulger was supremely loyal to the people of Southie, that he liked helping people, that assisting the locals made him feel good. It was said that Bulger didn't like bullies and he would put them in their place. It was said that Bulger, while not actually instructing anyone not to uphold the law, would encourage them to pursue their pleasure outside the neighborhood. Supposedly, if he heard that someone had burglarized a home in South Boston, he would grab the perpetrator and take him to school in Bulger Ethics 101—the first rule being that you could burglarize homes in swanky suburbs like Brookline and Wellesley but not in your own hometown. Men like Kevin Weeks were among the many who frequently promoted the Bulger propaganda, and the Rakeses had known Weeks for many years. The Rakeses, even if they didn't know Bulger, knew this reputation. But now, firsthand, the couple knew it was not true—Bulger had ripped the liquor mart away from them.

The other reason for the delay was a kind of paralysis. First there was the shock of it all, the suddenness of Bulger's takeover. Then came anger at the unexpected ambush. The next stage would have been acceptance— facing up to the reality that there was little they could do about their loss. But before their anger had a chance to settle into that kind of quiet despair, the Rakeses, especially Julie, decided to put up a fight. In hindsight, maybe she should have known better and been more clear-headed about facing up to the facts of life in South Boston. But no one, not the Rakeses, not their family, not anyone really, understood just how thoroughly Bulger had sewn up the neighborhood—and beyond, for that matter.

Soon after the midnight takeover, Julie and Stephen went to see her uncle, Boston police detective Joseph Lundbohm. Lundbohm, a veteran cop who'd joined the force in 1958, was now working in the homicide unit. He was Julie's mother's brother and lived in Quincy, just south of Boston, with his family. He'd attended Julie and Stephen's wedding and saw them occasionally at other family gatherings.

Lundbohm already knew about the new store the couple had opened; the good news had spread through the family. But he didn't know much else. He took his niece and her husband into his kitchen, and they all sat down. Mostly Julie talked, and she poured out her heart, telling her uncle, Lundbohm said, "about three men coming to her house and stating they were going to purchase the liquor store." The narrative included the part about Flemmi and the little girl and the handgun, and Lundbohm bolted upright—the threat was unmistakable. Talking about it again upset Julie. Once she was done, Lundbohm let a few minutes pass to allow her to calm down.

Julie asked her uncle if there was anything he could do, if there was anyone they could talk to. Lundbohm replied that he knew someone whom he "trusted who was an FBI agent." Lundbohm's thinking was that this sort of extortion was a perfect fit for the FBI. After all, the federal agency had more resources, in terms of manpower and technical capability, such as fancy electronic surveillance equipment. Moreover, Bulger and Flemmi were organized crime bosses. The FBI, not the Boston police, specialized in developing cases against organized crime. The FBI was the big time, and best of all, the agent Lundbohm knew was on its Organized Crime Squad.

The Rakeses gave their okay and left.

Lundbohm soon called the agent. Within a few days the two law enforcement officials were seated at breakfast in a Boston restaurant—on the one side Boston police detective Lundbohm, and on the other FBI agent John Connolly.

Following some small talk, the agent asked what was on Lundbohm's mind. He told Connolly everything—about his niece and husband having just opened this new business, and then the gun, the girl, and the money. Connolly listened. This was a crime that could not be justified, as others had been, as necessary for Bulger to maintain his position in the underworld in order to provide the FBI with intelligence about the Mafia. Bulger's move on the Rakeses had nothing to do with the Mafia.

Faced with this dilemma, Connolly opted to go with what was now reflex. The FBI agent let the police detective finish and then said, "Would Rakes be willing to wear a wire?" Of all the available options, he'd thrown out the most intimidating. Connolly said nothing about wanting to bring in the Rakeses for a debriefing with FBI agents. Nothing about how the bureau might want to proceed cautiously to further investigate Bulger. He was playing hardball, as if the only option was the most dangerous and least likely to be enthusiastically received.

"They'd be afraid to," Lundbohm replied instantly. Lundbohm knew— indeed every cop knew—that wiring up someone to see Whitey Bulger was high risk and extremely dangerous. Police agencies couldn't even convince wiseguys who had been turned into informants to wade into Bulger waters with their bodies wired up for sound. The idea of putting civilians at risk like that was reckless. The Rakeses were amateurs. Besides, still fresh in the minds of cops like Lundbohm was the murder of Brian Halloran two years earlier. The story was all around that he was shot down right after going to the FBI. Lundbohm waved off Connolly's talk about body wires. It was like asking someone to jump off the Tobin Bridge.

"I don't think so. I would advise against it."

"Then I'm not sure if much can be done, Joe." The meeting was over. "But I will look into it."

Connolly never did. Connolly did not write up Lundbohm's information in a FBI report. He did not share the information with his new squad supervisor, Jim Ring, even if only to discuss how to handle the accusation against two of their secret informants. Instead, on his own, Connolly decided that extortion by Bulger and Flemmi was not going to be any of the bureau's business, a decision that was certainly not his alone to make. "I would definitely have expected him to come to me," Jim Ring said later. "That's his entire job. There was an allegation that there was an ongoing extortion. That's what he's supposed to do. He's supposed to come and talk to me. He doesn't have the authority to go out and handle that on his own."

Connolly did share what he knew with one person, though. He told Whitey.

Following his breakfast with Connolly, Lundbohm called Julie Rakes and told her that, even though he'd rejected Connolly's idea to have Stephen wear a body wire, the matter was now in the FBI's hands, and the FBI would be in touch.

But just days after Lundbohm's meeting with Connolly, during a visit to the Lundbohm home, Stephen Rakes pulled Lundbohm aside, out of earshot of Julie Rakes and Lundbohm's wife. Rakes was nervous as he huddled with his wife's uncle.

"Whitey said to back off," Rakes told Lundbohm. Whitey, a shaken Rakes continued, had stopped him in the street in South Boston and said, "Tell Lundbohm to back off."

In an instant, Lundbohm had a single thought: Bulger knew about his talk with Connolly. And more than ever Julie and Stephen were in jeopardy. The truth smacked them in the face—all roads led to Bulger.

Stephen Rakes folded soon after the warning. Bulger summoned him to the liquor mart several times during the weeks that followed, and Rakes signed the documents so that the takeover of their liquor mart appeared on the up and up. Rakes at one point had the gall to mention the additional $25,000. Bulger began screaming at him, and the money was never mentioned again. The conveyance was made out to Kevin Weeks alone, although Weeks filed documents later listing an equal ownership to Bulger and to Flemmi's mother, Mary. Stevie Flemmi later said that the liquor mart was proof he and Bulger were in a legitimate business—an absurd claim that was almost humorous if not for the dark extortion behind the takeover.

Even before the actual passing of the papers, Weeks showed up in the store and took over behind the counter, Bulger hovering nearby. The sign out front was soon changed from Stippo's to the South Boston Liquor Mart. Then a large, green shamrock was painted on the cement exterior. Eventually, on a referral from John Connolly, the FBI in Boston began buying liquor for its Christmas party from Bulger's liquor mart.

Rumors spread quietly through South Boston. There was hushed talk that Stephen Rakes had been held from his ankles over the Broadway Bridge. There was a rumor about a gun being put to Stephen's head, a rumor that he'd lost the store in a card game. But Rakes now mostly brushed off all the gossip and just kept his head down.

To support themselves, Stephen and Julie dipped into the paper bag full of cash hidden in the hope chest at Julie's mother's house. They treated their wounds with a few splurges—a new Dodge Caravan, a road trip to Disneyworld, and the next year they used some of the cash as part of a down payment to get out of South Boston and purchase a home in suburban Milton. Their son Colby was born on June 5, 1984. Stephen Rakes had taken heed; he'd backed off.

While the Rakeses were in Florida, a rumor started that Bulger had killed Rakes. Weeks tracked Rakes down at Disneyworld and ordered him back. Rakes left his family, flew home, and, to quiet the talk, stood next to Bulger, Flemmi, and Weeks at a busy intersection so that passersby could see he was alive.

Rakes fell into line, behind so many others in Southie. He was eventually summoned before a federal grand jury investigating extortion and money laundering at Bulger's liquor store. He was called twice, in 1991 and 1995. Within days of the latter, Bulger pulled up next to him as he was walking in South Boston and called out of the passenger's window: "Hey, I'm watching you." But Whitey actually had little to worry about from Stephen Rakes. In both appearances before the grand jury he described how he'd happily and voluntarily sold his store to Kevin Weeks just a few days after opening it up. The reason? Rakes, under oath, said he was in over his head, had fallen too far in debt, and didn't like the many hours he had to log in order to run the business. He testified that Weeks paid him $5,000 and that he took out another $20,000 he'd put into the store, for a total of $25,000. They were silly lies that no one believed, despite Rakes's best effort to sound relaxed and convincing. And the lies came with a price.

Rakes was charged with perjury and obstruction of justice, and in 1998 he was convicted of both in U.S. federal district court. For Rakes it was the ultimate double jeopardy—the government that did not protect him went after him, while Whitey walked away. But it was a fate Stephen Rakes had come to prefer to facing Bulger.

CHAPTER TWELVE

The Bulger Myth

Detective Dick Bergeron of the Quincy Police Department pulled himself closer to the manual Royal typewriter that sat atop his gunmetal desk. Typing was not his calling in life; working the streets, stalking gangsters was. He shifted uneasily in the chair and then pecked at the keyboard.

The detective typed the words: "TOP SECRET."

He typed the words: "SUBJECT: Proposed Targets of Investigation for Sophisticated Electronic Surveillance."

He typed the names of the two targets:

 I. James J. (AKA "Whitey") Bulger.
   D/O/B: 09–03–29.
   SSN: 018–22–4149.

 II. Stephen Joseph (AKA "The Rifleman") Flemmi.
   D/O/B: 06–09–34.
   SSN: 026–24–1413.

It was June 19, 1983, and scattered across Bergeron's desk were stacks of notes and surveillance reports. Bergeron was shuffling through the material to compose a seven-page, single-spaced report for his Quincy police superiors about the two "notorious organized crime leaders." The time had come for the cops to do something about them.

Bergeron had been watching Bulger and Flemmi for months. Bulger, he had learned, was not just the boss of illegal rackets in South Boston but now controlled organized crime in the city of Quincy and "beyond into the South Shore." Moreover, by following Whitey, Bergeron and the other detectives in his organized crime unit had learned that Bulger had now moved right into their midst. As Bergeron wrote: "Subject Bulger is residing in a condominium at 160 Quincy Shore Drive, Quincy, which is located in a luxury apartment complex called Louisburg Square. The apartment or unit number is 101." The condo, he'd found, was not listed in Bulger's name. The owner was Catherine Greig, a Bulger girlfriend. The purchase price for the unit in 1982 was $96,000—cash, no mortgage. "The shades in said unit are usually pulled down, and cardboard is taped to the small windows in the outside entry doors."(Unknown to Bergeron at the time was the condo's eerie proximity to a gravesite. The new address was just about a hundred yards away from where Bulger and Flemmi, eight years earlier, had buried the corpse of Tommy King along the banks of the Neponset River.)

The cops had learned that Bulger ran the rackets in Quincy and was now often spending his nights there—reason enough to take action against him. But Bergeron had come up with an intriguing and altogether new twist about the crime boss. By consulting with his own network of underworld informants, Bergeron had learned that Bulger and Flemmi "now appear to have broadened their horizons into drug trafficking." With their "expansion into the drug market," wrote Bergeron in flat, official prose, "they will be helping people destroy their lives."

Bergeron finished typing his report, handed it off to his boss, and returned to the street. He and other detectives continued to follow Bulger as the gangster moved between their city and South Boston and as he met regularly with Flemmi, a few other select gangsters, and George Kaufman, the associate who often served as a front for them as the owner of record of their garages. In early 1984 Bergeron watched Bulger and Flemmi replace the sign out in front of the liquor mart at the rotary with a new one: South Boston Liquor Mart.

Eventually Bergeron's written proposal worked its way through various law enforcement channels, landing at the federal agency specializing in drug cases, the DEA. Bergeron's report was consistent with the DEA's own intelligence. The DEA had busted a major drug dealer, Arnold Katz, who had told DEA agents about Bulger's business ties to another major drug trafficker, Frank Lepere. Lepere was the dealer the state police had seen with Bulger at the Lancaster Street garage during surveillance in 1980. Now Katz was disclosing to the DEA that during the early 1980s Lepere had forged an "alliance with Whitey and his partner, Stevie Flemmi, in which Lepere agreed to pay Whitey and Stevie whenever he smuggled a load of narcotics in return for protection." Katz said Lepere had told him all about the deal himself, including how he delivered cash payments to Bulger in a suitcase.

The DEA had more. Early in 1981 a confidential informant had reported that Bulger and Flemmi were on the move—"attempting to control drug trafficking in the region by demanding cash payments and/or a percentage of profits for allowing dealers to operate." With the arrival of the secret Quincy police report, two DEA agents, Al Reilly and Steve Boeri, were assigned to work with Bergeron. Reilly and Boeri quickly added to the growing pile of Bulger intelligence. In February 1984 Reilly met with one of his informants, named "C-2" in DEA reports, who told him that coke dealers were complaining about having to "pay protection money to Whitey." The informant identified a pub owner in South Boston who paid Bulger for the right to sell "small quantities of cocaine and heroin from the bar." Then agent Boeri met with one of his informants, named "C-3," who'd known Bulger for two decades and said the ambitious gangster "most recently" had taken control of "drug distribution in the South Boston area."

The drug theme was reiterated by "C-4," as well as by other underworld sources, and by early 1984 the pieces were falling into place for a joint investigation into Bulger's drug activities. The case, called Operation Beans, would mainly involve the DEA and Quincy detectives.

It had come from bottom-up police work, especially through the often mind-numbingly tedious efforts of Bergeron and his colleagues. Piling up night after night of surveillance throughout 1983 and early 1984, Bergeron had learned a lot about Bulger. Going through the trash at the condo, Bergeron might find a grocery list intact, in Greig's swirling cursive hand-writing—"asparagus, chicken breasts, sherbet, ricotta cheese, olive oil"—but he'd also find Bulger's papers torn into tiny pieces or burned to ash. He'd learned that Bulger was "habit-oriented"—leaving the condo in Quincy at about the same time each afternoon for dinner at Theresa's house in South Boston. Then a full night of secret business meetings, mostly at the liquor mart. Then home to the condo. If it was sunny the next day, he'd often appear on the second-floor patio in the early after-noon for a breath of fresh air, sometimes still clad in pajamas.

Bergeron uncovered a man leading two lives. It was apparent that Theresa did not know about Catherine. But besides his women, Bergeron was witness to another Bulger double cross—one against his neighbor-hood. Bulger had an iron grip on drugs moving through South Boston and beyond. He made dealers pay "rent" on every gram of "Santa Claus," a Southie code name for cocaine. He extorted a share of everything from nickel bags to kilos, loose joints to burlap-wrapped bales of marijuana. Just across from the liquor mart, certain apartments in the Old Colony project, a project near where Bulger had grown up in Old Harbor, had vis-itors tapping at the door at all hours of the day and night. Young men, even some mothers, were selling drugs out of the homesteads—angel dust, mescaline, valium, speed, coke, and heroin—and nothing moved without Whitey's okay. (Paul "Polecat" Moore, one of Bulger's underlings in the drug business, kept a place in Old Colony.) Bulger might often refer to drugs as "fuckin' shit," but his disgust didn't stop him from making big money off the drug trade, which smoked hotter in the two projects at the rotary than it did in the more middle-class streets of City Point. It got to where "P-dope," a heroin mixture, cost only four dollars a hit—cheaper than a six-pack.

It would take another decade before the code of silence began to break, when victims' groups would sprout up and begin pushing back against the Bulger tide, when social workers would hit the streets to take hold of the neighborhood kids and urge them to quit snorting coke and shooting up the heroin, when former addicts would stand up. There was the Southie eighteen-year-old who openly described how he hadn't seen his dad in eight years, how his mother had died from an overdose, how he'd even tried once to hang himself in the hallway of his project. But after all that, he actually considered himself lucky: he hadn't shot up in fourteen months. There was a nineteen-year-old named Chris who described his seven years lost to drugs—a spiral that began with booze and pot, then LSD, coke, and heroin. He'd served time but was now determined to go straight. "There's nothing out there for me if I go back, nothing but a grave with my name on it." Patrick, a thirty-nine-year-old recovering addict, talked about the slippery slope that teen junkies followed: "When they're fourteen or fifteen, they start out snorting it. They'll say, 'I'd never stick a needle in my arm.' Then, once they do that, they'll say, 'I'll never use a dirty needle.' Before long they'll use a rusty nail to get high."

The thaw was not only about recovery. Too often there was bad news. Shawn T. "Rooster" Austin, a twenty-four-year-old who'd grown up in Old Colony, was found dead one morning in a rooming house from a suspected drug overdose. The empty bag of heroin and a syringe without a needle were discovered near the corpse. "I can remember him as a little boy on his bike," said a tenant at Old Colony, adding that she'd seen Rooster just a few weeks earlier. "He was saying that all his friends were dying, that all he was doing was going to wakes. Now, to think...." Patricia Murray, a twenty-nine-year-old Southie woman, was a high school dropout and a hard-core heroin addict when she was picked up on prostitution charges in the late 1980s. "Do you think I like going out on the street?" she said at the time, her thin legs covered in a maze of sores. "Well, I don't."

But in the 1990s, for the first time, people were fighting back. Michael McDonald, who also grew up in the Old Colony project and would later write a best-selling memoir about life in Southie, founded the South Boston Vigil Group. Drugs had ripped apart his family, and two brothers died playing with the fire that Whitey stoked. "There's a lot of pain in this neighborhood that's been ignored by us," he once said. "If you look at this community the way you look at an addict, we're at the stage where the addict admits he has a problem."

Former addicts like Leo Rull emerged as frontline troopers in Southie's new war on drugs. Back when he was eighteen in the mid-1980s, he was heavy into angel dust and coke, and a decade later he described himself as "a man on a mission," trying to save the lives of a new generation of project kids, at times rushing those who'd overdosed in alleyways to emergency rooms and then counseling them afterward. Rull worked for an agency with a federal grant that was trying to break the cycle of poverty and drugs in the poorest sections of Southie and Roxbury, an ironic pairing given their past animosity. During busing one of the Southie chants had been that Roxbury was plagued with troubles not found in the neighborhood whose twenty-nine thousand residents—and especially its pols—saw it as the best and most blessed place to live.

Later in the 1990s the city of Boston was planning to open the state's first detox and treatment center geared exclusively for adolescent drug users. Inside the former rectory at St. Monica's Church at the rotary near Whitey Bulger's liquor mart, Catholic Charities had opened Home for Awhile, a halfway house with a dozen beds for boys aged fourteen to eighteen sent on referrals from the South Boston courthouse or detox centers.

Even if some believed that blacks and busing were the twin forces killing the neighborhood, that wasn't the whole of it—one of their own was at it too. Southie had suffered in Whitey's hands. This was the reality that Bergeron knew, that DEA agents knew, that state troopers knew, that drug dealers all around knew. If you wanted to supply Southie, one dealer later told an undercover DEA agent, "you either pay Whitey Bulger or you don't deal or you end up dead."

But back in the 1980s these were truths the old neighborhood was reluctant to confront. Instead, everyday people clung to the notion that Whitey was their protector. More powerful than any politician, he could police and preserve. To think this way gave them a lift; the ache for a protector had never been greater than after busing, when much of Boston and even the nation unfairly looked down on Southie as a racist, backwater town. Whitey might rarely be seen, but his presence was palpable and, for many, a source of comfort. He might even send flowers or contribute to the funeral expenses of a family who'd lost a member to drugs or violence. He had the right touch that way—sticking to the shadows. His hands were clean. Drugs and prostitution might be "a way of life in other sections of the city, but they will not be tolerated in South Boston," the South Boston Information Center boldly declared in one of its newsletters, even as crime statistics showed that the neighborhood was just like any other in the city—awash in drugs. Yearly drug arrests were tripling in Southie between 1980 and 1990. Narcotics cases doubled in South Boston District Court from 1985 to 1990, and one Boston police detective said he thought there was more coke in Southie per capita than anywhere else in Boston. In the end the neighborhood's personality—its reserve and deep mistrust of outsiders—simply served Whitey all the more.

But just as the neighborhood was in denial, the FBI in Boston did not want to know the true story about drugs and Bulger and the forgotten casualties like Patricia Murray. Circulating instead on the streets of Southie and in the corridors of the FBI was a warm, do-good version of Whitey: Whitey hated drugs, hated drug dealers, and did his best to make Southie a drug-free zone.

It was a classic collision of reality and myth.

■ ■ ■

THE anti-drug Whitey Bulger was always one of the most stubborn and durable stories about the crime boss. It was a position that Bulger, along with John Connolly, staked out by using a linguistic sleight of hand. To the self-styled moral gangster, drug money was separate from the drugs themselves. He could extort "rent" from dealers, loan them money to get them started, and demand that they buy from wholesalers with whom he and Flemmi were associated. He'd make the world safe for drug dealers in return for a piece of the action, but he didn't personally cut the coke or bag the marijuana. That distinction became the basis for the Bulger ballyhoo: Bulger didn't do drugs.

It was a tortured kind of semantic somersault, but there was precedent: Bulger's attitude about alcohol. Bulger drank only occasionally, and when he did, just a glass or two of wine. He hated to see other people drink. Even on St. Patrick's Day he would complain about celebrants drinking at midday. He once said "he didn't trust anyone who drank." Drinkers, he said, "were weak" and might rat him out.

During their two decades together, the only time Bulger hit Theresa Stanley was after she stayed out late drinking wine at a friend's house. If she sipped two drinks, he'd act as if she'd guzzled a dozen. "I almost got killed for drinking a couple glasses of wine," Stanley recalled. Yet at the same time he was berating his girlfriend for wine-tasting Bulger was emerging as the neighborhood's biggest liquor supplier. He happily emptied the register at the liquor store he'd taken over from Stephen and Julie Rakes and once bragged to a patrolling Boston cop, "We have the busiest liquor store around." There were those who weren't fooled by the hypocrisy. The increasing numbers of dopers and junkies joked about the poster hanging in one of the stores Bulger controlled: "Say Nope to Dope." The liquor mart Bulger had taken over was nicknamed the "Irish Mafia store."

Eventually Flemmi himself was caught red-handed trying to push the phony wordplay. He claimed under oath that he could not be prosecuted for the illegal gambling operation he and Bulger ran during the 1980s because the FBI knew about it and had even "authorized" it. As part of the claim, Flemmi described the gambling operation: he and Bulger mostly required bookmakers to pay them "rent" for protection. "So part of the gambling business was shaking down bookmakers?" Flemmi was asked by a prosecutor. Flemmi replied, "That's correct."

Then the prosecutor pounced: "If you were shaking down drug dealers, you'd be in the drug business, right?"

"I assert the Fifth on that," Flemmi responded.

Flemmi was stuck. Faced suddenly with extending the same logic to drugs, Flemmi blinked. If he hadn't, he would have undercut the comfortable fiction that had served him and Bulger for years—the claim they were not involved in drugs.

Under the FBI's informant guidelines, Bulger's drug activities should have led to an abrupt end to the deal he and Connolly and Morris had worked so hard to preserve. Instead, the developing underworld intelligence putting Bulger together with drugs had to be discounted and deflected, and what better way to accomplish that than by cultivating a definition of drug activity that separated the money from the merchandise? Then Bulger, Flemmi, and Connolly could share a refrain: shaking down drug dealers did not make Bulger the person he in fact was—a drug lord.

. . .

RIGHT from the start, Bulger and Connolly had begun drawing a portrait of Bulger as the anti-drug gangster. During the crucial powwow on November 25, 1980, when Larry Sarhatt was conducting his suitability review of Bulger, the gangster proclaimed that he was "not in the drug business and personally hates anyone who [is]; therefore he and any of his associates do not deal in drugs." Inside the bureau Bulger's words went untested: if Bulger said so, it must be true. And in January 1981, as other police agencies were documenting Bulger's alliance with the drug trafficker Frank Lepere, John Connolly was padding the FBI files with the opposite. Connolly reported that Bulger and Flemmi were actually distancing themselves from Lepere because of the latter's drug predilection. Bulger, wrote Connolly, had formerly associated with Lepere but more recently had "broomed him due to his involvement in the marijuana business."

It was a Teflon coating that came in handy in 1984.

The FBI was not a major participant as the DEA and the Quincy police put together Operation Beans. But as a matter of courtesy, the Boston FBI had been notified by the DEA of its intentions. The Boston office now faced a dilemma: what to do with Bulger and Flemmi? To decide, FBI managers in Boston naturally turned to the agents in the best position to gauge what Bulger and Flemmi were up to: John Connolly and Jim Ring, who'd taken over from John Morris as supervisor of the Organized Crime Squad. The fortyish Ring had been fighting the Mafia in New England for nearly a decade, but mostly from Worcester, a city in central Massachusetts viewed by agents as a minor league outpost. From the moment he took over the squad, Ring recalled, Connolly insisted that Bulger and Flemmi "weren't involved in drugs, they didn't do drugs, and they hated drug dealers, and that they would never allow drugs in South Boston." When managers began raising questions, Connolly, fixed in place as the bureau's authority on all things Bulger, came armed with his FBI files discounting any possible link between the gangster and drugs.

Having to notify FBI headquarters in Washington, D.C., about the DEA's plans, the Boston office fired off a two-page telex to headquarters on April 12, 1984, explaining that the DEA was targeting Bulger and Flemmi, "whom DEA alleges are individuals who control a narcotics trafficking group." But the FBI in Boston urged calm. It labeled the DEA's allegations "unsubstantiated, and DEA has furnished no specific information relative to their involvement." Bulger, the telex concluded, should not be "closed due to the past, present and future valuable assistance."

Ring authored a more detailed memo later in the year explaining the Boston office's hands-off position toward Operation Beans, and once again the FBI in Boston displayed its backing for the anti-drug version of Bulger. "The predication" for the DEA's investigation, wrote Ring in October, "although it may be correct, is not consistent with our intelligence regarding the activities of these individuals." Guided mainly by Connolly but also by Ring, the FBI brass in Boston would simply not accept the drug talk building around Bulger.

But behind Ring's back, even Connolly was apparently engaged in hushed FBI talk about Bulger and drugs. In early April 1983 fifteen tons of marijuana were seized from a warehouse at 345 D Street in South Boston. The marijuana belonged to a trafficker named Joe Murray, and after the raid Connolly and agent Rod Kennedy got to talking. Connolly described specifically for his colleague how Bulger profited from Murray's drug business, Kennedy said later.

"The conversation was basically that Joe Murray was required to pay rent to Mr. Bulger and Mr. Flemmi for having used South Boston as a storage warehouse for his drug activity," Kennedy recalled. He said Connolly told him that Murray had paid Bulger and Flemmi between $60,000 and

$90,000 for that particular load. "It was like rent money for having used, you know, having gone into South Boston and using that area for illegal drug activity," said Kennedy, adding that this amount was on top of more regular tribute.

But that was off the record. In a report he filed after the bust, Connolly did not write a word about the payments Murray was making to Bulger and Flemmi. Instead, Connolly stated that the "Murray crew" was worried about Bulger being "upset with them over their storing grass in his town."

Kennedy, who worked briefly as the bureau's liaison with the DEA for Operation Beans, did share some of his intelligence about Bulger's drug activities with DEA agents Reilly and Boeri. (Kennedy had an informant who'd told him Bulger relied on a South Boston drug dealer named Hobart Willis to serve as his go-between with Joe Murray.) But Kennedy never told anything to FBI supervisor Ring. Nor did Kennedy tell Ring or the DEA agents about Connolly's disclosure regarding Joe Murray and Bulger. That was Connolly's responsibility, not his, Kennedy felt. Besides, Connolly had probably expected him "not to pass it on," and he didn't want to cross Connolly.

Eventually more FBI agents in Boston would have informants telling the bureau about Bulger and drugs. By the mid-1990s even some of Bulger's own rank-and-file dealers—like Polecat Moore—had decided to testify against him. And other dealers too. David Lindholm told investigators that in 1983 he was summoned to East Boston, where Bulger and Flemmi held a gun to his head to persuade him to pay them their share of his illegal drug action. In 1998 federal judge Mark Wolf ruled that Flemmi lied to FBI supervisor Jim Ring in 1984 in denying his and Bulger's drug involvement. "It's my understanding that he [Flemmi] was at least involved . . . in extorting money from drug dealers," Wolf said on September 2, 1998.

But Connolly never let up. He had played a key part in creating the myth, and he clung to it. "Well, you know, I've never seen any evidence that they ever did get into drugs," he boasted in 1998—six weeks after Judge Wolf's comments in court. Never mind the evidence, the testimony, the federal judge's findings. "I mean, to get involved with a drug dealer, to collect rent from them—they are the lowest form of animal life. A guy like Flemmi or Bulger is not ever going to put himself in a position to be dealing with these guys."

Denial is not a river in Boston.

. . .

BERGERON soon developed another reason for wanting to take Bulger and Flemmi down. He believed he'd lost a promising informant to them. It began one Sunday night in early October 1984 when the detective got word he better hurry down to the station. He arrived and learned that some other cops on the Quincy force had brought in thirty-two-year-old John McIntyre, an army vet with a string of minor run-ins with the law, for questioning after he was found trying to break into his estranged wife's home. Held in one of the claustrophobic, poorly lit cells, McIntyre's talk soon went way over the heads of the patrol officers. The man was rambling on about marijuana, mother ships, gunrunning, and, most shocking, the *Valhalla*.

The fishing trawler *Valhalla* had left Gloucester, Massachusetts, on September 14 for a few weeks of swordfishing. At least that was the cover story. In fact the trawler was carrying seven tons of weapons valued at a cool million—163 firearms and thousands of rounds of ammunition—destined for the IRA in Northern Ireland. Two hundred miles off the coast of Ireland, the *Valhalla* met up with a fishing boat from Ireland, the *Marita Ann*. The cache of weapons was transferred, and the operation seemed a success. But the Irish Navy had been tipped off and intercepted the *Marita Ann* at sea. The seizure of an IRA-bound arsenal made front-page news on both sides of the Atlantic.

Bergeron summoned Boeri, and they sat with McIntyre in the office of the chief of detectives at the Quincy police station, a tape recorder running. Bergeron sat transfixed as the names of some of the men he'd been targeting came tumbling off McIntyre's lips: Joe Murray, the major drug smuggler who worked out of Charlestown, and Patrick Nee of Southie, who worked as a liaison between Bulger and Murray. Identifying himself as a member of Murray's "cell," McIntyre described a number of marijuana smuggling operations. He talked about how in the past couple of years Murray's group had merged with the "South Boston organization," and that meant Nee was around more often because "they wanted to bring some of their own representative people over, so they could keep an eye on everything."

With regard to the botched IRA gunrunning mission that was so recently in the news, McIntyre confessed that he'd actually helped load the weapons and then served as the boat's engineer, and he said that six men went along on the voyage—himself, a captain, an IRA member named Sean, and three guys from the Southie crew. He didn't know them except by nicknames, and he didn't like them. "You can tell them right away. All of them wear scally caps. They got the Adidas jumpsuits, and they ain't got a speck of dirt on them. They don't know the first thing about a boat. Every day they got to take two, three showers. These fuckin' guys, running around flossing their teeth, takin' showers. There was a storm so bad out there that me and the captain were driving about two days, three days. They wouldn't even come out of their cabins."

Murray, Nee, and "the guys from the liquor store" were behind the arms shipment, and, McIntyre added, theirs was a gang no one should take lightly. "They would tie you right up with piano wire to a pile and leave you there. That's their idea of a joke."

The night the *Valhalla* left port, Kevin Weeks had stood watch on a nearby hill. Kevin was tough, said McIntyre, but then there was "one guy above him." Cross him, said McIntyre, and "he'll just put a bullet in your head." Bergeron could see McIntyre was shaky, almost petrified. "I'd like to start living a normal life," he'd said earlier. "It's almost like living with a knife in you. The last few years you don't know where you're going to end up or what kind of demise you're going to come to. I mean, I didn't start out in life to end up like this."

He never actually uttered the name of the "one guy" above Weeks who oversaw the drug smuggling and the *Valhalla*, but everyone else in the room knew exactly whom he meant: Bulger.

Bulger was considered to be a chest-beating IRA sympathizer. But eventually some investigators came to believe that Bulger, just as he'd betrayed his neighborhood with his phony anti-drug posturing, had also betrayed the IRA. He might have played a key role in rounding up the weapons to sell to the IRA, but after taking payment he dropped a dime. "Whitey waved good-bye to the *Valhalla*, then made a phone call," said one official later. Even if true, Bulger was not the only leak. The former head of the IRA in Kerry later admitted that he'd compromised the gun exchange at sea. Sean O'Callaghan, an assassin-turned-informer, said he did so to get revenge against the IRA. He immediately became a marked man for admitting his perfidy.

Bergeron at the time knew none of this. He was soaking up McIntyre's words and feeling as if he'd won the lottery. "Seemed like an awful big gift at that particular point in time," he was thinking. "This guy had a mountain of information." Over the next several days he and Boeri notified the DEA, customs, and even the FBI. McIntyre was willing to cooperate, and plans were made to use him to gather more information about the gang's drug trafficking. Then one day a few weeks after this seemingly huge break, McIntyre left his parents' house in Quincy saying he was heading off to see Patrick Nee. McIntyre was never seen again. His truck and wallet were found abandoned in a parking lot. Bergeron was crushed. It was Halloran all over again. It was Bucky Barrett all over again. Disappearances that followed talk about Bulger and Flemmi. There was even one more disappearance that autumn that fell outside Bergeron's jurisdiction. Stevie Flemmi and Deborah Hussey were having a bad time of it. The couple was fighting a lot, and Hussey was threatening to tell her mother about her affair with Flemmi. Of course, this would have made things difficult for Stevie. Suddenly Deborah Hussey disappeared. Like Debra Davis before her, she was twenty-six. Flemmi went home to Marion Hussey in Milton. He wasn't about to tell Marion he'd just buried Deborah in a basement in South Boston, a location he and Bulger had already used to dispose of John McIntyre's body a few weeks earlier, and before that, Bucky Barrett's. Instead he just shrugged his shoulders and did his best to console the girl's mother.

■ ■ ■

BERGERON believed Bulger and Flemmi had murdered McIntyre. He didn't know exactly how they'd found out about his cooperation, but he suspected the FBI. Bergeron and, especially, DEA agents Reilly and Boeri already knew about the rumors circulating throughout law enforcement in the Boston area that Bulger and Flemmi were informants for the FBI. In planning for Operation Beans, they had consulted with trooper Rick Fraelick, who provided the new team of investigators with photographs of the targets, informant reports, and other intelligence that state troopers had assembled. He also gave them a full accounting of the failed bid at electronic surveillance at the Lancaster Street garage in Boston. Fraelick was convinced the FBI had "dimed them out."

The new investigators were not naive. They harbored suspicions about Bulger's possible ties to the FBI. But no one had hard proof. From their own informants, they also knew that Bulger was supremely confident, that he liked to boast about outfoxing anyone who might try to pursue him. Bulger would rank on the state troopers, calling the failed Lancaster Street garage effort "a joke." It was similar to the wiseguy bluster the troopers had witnessed from their perch in the rooming house, spying Bulger posing outside the garage, sucking in his stomach.

In fact Bulger had taken the Lancaster Street garage challenge to heart. Post-Lancaster, the ever-wary Bulger and Flemmi had grown increasingly careful in their ways. Bulger installed a sophisticated alarm system in the condo he shared with Greig. He did the same with the 1984 Black Chevy Caprice he and Flemmi drove. (The car was registered to Kevin Weeks's sister Patricia, who worked as a clerk for the Boston police.) In the condo Bulger now always had the TV and stereo turned up. In the car he always blared the radio and a police scanner crackling with noise to mask his low talk. Then at the end of his day Bulger parked the car right up against the condo's door, where he could watch it.

Moreover, Bulger and Flemmi had further insulated themselves, especially Bulger. Instead of exposing himself to a steady stream of underworld figures—as he had each day at the Lancaster Street garage—Bulger pulled back. Bulger, one informant told investigators in 1984, "will converse with subordinates only when necessary. Subordinates cannot directly contact Bulger and Flemmi. Contact is directed to George Kaufman, and Kaufman will relay information."

The extra Bulger caution was in addition to his already well-established countersurveillance habits, such as the driving techniques he employed to check to see if anyone was following him: suddenly pulling over; suddenly reversing direction, especially on a one-way street; suddenly veering from the high-speed lane on the highway to take an exit. Bergeron and DEA agents Reilly and Boeri took note that Bulger and Flemmi seemed to function on high alert at all times.

Bulger and Flemmi and the new investigators periodically bumped into one another. Bergeron and Boeri were tailing Bulger one summer night along Dorchester Avenue in Southie when Bulger spotted them. Bulger waved and smiled. But Whitey wasn't always so jaunty. Bergeron and another detective one night set up surveillance at the condo in Quincy with a white Ford van the DEA had provided. It was 2:02 in the morning, and Bulger came out of unit 101, got into his car, and drove around the parking lot while staring suspiciously at the van. Then he parked, got out, and looked into the van's rear window. He walked all around the van, checking out the front plate. Visibly agitated, he went back inside the condo. Investigators hustled over to drive the van away, and as they did, Bulger appeared in the rearview mirror in a car that pulled out of the shadows by the Dumpster.

The investigators realized from these cat-and-mouse encounters that Bulger and Flemmi were aware of their interest in them. But even while recognizing that Operation Beans was unfolding in a high-risk atmosphere, they never thought of not going for it. Bergeron, Boeri, and Reilly had frequently worked over the possibility that Bulger and Flemmi were FBI informants. But in the end, so what? The bottom line in 1984 was actually quite simple. Bulger and Flemmi, Reilly concluded, "were the strongest organized crime figures remaining in Boston, since the recent downfall of the Angiulo organization." Even if they were informants, noted Reilly, "informants aren't given any particular free pass." They all recognized it would be a lot easier to build a case if they could line up witnesses to testify in court against Bulger and Flemmi, but that wasn't realistic, not with Bulger's insular lifestyle, not with the widespread fear of Bulger that persisted in the underworld, not when men like John McIntyre disappeared off the face of the earth. Thus, the central game plan for Operation Beans was to capture Bulger's own words. For much of 1984 the investigators worked to assemble the probable cause they'd need to win a judge's okay to install bugs.

Even though the FBI was notified as a matter of courtesy in April 1984, the goal in putting together Operation Beans was to limit the FBI's knowledge and participation in the drug investigation. "I wanted to keep it away from the FBI and go on with it," said Reilly. The case, he said, was, "DEA initiated, DEA sustained, DEA funded. We did everything." The whole operation was specifically set up to try to keep certain Boston FBI agents from knowing about it. That autumn, when agents from the FBI's crack "tech team" arrived from New York City to consult with the DEA on installing a bug in Bulger's car and condo, the out-of-town FBI agents were ordered not to check in with the Boston FBI office. The two local FBI agents who were eventually loaned to the DEA to help monitor the bugs were newcomers to the city. The office for Operation Beans was even moved off-site to the Fargo Building in downtown Boston, away from the John F. Kennedy Federal Building, where DEA agents and FBI agents often passed each other, ate lunch together, and might gossip about cases.

■ ■ ■

BUT the FBI did know, and the way Flemmi saw it, the FBI's role in Operation Beans was "no more than a surreptitious effort to ensure that the investigation was ultimately unsuccessful." Connolly, it turned out, had caught wind of Operation Beans right from the start—early on in 1984, even before the investigation had a name and before the DEA had assembled its plan of action. Immediately after the telex was sent from Boston notifying FBI headquarters about DEA's planned investigation, a top FBI official in Washington, D.C., named Sean McWeeney picked up the telephone to call Jim Ring. McWeeney was chief of the Organized Crime Section at FBI headquarters.

Instead of Ring, John Connolly took the call.

"Aren't these our guys?" McWeeney asked the handler.

And if Connolly knew, Bulger and Flemmi knew. They continued to meet regularly throughout the year, and, said Flemmi, the talk often turned to the intensifying interest the DEA and Quincy police showed in them. They had a kind of cross-fertilization going, each sharing with the other whatever information they'd picked up. Connolly got additional information from other agents, either directly or through Ring. It would have been helpful to have John Morris's input as well, but not only was Morris no longer running the squad, he was out of town: the former supervisor had been dispatched to Florida on a special assignment and would not return until early 1985.

During one key session in September 1984, Bulger and Flemmi and Ring and Connolly huddled at Connolly's apartment in South Boston. Connolly's apartment had been chosen because of all the cops spotted skulking around Bulger's condo all hours of the night. The foursome, recalled Flemmi, had an "animated discussion" about Operation Beans. Flemmi and Bulger made their self-serving denials to Ring about the drugs. Ring and Connolly told them not to worry, insisting that he and Bulger "hang in there and stay, you know, stay on the team." In addition, Bulger and Flemmi were told that Operation Beans was working out of the Fargo Building in Boston. This enabled Bulger to stake out the building and pick up the makes, models, and plates of the undercover cars the investigators were driving.

By the time DEA investigators, on Christmas Eve, won a court order to place a wiretap on George Kaufman's telephone, Flemmi and Bulger were one step ahead. John Connolly had provided a holiday treat: a warning about the telephone wiretap. Thus, instead of capturing criminal conversations, all DEA agents Reilly and Boeri overheard was Flemmi talking nonsense or in code to George Kaufman. The agents never picked up Bulger using the phone at all.

Given the heads-up, it was a wonder that Bergeron and the DEA's Reilly and Boeri actually succeeded in planting microphones in Bulger's car and condo. But they did do it, briefly, for a few weeks in 1985. The DEA agents and Bergeron had been left to their own devices after the FBI technical team called in for a consultation was unable to offer any surefire method to implant a microphone in Bulger's car and condo. Both contained sophisticated alarm systems designed to detect any intrusion inside the condo or the car. The technical team, looking at the condo and the car from a distance, concluded that unless the local agents could come up with the codes to defeat the alarms, there was no way agents could sneak inside to install the bugs. The other option the FBI mentioned was replacing Bulger's car with an exact duplicate wired for sound. Reilly considered that proposal ridiculous. After a day the FBI tech team returned to New York. Their anemic proposals simply fueled Reilly's worries about the FBI, even if the tech team had been ordered not to tell local FBI agents about being in town. "I thought they didn't put their best effort forward."

So Reilly, Boeri, and Bergeron took matters into their own hands. They obtained a Chevy exactly like Bulger's and began studying it, looking for a way to insert a bug without having to break into the car. They found a point of entry low on one of the door panels, and they practiced drilling into it until they could install a microphone that worked. They took the same approach with the condo—they practiced drilling into window sills to plant a bug from the outside.

In early 1985, under the cover of darkness, the agents got a bug insert-ed into the condo's window. "The bug worked fine," Bergeron said. The problem, he said, was that Bulger blasted the stereo and television once Flemmi arrived, and the two gangsters would go upstairs to talk business. The attempt was a bust.

Then, on February 2, 1985, while Bulger slept, the agents installed a bug in the door panel of the black Chevy. But the next day, after Bulger got into his car and drove into South Boston, all the agents got was an earful of road noise. The microphone was picking up the bump and grind of the car's wheels turning along the highway. Even after repositioning the bug the next night, the agents were faced with a persistent "lack of clarity" in catching Bulger talk. Part of the problem was that the technology they'd been forced to use had severe limitations. They were using a tiny device that transmitted a signal to a surveillance vehicle, where the actual record-ings of the conversations were made. This meant that their ability to tape anything depended on keeping the van close to Bulger's car—no easy task. Moreover, the agents were always competing with the road noise and Bulger's habit of playing the car radio as he and Flemmi chatted quietly, managing their affairs in a general state of wariness.

It was a constant struggle to decipher who exactly was talking in the car and what they were saying. The best night came on February 17, 1985, with the two DEA agents and Bergeron tailing Bulger and Flemmi to a meeting with George Kaufman at Triple O's. It was after 10:00 P.M. when Bulger and Flemmi emerged from the bar and drove off. Fighting through the radio and road noise, the agents then heard Bulger and Flemmi talking about the revised underworld order. They heard the gangsters talking about Howie Winter, who was due soon to come out of prison. "Fuck Howie," Bulger said.

The agents heard the talk veer briefly toward drugs.

"This fuckin' coke deal," said Flemmi.

"I'm running the business and everything over the phone," replied Bulger.

It was tantalizing stuff, but never more than a tease. They got snatches of talk about money, about "drug outlets," and about Bulger's gambling operations. They even captured what they thought was a reference to one of the local FBI agents, but they didn't know what it meant: "Connolly has been a little fuckin' nervous," Flemmi remarked at one point.

The agents kept at it nonetheless, but as the nights passed they were never able to get enough words strung together to put together a criminal storyline. They saw Bulger sitting in the car with Patrick Nee, who worked as messenger between Bulger and Joe Murray, but they couldn't quite capture what was said. They watched a Bulger subordinate climb into the car and deliver a pile of money to the crime boss, but once again, their talk was broken up. They listened to an angry Bulger curse another underling for daring to come for him at Theresa Stanley's. Bulger read the miscreant the riot act, saying he would "clip" anyone who came there. Family had nothing to do with business, he said.

No investigation had ever caught Bulger on tape before, even in fractured form, but the investigators realized that if they wanted to make a case they could take into court they were going to have to improve the quality of their recordings. On the morning of March 7, at 2:40 A.M., Reilly and Bergeron made a final attempt to tinker with the position of the microphone. "We thought he was asleep because normally he would be asleep around two-thirty in the morning," recalled Reilly. "We came around the building, and he came out of the condo. He saw us, and we saw him, and we took off and ran." Bergeron said an agitated Bulger jumped into his car with his girlfriend Greig and began driving in circles around the parking lot. "He began driving around like a madman, screaming at Greig, real hyper and suspicious and screaming he knows all about the cops."

Flemmi was out of town, in Mexico, and a jumpy Bulger hunkered down. Eluding the investigators, he met with John Connolly the very next day, on March 8. Then, three days later, DEA agents Reilly and Boeri followed Bulger as he drove his black Chevy into a garage beside the liquor mart in Southie.

The next words they heard from Bulger signaled the end.

"He's right—they did put a bug in the car."

The agents jumped out of their van and raced in to retrieve their electronic surveillance equipment. The last thing agents ever wanted was for targets to know exactly what kind of technology was being used against them. They found Bulger tearing open the door panel and Kevin Weeks standing nearby holding a radio frequency detector that located bugs just like the bug the DEA had used. Facing down Reilly, Boeri, and two other DEA agents inside the garage, Bulger resumed the take-charge bounce that usually characterized his interplay with cops. He said he was surprised they'd been able to install a bug. "I got a pretty good alarm system," he said as Reilly stepped forward and fumbled around the door panel to pull out the microphone. Bulger mentioned he knew something was up after bumping into Bergeron and Reilly in the condo's parking lot a few nights earlier. He did not, however, mention his FBI contacts.

Boeri noticed that Bulger wore a fancy belt buckle—inscribed with the words "ALCATRAZ: 1934–1963." Making small talk, the agent pointed out the handsome buckle, but Bulger didn't dare mention how he'd come to possess it.

The crime boss and the agents kept up their banter, with Bulger nagging them for details about when the bug was installed and how long it had been running. He guessed "seven or nine days." Weeks offered his guess the bug had been in place for about two months. They probably had a bug in his car too, Weeks added.

"You want to buy my car—cheap?" Weeks wisecracked.

Boeri asked Bulger where Flemmi was.

James J. "Whitey" Bulger Jr.

Former FBI agent John Connolly

Stephen J. "the Rifleman" Flemmi

Donato "Danny" Angiulo and Bulger, right,
in a garage on Lancaster Street, circa 1980

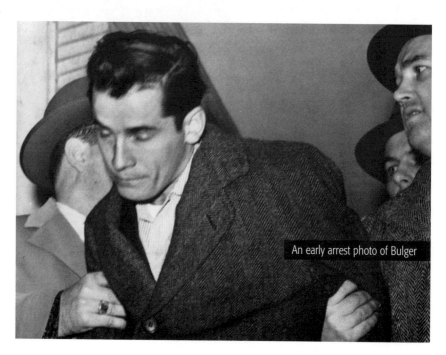

An early arrest photo of Bulger

Frank Salemme, left, and Robert Deluca, far right, seen meeting on Day Boulevard in South Boston, circa 1990

Flemmi

Gennaro J. Angiulo, mafia chief, entering federal court in Boston on racketeering charges in 1983

John Connolly Jr. points as he and another agent take Francesco "Frankie" Angiulo to court

Boston FBI supervisor James Ring, FBI Director William Sessions, and FBI agent John Connolly, celebrate the March 1990 Patriarca indictment

John M. Morris, former FBI supervisor

Millionaire Roger Wheeler was gunned down on May 27, 1981 by Bulger hit man John Martorano

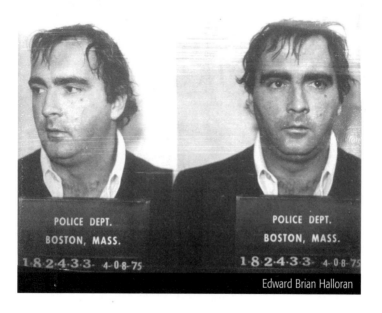

POLICE DEPT.
BOSTON, MASS.
1·8·2·4·3·3 4-08-75

POLICE DEPT.
BOSTON, MASS.
1·8·2·4·3·3 4-08-75

Edward Brian Halloran

By 1984, Bulger controlled these two South Boston businesses as a base for his underworld empire

Catherine Greig and Bulger, 1988

James J. "Whitey" Bulger

FBI TEN MOST WANTED FUGITIVE

RACKETEERING INFLUENCED AND CORRUPT ORGANIZATIONS (RICO) - MURDER (18 COUNTS), CONSPIRACY TO COMMIT MURDER, CONSPIRACY TO COMMIT EXTORTION, NARCOTICS DISTRIBUTION, CONSPIRACY TO COMMIT MONEY LAUNDERING; EXTORTION; MONEY LAUNDERING

JAMES J. BULGER

Photograph taken in 1994   Photograph taken in 1994   Photograph retouched in 2000

Aliases: Thomas F. Baxter, Mark Shapeton, Jimmy Bulger, James Joseph Bulger, James J. Bulger, Jr., James Joseph Bulger, Jr., Tom Harris, Tom Marshall, "Whitey"

DESCRIPTION

Date of Birth:	September 3, 1929	**Hair:**	White/Silver
Place of Birth:	Boston, Massachusetts	**Eyes:**	Blue
Height:	5' 7" to 5' 9"	**Complexion:**	Light
Weight:	150 to 160 pounds	**Sex:**	Male
Build:	Medium	**Race:**	White
Occupation:	Unknown	**Nationality:**	American
Scars and Marks:	None known		

Remarks: Bulger is an avid reader with an interest in history. He is known to frequent libraries and historic sites. Bulger is currently on the heart medication Atenolol (50 mg) and maintains his physical fitness by walking on beaches and in parks with his female companion, Catherine Elizabeth Greig. Bulger and Greig love animals and may frequent animal shelters. Bulger has been known to alter his appearance through the use of disguises. He has traveled extensively throughout the United States, Europe, Canada, and Mexico.

CAUTION

JAMES J. BULGER IS BEING SOUGHT FOR HIS ROLE IN NUMEROUS MURDERS COMMITTED FROM THE EARLY 1970s THROUGH THE MID-1980s IN CONNECTION WITH HIS LEADERSHIP OF AN ORGANIZED CRIME GROUP THAT ALLEGEDLY CONTROLLED EXTORTION, DRUG DEALS, AND OTHER ILLEGAL ACTIVITIES IN THE BOSTON, MASSACHUSETTS, AREA. HE HAS A VIOLENT TEMPER AND IS KNOWN TO CARRY A KNIFE AT ALL TIMES.

CONSIDERED ARMED AND EXTREMELY DANGEROUS

IF YOU HAVE ANY INFORMATION CONCERNING THIS PERSON, PLEASE CONTACT YOUR LOCAL FBI OFFICE OR THE NEAREST U.S. EMBASSY OR CONSULATE.

REWARD

The FBI is offering a $1,000,000 reward for information leading directly to the arrest of James J. Bulger.

"He's around," Bulger lied.

The talk went around in circles. Hey, announced Bulger at one point to the DEA agents, "We're all good guys."

How so?

"You're the good good guys. We're the bad good guys."

The agents took their equipment and went home. Two days later Boeri and Bergeron were driving past Theresa's house when Bulger waved them down. He kept up his gangster panache, advising the investigators they shouldn't believe all the things they heard about him. He showed them that the car panel had come loose and asked for their help securing it.

"Pretty ingenious installation," Bulger told Boeri, returning again to the bug, fishing for information.

Flemmi returned from Mexico and ran into Boeri and Reilly in the parking lot of the Marconi Club in Roxbury, where he often hung out. They talked about the "excitement" earlier at the garage over the bug. Flemmi asked about the quality of the transmissions. "Doesn't the cold weather affect the batteries?" he taunted. The agents said everything worked fine. They weren't going to give an inch.

Flemmi urged that they all get along. Instead of chasing each other, they should be scratching each other's backs. "Whaddya want?" he joked. "We don't need Miranda. We can wrap a rope around anyone's neck. Just tell us what you want." Then he asked where all this was headed. He hoped the agents were not going to bother them much longer. "You're not going to make Jimmy and me a lifetime investigation?"

"Well, we're really just getting started," said Boeri.

Bulger and Flemmi knew this was bluff. The two gangsters had already huddled again with Connolly. "John Connolly said that Jim Ring told him that the DEA investigation was collapsing, or it collapsed, words to that effect," Flemmi said. "Connolly told me. We had frequent meetings at John Connolly's house, independent of the meetings we had with supervisors."

In the garage, the moment Bulger had uttered the line "He's right— there is a bug in the car," DEA agent Reilly was convinced that the FBI had tipped off Bulger. Reilly had his suspicions but couldn't prove exactly who in the FBI Bulger was referring to. But the words were like the exclamation point to long-harbored concerns about Bulger's ties to the FBI. From then on, Reilly, Boeri, and Bergeron all believed their effort was compromised.

Even so, no governmental inquiry was ever undertaken to examine this belief. No postmortem was conducted to try to find out exactly why Operation Beans failed. Everyone walked away, moved on. It was as if yet another investigatory dud gave rise to a numbness, with police agencies now unwittingly ready to accept the FBI's protective shield of Bulger and Flemmi as a fact of life, the way things were in Boston, part of the city's fabric.

Outwardly, the gangsters made the best of it. "I didn't think they appeared to be concerned," Ring recalled. Bulger and Flemmi acted like the car bug was a pretty funny joke. "It was more a matter of, I guess I'd have to call it 'Gotcha.'"

The truth was that the close call was no laughing matter. The year-long chase had proved grueling. Bulger and Flemmi had felt harassed at every turn. Despite the FBI, the DEA had actually managed to accomplish a first—a bug on Bulger. Detective Bergeron and DEA agents Reilly and Boeri had revealed the man behind the myth, though not in a way that could result in a criminal indictment. But what Bergeron and the agents knew would remain locked in confidential law enforcement files. John Connolly, Bulger, and Flemmi resumed their anti-drug mantra. They had beaten the DEA's Operation Beans.

But it had been way too close for comfort. The scrutiny was tiring, and not the good life the gangsters had in mind as part of their deal with the Boston FBI. So, in April 1985, just days after Flemmi's repartee with the DEA agents at the Marconi Club, Bulger and Flemmi were looking for reassurance that things were okay and would stay that way. John Morris was back in town, and it was time to pay him a visit.

CHAPTER THIRTEEN

Black Mass

Tight-lipped and intense, the John Morris of 1985 was still enjoying the glow of having overseen the successful bugging of Mafia headquarters in early 1981. He was viewed as a seasoned veteran, thoughtful and determined. He was also leading the double life of a libertine, as were the other members of the cabal—John Connolly, Whitey Bulger, and Stevie Flemmi. Each had a public pose that contrasted sharply with a private reality. Morris and Connolly were FBI agents by day who at night caroused with the two gangsters they now zealously protected, even if it meant bending rules and breaking laws. Bulger and Flemmi feasted off reputations as the ultimate stand-up guys who cunningly outwitted the police at every turn, when in fact they had for years given the FBI tidbits about underworld friends and foes and enjoyed a protective shield from the nation's top law enforcement agency.

Morris was essentially in Bulger's back pocket—having solicited and taken $1,000 in 1982 to fly Debbie Noseworthy to Georgia. And during the

early days of 1984, amid the start-up of the DEA's Operation Beans, Morris
had taken a second bite from the apple Bulger held out for him.

"Connolly called me and said, 'I have something for you from these
guys. Why don't you come on over and pick it up?' I went over; I picked it
up. It was a case of wine. On the way out he said, 'Be careful with it,
there's something in the bottom for you.' So I took the case of wine, and
then when I opened the case I found that there was an envelope on the
bottom that contained $1,000 in it." It was as if Morris needed more mo-
ments like this one to keep the high going. The concern was not whether
he should march into the office of the special agent in charge of the
Boston office and turn them all in; instead, his narrow eyes darted this way
and that to make sure no one was watching. He picked up a corkscrew,
opened a bottle, pocketed the Bulger money, and savored it all.

But if Bulger saw the case of wine as a second premium on his FBI insurance plan, he was suddenly disappointed. The FBI that considered
Morris a model of integrity dispatched the supervisor off to Miami to
oversee a special team of agents investigating—of all things—the corruption of an FBI agent in Florida. The timing was horrible, given the de-
tectable increase in scrutiny Bulger and Flemmi were getting from the
drug agents and the Quincy police. Throughout the remainder of the year
and into early 1985, Bulger and Flemmi weathered Operation Beans with
the help of Connolly and, to a lesser degree, Jim Ring. It had not been
easy, however, and now that federal drug agents were stymied and John
Morris was resurfacing, it seemed like the time for a reunion. Time to clarify their secret alliance over a good meal. Time to review some old business—Operation Beans—as well as discuss pressing new concerns, such as
the long-delayed, upcoming racketeering trial of the Mafia's Gennaro
Angiulo, featuring the FBI's extensive tape recordings of Mafia talk at 98
Prince Street. The trial—the biggest criminal trial in Boston in decades—
was finally due to start any week, and Bulger and Flemmi had a list of
worries about the tapes.

Going into the dinner, Connolly had already disclosed the fact that
Mafia leaders Jerry Angiulo and Larry Zannino often got to talking on the
tapes about Bulger and Flemmi, "conversations," said Flemmi, about
"different criminal acts." Of particular concern to Flemmi was the Mafia

talk about his role in the 1967 slayings of the three Bennett brothers. But there was plenty more. Connolly provided a full telling of the wiseguy dialogues. "The Bennetts were mentioned on the tapes," Flemmi said, and John Connolly also "mentioned the gambling, if I can recall, some bookmakers on there that were—that we were involved with. I think Jerry [Angiulo] mentioned the fact that Whitey had all of South Boston, Stevie had all of the South End, and we were extracting X amount of dollars from bookmakers. He mentioned an amount—Whitey probably gets . . . $50,000 a week from extracting payments from bookmakers."

Flemmi and Bulger were alarmed. Prior to the 1981 bugging of the Mafia, this was the exact situation Bulger and Flemmi had voiced concern about—that even if they avoided appearing at 98 Prince Street the Mafia bosses would nonetheless talk about their mutual business interests. They needed reassurance of a promise Morris and Connolly had made at the time, that in return for their help against Angiulo the tapes would not be used against them.

While Morris was off in Miami, the gangsters had talked all of this over with Connolly, asking the FBI handler about the precise danger the tapes posed to them. Connolly tried comforting them. "That's when he said not to be concerned about it," Flemmi recalled. But better to hear the same from Morris, to have the promise restated.

"The meeting was set up by John Connolly," Flemmi recalled. Connolly got in touch with Bulger, and Bulger lined up Flemmi. "We just became available." They picked a weekday night in early spring. The city was emerging from the darkness of winter, and the weather was mild, hinting at summer. Connolly picked up Bulger and Flemmi in a South Boston parking lot. He said another old friend would be joining them, Dennis Condon, the former FBI agent who'd been with them all at the start of their deal in 1975 and was now a high-ranking public safety official overseeing the state police. Condon was an elder statesman, a veteran of FBI tricks from the 1960s. "They knew each other," Morris recalled, "and Connolly and I felt that Condon would enjoy the opportunity of seeing them." It went without saying that having Dennis Condon attend what was essentially a fifty-thousand-mile checkup in the FBI's Bulger deal made sense. Condon was ex-FBI and now sitting atop the state police, and

Bulger and Flemmi were constantly distracted by the attention they were drawing from other police agencies. Why not try to touch as many bases as possible?

Driving into the rush-hour traffic, Connolly, Bulger, and Flemmi headed out of the city for dinner with John Morris.

■ ■ ■

MORRIS, meanwhile, was busy puttering around the kitchen of his Lexington home. He seasoned the steaks and got the meat ready for the oven. He set the table in the dining room for five. His wife Rebecca would not be joining them. "I refused to cook dinner for them," she said later. John might be upbeat about his dinner party, but his wife was downcast. They circled one another in the kitchen, wary and mistrustful. Her head shaking, she voiced again her strong opposition to having two gangsters in their home—what about their son and daughter? John tried calmly to explain again the necessity of maintaining Bulger's and Flemmi's trust. Rebecca knew nothing about the Bulger money or any of the other peculiarities of her husband's ties to the crime bosses. But she knew something wasn't right. Rebecca had been an FBI wife long enough to sense that something was irregular about the long-running arrangement.

So she would have none of it. John might try to soften the terms of the disagreement by always referring to Bulger and Flemmi as "the bad guys," a kind of concession to her that he never forgot who Bulger and Flemmi were and that, rest assured, he knew exactly what he was doing by having them over. He even tried saying he was actually concerned about John Connolly and Connolly's closeness to Bulger, and that he, as Connolly's friend and former supervisor, had a duty to keep an eye on things. But Rebecca was not impressed. She didn't want them or their gifts in her house.

The maple trees in the yard were sprouting buds and inside the kitchen John Morris was doing his best to let the marital tension drain from him. He was feeling pretty good otherwise, riding a professional high from the Florida special assignment he was in the process of wrapping up. Morris thought about what he'd done down south. The agent he'd investigated,

Dan Mitrione, had been considered a role model—smart, always physical-
ly fit, an ex-marine and Vietnam vet with solid law enforcement blood-
lines. He was the son of a former police chief and State Department
employee who had been murdered by terrorists in Uruguay in 1970. In the
early 1980s Dan Mitrione had begun working undercover as part of a
major FBI drug investigation. Mitrione worked his way into the inner circle of a major cocaine cartel. But he fell under the spell of the key smuggler, an older man who began treating Mitrione like a son. Mitrione
eventually began aiding the smugglers he was supposed to catch. By 1984
Mitrione was under investigation.

John Morris was in charge of a team of FBI agents assembled from
around the country and sent to unravel the mess. By the fall of 1984
Mitrione had confessed to the special task force that he'd taken $850,000 in
bribes from the drug smugglers. Mitrione pleaded guilty in federal court
and was sentenced to serve a decade in prison. The federal judge, at his
sentencing, was clearly dismayed at the undoing of an agent with such an
exemplary career. "The Lady of Justice may have a blindfold on, but she
also has a tear on her cheek today," the judge said from the bench.

Morris had come home to applause from superiors for a job well done.
But it had to be an eerie experience. He'd gone off to Florida within weeks
of accepting wine and $1,000 from Bulger. He realized that the dirty
money he had taken amounted to chump change compared to Mitrione's
eye-popping $850,000. But imagine the fallout if the FBI brass realized
they had sent one corrupt agent to investigate another. And there were
other secrets to keep, including hiding from Rebecca the romantic affair
with his secretary Debbie.

The husband and wife maintained their big chill in the kitchen of
their suburban home when, around seven o'clock, the doorbell rang. The
special guests had arrived. Rebecca stiffened. John surveyed the kitchen,
saw the meal was coming along fine, and headed to the front door. "I felt
that my house was a very safe place," Morris said about hosting gangsters
at his home. "I did not think that they were an immediate threat to my
family. I was concerned later on about them knowing where I lived, but
at the time I was not concerned for the safety of my wife and children."
It would be good to see Connolly, Bulger, and Flemmi again. He had

already picked up talk from the office that the group was not all that happy with Jim Ring.

Morris pulled open his front door. He heartily greeted his guests. There were handshakes all around. Welcome, welcome. The gangsters had brought along not just wine but a bottle of champagne as well. John Morris and Flemmi headed into the kitchen to put the bubbly on ice. Rebecca Morris stood at the sink washing her hands. The moment Flemmi entered her kitchen she turned off the water and abruptly left the room. Morris shrugged. He turned his attention to his guests, offered a thin, wan smile, and asked how things were.

■ ■ ■

THE trio of Connolly, Bulger, and Flemmi was just as happy to see Morris as Morris was to see them. Especially Connolly. Jim Ring had been a tough mark. Connolly had tried his best to get off on the right foot by arranging get-togethers so everyone could get to know one another. ("John Connolly came to me and used the expression, 'The boys want to meet with you,'" Ring said later.) But Ring had studied Connolly, grown increasingly concerned at the agent's breezy style, and was left momentarily speechless at the end of the dinner at Mrs. Flemmi's house when, "as we were leaving, Whitey Bulger's brother, Bill Bulger, came into the kitchen to give him some photographs.

"'What the hell is going on?'" Ring blurted at Connolly afterward about the pileup of breaches in protocol—the casual dinner atmosphere with two crime bosses, the involvement of an informant's mother, the entrance of one of the state's most powerful public figures. No one in the room had even blinked—one big happy family. Connolly didn't understand Ring's question. He simply pointed out to his supervisor that Bill Bulger lived next door—that was the explanation for the unexpected drop-in.

Ring's dismay had culminated in private sit-downs with the Boston office's star handler of informants. The supervisor's list of grievances covered just about every basic ground rule the FBI or any police agency had on how to work informants. "I had a meeting with John Connolly in my office," Ring said later, "and I told him that what I was observing was contacts with Mr. Flemmi and Mr. Bulger with mistakes made that a first-year agent wouldn't make." Ring complained that Connolly's friendly manner was way over the top, that instead of treating the two informants as criminals he treated them as if they were colleagues at the FBI office.

Ring immediately noticed that information was flowing the wrong way—to Bulger and Flemmi. Connolly, Ring said, "gave away too much. He could have rephrased the question in a different way. You could have buried the question among five others, and the one thing—I think it was the second meeting—that struck me was Connolly turned to me and said something to the effect, 'Oh, tell them about such and such.'"

The meetings at Connolly's home in South Boston were also a problem. "It was crazy," Ring said. He ordered Connolly to stop hosting Bulger and Flemmi at his home. Connolly responded like a merry schoolboy prankster determined to fool the stern, humorless schoolmaster. He sought out another agent, John Newton, and asked if he could move the gatherings to his South Boston apartment. Newton, the agent Connolly had befriended upon his arrival in Boston, was happy to help. Newton opened up his home to his FBI friend, and when they all showed up for these unauthorized encounters, Newton would take his two dogs out for a stroll. The considerate Bulger eventually began bringing along dog biscuits.

Connolly then reported back to Ring that he'd obeyed the order and halted the practice of meeting at his house. But word got to Ring that Connolly had simply pulled a fast one, relocating down the street. "Unprofessional, stupid, not the way business is done by FBI agents. I was just not happy," Ring said. "Why go into a neighborhood where two people are known? You can go to New York City. You can go to Canada. Go someplace. This is being lazy."

And Ring didn't even know about the dinner parties—at Nick Gianturco's house, at John Morris's house. In addition, Ring noted that seeing two informants together—an accepted fact at this point in the history of the FBI's deal with Bulger and Flemmi—was highly irregular. "If you could control the situation," noted Ring, "you'd meet Bulger and Flemmi separately." But of course the FBI was not in full control.

In response to Ring's criticisms, Connolly unleashed his well-rehearsed defense of Bulger and Flemmi as indispensable to the FBI's war on the

Mafia. Included was Connolly's patented story that pulled the heartstrings of every FBI agent—how Bulger and Flemmi had saved Nickie Gianturco's life.

But Ring even had the gall to question this piece of Bulger hype. Rather than take Connolly at his word, he went and asked Gianturco about the tale. "I asked him, what was the story? And he went back and related that there was this undercover operation which he had been in, that there was some scheduled meeting he was supposed to attend, and that reportedly Mr. Bulger and Mr. Flemmi had sent him information warning him not to attend.

"I was saying to him: 'You didn't answer my question. My question was, "Are you reporting to me that you believe that these two people saved your life?"' And I recall his response being that the case was over." Ring never got a straight answer.

For all of his concerns, Ring kept the matter between himself and Connolly. He did not document his criticisms or share his concerns at the time with any of the other FBI supervisors in the Boston office. He did not discipline Connolly. Ring didn't think discipline was warranted "for doing something stupid. What I thought I needed to do was to manage the people that I have and start doing that." Instead, Connolly's personnel files continued to fill with glowing reports about his work.

No surprise, then, that in the spring of 1985 at Morris's house Jim Ring was not standing in the kitchen alongside Bulger, Flemmi, and Connolly. In fact, around the time of the dinner Ring and Connolly had even discussed the issue of "Mr. Bulger and Mr. Flemmi not liking me," recalled Ring, "and my position being I really didn't care, because they were informants." But Morris did care about being liked—by everyone.

■ ■ ■

"CONNOLLY, Flemmi, and Bulger had arrived together," Morris recalled. Dennis Condon showed up thirty minutes later, around 7:30 P.M. He had driven directly from his executive office at the state Public Safety Department in Boston. Morris hustled from living room to kitchen, the dutiful host and cook.

The men headed into the dining room. It had been years since Bulger and Flemmi had seen Condon. The night in Lexington marked "the first meeting that I've had since 1974 with Dennis Condon," Flemmi recalled. The year 1974 had certainly been a pivotal one for Flemmi. He'd returned to Boston after spending nearly five years on the lam, a forced departure triggered by his indictment in 1969 for a car bombing and the William Bennett murder. Flemmi believed that Condon had paved the way for his eventual return from Canada by seeing that the two major felony charges were dropped along with a third charge that had been added as soon as he fled the country to avoid prosecution. After Flemmi's return there had been the get-together with Condon at the coffee shop as part of his handoff to the very useful Connolly. In Flemmi's eyes, Condon had been the stage manager behind many of these moves, and he was grateful. "I hadn't seen him for quite a while. I asked him how he was doing, how he felt. I thanked him for disposing of the federal flight warrant that I had. I asked him how Mr. Rico was, who was a partner of his, and I says, 'If you ever have the opportunity to see him, say hello for me.'"

The men took their seats at the table. Morris served up the steak. The men poured more wine. For the first hour or so they chatted about old times.

"It was light banter," Flemmi recalled. Bulger recounted stories from his time in federal prison during the late 1950s for robbing banks. "Most times he does most of the talking," Flemmi said about Bulger. "Quite a variety of subjects. He's very knowledgeable, very intelligent. He kind of captivates his audience."

But if Bulger was a chatterbox, Condon was not. The graying veteran of Boston's law enforcement circles sat there picking at his food and listening politely. He felt ambushed, he said, surprised to find Bulger and Flemmi in Morris's home. He'd gotten his invitation during a telephone call late in the afternoon—c'mon and swing by on your way home. He said that all he'd been told was that Morris and Connolly were going to be there, "and a couple of people were coming by, and they'd like to say hello."

Of course there was an outward collegiality to the occasion, the appearance of a simple gathering of old friends sharing wine and war stories. But beneath the easygoing veneer were pressing concerns that Bulger and

Flemmi had about their protection. In a way each law enforcement official present at the dinner was a symbol of the history and the scope of the alliance. The past, the present, and, they hoped, the future were represented at the table in Condon, Morris, and Connolly. But Condon, who potentially covered two police agencies, the FBI and the state police, was hardly having a regular old time. Morris said about Condon, "I could tell from the way he looked when he came in . . . he didn't look real comfortable."

"I thought that it was extremely unusual that Mrs. Morris was there and I was there, and neither of us at the time were members of the FBI," said Condon. "I also felt that in the position that I occupied I shouldn't have been there."

Dennis Condon did not protest to anyone at the time, did not pull Morris and Connolly aside and ask for an explanation. "I hung in there for, I would say, for politeness and diplomacy." (He would also keep the dinner a secret, telling no other official about it for at least another decade.) But the others at the table that night got no hand-holding from him. Finishing his food, Condon made his exit less than sixty minutes after he'd arrived. Flemmi was taken aback. To him, Condon "didn't seem to be uncomfortable," and he was sorry to see him leave.

The party was now minus one.

Even so, Bulger and Flemmi still had Connolly and Morris at hand. They poured more wine and got down to business.

John Connolly, Flemmi said later, provided updated accounts on who the two crime bosses should avoid in their underworld activities. He disclosed the identities of several police informants. The talk then turned to the upcoming Mafia trial, the FBI's tapes, Bulger's possible vulnerability, and, most important of all, the keeping of promises the agents had made.

"I don't know who raised it," said Flemmi. "We were concerned because we believed our names would be, during conversation at Prince Street, would be mentioned regarding criminal matters.

"I knew at that particular time there was conversation on them wiretaps between Jerry [Angiulo] and Larry [Zannino], and they were discussing Jim Bulger and myself. I was concerned about them at some point in time being used against us. I asked John Morris and John Connolly about that. And they said to me that that would be of no concern because I was not going to be prosecuted for anything that would be on those tapes.

"Well, when we were discussing the tapes, the flow from that conversation led into a statement that John Morris made to me and Jim Bulger."

It was better than any promise Morris and Connolly had ever made to them. Morris, his wine nearby but clearly sober, said: "You can do anything you want as long as you don't clip anyone."

Flemmi liked what he heard. "I said to John, I says, well, I says, 'John, can we shake on that?' And he says, 'Yes.'

"And we shook hands, and Jim Bulger shook hands."

They had finally reached a champagne moment.

■ ■ ■

THE DINNER lasted three hours but did not run late. Bulger, Flemmi, and Connolly drove away around 10:30 P.M. Morris tidied up before heading off to bed.

Condon may have departed prematurely, unable to enjoy the highlight of the night, but Bulger and Flemmi nonetheless left feeling pretty good. The gangsters thought their FBI agents had sanctioned what they did best: committing crime.

"That's the way I interpret it," Flemmi said later of the wonderful life he'd been promised. "Short of murdering someone, I think that, yes, they could give that kind of assurance."

In Flemmi's mind, the two agents had reaffirmed a group protection policy featuring a full menu of services: snuffing out trouble before an investigation could even get going, as the agents had done in the past in matters involving the Melotone vending machine executives, Frank Green's extortion, the many unsolved murders, and the takeover of the Rakes family liquor store; tipping them off to wiretaps against them, as they had done in the state police's Lancaster Street garage case and, most recently, the DEA's Operation Beans; pulling them out of any indictment that actually made it to the development phase, as they had done in prosecutor

Jeremiah O'Sullivan's horse race–fixing case; and finally, if all else failed and Bulger and Flemmi were actually facing indictment, giving them a head start.

It was as if at the tenth anniversary of their secret deal they all renewed their vows. Bulger and Flemmi could leave the table feeling recharged. Ring might be unpredictable and therefore unreliable, but they could count on Morris and Connolly. The timing for this revived good cheer turned out to be fortuitous too. Though no one realized it that night, another Bulger, brother Billy, was about to have his own need for a friendly FBI.

CHAPTER FOURTEEN

Shades of Whitey

By 1984 Billy Bulger was securely on top of the state senate, running it smoothly and firmly with vinegar and honey. Yet he had ignored his private law practice with a boyhood friend from Old Harbor and was having trouble financing his hectic household of nine children. He worried about the roof falling in on a house full of kids and about paying their tuitions. He fretted that his battered car would drop dead by the side of the road, stranding his wife Mary as she gamely transported youngsters hither and yon. Even though he earned between $75,000 and $100,000 that year, he was swimming upstream, with more money going out than coming in. In his memoir, he lamented that while he was not bankrupt, he was "not far from it."

Then, according to Billy, a miracle client walked into his downtown law office out of the blue. Two brothers wanted to buy back property from a customer, and Bulger got them a $2.8 million loan from a friendly South Boston bank to do it. In exchange for his help in negotiating the loan and the property buyback, Billy was offered a prodigious fee. The prospect flooded Bulger with happy visions of hearth and home. "A new car for Mary...a new roof."

After paying sporadic attention to the buyback, Bulger settled it in 1985 and agreed on a deferred fee of $267,000, more than enough for Mary and Bill to stop worrying about the car and the tuitions. But the cash flow problem persisted because Bulger agreed to take the fee in 1986. He told his law associate from South Boston, Thomas Finnerty, that he would be among the "impoverished rich" until his money came through.

But Tom leaped to the rescue. He offered to give Bulger a $240,000 loan against the fee. Bulger was ecstatic, but his relief was short-lived. A few weeks after taking the loan, he learned that Finnerty had been working with Boston developer Harold Brown. Bulger flushed with alarm when he heard that Finnerty was dealing with the likes of Brown and warned him that the disreputable landlord was trouble. But Finnerty laughed it off and teased Bulger about being a compulsive worrier. Besides, he said, a $500,000 fee from the developer was already in a trust fund Finnerty had set up.

Recoiling at the mention of the fund, Bulger realized that his recent loan came from Brown money. "You didn't tell me that," Bulger objected. "I'm paying it back—and right now. I want no connection, however remote, with Brown." Back went the Brown money, with repayments totaling $254,000 with interest by the end of 1985. Mary was told to put plans for easy street on hold.

The next year Bulger felt more than justified in his cautious reaction when Brown was convicted of bribery in federal court. Brown began wearing a wire for the FBI, seeking out conversations with politicians. Bulger and Finnerty joked about avoiding Brown in a rainstorm for fear of being electrocuted. They had a good laugh.

■ ■ ■

BUT Harold Brown told an entirely different story.

The Bill Bulger case started in 1983 when federal investigators caught a corrupt city inspector taking a bribe and converted him into an undercover agent. In 1985 he put on a hidden wire to record conversations and revisited regular customers, including Harold Brown. The hands-on landlord paid the inspector $1,000 to "lowball" the cost of a housing project so that Brown could save $24,000 in permit fees.

Brown then walked into a trap after being subpoenaed before a grand jury. He did not know he was on tape with the inspector and thought he was up against some bumbling police work. He tried to lie his way out of it, telling grand jurors he never gave anyone a dime and perish the thought. He was quickly indicted for perjury and bribery and just as quickly turned into a government agent, wire and all. He was looking for a plea bargain that would get him out of doing prison time. The prosecutors asked Brown, what do you have? Brown said Tom Finnerty and Bill Bulger.

Brown's bruising encounter with Finnerty had its origin in the mid-1970s when Brown saw the potential for a skyscraper at the run-down lower end of State Street, one of downtown Boston's colonial-era boulevards. He began buying up property one decrepit lot at a time. As the state's largest landlord, with holdings worth between $500 million and $1 billion, Brown foresaw the building boom of the 1980s and waited for it to reach him.

The push to develop the site started in 1982 when the city, reeling from the first year of a new statewide reduction of property taxes, found itself stuck with a $45 million bill from tax abatements due commercial property owners. Mayor Kevin White needed help from the legislature to get bonding authority to underwrite rebates, and Bulger pushed it for him— with the proviso that the city would sell property to the state to launch a convention center authority. The new state agency was immediately controlled by Bulger and White appointees.

Another part of the legislation required the city to sell five parking garages, including one that became part of Brown's project. The garages were not auctioned off to the highest bidder but transferred to the city's redevelopment authority, which could sell them to developers as it pleased. It was a closed shop, and Bulger was part of the planning process.

After White and Bulger struck their deal, Brown and his partner, a prominent architect, became the odds-on favorites to develop the State

Street site. The designer had the endorsement of the Boston Society of Architects, and Brown already had most of the land. Then Brown was approached by a White confidant, former Massachusetts attorney general Edward McCormack. McCormack asked for an outlandish stake in the project in exchange for monitoring the city hall approval process. When that was rejected, Finnerty suddenly appeared as a lesser-known lawyer willing to take less money.

At the time Finnerty began negotiating for a piece of the skyscraper, he was a criminal defense lawyer with no track record in big-time real estate. The crossover is so daunting that it is seldom tried in Boston. The two law specialties require two different skills—low-key urbanity versus hard-nosed advocacy. Finnerty, a former district attorney, was in the brassy South Boston tradition and had little in common with the muted lawyers from white-shoe firms who usually handled downtown developments. Brown danced with Finnerty for months, never saying no, never saying yes, pushing the project along its route in city hall as they talked between late 1983 and February 1985.

When Finnerty saw Brown racing to the finish line on his own, the negotiations became more intense. Brown capitulated in 1985, agreeing to "buy" Finnerty's self-proclaimed interest that never existed for about $1.8 million. Finnerty never appeared at any design or development hearing on the project and did not represent Brown when another developer sued him over the size of the office tower.

Nevertheless, Finnerty deposited the first installment of $500,000 in July. In a rapid sequence, Billy and Tommy, the two old friends from Old Harbor, split $450,000 in August and $30,000 more in October. But a month later the other shoe dropped for Bulger. In November Brown was indicted by a federal grand jury for bribing the city inspector and "other public officials." Bulger returned his money to the trust three days later, calling it a repaid loan.

By the time the transactions became a public controversy in 1988, Finnerty had dropped any pretense of being a real estate lawyer for the massive project. He said he had joined the Brown development team to bring it respectability, using his law enforcement background to overcome Brown's past association with arsonists. His price for respectability was

$1.8 million, and he actually filed suit against Brown to get all of the money.

But a few weeks of public clamor about the deal was more than enough for the low-profile landlord. He suddenly folded, settling the suit. Brown called it a pragmatic decision to pay less in the long run. "I am a businessman, and it is not my job to pursue investigations," he said. He never uttered another word about it.

Despite his defiant public stance, the controversy around the skyscraper at 75 State Street was an intense ordeal for Bulger. When the furor was at its height, the senate president was briefly stalked "by the black dog of melancholy." At the end of 1988 he slipped out of the State House and walked over to Boston Common, where he sat glumly on a park bench. He watched people eating lunch on nearby benches and, in his disconsolate reverie, became angry at their indifference to media misconduct. He thought: "Don't any of these people walking our streets or the paths in our parks . . . see what the media are doing in this city?" The episode passed quickly as he realized that strangers had no reason to be aroused by his problems. The angst departed, and he headed back to his office "with a lighter step, ready for whatever awaited."

Bulger filed an affidavit stating that he borrowed money from Finnerty without knowing its origin. Over time Billy's version of the scandal became an accepted part of his bloodied but unbowed image in South Boston. Once again Billy Bulger had stood up to outsiders and been victimized by the media for it. As always, he came out on top.

But Bulger's brief on 75 State Street holds up only if the facts are discarded. Bulger was not the innocent victim. The slumlord was. And just as the FBI had protected Whitey Bulger for fifteen years, the bureau stepped in to keep William Bulger out of harm's way.

During a federal review of several downtown developments, including 75 State Street, investigators uncovered records that shattered the senate president's claims. The documents—which remain buried in federal files— show that Bulger actually kept a full share of Brown's money. Although Bulger "repaid" the loan, Finnerty washed the money back to Bulger through other law firm accounts. Through this circuitous route, Bulger received about half of the original $500,000 down payment.

Moreover, Bulger did not get anywhere near the $267,000 fee he said stood behind the loan as collateral. The law firm records show that he received less than half the claimed amount, or $110,000.

The records would not prove extortion, but they destroyed his tale of borrowing money to fix the car and roof for Mary. Instead of putting the money into household improvements, Bulger invested it in a tax-free bond fund. If this got out, it would not sit well with Southie. After all, Billy would not be Billy if he took the money. Taking the money would be shades of Whitey.

■ ■ ■

BUT Bulger had some help within the FBI. Despite the public clamor, the Brown extortion claim was already a closed matter in the bureau. The same John Morris who had protected Whitey Bulger and taken money from him was now on the case as supervisor of the squad overseeing public corruption crimes. In 1988 Morris moved quickly to head off damage to Billy Bulger by shutting down the case a few days before the *Boston Globe* published a front-page story about the deal behind the skyscraper.

Once again, Morris had to wrestle with his conscience. The persistent Brown case was another in a lengthening line of decisions that required him to calculate the risk of doing the right thing against the certain wrath of a ruthless crook who had bribed him multiple times and slowly seduced him with fine wine and a curious camaraderie. But Morris knew Whitey Bulger would not hesitate to use his weakness against him. Indeed, at the most recent dinner party Morris held for the informants (a small gathering at Debbie Noseworthy's apartment in Woburn), Whitey upped the stakes. After John Connolly and Stevie Flemmi had left the apartment, Morris saw that Bulger was hanging back by the coat rack. "As he was putting his coat on," Morris said, "he pulled out an envelope and gave the envelope to me. He said, 'Here, this is to help you out,' and walked out the door." Inside the envelope was $5,000 in cash.

With this recent exchange in the background, Morris closed the 75 State Street file. But the skyscraper story lumbered on, especially after it was learned that the FBI had never even questioned Billy Bulger.

Massachusetts attorney general James Shannon called for a renewed federal effort to clear the air.

Enter John Connolly. With Billy Bulger now squarely on the firing line, Connolly took Morris aside and pressed him on whether the senate president should agree to be interviewed. Morris recalled that "Connolly approached me and asked me what the senate president should do, that he's been asked to submit to an interview and what did I recommend that he do?" Morris told him that Bulger should do it because the uncorroborated Brown allegations made for a soft case. "I didn't feel that the case was very strong," Morris continued. "I didn't think that he could hurt himself. I thought it would be to his advantage to submit to the interview and put an end to the public clamor." The premise for the renewed investigation became Bulger's best interest rather than no-holds-barred work in the trenches.

Having covered up for Whitey to the point of warning him about other FBI informants, Connolly now swooped in to run interference for brother Bill—his real hometown hero. Whitey was mostly business. But Billy was something of an idol. Over the years Connolly had masked his relationship with Whitey, but never his friendship with Billy—Connolly wore that on his sleeve, exulting in his ties to the altar boy from St. Monica's. Connolly believed that his friendship with Billy had convinced Whitey to become an informant. He called Billy a "lifelong friend . . . a mentor . . . a very close friend." And Connolly worked the relationship hard inside the FBI, parading agents through Bulger's senate office to meet the president in person. Bulger once introduced him to his fellow senators during a session, and Connolly was given a standing ovation. Knowing that many agents are like aging ballplayers who fear life after the glory years, Connolly often told colleagues that Bulger could help them get high-paying jobs when they retired. No way was Connolly going to allow a hostile FBI interview of Billy, let alone a no-holds-barred probe for the truth.

In these circumstances, it was not surprising that the second FBI investigation consisted solely of an interview with Bulger in his lawyer's office. Prosecutors and an FBI agent listened to a two-hour speech from Bulger in which he denied any connection with Brown and stuck by his loan and fee story. He said that Finnerty "swore" to him that he never invoked Bulger's name to gain an advantage. And Bulger added a new twist to the loan. This time around it was not about meeting household expenses but about taking preemptive action because he didn't trust Finnerty to give him his full share of the fee. Bulger simply wanted his money while the getting was good.

■ ■ ■

BULGER'S friendly FBI interview became the basis for shutting down the investigation forever. Jeremiah O'Sullivan, who had become interim U.S. attorney, said the case showed power brokering but did not rise to the level of extortion. Asked if he was leaving the impression that wrongdoing had occurred without being addressed, O'Sullivan said it wasn't his job and that further action should come from state authorities.

Despite his behind-the-scenes interventions for Whitey Bulger, O'Sullivan did not recuse himself. He had looked the other way on race-fixing and alerted the FBI to the state police surveillance at Lancaster Street. He'd played a key role in saving Bulger from Sarhatt's internal FBI review and then was the one who banished the doomed and desperate Brian Halloran from the witness protection program. Now the cocksure prosecutor proclaimed the Bill Bulger case dead on arrival, not even a close call. It would be O'Sullivan's valedictory from law enforcement.

One of the matters that O'Sullivan discarded to lesser agencies was the downside of Bill Bulger's stay at the State House. Belying Bulger's public persona of rock-solid rectitude were steep legal fees for dubious services. For example, in addition to the $250,000 in Brown money funneled back to him by Finnerty, Bulger had split fees with a State House lobbyist who brought him influence-seeking clients. The lobbyist was Richard McDonough, the son of a legendary political rogue, Patrick "Sonny" McDonough. Although the son lacked Sonny's gruff charm, he was a street-smart hustler who had learned well the byways of the State House. Indeed, it was Dickie McDonough who had originally brought Bulger the magical case from the contractors in need of the $2.8 million bank loan.

And it was Dickie who received $70,000 in return for the referral. He also brought Bulger another client, a California weight loss company that sought assistance in getting one of its products off the Food and Drug Administration's carcinogenic list. The company thought that Bulger could help with the FDA, but all he could do was get an appointment with minor bureaucrats in a different agency. Despite the lack of results, Bulger and McDonough split a $100,000 fee.

In their interviews with federal investigators, neither Bulger nor McDonough could produce paperwork to support the fees. McDonough knew next to nothing about the work done for clients that indirectly paid him $120,000.

Two months after O'Sullivan slammed the door on any further investigation, the senate president was the guest speaker at a retirement party for FBI agent John Cloherty. Cloherty had handled press relations when the bureau closed its review of 75 State Street. He was also a former member of the Organized Crime Squad under Morris and a friend of Connolly's. It was a rollicking good time.

■ ■ ■

ABOUT a year after Bill Bulger and Tom Finnerty split up $500,000 from the state's largest landlord, a small South Boston realtor received an offer he couldn't refuse. Once again money allegedly was demanded under duress, but the terms were starkly different in Southie. Raymond Slinger's alternative to paying $50,000 was to get blown away by a shotgun.

Slinger thought he might be on to something good when his dealings with Whitey Bulger began in the fall of 1986. Bulger stopped by his office unexpectedly for a short primer on how to cash in on the suddenly surging local real estate market. They chatted for about twenty minutes, and Slinger may have seen himself working with Bulger in some real estate deals.

But it was not to be. Six months later Slinger was summoned to the dreaded Triple O's bar. He gingerly entered the dank, claustrophobic barroom, with its warped floorboards and low ceiling, its dark walls and sticky tabletops. It was a place where someone was always playing pool while nursing a drink and solitary patrons stared into their shot glasses and beer chasers. Slinger was ushered to the second-floor office, where Bulger was waiting for him, arms folded. He looked up and announced, "We got a problem."

Bulger said he had been hired to kill Slinger, an assignment that would require him to arrive at Slinger's Old Harbor Real Estate office "with shot-guns and masks and so forth."

Bulger would answer no questions, including who it was who wanted Slinger dead or why. He would only talk about what could be done about it—pay Bulger to cancel the contract. Slinger, who had some large debts and his share of enemies, gulped and asked if he could be out from under for $2,000. But Bulger laughed at him and said his boots cost more than that.

BULGER: "$50,000 would be more like it."

SLINGER: "I don't have that kind of money."

BULGER: "Well, I think you better find it."

Slinger went straight to the downstairs bar to fortify himself before re-turning to his East Broadway Street office. He made a desperate call for help to city councilor James Kelly. After Kelly talked to Bulger, he told Slinger everything should be okay.

But it wasn't. Two days later Slinger heard from Kevin O'Neil, the Bulger associate who ran Triple O's. O'Neil told him "the man" wanted to see him again. Sensing the worst, Slinger returned to Triple O's with a rac-ing heart and a gun borrowed from a friend. Once inside, two of Bulger's henchmen seized him immediately, pushing and shoving him up the stairs to the second floor, where a ranting Bulger was waiting. Slinger recalled that they "grabbed me and pulled me upstairs, frisked me, opened my shirt, took my gun away, and started belting me, beat me up." Out of the melee, Slinger had the clear memory of Bulger kicking him.

Bulger and his underlings sat Slinger down hard in a chair. They made sure he was not wearing a wire and then upbraided him for talking to Kelly. Bulger took Slinger's gun and placed the barrel pointing down on the top of Slinger's head, explaining that the bullet would go down the spinal column and not cause a bloody mess. Bulger then ordered an aide to get him a "body bag," and Slinger nearly passed out from fright. "I thought I was done."

The moment passed, and Slinger was given a second chance to come up with the money. With a ripped shirt and scarred psyche, Slinger stumbled to the downstairs bar again. When he got back to his office, he called his sister and wife and lined up loans for a $10,000 payment. He also agreed to a weekly payment schedule.

About two months after he was slapped around and terrorized by Bulger, Slinger began to stagger under the burden of making the weekly $2,000 payments, which he put in a paper bag and handed over to O'Neil in a car outside the realty office. Slinger had paid half the debt, but he was so desperate that he turned to law enforcement. In the spring of 1987 he reached out to the FBI.

Without making an appointment, two agents showed up at the Old Harbor Real Estate office one day. Slinger opened his door to John Newton and Roderick Kennedy.

Later Newton would say that Slinger was willing to testify about a "shakedown" by Kevin O'Neil. But he claimed that Slinger never mentioned Bulger's name. For his part, Kennedy could not remember a single detail about the interview, including whether it happened at all. And in an extraordinary departure from standard procedure, neither agent wrote a report on the session with Slinger.

In a classic example of what not to do with such a case, Newton discussed Slinger's account with his boss, who talked it over with the assistant agent in charge. The top-level managers promptly dropped it, ignoring internal guidelines that they either refer it to prosecutors or explain their decision not to use it to FBI headquarters.

Ironically, the unproductive FBI interview helped Slinger get off the hook in his unexpected business relationship with Whitey Bulger. After the agents left his office, a worried Slinger immediately called O'Neil to cover himself by explaining that the unexpected visit by the FBI was none of his doing. O'Neil called him back the next day and told him he could cancel his installment plan. The $25,000 would be payment in full, a rare half-price sale from Bulger Enterprises.

Some years later Newton admitted that the bureau passed on what would have been a great extortion case. He was asked in court if there was a connection between the case dying and Bulger being an informant.

When an informant is involved in a crime, he said, "either you're going to go ahead with this investigation or you're going to have to figure something out."

The something figured out was agent John Connolly telling Whitey to back off on the balance due from Slinger. That was what being a loyal friend was all about.

CHAPTER FIFTEEN

Connolly Talk

Late Monday morning, February 8, 1988, FBI agent John Connolly strode out of a hardware store near his FBI office and bumped into Dick Lehr, a reporter for the *Boston Globe* (and one of the authors of this book). Connolly had been at the store getting some duplicate keys made while Lehr was crossing town en route to an appointment with a source.

It was a chance encounter on a crisp winter day.

Connolly, recognizing the reporter, stopped on the sidewalk to say hello. They didn't know each other very well, although Connolly was well known by a corps of reporters in the Boston media who covered organized crime as a regular beat. Of all the FBI agents in Boston, Connolly was the most accessible, the agent most eager to talk to the media about his work and the FBI.

Crime was not Lehr's beat. But he had met Connolly the year before, in 1987. He was part of a team of *Globe* reporters who spent months interviewing FBI agents from the Organized Crime Squad about the Angiulo bugging. Lehr and the reporters had met with nearly a dozen agents—

Connolly, John Morris, Ed Quinn, Nick Gianturco, Jack Cloherty, Shaun Rafferty, Mike Buckley, Bill Schopperle, Pete Kennedy, Bill Regii, and Tom Donlan. The series had been a hit with both the newspaper's readers and the bureau, for it showed the FBI at its technical best: breaking into the Mafia's inner sanctum to plant a listening device. Lehr had not seen or talked to Connolly since the newspaper project a year earlier. There was a round of greetings, and then the reporter asked the FBI agent how things were going.

Connolly, jingling the shiny keys in his hand, didn't hesitate. He began talking about a new FBI bug, one targeting the post-Angiulo mafiosi who were jockeying for position and power. Connolly said that for about six months, from late 1986 to mid-1987, the FBI had monitored the new Mafia lineup conducting business in the back of a grinder shop located in a shopping plaza at the foot of a Boston landmark, the Prudential Tower.

"It was great," the agent said about the bug that agents installed inside Vanessa's Italian Food Shop.

Lehr listened intently, realizing right away that the information might make for a great story. But the reporter was also taken aback by Connolly's loose manner. There was no talk of the conversation being "on background" or "off the record" or restricted in any of the ways information can be when passed along to reporters. To the agent, talking about Vanessa's seemed to be the same as talking about the Boston Bruins, who the night before had beaten the Calgary Flames, 6–3, to take over first place in their division in the National Hockey League. Or politics. The Democratic Party's Iowa caucus was under way that very same day, featuring a challenge by Massachusetts governor Michael Dukakis to the front-runner status of Richard Gephardt. Connolly, it appeared, was used to putting tidbits into orbit and not having them traced back to him.

There had been no press coverage whatsoever of an FBI bug inside an eatery in the city's Back Bay neighborhood. If anything, Boston reporters who covered crime had been puzzling over the status of the Mafia in the aftermath of the 98 Prince Street operation. It was known that a certain amount of Mafia disarray naturally followed the removal of a long-standing Mafia leader like Angiulo, and the names of a number of relatively unknown Mafia figures had begun to circulate. There was Vincent

M. Ferrara, who combined a degree in business administration from Boston College with "a taste for blood"; an older mafioso named J. R. Russo; and Russo's half-brother, Bobby Carrozza of East Boston. Those three men were serving as *capo de regimes,* or lieutenants, in the struggling Mafia, but not a lot was known about them. In addition, Cadillac Frank Salemme was finally coming home, released from federal prison after serving fifteen years for the 1968 bombing of a lawyer's car, the assassination attempt for which his accomplice and pal Stevie Flemmi had never been prosecuted.

Outside the hardware store, Connolly was buoyant about the bureau's ability to track the Mafia from its traditional base in the North End to the upscale plaza in the Back Bay. Vanessa's Back Bay location constituted an altogether new twist, an unlikely spot for the Mafia, churlish bulls in a china shop. Polished shoppers and young urban professionals might be catching a quick bite at the counter while at the same time, in the back room, a fiery Ferrara was spewing vulgar ultimatums to bookmakers as he explained that a new Mafia day was dawning.

The windowless room was isolated and could only be reached by a convoluted route. The gangsters would park their cars in the Pru Center's underground garage-maze, and no one could follow them without being made. Connolly delighted in the fact that the brazen Ferrara, Russo, and Carrozza all thought they'd found a place to meet that was impenetrable, and he relished the prospect of bringing down Ferrara. Ferrara was "arrogant" and "cocky," "a real troublemaker." He was hated by his peers for his vicious streak and disrespectful way. In fact, noted Connolly, Ferrara would be dead already if word hadn't gotten around Boston's underworld that the FBI was after him. The other wiseguys, said Connolly, could "sit back and let us chew him up."

Subsequently, Lehr teamed up with fellow reporter Kevin Cullen and, after more reporting to confirm Connolly's account, wrote a front-page piece about Vanessa's that ran on Sunday, April 17, 1988, and started out: "It was a perfect spot. The cops couldn't tail you, and you could park your car in the underground garage, walk to a freight elevator and ride up in secrecy." Though the article included a lot of information, the reporters didn't have the actual recordings from the Vanessa's bug. That meant they couldn't hear Connolly's favorite recording: Ferrara's shakedown of "Doc" Sagansky.

"We got a lot of guys in trouble, Doc," Ferrara told Sagansky. Ferrara was going for the soft touch in his approach to his target, who, at eighty-nine, was the elder statesman in the world of bookmaking. Born at the end of the last century, Doc was a practicing dentist as a young man, a graduate of Tufts Dental School, but he became a millionaire as the city's premier bookmaker. By the 1940s he was regarded by police as the "financial top man" in the city's rackets and held ownership interests in two Boston nightclubs and a loan company. In 1941 he'd loaned $8,500 to James Michael Curley, the legendary Boston mayor and then congressman. In return, Sagansky was named a beneficiary in a $50,000 life insurance policy that Curley had taken out as security for a loan. That the two were linked publicly raised a few eyebrows and made headlines. Sagansky's name had surfaced in every major gambling investigation in Boston since the Depression. In the storeroom of Vanessa's on January 14, 1987, Ferrara was trying to come off as reasonable with the old man, explaining the Mafia's hard times—five Angiulo brothers and many other soldiers gone, in jail.

"We have to help 'em," Ferrara urged. "Their families, lawyers. Some of us are in trouble." Ferrara wanted Sagansky and an associate who'd accompanied him, another aging bookie named Moe Weinstein, to start paying "rent." During the regime of Gennaro Angiulo, Sagansky had operated without having to do so. But Ferrara said those days were over, and he wanted a show of good faith in the form of $500,000. He told Sagansky that such a sum was nothing to a millionaire like him, and that Sagansky had "class." "Help us," Ferrara said.

Sagansky would not. Even though he was seated in the windowless storeroom surrounded by Ferrara and his muscle, Sagansky tried persuading Ferrara that his gambling business was kaput, that it had "plummeted to nothing."

Both sides cried poor for a while until Doc had enough. "I'm not gonna give you no bankroll," he said.

Ferrara exploded. Mob enforcer Dennis Lepore leaned down to get into the eighty-nine-year-old's face: "You don't have no alternative. We want something now. And you're lucky it ain't more. This is a serious request. You understand?" The venom poured from Lepore's lips: "What are we playin', a fuckin' game here, pal? You reaped the harvest all those fuckin' years! This is something you're going to pay now. We want it. We're not asking."

To induce cooperation, an angry Ferrara then threatened Sagansky that his pal Weinstein would be held hostage until he came up with the $500,000. Doc and Moe were given some time alone in the storeroom. "I'll never see you again," Doc said. "Now what should I do?" Weinstein stated the obvious: "Guess you're going to have to give it to 'em." The two old men promised to get the money, and Ferrara released them.

The next day, as investigators watched undetected from a safe distance, Weinstein carried a white plastic shopping bag into a restaurant at the Park Plaza Hotel. He handed the bag to Ferrara and Lepore. Inside was $250,000 in cash, the first installment. The two mobsters hurried back to the Vanessa's storeroom and gloated as they split up the money into six shares of $40,000. "Those assholes, this better be real money," a flush, cash-happy Ferrara joked to Lepore.

Even without all of the dialogue, the *Globe* story hit a nerve. FBI officials and federal prosecutors, particularly Jeremiah T. O'Sullivan of the Organized Crime Strike Force, were incensed. Their investigation of Ferrara was still ongoing, and they wanted to know how word about Vanessa's had gotten out. But the reporters had no obligation or reason to explain to the authorities where their story had started. They were not about to complain about Connolly's propensity for chatter.

■ ■ ■

IN FACT it turned out that Connolly wanted to talk a lot about Vanessa's, or, as it was confidentially referred to, "Operation Jungle Mist." The agent developed a kind of stump speech in which he described Vanessa's as the second in a "trilogy" of major Mafia bugs (the first being the 98 Prince Street bug) that the FBI would never have gotten if not for his work with Bulger and Flemmi. "They were without a doubt the two single most important sources we ever had," Connolly liked to say in a flourish at the end of this proclamation.

But as they so often did, Connolly's claims upon closer scrutiny proved to be overstated. Bulger and Flemmi were the unnamed informants Connolly referred to during his sidewalk moment with Lehr of the *Globe* in early 1988. In this regard, it *was* a shining moment of genuine, singular intelligence. The evidence from the tapes later helped convict Ferrara, Lepore, Russo, and Carrozza of extortion and racketeering. But most of the credit for steering the FBI toward Vanessa's actually belonged to Flemmi rather than to Whitey Bulger.

Even though Vanessa's was listed in city records as being owned by a couple from the affluent suburb of Belmont, the eatery was in fact controlled by Sonny Mercurio, a Mafia soldier and pardoned murderer. (Later Mercurio himself would become an FBI informant.)

In April 1986 Flemmi began telling Connolly about Vinnie Ferrara, and how Ferrara was working with Mercurio, J. R. Russo, and Bobby Carrozza out of the Italian eatery. Flemmi, not Bulger, was attending the meetings, where the pending business was sorting out the underworld action between the Ferrara faction and Bulger's gang. Following one meeting in early August, Flemmi explained that Mercurio was "friendly" with him and Whitey Bulger, "from the days when he was a messenger and liaison between 'The Hill' and Jerry Angiulo." Flemmi added that Mercurio was in charge of setting up the session between the groups to discuss changing the payoff on the illegal daily numbers games so that they could all rake in even more profits.

Flemmi attended another meeting a week later; afterward he once again provided Connolly with a full account—about the ongoing negotiations to change the payoff odds on the illegal numbers games and about plans to distribute illegal football betting cards during that fall's football season. He told Connolly, "The Mafia intends to chop up the whole city and state, if possible, by controlling all independent bookmakers." He reported that the "Mafia was on the march" into the suburbs and said that he'd made his way to the secret session "by taking an elevator up from level 5 to the service area."

The meetings continued, and Flemmi began providing more details about the storeroom's location, layout, and security. "The storeroom is located two doors from Vanessa's," he told Connolly on August 18, 1986, "which is used for the meet, is wired with an alarm system, but the system does not seem to be operative. In addition to the alarm system, the area is patrolled by a security service." During one of their late-night huddles at Connolly's home at the end of August, attended by Bulger and Jim Ring, Flemmi even drew up a rough sketch of the Vanessa's floor plan.

This kind of information provided ample probable cause for the FBI to win court permission to plant a bug inside the eatery's storeroom—and then some. The diagram, for instance, was somewhat over the top, Ring said later. "I think it's pretty stupid," the supervisor said about Flemmi's artwork. "I don't need a diagram to figure out how they got in there," he said. Better to have agents conduct surveillance than give away the FBI's plans to a criminal informant. "You get too far down a discussion like that with an informant, the informant is learning too much from your questions," said Ring. "Despite Mr. Flemmi's great skills," he added sarcastically, "the people we have are far better, and I relied upon our technicians to put the bugs in the right place so that they functioned."

By the time the FBI's bug began on Halloween, Flemmi had, not surprisingly or coincidentally, stopped attending the meetings in the storeroom at Vanessa's. Once again, the FBI would capture the Mafia while Flemmi and Bulger would remain invisible. "I wasn't intercepted because I knew it [the bug] was going to be in there," Flemmi said. Just before the bug began, "John Connolly did tell me it was in." For months policy meetings at Vanessa's had involved the two powerful organized crime outfits in Boston, the Mafia and the Bulger gang. But once the FBI tapes began rolling, it was as if Boston was strictly a Mafia town.

The Sagansky shakedown coincided with the arrival of a new special agent in charge for the Boston office. Jim Ahearn, himself a veteran of organized crime cases in California, arrived in November 1986 at the same time the Boston squad was piling up taped evidence against the Ferrara faction. He was immediately impressed by the Organized Crime Squad's work, and especially by John Connolly, who made sure others knew that the informants behind the bug belonged to him.

To rely on Flemmi at this time, however, the FBI also had to ignore mounting intelligence from other informants about the FBI's two crime bosses. "Stevie Flemmi, of the Winter Hill gang, has been looking around for numbers agents to take over during the period of [Mafia] confusion and weakness," one informant told John Morris on April 20, 1986. Flemmi began steering Connolly to Vanessa's at the same time he and Bulger were moving about the city, flexing their own muscle. "The Winter Hill people are presenting a challenge to the old Angiulo regime, and Flemmi has been all over the city," the informant went on. "The old Angiulo regime is not in a position to stop Flemmi."

In this regard, Flemmi's tip about Vanessa's proved self-serving, a way to keep a staggered Mafia back on its heels. The FBI could do the dirty work.

Then there was the third in the trilogy of FBI bugs that Connolly would invoke in the 1990s as proof that Whitey Bulger had all-world status. The bugging operation itself, which unfolded on a single night, October 29, 1989, indeed warrants a spot in the FBI's hall of fame. For the first time ever, agents that night secretly recorded a Mafia induction ceremony. Present were Vinnie Ferrara, J. R. Russo, Bobby Carrozza, thirteen other Mafia figures, and, most important, the reigning Mafia boss in New England, Raymond J. Patriarca, son of the deceased Raymond L. S. Patriarca. In the dining room of an associate's home in Medford, Massachusetts, the band of mafiosi went through their legendary ritual— the pricking of fingers, the sharing of blood oaths—that culminated in the "making" of four new soldiers. It was also a ceremony that was part of the mob's ongoing effort, post-Angiulo, to ease tensions between competing factions and establish a better working order.

"We're all here to bring some new members into our Family," welcomed the presiding Patriarca, "and more than that, to start making a new beginning. 'Cause they come into our Family to start a new thing with us." One by one, the four new soldiers were administered the oath of Mafia office. Each drew blood from his trigger finger for use in the ceremony. "I, Carmen, want to enter into this organization to protect my Family and to protect all my Friends. I swear not to divulge this secret and to obey, with love and *omerta*." Each was then told he had become a "brother for life," and each responded, "I want to enter alive into this organization and leave it dead."

Carmen Tortora, along with the other three, was also run through a test of loyalties: "If I told you your brother was wrong, he's a rat, he's gonna do one of us harm, you'd have to kill him. Would you do that for me, Carmen?"

"Yes."

"Any one of us here for that?"

"Yes."

"So you know the severity of This Thing of Ours?"

"Yes."

"Do you want it badly and desperately? Your mother's dying in bed, and you have to leave her because we called you, it's an emergency. You have to leave. Would you do that, Carmen?"

"Yes."

In the 1990s the famous induction ceremony became an integral part of Connolly's ode to Bulger. But once again, the facts got in Connolly's way. FBI files revealed that of the four informants the FBI used for its affidavit to win court approval to record the ceremony, Bulger was not one of them. For probable cause, the FBI relied almost exclusively on another of Connolly's informants, Sonny Mercurio. Sonny had all the hard information about the time and place of the Mafia induction—not Bulger. For his part, Flemmi was used as one of the four informants, but his contributions paled compared to Mercurio's. In fact, Flemmi later conceded that during the early autumn of 1989 the few tidbits of information he picked up for Connolly came only after the agent told him about the planned event. Until then, Flemmi didn't know anything about the scheduled Mafia ceremony. "He asked me to monitor all sources and to report to him any information that I obtained, which I did." Then, once the FBI had captured the ceremony on tape, Flemmi added that he was told about the bureau's success—a disclosure that may have seemed matter-of-fact to Flemmi but that violated FBI rules. Who told him? "John Connolly," said Flemmi.

If anything, Connolly's later stump speech reflected not only a habit for hype but also his knack for embellishing Bulger at the expense of Flemmi. Throughout the years Connolly sometimes filed duplicate reports for each —attributing the same information in the exact same words to both Bulger and Flemmi. The only difference between the two reports would be the typewriters used to write them. Other times the wording wasn't exactly the same but the information was, and both would get credit. To explain the duplication, Connolly said he wasn't especially careful about how he kept the books and that he considered them one source. "Oftentimes they blurred," he said. "The information almost came as one."

The technique benefited Bulger, for between the two, Flemmi was the one with long personal ties to the Mafia. Flemmi, not Bulger, had the juice; he was the frequent visitor inside Mafia dens. Flemmi, not Bulger, was then later able to describe to Connolly the layout and floor plans. Larry Zannino, Patriarca, and other Mafia leaders repeatedly tried to persuade Flemmi to join La Cosa Nostra. But by his "blurrings," Connolly spread the credit to include Whitey, pumping up—and thus protecting—his old friend from the neighborhood.

■ ■ ■

TIPS like Vanessa's were to be treasured, and unlike the other two FBI bugs cited by Connolly, Vanessa's was truly the result of working with Flemmi and Bulger. Without their intelligence, there would have been no Back Bay bugging of the new Mafia, no extortion of Doc Sagansky.

But by the late 1980s, at what price?

The deal between the Boston FBI and Bulger was by now so out of whack that any good that came the FBI's way was offset by a wave of concessions and corruption. Of course, such aspects of the deal never showed up in any of the official FBI paperwork—indeed, the annual reviews perfunctorily filed by Connolly and Morris always putatively put Bulger and Flemmi on notice that they fell under the bureau's guidelines just like any other informant. No favors. No license to commit crimes. No looking the other way. For example: "Informant shall not participate in acts of violence or use unlawful techniques to obtain information for the FBI or initiate a plan to commit criminal acts." Each year Connolly signed an internal FBI memo saying he'd given this and ten other "warnings" to Bulger and Flemmi, including: "Informant has been advised that informant's relationship with the FBI will not protect informant from arrest or prosecution for any violation of Federal, State, or local law, except where the informant's activity is justified by the Supervisor of SAC pursuant to appropriate Attorney General's Guidelines." And in all the FBI's files on Bulger and

Flemmi, covering hundreds of pages over two decades, no documents ever surfaced showing that the mobsters' crime spree was authorized.

Instead, Connolly and Morris and the Boston FBI office had fashioned a side deal, a fine-print, invisible-ink addendum of sorts. It was simple and relatively straightforward. It called for agents to commit crimes to protect the two informants. Up had become down.

Sometimes the FBI protective zeal extended beyond Bulger himself to include sidekicks on Bulger's rim. Bars on the lower end of West Broadway were letting out in the early morning hours of Mother's Day 1986. A *pop-pop* of gunshots rang out, and in a car parked across from the entrance of Triple O's, Tim Baldwin, twenty-three, of South Boston, an ex-con who'd just gotten out of jail, slumped forward, dead.

Within days Boston police homicide detectives had a suspect—twenty-six-year-old Mark Estes, another ex-con who'd been drinking inside Triple O's just prior to the killing. Police learned that two weeks earlier Estes had been beaten by Baldwin with a tire iron in a dispute over a girlfriend. Police had eyewitnesses to the shooting among the hundred or so people spilling out of the bars at closing time. The witnesses told police they saw Estes shoot Baldwin, saw Estes shoot at bystanders as he fled, and saw Baldwin commandeer a car driven by a woman in a futile attempt to escape.

But at a court hearing in late June the case against Estes hit a big-time snag. The witnesses recanted their identification. The murder charge was dismissed, and afterward police complained about the long-standing neighborhood "code of silence": residents would balk at cooperating with the authorities. "I'm from South Boston," shrugged one of the witnesses, trying to explain the turnabout to the judge. "We keep things to ourselves."

Prosecutors vowed to continue a grand jury investigation, and by Labor Day a subpoena to appear at the grand jury was issued to Kevin O'Neil. The Bulger protégé had been running Triple O's the night of the murder, and Sergeant Detective Brendan Bradley of the Boston police homicide squad said he had gotten information that O'Neil "knew all the details of the murder, including the name of the perpetrator." Prosecutors wanted O'Neil to go before a grand jury and give them Estes.

But the Bulger gang and the FBI saw the subpoena differently—as a nuisance. Bradley came into work on September 5, 1986, and found a telephone message. FBI agent John Connolly had called. Bradley returned the call. "Connolly said that he wanted to talk." They agreed to meet for coffee three days later in the lobby of the John F. Kennedy Federal Building, where the FBI had its Boston bureau.

Bradley arrived first. "Connolly came out of an elevator carrying a cup of coffee for himself." The agent was apologetic that his other hand was empty, saying, "The girls in the office love me and always buy me coffee." What's a popular guy to do? The two investigators went and got Bradley a cup and huddled off to the side. "What are you doing to my friend?" Connolly asked the cop.

The agent explained that he knew all about the subpoena served on O'Neil. O'Neil, said Connolly, was from a good South Boston family, and his brother was an injured Boston firefighter. He was "a good shit."

Bradley explained that they were talking about a murder investigation, and O'Neil could apparently help the police. Connolly was unmoved. "But he's a good guy." Besides, he said, the dead man was "a piece of shit."

The message was simple: a "good shit" beats a "piece of shit" any day.

Connolly did not "ask directly to withdraw the subpoena to O'Neil," but Bradley left with the impression "that was the purpose of the conversation." O'Neil eventually did appear before the grand jury, but he refused to testify. He cited his Fifth Amendment privilege against self-incrimination. Homicide detectives chased other leads; nothing broke and the investigation fizzled. Estes was a free man.

Immediately afterward, Bradley told a colleague and two homicide prosecutors about the disturbing lobbying on behalf of a Bulger protégé, apparently to "squash a grand jury subpoena." Years later one of the prosecutors said that he did not recall Bradley complaining about Connolly. John Kiernan, a self-described friend of Connolly's, said he did not "believe Connolly would ever do such a thing." But the other prosecutor clearly recalled hearing from Bradley right after the detective had had coffee with the FBI agent.

James Hamrock said he had actually considered subpoenaing Connolly to the grand jury "to testify about his role and knowledge of the matter." But to avoid worsening the already poor relations between the FBI and local prosecutors, Hamrock did not. Like others before him, he let the Connolly talk go.

∎ ∎ ∎

IN TERMS of FBI housekeeping, John Connolly was not acting alone in keeping the Bulger house in order. John Morris was now the supervisor of a white-collar squad that mainly pursued public corruption, and in early 1985 he was running an investigation that had started as an organized crime case. The original targets were two veteran bookmakers operating in the Roxbury section of Boston, John Baharoian and Steve Puleo. Baharoian ran a gambling business out of his run-down Avenue Variety on Blue Hill Avenue. The shelves were stocked with dust and goods with expired sale dates.

Investigators knew the convenience store was a front for one of the busiest bookie joints in that part of the city. They also believed that Baharoian paid tribute to Flemmi. But then investigators began to develop evidence that Baharoian was also bribing several Boston police officers for protection. Once that happened, the case was transferred to Morris's squad, with an expanded focus on the police corruption.

In the late winter of 1988 agents working for Morris were putting together a plan to install a wiretap on Baharoian's telephone. Morris's unspoken worry was that Flemmi, and possibly Bulger, would be caught on the tape. It was a possibility that stoked his worst fear—an arrest of Bulger and Flemmi leading to his own apprehension if the mobsters, looking for leniency, turned and traded him in. He decided he'd have to warn them off.

Morris told Connolly about the imminent danger, that Flemmi and Bulger needed to stay off the telephone and stay away from Baharoian. They should call a meeting, replied Connolly. Connolly, recalled Morris, "thought they would like to hear from me. He wanted me to give them that information as opposed to him giving them that information, or meet with them at least to discuss it with them personally."

Fine, said Morris. The four could meet. But there was one other worry haunting Morris. Even if these circumstances were not exactly the same,

Morris knew that on a prior occasion when he'd disclosed a secret investigatory effort to the group, the outcome had been bad, chillingly bad. "I don't want another Halloran," Morris told Connolly.

Connolly made arrangements for another get-together, this time at the Lexington town house Morris had moved into. It seemed that on every front Morris's life was bottoming out. His marriage was torn beyond repair, and he was worried sick about his teenage daughter. But as troubled as Morris was, Connolly just cruised along. Bulger and Flemmi seemed fine too. They had certainly come to expect this sort of input—tips about investigations, wiretaps, bugs, and the names of other wiseguys who were cooperating with the police. "As the need arose and I was in a certain situation," said Flemmi, "I would ask him [Connolly] a question regarding certain people, and he would advise me." It was as if the two agents were serving as their *consiglieri,* the Mafia's term for advisers.

But Morris's own reasons for protecting Bulger and Flemmi had multiplied. He was desperately looking to cover himself. "I was completely compromised at that point, and I was fearful that Mr. Flemmi might be intercepted, and that would be the beginning of the unraveling of what in fact had transpired between myself and them," Morris said. He knew he was breaking the law—obstructing justice. "I believe that the Baharoian matter clearly was a violation of regulations." But he saw his own neck on the chopping block if agents caught Flemmi or Bulger on tape. Connolly, Bulger, and Flemmi arrived at the town house, and Morris got right to it, telling the two informants "that we had already started a Title III on Baharoian, and I warned them to avoid Mr. Baharoian."

Flemmi appreciated the heads-up. "Morris said that he could keep me out of the indictment, but he couldn't do the same for other participants in that operation, meaning Baharoian and Puleo."

The FBI's wire on Baharoian was up from June 22 to September 26, 1988. That wiretap and other evidence resulted in the indictments of Baharoian, Puleo, and several Boston police officers. Baharoian eventually flipped and testified at trial against the police. Tapes were played, featuring the voices of bookies and cops. But not Flemmi's. Not Bulger's. They knew when it was safe to talk, and when to keep quiet.

CHAPTER SIXTEEN

Secrets Exposed

If Connolly was the Elmer Gantry of the Boston FBI office, an agent who used the power of his word to win converts, John Morris was another story. Unable to resist temptation but tortured by all the wrongdoing, Morris was like a kid at the wheel of a raceway video game who bumps his car against one wall and then overcompensates and veers at high speed back across the track, crashing into the opposite wall. Careening back and forth, unable to hold his place inbounds, he was approaching Game Over. By 1988 Morris's marriage was ruined. He'd risked his FBI career. Even his friendship with the proselytizing Connolly was taking a turn for the worse. Morris, after saying he would support it, had opposed Connolly's bid for promotion to supervisor. Connolly felt betrayed, with good reason. Morris had legitimate concerns about an agent who liked to come and go, could rarely sit still behind a desk, and handed in lackluster paperwork while serving as a manager for other agents.

More to the point, Morris's opposition stemmed from matters he would not dare mention. In his letter to the FBI's career board, Morris was not about to go into the corruption or explain that promoting Connolly would enhance the protection enjoyed by an increasingly dangerous Bulger. "I didn't think he should be a supervisor, period," was how Morris said he put it. "I didn't think he was fit."

The career board's decision against a promotion naturally upset Connolly. But then Connolly went into action. He went to Jim Ahearn, who'd been in Boston as the office's special agent in charge only a little over a year, since late 1986. Connolly and Ahearn had become fast friends. More than any supervisory agent who ran the Boston office, Ahearn was a boss Connolly could count on.

"They were," observed Morris, "very, very close." There were more than two hundred FBI agents assigned to the Boston office, and Morris watched the new manager do "things for Connolly that I have never seen done for an agent in my career." One of those things was making sure Connolly got what Connolly wanted. "I have never seen a SAC go to FBI headquarters and recommend somebody be made a supervisor when the career board recommended against it. Never." But Connolly got his wish, and during 1988 he was working as a drug task force supervisor. Jim Ahearn had come to the rescue.

Now, having crossed Connolly, Morris was more worried than ever about the agent's influence, which was cresting at an all-time high. "I was concerned it would absolutely destroy me." Morris felt he was falling out of the loop, becoming isolated. And fresh from leaking the Baharoian wiretap, he was also suffering a whiplash of guilt, careening back across the raceway.

Morris decided he would make a pledge to himself: "I wasn't going to do anything more, you know, in terms of protecting them to protect myself." Morris was going to put an end to it.

It was the late spring of 1988, and the timing of all the troubles haunting Morris coincided with the work by a team of *Globe* reporters about Bulger and the FBI. Lehr, Gerard O'Neill (the authors of this book), Christine Chinlund, and Kevin Cullen were all working on their series about the brothers Bulger. Cullen had put into play the notion that Whitey was an FBI informant as the only explanation for his charmed life.

The reporters kept asking around. Police veterans like Dennis

Condon, the high-ranking state police official and former FBI agent, shrugged off the inquiry during an interview that summer. Having provided a lot of material about the history of the Boston Mafia and the Winter Hill gang, Condon sat back and sighed. "Well, I left the FBI in 1977, and I never expected any help from Whitey Bulger or Stevie Flemmi," he said unblinkingly.

Jeremiah T. O'Sullivan, still the chief of the Organized Crime Strike Force, proved impatient and combative. "I don't buy it," he shot back when asked about the theory that Bulger served as an FBI informant. He then went on the offensive against the troopers and cops who had been talking to reporters. "There are a lot of people wandering around with blue lights and guns, making a nice salary. Many of those people aren't making cases, and they cause feuds, bitching and moaning."

Lehr may have bumped into Connolly on the street early in the year, and Cullen was talking to Connolly about other matters, but the team of reporters knew they could not expect help from him on this line of inquiry. Connolly was the FBI agent other cops were complaining about.

Instead, in May 1988, O'Neill called FBI supervisor John Morris. The two had gotten to know one another during the *Globe*'s series about the bugging of 98 Prince Street.

Morris took O'Neill's call, but he rebuffed the gingerly advanced notion that Bulger was an FBI informant. Morris did agree to meet for lunch. O'Neill had described the project about the Bulger brothers and said he wanted to get from Morris some background, what reporters like to call "color," about Whitey's life in Boston's underworld.

O'Neill and Morris met in June at Venezia's, a restaurant overlooking Dorchester Bay. Morris arrived, dressed nattily in a suit, and he seemed excited to see O'Neill. There was some small talk, and then O'Neill raised the need to ask again about Bulger and the bureau. "You have no idea how dangerous he can be," Morris said. It was as if Morris had come to the lunch ready for this moment. Bulger was an informant, Morris suddenly declared, and it was a deal that had become a terrible burden, one that he feared had corrupted the bureau and was going to end badly. The words poured off his lips, gathering momentum. Connolly and Bulger were close, perhaps too close. There were these dinners, Morris explained, he and Connolly had enjoyed at the home of the mother of Bulger's partner. At one, Billy Bulger had even walked in on the feast Mrs. Flemmi had prepared. (This was a separate dinner from the one later attended by Jim Ring.) "There we were, the two brothers on one side of the table and the two FBI agents on the other."

O'Neill sat there stunned. If there were any other sounds inside the restaurant—the noise of other diners and the waiters—neither man heard them. O'Neill had hoped for confirmation and got a confession. The FBI supervisor looked weary, ashen, and deflated; something inside him had given way. They wrapped up lunch, mixing chitchat and non sequiturs with references back to Bulger. Morris worried openly about what the *Globe* would do with the information and cautioned about the consequences of revealing an informant's identity—the danger that such a disclosure could pose to Bulger, to himself, to *Globe* reporters.

O'Neill said he wasn't sure yet what would come of it. But they both knew something had happened, something pivotal. This was the rare kind of information that precipitates movement in the way things are, information that causes a correction in the history of a city as it is understood by its citizens, so that ultimately one version of history is replaced by a more complete and truer one.

■ ■ ■

UNKNOWN to the reporters, Morris was already well informed about the *Globe*'s project even before O'Neill telephoned. Connolly had told Morris that Billy Bulger, the senate president, was cooperating and doing interviews focused on growing up in Southie. But Connolly had fresh concerns about an apparent turn in the journalists' reporting: word had gotten back that the *Globe* was asking around about Whitey and the FBI. Connolly suggested that because Morris knew O'Neill better than any of the other FBI agents, he should put in a call and spin O'Neill off of any trouble spots. Connolly, recalled Morris, "requested that I contact him to attempt to learn about the true direction of the articles and to set him straight."

The supervisor's decision to verify the *Globe*'s reporting was hardly high-minded. "My principal concern was my own skin," he conceded. "I was trying to minimize damage in my career." By his calculation, "outing" Bulger seemed to offer a new solution. Publicity might force the FBI's hand and lead finally to closing down shop with the two informants. If that happened, his own wrongdoing—"that I had accepted money, gifts, and in turn had compromised an investigation"—might be buried forever. There was also a darker possibility—that the Mafia or someone else would assassinate an "outed" Bulger. This would truly end any risk to Morris that Bulger would ever disclose his own wrongdoing. But Morris insisted that bringing about this "potential harm" was not his intent. "I wanted them closed," he said.

He also sensed, however, that he was just fooling himself to think that if only the FBI would close down Bulger then he would be safe. "My thinking there really wasn't very clear," he said. "I think that part of it, if Connolly were surfaced, that would mean that I would be surfaced; and I think at that point in time I in fact wanted my own involvement surfaced." Full of fear and self-loathing, Morris lacked the courage to confess to the authorities.

Back at the *Globe*, O'Neill shared his findings with the other reporters. Everyone was dumbstruck, and there was discussion about whether the information could run in the newspaper, whether it might spur under- world bloodshed. But before any decision about publication could be made, the reporters knew more work was required. They had only a sin- gle source. There are times when an unnamed but well-placed source is enough to go with a story, but a single source for this kind of explosive dis- closure did not cut it. Morris's information needed to be tested.

In July, O'Neill and Cullen flew to Washington, D.C., to see William F. Weld. Weld had just resigned from his post as head of the Criminal Division at the Justice Department in a much-publicized policy dispute with Ed Meese, the attorney general. Over lunch, and on background, Weld was careful and cautious. He said he'd heard the rumors from agen- cies like the state police. He even said he'd thought the rumors were true. But he had no proof, and he did not give the two reporters anything they could use in their story.

Then, during the last week of July, Lehr called Bob Fitzpatrick, a name he'd been given along the way. The New York native had joined the FBI in

1965. He'd worked in New Orleans, Memphis, Jackson, Mississippi, and Miami. He'd worked the Martin Luther King assassination. He'd worked several bombing cases involving the Ku Klux Klan. He'd taught at the FBI Academy in Quantico, Virginia. The now former agent had served as the FBI's assistant special agent in charge of the Boston office from 1980 to 1987. During that time he'd been Morris's boss and overseen the Organized Crime Squad. In 1988 he was working in Boston as a private investigator.

Lehr drove to Fitzpatrick's home in Rhode Island, and Fitzpatrick took him for a walk to a nearby beach. The day was muggy and overcast. The beach was empty. Far away in Atlanta, Democrats were nominating Massachusetts governor Mike Dukakis at their convention.

"What do you know?" Fitzpatrick asked abrasively.

"We know."

Pacing in the sand, Fitzpatrick seemed edgy. Then he started, and for the next few hours he talked about Whitey Bulger and the FBI, about Connolly and Morris.

"He became a fuckin' liability," Fitzpatrick said about Bulger. He said that during his tenure at the Boston office he'd had increasing concerns about the quality of Bulger's information and about Bulger's rise to the top as the biggest wiseguy in the city. "You can never have the top guy as an informant," he said at one point, his voice rising in anger. "You have the top guy, he's making policy, and then he owns you. He owns you!"

It began to rain, and the interview moved into Lehr's car and then back to Fitzpatrick's house. The wide-ranging discourse became a primer of sorts about informant handling, the dangers and benefits of the bureau's reliance on informants, a beachside course on informant dos and don'ts. He repeatedly voiced regret that what he saw as a major internal scandal had gone untreated. The few times Bulger was reviewed internally, the pro-Bulger forces prevailed.

"The FBI is being compromised. That's what pisses the shit out of me. I mean the FBI is being used." The root of the problem, he said, came down to the most basic seduction facing any FBI handler of a longtime informant. Connolly, he said, had long before "overidentified with the guy he was supposed to be running, and the guy took him." The agent, said Fitzpatrick, had "gone native."

■   ■   ■

TWO MONTHS later a four-part series about the Bulger brothers published in the *Boston Globe* included an installment devoted to what was described as the "special relationship" between Whitey Bulger and the FBI.

In the hectic weeks prior to publication, Cullen and *Globe* photographer John Tlumacki, acting on a tip from a local cop, succeeded in taking fresh photographs of Whitey Bulger late one sunny afternoon in a city park near Neponset Circle in Dorchester. Bulger was walking Catherine Greig's poodle, wearing his trademark sunglasses and baseball cap.

By this time too the FBI was well aware of the *Globe*'s storyline and took a shot across the newspaper's bow. Tom Daly, a veteran agent, called up Cullen one afternoon at the office. Daly acted miffed, wanting to know why Lehr had been trying to contact "Fat Tony" Ciulla, the former government witness he'd handled in the 1979 race-fixing case against Howie Winter. Then the conversation turned to Bulger. First off, Daly said that if he was ever asked, "this conversation never took place." (True to form, a decade later Daly denied calling Cullen.) Daly also said he was calling as a "friend," although Cullen barely knew him.

Daly wanted to know where the *Globe* was headed with the Bulger story. First he denied that Bulger was an FBI informant. Then he said that he wanted to make sure Cullen understood what he and his colleagues were up against. He said Ciulla, who was now in the federal witness protection program, had a warning for the *Globe:* "Whitey is a dangerous guy. You don't want to piss him off."

Daly said Ciulla had cautioned that Bulger would not tolerate anything written about him that either was untrue or caused his family any embarrassment. "The guy would never live with that," said Daly about Bulger. "He wouldn't think nothing of clipping you."

The intimidation tactic left Cullen briefly rattled. But by the next day the reporters and their editors had all agreed that Whitey Bulger did not get where he was by killing reporters. The story was seen as something that simply had to be published.

The series ran in late September 1988, a few weeks after Bulger turned fifty-nine, and included unequivocal denials from FBI officials. In public remarks, Jim Ahearn, the top agent in Boston, exuded certitude. "That is absolutely untrue," he declared. "We specifically deny that there has been special treatment of this individual."

Backstage, however, a scramble was under way to assess the fallout. "I read the article," said Flemmi, and "I discussed it with Jim Bulger." In early October they met at Morris's condo. "I went there with John Connolly and Jim Bulger," Flemmi said. It was too soon to wonder how the *Globe* got the story; their first worry was damage control. "He was upset about it," said Flemmi of Bulger. "But I don't believe he at that point in time said anything about who leaked the information. I don't think he knew."

"It was brief," continued Flemmi, the meeting marking the last time Bulger and Flemmi ever met with Morris face to face. The agents, recalled Flemmi, were "talking about distancing themselves from us." But Flemmi also detected that Connolly wasn't happy about this kind of talk and was under pressure. He was against a breakup. "John Connolly, he wanted us to hang in there, and we did," said Flemmi.

In fact, Morris and Connolly had already gone over the story and figured maybe they would all be okay. Even though the in-depth stories "left little imagination" regarding Bulger's status, the *Globe,* noted Morris, had never used the I-word: informant. The article called the deal a "special relationship." Working in their favor, the story was followed by the FBI's public denials. Maybe, they thought, they could ride it out. Maybe their best asset was Bulger himself, and the myth that he was the ultimate stand-up guy. "Connolly and I both thought the informant would be okay because no one in the underworld would believe it," said Morris, playing along once again to cover his tracks.

In the weeks after the story their hunch proved correct. Flemmi and Bulger went to work calling the story a hoax. The FBI agents, meanwhile, took the underworld's pulse. In late September, Sonny Mercurio passed along to Connolly that his associates were thinking the story was "bullshit." Mercurio said Ferrara and J. R. Russo were talking about hidden agendas, deciding the newspaper story was actually a bid to embarrass Billy Bulger. The agents wondered if the Mafia's quick dismissal was actually a reflection of the Mafia's fear of Whitey. If the mafiosi believed Bulger was an FBI informant, then they would have to take action; they would probably have to get rid of Bulger. Maybe the Mafia didn't want to believe.

In October yet another government source indicated that the disclosure was not provoking undue concern. The source, who was actually passing along word of Bulger's continued drug profiteering, mentioned that Bulger and Flemmi, although still "very concerned about the newspaper article," now believed they were "weathering the storm of present." The two crime bosses, said the tipster, had taken to calling the story a lie planted by their enemies and other informants who were out to get them.

It was the talk of the town for a while. By the end of October, however, the storm had passed. In short order, Connolly turned his attention to another important matter. He'd met her at the office nearly a decade before, and on November 5, 1988, Connolly walked down the aisle to marry Elizabeth L. Moore. The crowd watching the happy couple included many of Connolly's pals from the office, especially from the old Organized Crime Squad, among them Nick Gianturco, Jack Cloherty, and Ed Quinn. The affair was joyous, and John Connolly had begun to entertain thoughts of retiring. But even if he stuck around, despite the troubling publicity about the FBI's Bulger deal, the coast now seemed awfully clear.

■ ■ ■

BY THIS time Connolly and the others—including an unraveling John Morris—had honed their skills at deflecting trouble. They'd been doing it for thirteen years, getting better all the time. Now, to his enemies list of state troopers, drug agents, and cops whom he claimed hated him, Connolly added reporters. He couldn't understand any of it. What could there be not to like about an agent armed with colorful FBI stories about bringing the Mafia to its knees? To rebut the Bulger talk, he sought out a private meeting at one point with the top editor at the *Globe*. Connolly made his pitch. How could any of these stories be true, he explained to the editor, Jack Driscoll, *when he'd never even talked to Whitey Bulger.*

Connolly and the others had a strategy to weather the scrutiny of this new press coverage: just keep zealously working the street. They were confident that they could extinguish any brushfire that came their way, including another that was smoldering from within.

This one originated from Bill Weld. Before he left the Justice Department, he'd started getting telephone calls from a woman from Boston with intriguing insights about Bulger and the FBI. The first call came January 6, 1988, and the woman talked to one of Weld's assistants. She was "obviously scared and calling from a pay phone," and she promised to call again to give "information on who Stevie Flemmi and Whitey Bulger have on their payroll, i.e., Boston police and federal agents." Weld distributed a memo to a few high-ranking officials at Justice, and he scribbled in the margin next to the reference to Bulger, "OK, this checks out—maybe not a nut." Weld's office not infrequently got calls from people complaining about the CIA monitoring the fillings in their teeth, but Weld felt this wasn't one of those. The next call came on January 20, and the caller named "Agent John Connolly—FBI" and a Boston police official as the two who "sell wiretap information" to Bulger and Flemmi. Weld again scribbled in the margins: "I know all this! So this is on the up and up." The calls kept coming, on January 27, February 3, February 10, and they included mouthwatering lines like, "I have information on the Brian Halloran killing. It was done by Whitey Bulger and Pat Nee."

Despite his exclamatory jottings, Weld didn't know for certain if the tips were true, but he did think they should be taken seriously and pursued. "I had a sense that there might be a weak link there between Mr. Bulger and Mr. Connolly."

Weld resigned his post on March 29, but his former assistants continued to take the calls, on August 15 and October 27, during which the caller said that a second FBI agent, John Newton, also disclosed government secrets to Bulger. The tipster turned out to be a woman named Sue Murray, fronting for her husband, Joe Murray, the gangster who trafficked in drugs and stolen guns for the IRA and sometimes did business with Bulger.

Murray, imprisoned since his arrest in 1983, was looking to trade information for leniency.

Prior to resigning, Weld shipped "all the stuff up to Boston for further
investigation." But the referral landed right in the laps of Connolly's
friends and the longtime gatekeepers of the Bulger deal, people like
Jeremiah T. O'Sullivan and Connolly's new best friend, Jim Ahearn. The
Boston SAC oversaw an internal inquiry of Connolly that proceeded slowly throughout 1988 and into 1989. It was not to be handled by outsiders or
impartial agents from another office, but by Connolly's associates. It was
as if Connolly had been asked to look into the allegations himself.

Ahearn made it clear that he thought the information was baseless. In
a letter to FBI director William Sessions, he complained that this latest
questioning about Connolly's conduct was "but one of a lengthy series of
allegations over the years." Ahearn assured his boss he would not jump to
any conclusions, but in the next breath he did just that. He wrote Sessions:
"While I am not prejudging the current investigation, all others have
proven groundless and [agent] Connolly is held in extremely high esteem
by both the Criminal Investigation Division and myself for his accomplishments." The writing was on the wall.

Joe Murray was brought to Boston in June from a federal prison in
Danbury, Connecticut, for an interview with two agents from the Boston
office. Ed Clark and Ed Quinn sat across from Murray that day. Both
agents were friendly with Connolly, especially Quinn, who for years
worked closely with Connolly and just a few months earlier was raising a
glass in a toast to John at his wedding.

Murray told the agents he'd heard Bulger and Connolly traveled to the
Cape together and shared an apartment in the Brighton section of Boston.
He said a number of Bulger's associates, like Pat Nee, knew Bulger and
Connolly were close and that Bulger had Connolly on a string. "Connolly
was no problem," Nee indicated. He said "Bulger and Flemmi are responsible for the death of Bucky Barrett in 1983" and summarized what he
knew about the twenty-four hours leading up to Barrett's disappearance.

The Boston FBI agents nodded and took notes, but never asked any
follow-up questions—about Connolly, about Bulger's role in the Halloran

and Barrett murders, or about anything Murray had to offer about the crime boss.

Clark later described his assignment that day as if he were a mere stenographer, not a seasoned FBI interviewer. In his view, he was there to just listen to what Murray had to say and pass it on to somebody else who would evaluate it and decide whether any further action was warranted. Clark said he even thought to himself that Murray would "make a terrific informant." But instead of being cultivated, Murray was returned to his cell in Danbury. Clark said he was not asked to follow up on anything Murray said.

Meanwhile, Jim Ahearn and his deputies took Clark's typewritten report and forwarded it to headquarters, urging the top brass to slam the door shut on any further challenge to Connolly. The cover letter dismissed Murray's comments as "rumor and conjecture" and concluded: "Boston recommends that this inquiry be closed, and no administration taken."

It was done. The paperwork was buried—like Halloran's and Barrett's corpses—and the negative Connolly talk was rerouted into FBI oblivion. Yet another mere inconvenience.

■ ■ ■

CONNOLLY, Bulger, and Flemmi seemed to have a growing sense of entitlement: the city was theirs. Thus, Bulger was absolutely put out one day at Logan Airport when he and his girlfriend, Theresa Stanley, were detained as they were boarding a Delta Airlines flight to Montreal.

It was around 7:10 P.M. Using cash, Theresa had paid for two first-class tickets. Bulger, dressed in a black jogging suit, was carrying a black leather garment bag. Inside the bag was at least $50,000 in cash he was attempting to smuggle out of the country. But as the bag passed through the X-ray machine a security guard noticed several unidentified lumps. Zipping open the bag, the guard spotted bricks of cash—all $100 bills. Believing the amount was well over $10,000—federal law required the reporting of cash amounting to more than $10,000—the guard told Bulger and Stanley to step to the side; she would have to advise the state police.

"Fuck you," Bulger told the female security guard.

Bulger picked up the bag of cash and began walking quickly away. He handed the parcel to another man, saying, "Here, Kevin, take this." Kevin Weeks hurried out the door, climbed into a black Chevy Blazer, and raced off. Bulger stuck his foot in a revolving airport door to slow a second guard who had taken up the chase after the bag of money.

Bulger was arguing with guards when plainclothes trooper Billy Johnson of the Massachusetts State Police's airport barracks arrived. No one recognized Bulger, who was sneering at the guards, Theresa at his side.

"Hey, you, get over here," Johnson shouted.

Johnson identified himself, and one of the guards began to explain the situation, but Bulger interrupted and pointed at the guard. "Shut the fuck up," he said. "You're a liar." Johnson demanded identification, and Bulger produced a license: "James J. Bulger, 17 Twomey Court, South Boston."

The guard tried a second time to talk to Johnson, but Bulger again interrupted. "Shut the fuck up."

Johnson turned to Bulger. "You shut up." He pinned Bulger back against the wall, one of the few men who probably ever put his hands on the gangster. "One more word out of you, and I'm going to lock you up."

Bulger didn't back down. "That how you treat citizens?" he snapped. "That how you treat citizens?" Bulger shouted. Johnson ignored him. The trooper seized $9,923 in cash that Theresa Stanley was carrying. Customs officials were notified, but the amount was just below the reporting requirement. Eventually, after conferring with other agents, Johnson realized that he had no reason to detain Bulger. Maybe he could have tied him up on a disorderly conduct charge, but he decided that would be a "cheap pinch." He let Bulger and Stanley go. Bulger stormed off, hailed a cab, and was gone.

Life uninterrupted. Flemmi was now often taking a break from the crime beat—indulging in a passion for parachuting by attending army reunions and joining the International Association of Airborne Veterans. He began traveling worldwide to jump from planes—to South Africa, East Germany, Thailand, Israel. He renewed friendships with other Korean

War vets. Meanwhile, John Connolly's world was also humming along—a new marriage, a promotion to supervisor of a drug task force, and the prospect of retirement. Following the celebrated Mafia induction ceremony taping in late 1989, FBI director William Sessions traveled to Boston to personally congratulate the Boston agents, singling out Connolly for his handling of informants. Connolly was moving up and out—literally. In 1990, he sold his Thomas Park home and moved briefly into a South Boston townhouse, a six-unit complex where Bulger and Weeks also owned units. But Connolly now had his eye on the North Shore suburbs, and he soon purchased land in Lynnfield and built a large, two-story red-brick home.

Even though Jim Ring had instructed Connolly to quit meeting his informants inside his home, the get-togethers continued, if simply relocated to agent John Newton's house, or Nick Gianturco's. Gianturco once invited two star FBI agents from the New York office in town for a few days. Joseph D. Pistone, retired from the bureau, had written a book, *Donnie Brasco: My Undercover Life in the Mafia.* The book, published in 1987, became a best-seller and eventually was made into a movie starring Al Pacino. Joining Pistone was Jules Bonavolonta, a veteran Mafia fighter who eventually would write his own book too. Gianturco cooked up the meal, and Connolly proudly introduced Bulger and Flemmi to the out-of-town guests. "It was obvious," Bonavolonta recalled, that "Bulger and Steve were friends of Connolly's." Connolly began talking about how someday he'd like to write a book about his FBI triumphs.

Morris was now persona non grata. He was busy defending himself in 1989 against an internal inquiry into leaks to the *Globe* regarding the 75 State Street investigation. He refused to take a polygraph and was scrambling to lie his way out of trouble, writing up false reports and denying to the FBI brass that he was a leak, and all the while Connolly was leading the charge for his former friend's scalp. "He was suspicious of me," Morris said about Connolly. But Morris would survive the internal scrutiny with a censure and fourteen days of unpaid leave.

In back rooms at their liquor mart and the variety store next door, Bulger and Flemmi conducted the dirty work of their underworld empire, hauling in recalcitrant debtors for meetings, perhaps pulling out a weapon to illustrate a point they were trying to make about the price of tardiness. Out front, at holiday times, FBI agents showed up to pick up their Christmas cheer. "Dick Baker, Friend of John Connolly," was the note scribbled onto a receipt for the $205 in booze that agent Baker bought in 1989.

It seemed to Connolly and the others that everything was going their way. Deriding any criticism was Jim Ahearn. Indeed, soon after he came to Boston, he ordered a deputy to review Bulger's status to quell the nagging backbiting at the office. But the outcome—a hearty recommendation to keep Bulger—was hardly a surprise. The review consisted largely of a review of Connolly's files and talking to Connolly himself. Ahearn wrote to the FBI director on February 10, 1989, boasting that Whitey Bulger was "regarded as the most important Organized Crime informant for many years." (The memo did not even mention Flemmi by name, even though Stevie was the one with the best Mafia access.) Connolly, wrote Ahearn, has an "outstanding reputation as an informant developer and his accomplishments are well-known throughout Massachusetts law enforcement."

The SAC's memo to Sessions had a specific purpose: to protest the fact that the Drug Enforcement Administration and the Boston Police Department were conducting yet another drug probe of Bulger. Ahearn had only the day before learned of the joint investigation; worse still, the probe had been under way since 1987. Ahearn was beside himself—angry about being left out of the loop, and incensed that the second-class DEA would dare treat the Federal Bureau of Investigation that way.

But the decision to leave out the FBI had been carefully considered. "I was quite happy to have the FBI out of that investigation," said Bill Weld, the chief of the Criminal Division in the Justice Department at the time. "I thought there might very well be a problem somewhere in the FBI. I thought it was at a low level, the John Connolly level. I thought it was historical, but that's still a problem."

But Jim Ahearn didn't care. He told the FBI director that the DEA's conduct was "reprehensible." He was "deeply disappointed." His words were "in your face": the Boston office and John Connolly were above reproach, and Whitey Bulger was the best thing ever to happen to the FBI.

It was a high-water mark in Bulger hype and FBI bravado. And once again Whitey weathered the squall in his back yard. The DEA investigation lopped off top enforcers such as John "Red" Shea and Paul "Polecat" Moore and snared scores of dealers. But no Whitey. Now it was time to coast home. Nearing retirement, Connolly wrote a report saying that Bulger and Flemmi were also thinking of calling it a day, "packing it in and going into various legitimate businesses that they own." Flemmi, for one, was spending more than $1 million—in cash—to buy up a slew of real estate in the affluent Back Bay neighborhood.

But what Connolly considered "legitimate business" a new team of federal prosecutors would soon regard as money laundering. Despite how it seemed at decade's end, Connolly and the gang would never have it so good again.

PART THREE

Some things are necessary evils,
some things are more evil than necessary.

JOHN LE CARRÉ, THE RUSSIA HOUSE

CHAPTER SEVENTEEN

Fred Wyshak

The 1989 Mafia baptism captured by the FBI on tape seemed like a scene out of *Saturday Night Live*—as burly men took stilted oaths and burned holy cards. But it was a deadly serious event in the history of the New England mob, a last-gasp attempt by the beleaguered boss, Raymond Patriarca of Rhode Island, to bring warring Boston factions together. "Junior" was a pretender to the throne once held tightly by his deceased father, and he hoped that adding some new blood to the ranks would help calm Boston's troubled waters. Notable Boston Mafia malcontents Vinnie Ferrara and J. R. Russo were there, nodding and smiling. Leaving the show of unity, Ferrara said, "Only the ghost knows what really took place over here today, by God."

Not quite. Whitey Bulger was rubbing his hands on the sidelines, glee-fully aware that another Mafia cadre was about to bite the dust by putting racketeering evidence on tape for the feds. Once again top mafiosi would soon face the music played in court and have little choice but to plead guilty to long terms. Patriarca, with the lightest criminal record, was sen-

tenced to eight years; Russo got sixteen years; and Ferrara was dealt the
stiffest sentence of all—twenty-two years. Once again Whitey and Stevie
had helped target their enemies and then got out of the way.

The shattered mobster hierarchy also paved the way to the top for
Stevie's old partner from the 1960s, Cadillac Frank Salemme. Just out of
jail, Salemme was planning a rapid ascension. He revived a loose alliance
with Flemmi, a reunion of their two-man death squad of the late 1960s
when they carried out hits for Larry Zannino. Salemme would soon manage to survive a clumsy assassination attempt against him outside a pan-
cake house, for which he blamed Ferrara. But the gunfire did not slow his
ambitious program to take over the Mafia and ally himself with Flemmi
and Bulger.

The law enforcement terrain began to shift as well. For starters, John
Connolly stepped down at the end of 1990. He was feted by his colleagues at a raucous party before making a soft landing as head of corporate security at Boston Edison, a company that had long curried favor
with Senate President William Bulger. Around the same time, Connolly
moved into a condo building in South Boston that had adjoining units
belonging to Kevin Weeks and Whitey Bulger. Connolly quickly moved
up the corporate ladder to the job of in-house lobbyist and an executive
salary of about $120,000. From a Prudential Tower office above Boston's
Back Bay, Connolly worked with legislators at Bulger's state house and
did some Washington lobbying for the utility. But his interests stayed
parochial. His office wall, decked out with photos of local politicians
and sports figures, had a special place for Ted Williams, his boyhood
icon.

Without Connolly in place, Bulger began to scale back and focused on
South Boston holdings rather than looking for new business. He even
forged a uniquely Whitey Bulger retirement plan: he "won" the state lottery. After a winning ticket was sold at his Rotary Variety Store, Bulger informed the $14.3 million jackpot winner that it would be in his best
interests to acquire a new partner. Whitey and two allies left the customer
half of the proceeds. Bulger claimed about $89,000 a year in after-tax in-
come for himself—a stipend that could support his lifestyle against audits
by the increasingly snoopy IRS. Investigators later found that Bulger paid

the ticket holder $700,000 in dirty money to get an official cut worth $1.8 million over the next twenty years.

For his part, Flemmi launched his 401k plan with real estate trusts he controlled through relatives and in-laws. The 1990s marked his whole-hog immersion in Boston's toniest neighborhood, the onetime Brahmin bastion of Back Bay. In 1992 he sunk $1.5 million in cash into a six-unit condominium building and two smaller units and some residential property in surrounding suburbs.

As the new decade dawned, the Mafia was dissolving once again, and the Bulger-controlled Winter Hill gang was moving upscale and uptown. On both sides of the line, the key players began harvesting the fruits of the 1980s.

Whitey Bulger had legitimate income for the first time since he was a courthouse janitor.

Stevie Flemmi made $360,000 on the resale of his Back Bay building.

John Connolly landed a big job at a major utility.

Jeremiah O'Sullivan was charging $300 an hour as a defense lawyer at a white-shoe Boston firm. And the FBI's Jim Ring soon followed him there as an investigator.

Only John Morris struggled as the decade began. He'd barely escaped the investigation of 75 State Street leaks to the *Boston Globe*. Regaining his balance, Morris moved on to Washington with an assist from a rising star in the bureau, Larry Potts, who had once worked in Boston. Morris then finally got the promotion he had been after and became assistant agent in charge of the Los Angeles office.

■ ■ ■

THEN along came Fred Wyshak. Born in Boston, Wyshak was new old blood who had returned home after a decade as a crime fighter in the rough and tumble of Brooklyn and New Jersey. He arrived at the U.S. Attorney's Office in 1989 with a reputation as a case maker who did not suffer fools or mince words. He had no time for or patience with agents who dogged it or didn't get it. Unlike the more typical federal prosecutor with an Ivy League background and no street sense, Wyshak had no stepping-stone jobs in mind. He just wanted to make cases—the bigger the better. Within weeks Wyshak had but one question: how come no one is doing this Bulger guy?

He had been told that Bulger was just about ungettable, that he was smart and shifty and never talked freely on the phone or dealt directly with anyone who would roll, that he had regularly outfoxed the DEA, the state police, and, most recently, the Boston police. Besides, Wyshak was told, Bulger's not worth it. Why not check out the new Mafia boss, Cadillac Frank Salemme, the next big case?

Wyshak smiled his small smile while his skeptical eyes said, "Really?" He had seen the real Mafia in New Jersey, and Angiulo successors like Salemme seemed like penny ante bookies. In fact Wyshak was coming off a major victory in Newark, a conviction of the city's Mafia head, a man who had so dominated the trade unions that he annually extracted millions of dollars from contractors dependent on union labor and work terms. As a prosecutor in his midthirties, Wyshak hadn't thought twice about calling the special agent in charge of the Newark FBI office and saying, "Let's go."

Wyshak knew the difference between big and little fish, and as he looked over the Boston underworld, he kept coming back to Bulger. The question lingered and tantalized. Why did no one seem to care about such a natural target?

When he arrived in Boston as a thirty-seven-year-old prosecutor, Wyshak had a decade's experience in making cases in Brooklyn and Newark by getting defendants to roll against each other. He also knew how to assemble and manage a massive racketeering case against several underworld leaders. He could do the paperwork, and he could fight in court. He learned to keep ahead of defense lawyers and developed an instinct for which defendants would fold and which would hang tough.

But while Wyshak brought his considerable playbook to town, nothing prepared him for the backstage politics of Boston. His jock mentality had a New York edge that often cut two ways. Not everybody liked him. A case maker who was always pushing a game plan, he gravitated to workers, not talkers. He disdained one agent as a "donkey stuck in mud." In one of the first meetings with the best ally he would have in Boston—the long-suffering state police—Wyshak rubbed against one detective as "an arrogant son of a bitch, a kid from New Jersey telling us how everything works." Yet to a small circle of friends Wyshak was a closet comedian who made lunch a riotous event with snide asides. He joked about how everybody hated him, including his own family. And when the punch was spiked at one office Christmas party and secretaries were crashing into walls, it was Wyshak taking it in with mischievous eyes.

Although Wyshak worked out elaborate strategies long in advance, his basic approach was not hard to figure out. With a heat-seeking instinct for the weak link in any criminal enterprise, he used Hobson's choice as a weapon. Be a defendant or be a witness. Get on board or pack for prison. Robert Sheketoff, a defense lawyer who worked against Wyshak, came away respecting his tenacious intelligence but viewing him as a zealot. "I don't understand how the government can crush a human being on the theory that if they crush enough human beings you get a greater good," Sheketoff said. But about Wyshak's strategy he could only grimace and say, "Hey, it's working."

Over the years Wyshak battled judges and defense lawyers with arms flailing, voice rising, chin jutting. In one typically stormy sidebar conference an exasperated judge once threw down his glasses on his bench and stammered at Wyshak, "You stop. You stop."

Wyshak greeted witnesses with perfunctory goodwill and then got right to it. He once turned on an FBI agent with machine-gun intensity. "Tell us what you really think," Wyshak demanded of the agent, who, like nearly everyone in the bureau's Boston office, detested the prosecutor. Every time the agent began to respond, Wyshak fired another question while the judge futilely insisted, "Let him answer, let him answer."

At first, Brian Kelly was yin to Fred Wyshak's yang. Though Kelly did not have the experience that Wyshak brought to a big case, the young prosecutor wanted to do them badly. They shared an irreverent disregard for office politics, though Kelly had the more traditional background for the job of federal prosecutor and was an archconservative, distinctive even in a Republican shop. (An honors graduate of Dartmouth College, he was to the right of the *National Review*.) And unlike a lot of the career-obsessed attorneys in a competitive office, Kelly didn't particularly care if he lost some cases as a way to learn something. But most of all, he could roll with

Wyshak's tart tongue and sharp elbows. He could even make Wyshak laugh and slow down. When others huffed off muttering, "I can't believe he said that," Kelly would smile and say, "Cut the shit," or, "What makes you so smart?" Kelly had a nickname for everyone, and Wyshak was "Fredo," just like the over-his-head brother in *The Godfather*.

In addition to having an even temperament, Kelly could get people to row in the same direction and was able to rebuild some of the bridges that Wyshak incinerated. After a couple of years the prosecutors became as inseparable as Bulger and Flemmi, playing off each other in and out of court. Most of all, they enjoyed the courtroom shoot-outs, and they enjoyed a challenge. They would get both in taking on Whitey Bulger.

Both Wyshak and Kelly had instinctively rejected the unspoken view that the FBI was the best client in the office. Both had worked in U.S. Attorney's Offices where prosecutors worked with agents from several federal and state agencies, not just the FBI. And it fit with Wyshak's mantra. No screwing around. Try the cases. Win some. Lose some.

After a while another prosecutor, James Herbert, joined the Wyshak-Kelly team, arriving as the best writer in the office. Like his writing, he was orderly, clear-minded, and to the point. Not as madcap as his new colleagues, Herbert was a levelheaded scrivener making his way around the courtroom. He had an Ivy League résumé more typical of the office's lawyers, the kind that ran three pages to Wyshak's four paragraphs.

■ ■ ■

THE first obstacle Wyshak encountered as he set out on the Bulger highway was a mind-set. Many in the U.S. Attorney's Office wanted to stay religiously focused on the Mafia and follow the FBI's lead, a long gray line headed for a decade by Jeremiah O'Sullivan and then, in his wake, by assistant U.S. attorneys Diane Kottmyer and Jeffrey Auerhahn. (The pro-FBI contingent was led by Jim Ring and Kottmyer, a competent assistant in the Angiulo case and a dour O'Sullivan disciple addicted to the FBI.) Wyshak's early effort to target Bulger was never opposed directly. The response was never, "That won't work." It was, "Interesting. Let's talk more."

Then Howie Winter strayed onto the playing field. By the end of 1989

Howie had been out of jail for a few years and was living in exile in rural Massachusetts, working at a garage and staying out of Boston while he was on parole. Winter had fallen on hard times and was collecting workmen's compensation from a garage injury. But the lure of the kind of easy money he had made in the 1970s proved irresistible, and soon enough the state police and the DEA got a tip that Howie was moving cocaine. The detectives took the case to Wyshak, the outsider with no history or agenda and no ties to the FBI. Wyshak immediately formulated one of his game plans: an aging and wired Howie talking to Whitey about "Santa Claus."

But they had to catch Howie first. The snitch network reported that Howie was foolishly taking some orders over the telephone. After sufficient "probable cause" detective work, Wyshak obtained court authority to do a wiretap on Winter's phone and then held a meeting among federal and state investigators to go over "minimization" rules for investigators listening in on the calls.

The bug was compromised the first day it went up. All investigators had was Howie goofing around on the phone. An informant told them that Howie warned him away from telephone contact. It was a fast education for Wyshak in the ways of Boston law enforcement.

Wyshak had gone about the Winter investigation the way he did in Brooklyn—setting a course of action with several agencies in on the details. In New York it had been possible to collaborate over a cross-section of investigators. But not in Boston. So Wyshak was forced to adopt the prevailing need-to-know strategy. After putting out word that the Howie case was kaput, he began working in earnest on a new plan with a chosen few. Using what a colleague calls "great instincts," he zeroed in on one of Winter's cocaine suppliers as someone who would roll. The supplier was a fortysomething ex-convict who had just started a new family and had a wife and baby at home. The investigators built a cocaine trafficking case against him, then gave him the choice: doing heavy prison time or coming on board with prosecutors and staying home with the new family. The dealer was wearing a wire within a year, talking to Howie about distributing kilos of cocaine. In 1992 Howie was arrested as he attempted to sell coke. In a flash, Howie was looking at a minimum of ten more years in prison and as many as thirty if Wyshak

could convince a judge that his earlier convictions for race-fixing and extortion made him a career criminal.

Howie was taken to a motel and interrogated by Wyshak, state police
detective Thomas Duffy, and DEA agent Daniel Doherty. As if Winter
didn't know, they explained his predicament. He was told: we're really
after Whitey Bulger, who, by the way, hasn't done you any recent favors.
Can we work something out here? Howie listened hard and watched the
question hang in the air. He asked to speak to his wife, Ellen Brogna,
about it. "Become a rat?" she asked him in horror. "You should tell them
to go fuck themselves." So that's what Howie did.

In May 1993 Winter pleaded guilty and was sentenced to ten years.
Once king of Winter Hill, he left court dressed in a drab gray suit on a
drab gray day, a sixty-two-year-old gangster looking at a decade in prison,
carrying all his belongings in a brown paper bag. A convicted drug dealer
with a strong wife—but no rat.

Wyshak had bagged a big target in Howie even if it didn't get him to
Whitey. And the plea bargain meant much more than one more Winter
Hill figure behind bars. It forged a lasting alliance between the high-
energy prosecutor and the state police detectives and DEA agents who
were aching for another shot at Bulger. For his part, Wyshak just wanted
to make cases. So they saddled up.

■ ■ ■

THE Wyshak posse picked up the trail that had been blazed back in the
early 1980s by state police detective Charles Henderson. Henderson had
overheard suburban Jewish bookies on wiretaps talking about "Whitey"
and "Stevie." As head of the Special Service Unit, Henderson had arrested
all of the bookies at one time or another and now knew they were paying
rent to Bulger. Whitey annoyed the combative detective on a personal
level. He also realized Bulger was getting a pass on his extortion, that no
one else in law enforcement gave a rat's ass about it except the state police
and a few local prosecutors. (In fact the FBI had a formal policy of not
stooping to chase lowly bookies.)

But Henderson saw the bookies as a bridge to Bulger and knew that
they would be vulnerable to a concerted assault—if one could ever be

mounted. Henderson knew well the bitter legacy of the Lancaster Street garage and even something about the Halloran murder aftershocks. But most of all, he was a visceral cop who decided he'd had enough of this bully who swaggered out of South Boston on a pass from the FBI. Henderson did some long-range planning. He needed bookie cases that would enable police to take control of gambling profits by using forfeiture statutes. It was a sure way to get a bookmaker's full attention. And he needed to hand the bookies over to federal prosecutors like Wyshak as witnesses against Bulger for some kind of racketeering case. As he began plotting his way at the end of the 1980s, he realized that politics was at least as important as evidence.

By 1990 Henderson saw that the timing was finally right. He had just been promoted to head of the uniformed state police. And there was a new lineup at the top of law enforcement that could work together. The new state attorney general, Scott Harshbarger, the new district attorney in Middlesex County, Thomas Reilly, and U.S. attorney Wayne Budd were friends who could work together. One factor plaguing earlier efforts against bookies and organized crime had been the fragmented jurisdictions of county district attorneys. It made it hard to chase bookies with phone taps across county lines. So one of the first moves Henderson made in his new job was to have Harshbarger's office obtain blanket court authority to chase bookies across county lines. Henderson's second was to appoint his protégé, Thomas Foley, as head of the Special Service Unit.

The plan was to make cases against bookies that could be handed off to the feds, who could use their tougher sentences to turn bookmakers, accustomed to paying $3,000 fines in state court and never going to jail, into witnesses. The middle-class bookies were more businessmen than archcriminals, and there were not many who would stand up to ten years in a federal prison.

The effort got under way in Middlesex County, chosen because of its heavy betting (it was the state's most populous county) and because the state police worked well with Reilly, who had been a longtime prosecutor there. Phone taps went up in 1991 and multiplied quickly as one bookie led investigators to another. There soon was an embarrassment of riches, and the state police had to make a fast decision—whether to chase both Bulger's gang and Mafia bookies. In some fancy footwork, the investigators slyly handed off Mafia bookie "Fat Vinny" Roberto to the FBI but quietly retained control of Chico Krantz and his crew of Jewish bookies paying Bulger.

While Roberto eventually fizzled, state investigators made dramatic progress with Chico, especially when a search warrant uncovered the keys to Chico's cash box. Krantz played it cozy, but he was intrigued by the idea that he could stay out of jail and get some of his money back if he did a little talking. Whitey was where things bogged down.

Foley was ideally suited for carrying out the next step in the delicate mission. Having worked on special assignment since 1984 with the U.S. Attorney's Office and the FBI, he knew how to ease the case to federal prosecutors who wouldn't just turn things over to the FBI for more legwork. Foley took his pitch and Chico's predicament down the hall to Fred Wyshak. Foley convinced him that a criminal merger had taken place and power had shifted to Bulger's gang. Wyshak was so impressed he didn't make a wisecrack.

■ ■ ■

BRINGING in skittish bookies looking for a deal to stay out of jail was one thing. Slipping under Bulger's stranglehold on drug dealing in South Boston was quite another. Throughout the 1980s Southie had been an impregnable fortress. But now a crack began to show.

Timothy Connolly was a mortgage broker trying to outrun his roots as a South Boston tavern owner. He had a simple story of extortion to tell about Bulger putting a knife to his throat for money. But the U.S. Attorney's Office tried to turn Tim Connolly's solid single into a home run. They constructed an elaborate plan to infiltrate Bulger's financial operation, a doomed effort that fell far short of the mark. Just as some in the FBI would have liked, Timothy Connolly was forgotten—almost.

Four years later, in 1994, Brian Kelly bumped into an investigator in a courthouse corridor. "Don't forget the Tim Connolly stuff," the investigator said. "It's good." Kelly looked at him blankly. Tim Connolly? Tell me about him, Kelly asked.

It had all started, the investigator recalled, in 1989. A car almost cut

Tim Connolly off as he walked along a South Boston sidewalk on a sim-
mering summer day. It screeched up the curb, and Connolly squinted into
the sun to see inside. With a rush of adrenaline, he saw Whitey Bulger and
Stevie Flemmi glaring out at him. The driver barked to meet Bulger at the
Rotary Variety Store and sped away.

Tim Connolly was flummoxed. What's this? he thought with a gnarled
stomach. He got an emphatic answer the second he made his way into the
dark storage room in the back of the variety store. "You fucker," Bulger
screamed at him, pulling a knife from a sheath strapped to his leg. Bulger
began viciously stabbing empty cardboard boxes stacked against the wall.

Tim Connolly's hanging offense was that he had taken too much time
in arranging financing for someone who owed Bulger money from a busted drug deal. Tim Connolly had simply not moved fast enough.

Holding the knife against Connolly's throat as Flemmi watched the
door, Bulger slowly simmered down. As with similar tirades, Bulger's fury
seemed calculated, another episode in the Bulger production called "A
Second Chance." "I'm going to let you buy your life," he said. It was the
classic Bulger scenario and price all over again—$50,000 and how-you-get-
it-is-your-problem. Once again a terrified victim was thankful to be paying
Whitey for not killing him.

Tim Connolly pleaded for some time and said he had to go to Florida
in the next few days. Bulger set the terms: Twenty-five large before he
went, and twenty-five on his return. Tim Connolly borrowed $25,000 and
brought it in a paper bag to the store. As he left, an appeased Bulger told
him, "You are now our friend."

When Tim Connolly returned from Florida, he took $10,000 more to
the store. But Bulger had no time for him now and motioned him to his
associate, Kevin Weeks. After taking the money, Weeks looked up and
said, "Where's the rest?" Coming, Connolly said wearily. Coming.

But in fact Tim Connolly was going. Desperate to get away from a killer
debt, he began talking with a lawyer who could get him to federal prosecutors. Like Brian Halloran, he was looking for a safe haven. But the bloody
history showed that nothing involving Whitey Bulger was simple or easy.

Within a matter of weeks Tim Connolly was swept up again, this time
on the other side of the line. The DEA and Boston police were wrapping up

their investigation into South Boston and Tim Connolly was subpoenaed to talk about a second mortgage he arranged for one of Bulger's dealers.

Using phone taps and shoe leather, detectives had worked their way up from a street dealer to the highest level in Bulger's cocaine network. The evidence included taps on the phone of a dealer who had lost money in a deal involving Bulger—the same dealer who got Tim Connolly summoned to the variety store. The detectives knew nothing of the threat to Tim Connolly but wanted to find out if he was financing drug deals through his banking connections. What the local police also didn't know was that Tim Connolly was already dealing with the FBI after making his way to the U.S. Attorney's Office.

But as always seemed to happen when events veered dangerously close to Bulger, there was a derailment in federal offices. One of the top prosecutors in the U.S. Attorney's Office, A. John Pappalardo, decided to use Tim Connolly to get into Bulger's finances. He turned Tim Connolly over to two handpicked FBI agents who had no ties to John Connolly. They wired the mortgage broker as a way to get an inside look at Bulger's money laundering. But then Whitey Bulger suddenly stopped dealing with Tim Connolly.

In the end Tim Connolly was not used in the DEA and Boston police case against Bulger Drug Network because they never knew about the extortion in the back room. And the FBI's attempt to use Tim Connolly on Bulger's money laundering never got off the ground. But if investigators and even some prosecutors never knew Tim Connolly's value when it counted the most, the same cannot be said of Whitey Bulger. He knew all about the threat that Tim Connolly posed, almost immediately after the FBI had him wired.

Stevie Flemmi said that after Tim Connolly was sent to the FBI, "Mr. Bulger told me that Tim Connolly was wired up and that he was directing [at] us as a target . . . the information came from the FBI." Flemmi was quite certain the tipoff came from John Connolly.

Kelly took all of this in. It was a lesson in how hard it would be to bring a case—any case—against Bulger. But it was also a reminder that perhaps, just perhaps, it could be done.

CHAPTER EIGHTEEN

Heller's Café

On a November day that warned of winter, a state cop took a slow drive by a forbidding brick building with iron bars on the windows and an oversized Schlitz Beer lantern above the front door. Detective Joe Saccardo began nodding to himself as he rolled by slick cars on a skid row. Too many Cadillacs for downtown Chelsea, he thought. Heller's Café is a bookie joint all right.

But inside the tavern the proprietor was doing more than logging betting slips. Michael London was shuffling checks, tallying part of the $500,000 in paper he converted into cash each week for the region's biggest bookmakers. London was just hitting his stride as a back alley banker in 1983. Starting with a small book in a barroom inherited from his father, London had moved up the gambling chain by turning hot checks into cold cash. Bookies now called him "the Check Man." At the beginning of the 1980s he began shifting away from a local clientele to the big sports-betting network run by Jewish bookmakers with ties to Winter Hill and, to a lesser extent, the Mafia. London had become the man to see when bookies and businessmen wanted to hide profits from the Internal Revenue Service.

When Saccardo pulled over to a curb, he did some tallying of his own. He had a dozen license plate numbers from the sleek cars that ringed Heller's Café. Back at the office the state police computer took the numbers and spat out a who's who of Boston bookmaking: Chico Krantz, Jimmy Katz, Eddie Lewis, Howie Levenson, Fat Vinny Roberto. Even Joey Y—Joseph Yerardi, a wiseguy more than a bookie who put money on the street for Winter Hill and was allowed to collect rents of his own.

Bingo. Saccardo had found much more than a bookie joint. He had discovered the mob's bank, a place where gamblers' losses—in five-figure checks made out to cash or joke names such as Ronald Gambling or Arnold Palmer—were converted into payouts and profits. At its height the bulletproof teller booth in the back of a saloon converted $50 million a year into cash. It also yielded about $1 million in fees to London, who was raking it in on a back street under a tired bridge in a run-down city.

Fittingly, it was left to Joe Saccardo of the Massachusetts State Police to target Boston's version of Meyer Lansky. London juggled two accounts in a local bank with about $800,000 in family money and withdrew up to that amount each week as the checks cleared. It was a good deal all around. The local bank got use of the money without having to pay interest, and it winked at London having to report cash transactions of more than $10,000 to the IRS. He worked the system to buy a house in Weston, the wealthiest suburb in Massachusetts, and a summer home in West Hyannisport not far from the Kennedy family's compound.

Though most of London's bookmaking customers were affiliated with Bulger's gang, he was drawn to the brash braggadocio of Vincent Ferrara, a flashy capo who became such a regular at Heller's that he had his own table. London saw Ferrara as a comer in the Mafia and hitched his red tavern to Vinny's rising star.

London and Ferrara were simpatico, understanding enough about money to see it as more than cash-in-the-pocket and a new car. London began helping to round up freeloader bookies for Ferrara, giving them intimidating pep talks. "You gotta pay one side or the other these days," he

told them. "I'm just letting you know how it works so ya don't get hurt."
Over time London became the poor man's version of the Wall Street broker who pushes clients toward an investment banker who gives him kick-
backs. The two men had similar tastes. They both bought the same silver
two-seater Mercedes, and Ferrara convinced London to take one of the
small boutique dogs he bought in New York for $5,000. They also shared
loan-shark profits.

■ ■ ■

AFTER Joe Saccardo brought the who's who license plate printout to his
bosses, they knew what they had. Instead of settling for a fast gaming
raid, they called for reinforcements. A task force of state police investigators and FBI and IRS agents was formed. At times the various agencies did
little more than get in each other's way. It took three years of fits and
starts before bugs were spliced into the teller's cage inside Heller's Café
and taps were placed on two phones. Investigators monitored bugs from a
nearby construction trailer for the last two months of 1986. When it
ended, no one was quite sure of what they had, though they knew this
much: Vinny and Mike had a problem. In December the police team
rousted the bar, pushing everyone against the wall. But the jammed-up
clientele was nothing compared to the boxes of checks carted away to FBI
headquarters in Boston.

Soon afterward London told Jimmy Katz, a bookie whose own day
would come, "It's gonna be a big problem. Not, not immediately. But it
will happen." London knew that the boxes of checks from 1980 to 1986
would tally $200 million.

Though the confiscated boxes of checks and reels of tape were as rich
a vein of evidence as police could have carried away, the whole case
bogged down at the FBI in 1987. The bureau was sure there was a Mafia
capo in the big stack of stuff but was halfhearted about investigating further. In the U.S. Attorney's Office, Jeremiah O'Sullivan had just finished
the Angiulo case and was ready to take on reckless newcomers. As federal
prosecutors reviewed the tapes, O'Sullivan cherry-picked them for his
strike force and tossed the rest back. His assessment: we'll take Vinny, and

somebody else really should do London. And, oh, there might be some other stuff in here too.

．．．

INDEED there was. Only doing Ferrara meant taking a pass on the bookies in the line at Mike London's cashier window who were being extorted by Whitey Bulger and Stevie Flemmi. London once told Chico Krantz, the premier bookmaker with a long-term deal with Bulger, to "shop Italian." "Stevie can't hold [Vinny's] jockstrap. Vinny will work for ya . . . a collection agency, personal protection. Stevie don't do nothin. This guy here will go to bat for you." In another Mike London speech, a bookie nicknamed "Beechi" got the sad facts of life: pay Ferrara or "the other guys are gonna get your name . . . Stevie and Whitey." But nobody in federal law enforcement seemed excited about the evidence implicating Bulger and Flemmi.

After O'Sullivan culled Vinny out of the tapes, the boxes of checks collected dust. Several prosecutors had taken one look at the evidence room and kept on going. No one wanted to wrestle a messy paper case to the ground to convict a Chelsea tavern owner. Joe Saccardo finally prevailed on a young eager prosecutor named Michael Kendall to take a look.

If the storage room was overflowing, the quality of the seized evidence was remarkable. Kendall had the patience to assemble the paper and prepare a chart showing how $200 million in gambling losses and loan-shark payments got turned into cash. Two years later London was convicted of money laundering and racketeering and sentenced to fifteen years.

．．．

CHICO KRANTZ was only a footnote in the London indictment, but Saccardo began to lobby for a second wave of prosecutions out of Heller's Café—all the bookies who were paying rent. He didn't know what the crimes should be, but he began to wonder if something in the mix could be used against Bulger. Kendall begged off, however, citing his caseload.

Then one of those mundane but magical things happened. Kendall recalled that Fred Wyshak had done a similar check-cashing case and went to talk to him about Chico Krantz. As luck would have it, Chico was just coming into focus out of a separate broad-based bookie investigation by state police in the Special Services Unit headed by Sergeant Tom Foley. The state police had set out to find bookies who dealt with Whitey Bulger, and as in Heller's Café, Chico was at the head of the line.

Suddenly Chico, the whiz kid of betting lines, was overlapping himself as the perfect witness against Whitey Bulger. He had been paying tribute to the insular Bulger for nearly twenty years. He was one of the first to know about the new system of monthly rent payments when Bulger explained it to him in 1979. He was threatened with death by Bulger when he dragged his feet on paying a debt to another bookie. And his long history of payments to Bulger measured the expansion of Whitey's empire. Over the years Chico's monthly rent had climbed from $750 to $3,000.

Chico's undoing began just about the time Mike London was indicted in 1990. State police targeted a bookie network with Mafia ties. Fat Vinny Roberto and his brothers handled daily action from thirty-five bettors who wagered up to $500,000 a week. But the big payoff from the Roberto investigation was the discovery that Krantz was his everyday boss, even setting the Roberto brothers' work hours. Best of all, undercover state police followed Roberto to Chico's suburban home, where he dropped off a package. A search warrant got them inside Krantz's home, where they found keys to bank deposit boxes that were filled with $2 million in cash.

After Krantz was arrested on gaming charges in 1991 at the state police barracks outside Boston, he sought out Sergeant Foley. How come the police went to my house this time? Krantz asked.

Foley shrugged.

Where's this thing going?

Foley shrugged again.

About a week later, with Krantz out on bail, Foley met with the master bookie at his Florida home, and they talked for two days about bookmakers and the Bulger gang. Krantz didn't give up too much, talking in general terms about Flemmi, George Kaufman, and Joe Yerardi. But Krantz did agreed to be a "CI," or a confidential informant.

With an ambivalent Krantz waiting in the wings, prosecutors and state

police began to chase down leads from the Heller's Café tapes and the related Middlesex County case that started with Fat Vinny Roberto. Wyshak
soon focused on four check-cashing operations in greater Boston, including Heller's. The investigators collated boxes of checks, much as Kendall
had done in the London prosecution, isolating and tallying rafts of checks
that exceeded the $10,000 limit that have to be reported to the Internal
Revenue Service.

Now the pressure on Krantz went up a notch. The state dropped the
gaming charges against him in 1992 and turned the evidence over to the
U.S. Attorney's Office. In September, Foley told Krantz that he and his
wife, who cashed checks for Chico while he was sick, were going to be indicted for money laundering. Foley even showed him draft copies of indictments. Chico sighed and asked to sleep on it.

The next day Krantz got a new lawyer and finally stopped playing
games. He graduated from CI status to the witness protection program.
He filled in holes in his earlier statements and finally talked about Whitey
Bulger and his one-way loyalty.

In November, Chico and seven other bookies from Heller's Café were
indicted for money laundering in a massive check-cashing scheme. About
the same time that London was sentenced in 1993, Chico Krantz slipped
into another federal courtroom under tight security and pled guilty. He
formally forfeited his $2 million in cash, with a wink and a nod on half of
it that the government agreed to give back if he cooperated. And he admitted guilt on washing $2 million in checks, much of it at Heller's. He
also became number one on the witness list in the developing case against
Bulger and Flemmi.

Jimmy Katz, who had also washed big money through Heller's, found
himself mired in the quicksand between Fred Wyshak and Stevie Flemmi.
Just before Katz went to trial, Flemmi met him at a hamburger joint in
downtown Boston. Flemmi offered him the parable of Eddie Lewis, another bookie in the Chico camp. Lewis had refused to give immunized testimony to a grand jury about rent and had gone off to do eighteen months
for contempt. Stevie then got to the point: if Katz went off quietly to jail
like stand-up Eddie, he would be well taken care of in prison. It would be
worth his while.

They parted, and Katz went to trial. But he lost and was sentenced to four years. As his wife and daughter cried quietly beside him in the courtroom, Katz said he was standing on principle by refusing to cut a deal with Wyshak. "I won't do that," he said. "The government is turning everyone into rats. It'll become Russia. Every other day they call me: 'You wanna go with Chico?'"

Katz went off to prison in Pennsylvania. After he settled in and made a few friends, he was abruptly transferred to a spartan holding cell in Massachusetts. He was put in front of a grand jury to answer questions about rents. If he refused, it would mean eighteen more months in prison.

After a year in jail Katz rolled, deciding he did "wanna go with Chico" to the witness protection program after all. He became another key witness against Bulger and Flemmi.

■　■　■

JOE YERARDI was next up in the march toward Winter Hill. Going after Joey Y was cutting closer to the bone. Krantz and Katz paid to be left alone. But Yerardi was a leg-breaker who worked for Bulger and Flemmi, putting over $1 million of their money on the street and collecting their debts. Yerardi did run some bookies, but loan-sharking was his thing. And his criminal record was far different from the other customers at Heller's. There were firearm violations and several assault and battery convictions in state court.

Yerardi's main line of work had become handling usurious loans for the bad-to-the-bone Johnny Martorano. His formal ties with Flemmi and Martorano made him a prime target for Wyshak as he assembled his witness list. Yerardi knew that too. And so did Stevie and Whitey.

By the middle of 1993, with Krantz in hand and Katz up against it, the writing was on the wall. A grand jury was going strong, and indictments were in the air. Whitey pulled Stevie aside: time for a vacation. Stevie lit out for Canada, just as he had two decades earlier. Bulger took one of his slow drives across America with Theresa Stanley.

And Yerardi fled too, heading to Florida with $2,500 sent him by Martorano. But he made the mistake of using an old alias from

Massachusetts, and six months after he was indicted the Massachusetts State Police found him living in Deerfield Beach as Louis Ferragamo. The fatalistic if bumbling Yerardi asked the troopers, "What took you so long?"

Joey Y became the Gordon Liddy of Heller's Café. He continued making loan collections while under house arrest and never complained about the United States becoming Russia. He could have croaked Flemmi, with whom he had extensive dealings. In fact Stevie was on a tapped line talking business with Yerardi. But Yerardi stood up, taking an eleven-year sentence as the price of saying no to Wyshak, and law enforcement had to move forward with Chico and Katz and others who lined up at the cashier's cage in Heller's Café.

■ ■ ■

THE BOOKIE brigade had become the soft underbelly of the Bulger gang. It kept Whitey and Stevie on the firing range and shifted the prospect of indictments from the outlandish to the inevitable. And it left the FBI scrambling for a piece of the action, if only to avoid the embarrassment of sitting on the sidelines while a major case was made against the most renowned gangsters in Boston by the Massachusetts State Police. The bureau saw the train leaving and jumped on board at the end.

By the middle of 1994, with London and Yerardi in prison and all the Heller Café tapes deciphered, prosecutors began assembling the rest of the racketeering case that involved historical evidence from 98 Prince Street, Vanessa's Italian Food Shop, and the 1989 mob induction. This required the FBI to designate someone to help round up the material, and that job fell to Edward Quinn, the hero of the Angiulo case who now headed the Organized Crime Squad.

Though Quinn commanded respect from other investigators, the intramural jockeying continued and showed itself in a spate of news stories, several from the FBI, that reported promising developments in the quest for Bulger. Stories with unnamed sources said, "It's getting close to Bulger, but it's not quite there." The analysis could be read as a warning for Bulger to stay gone. And behind the news stories, John Connolly had been keeping

Bulger and Flemmi updated on grand jury progress. In particular, they discussed the Yerardi investigation, which had veered toward Bulger's gang.

. . .

THOUGH bookies were the mainstays in the percolating case, prosecutors also finally broke through the South Boston code of silence. In addition to Timothy Connolly's testimony, there was the momentous flip of true believer Paul Moore, a skilled boxer and renowned street fighter whose nickname "Polecat" derived from his fast hands and feet. Moore had headed one of Bulger's cocaine distribution networks and was the real deal, a genuinely tough guy who had pled guilty in the 1990 drug case. He went off to do nine years at a federal prison in Pennsylvania, tight-lipped but buoyed by expectations that were also part of the code—a good lawyer, family support, home insurance. But after a few years in prison he felt that his questions about an appeal were falling on deaf ears. His wife was not getting the support she needed. And a bank foreclosed on his home.

In 1995 Moore had the epiphany that comes to those sitting in a prison cell while other more deserving candidates are walking the streets back home. By this time he was hearing stage whispers from the prison network that Whitey was a rat. He began asking himself the rhetorical question that prosecutors count on: what am I, an asshole? The process accelerated when Moore was hauled before a grand jury and faced another year and a half in prison if he didn't answer questions about Bulger. Breaking with Whitey the Rat was the easy part. The code was a different story. But Moore had had enough. He asked one thing: put me near the water so it will be as much like South Boston as a modest house and a small shoreline can make it. He entered the witness protection program as someone who would testify against Bulger.

. . .

AS THE doggedly determined prosecution moved forward, the strategy remained the same, even as the witness list was reshuffled. Katz and a half-dozen bookies replaced Krantz, who was diagnosed with the leukemia that eventually killed him. Paul Moore and loan officer Timothy Connolly replaced the adamant holdout Yerardi as belly-of-the-beast witnesses.

But the heart of the matter remained the mundane business of Bulger and Flemmi shaking down vulnerable bookies from Heller's Café. Though the bookies had dealt mostly with Bulger's out-front man, George Kaufman, most had endured at least one moment alone with the marble eyes of Whitey Bulger or the unfriendly smile of Stevie Flemmi. The "other" crimes that supported racketeering charges against the pair reached back into the ancient history of Bulger's early work in Winter Hill's sports-betting network in the 1970s. Flemmi's racketeering was linked to gangland murders from the 1960s.

Frank Salemme was the next mob figure to get into trouble. Despite his years on the mean streets, Salemme remained oblivious about the dangers of his boyhood friend Stevie Flemmi. He had no clue that he had spent fifteen years in jail for attempted murder because Stevie tipped off the Boston FBI about where to find him.

After his 1988 release from prison, Salemme soon began taking the easy money that Stevie pushed his way from independent bookies who had broken free from the Ferrara network. It left Salemme as vulnerable to bookie extortion charges as the Bulger gang. But Salemme fell into another deep hole on his own. About a year out of prison he began working on an ill-advised deal brought to him by his son. He allegedly began extorting a Hollywood production company that wanted to avoid paying expensive union workers as it made a movie in Boston and Providence, Rhode Island. For a price, Salemme got the Teamsters to go along. The fatal catch: the head of the production company was an undercover FBI agent. The spider's web had caught Cadillac Frank.

■ ■ ■

BY THE middle of 1994 prosecutors had assembled a sturdy, intricate mosaic to support racketeering charges. The plan had been to arrest Bulger,

Flemmi, and Salemme in rapid succession to avoid escapes by any of them. But while, by mid-December, Salemme could still be found at his usual haunts, Stevie and Whitey had been in and out of town for several weeks. The FBI insisted that Salemme, as the Mafia man of the moment, be arrested first. But top officials at the U.S. Attorney's Office overruled the agents, concluding that the case was about Bulger and Flemmi. Indeed, most of the evidence concerned Flemmi, since he was the man in the middle, standing at the junction of Bulger and La Cosa Nostra. Fittingly, the arrest warrant for Flemmi charged him with extorting money from Chico Krantz.

As 1995 got under way the latest law enforcement intelligence was that Flemmi had been seen at Quincy Market, a tourist shopping center in downtown Boston where Flemmi's two stepsons were renovating a restaurant. It was staked out by state troopers Thomas Duffy and John Tutungian and DEA agent Daniel Doherty, who were all part of the ad hoc team that had first gathered in Fred Wyshak's office. Their orders were to arrest Flemmi the minute he "went mobile" by getting in a car.

In winter's enveloping nightfall, the arrest team moved into action when Flemmi and a young Asian woman left Schooner's Restaurant and got into a white Honda at 7:00 P.M. The team boxed them in with two cars and then raced at the Honda with guns drawn. After instinctively trying to hide under the dashboard, Flemmi calmly got out of the car and asked for permission to call his lawyer. The detectives relieved him of a knife and some mace and unsuccessfully tried to persuade the woman to accompany them to FBI headquarters, if only to keep her from warning others. But she knew the drill and refused to go without a warrant.

■ ■ ■

ALTHOUGH the FBI had brought in its elite Special Operations Group to do surveillance on Salemme with a helicopter, he escaped that night. Cadillac Frank fled to West Palm Beach, Florida, a favored sanctuary for mafiosi on the run. He would eventually be arrested there eight months later, but his easy escape fueled the barely suppressed anger of investigators working the same case. One denounced the Special Operations Group as an over-the-hill gang. "They suck," he said bitterly. "It's part of the facade over there. Those guys are looking for retirement homes. And they're nine-to-five. Once their shift ends, they're out of there. They have no personal interest in the case."

For his part, Stevie Flemmi was an unflappable presence inside FBI headquarters, a calmness rooted in his belief that thirty years of FBI service would save him. He was expecting a quick bail and a night flight to Montreal. It was only as the night wore on with no side door opening that he realized he was all alone in his adversity. He thought that John Connolly or Paul Rico would help, as they had in the past. But Flemmi was like the Hollywood celebrity arrested for drunken driving. Protests about his importance would only make things worse. No one could save him now. He belonged to trooper Tom Duffy.

Flemmi had expected more because Connolly had kept him posted on grand jury developments throughout the year, at times using his continuing contact with the bureau's Organized Crime Squad. But both Connolly and Morris, who was also close to retirement and working in Los Angeles, had left the scene and taken their early warning system with them.

In fact there had been a wholesale changing of the guard within the U.S. Attorney's Office and the FBI that left Bulger's barrier beach unprotected. But hardly abandoned.

Bulger had become a dirty little secret that evolved into a tacit policy administered by new players who may not have fully understood the history but held fast out of institutional loyalty. They viewed any attempt to change the system as a challenge by upstarts who had the bad taste to urinate inside the tent. The lingering commitment became grounded in the fear that Bulger had become a time bomb by attracting too much public attention, especially after the 1988 *Boston Globe* article. The fierce personal friendship of John Connolly was replaced by the knee-jerk protectionism of one special agent in charge after another. The credo became: Bulger may be a skunk, but he's our skunk.

But Flemmi's arrest by state police told the FBI that the gig was up. And when it realized what had happened, the bureau backed away as quickly as it could. The only contact Flemmi had with his old allies after his arrest was when he hailed agent Edward Quinn at a bail hearing. The awkward encounter made Flemmi realize that he was no longer a prized informant. He was just another unhappy wiseguy in a courtroom.

"What's going on here?" Flemmi asked the startled Quinn as he walked by. "How about a break on bail?" Flemmi persisted in a plea that meant "Get me outta here."

But all Quinn could do for him was get him a Coke.

Even then, as Quinn edged away and the government's lawyer got in between them, Flemmi thought there might be a magic parachute. His mind drifted over the years of FBI intervention, back to how Paul Rico got attempted murder charges dropped in state court. Flemmi remembered being tipped off to state police bugs in the Lancaster Street garage, and the time he and Whitey were let out of the race-fixing case. And how the FBI in Boston helped cover up Winter Hill murders in Boston, Tulsa, and Miami. Surely his friends, Jim Bulger and John Connolly, would "get this all squared away."

But the most Flemmi ever got were prison visits from Kevin Weeks, Bulger's friend from South Boston, who conveyed the commiseration of John Connolly. The agent wanted Flemmi to know how badly he felt about the FBI letting them both down.

Flemmi never heard another word from Bulger.

■ ■ ■

BULGER quickly adapted to life on the lam. The wild teenager who sought attention by walking a pet ocelot around the Old Harbor housing project had developed the low to the ground discipline of an army ranger hiding in the jungle. When it was clear that indictments were on the way, he cut all ties with South Boston, except for an occasional call to prearranged pay phones.

Though Bulger was never known for sentimental attachments, it surprised Flemmi that he never heard another word from Bulger as his partner moved from one small city in middle America to another. Still, Bulger had done more for Flemmi than he did for most. He had warned him to stay out of Boston, and Flemmi had foolishly ignored him. It was a dumb mistake, and Whitey didn't make those.

But Bulger had almost slipped up too. In January, shortly after trooper Tom Duffy put his gun to Flemmi's temple, Bulger had been driving toward Boston himself. Theresa Stanley had grown tired of traveling on their extended "vacation." Since the fall of 1994, while Bulger waited to see what would happen in Boston, they had traveled to Dublin, London, and Venice and then toured the southwestern United States. But Stanley was bored with sightseeing and tired of being alone with the aloof Bulger and his long silences. She missed her children and South Boston. In the last couple of weeks Stanley had hesitated to even ask simple questions like, where are we going now? It would only start an argument.

So in January 1995 they were making their way to the edge of Boston in stony silence, driving along route 95 in Connecticut, when Stanley heard a radio report about Flemmi's arrest. Bulger took the next exit and headed back to New York City, where they checked into a Manhattan hotel. Bulger hung out at the hotel pay phones, getting whatever information he could. Theresa didn't bother to ask him what was going on.

The next day they drove to a parking lot south of Boston where Stanley got out to wait for her daughter. Bulger said, "I'll call you," as he roared off forever. She never heard from him again.

Instead of heading off alone, he picked up his other girlfriend, Catherine Greig, and disappeared into rural America as a balding retired everyman with a younger wife.

On the road again with a different woman, Bulger lived for a while in the Louisiana bayou country and has reportedly been seen in the Midwest and Florida and even Mexico, Canada, and Ireland. Investigators traced phone calls he made from a New Orleans hotel and a restaurant in Mobile, Alabama. He stayed in touch with Kevin Weeks and some family members and even ventured back to the Boston area on a couple of occasions to rendezvous with Weeks. The meetings, which came early on, later in 1995 and in 1996, enabled Weeks to provide Bulger with some false identification and new intelligence about the ongoing investigation. Kevin O'Neil did his part too, funneling nearly $90,000 into Bulger's bank account soon after Bulger was forced to flee. But no one outside his tight circle heard from him once he dropped off Theresa Stanley.

■　■　■

EXCEPT John Morris.

Morris's last FBI station before retiring at the end of 1995 was training director at the FBI Academy in Virginia. One October afternoon his secretary told him that an insistent "Mister White" was calling. Ten months on the lam, the brazen Bulger was calling from a pay phone on the road.

He had a short message for Vino: If I'm going to jail, you're going to jail.

"I'm taking you with me, you fuck," Bulger said.

"I hear you," said Morris. That night John Morris suffered a major heart attack. Bulger had nearly killed him with a phone call.

CHAPTER NINETEEN

In for a Penny, in for a Pound

Their cells were side by side on the mezzanine level of cellblock H-3 at the Plymouth County Correctional Facility, number 419 belonging to Cadillac Frank Salemme and number 420 to Mafia soldier Bobby DeLuca. The seven-by-nine-foot cells had gray cement floors and walls painted a dull white. It was late summer 1996, and the racketeering case against the Mafia and Bulger and Flemmi, albeit with Bulger in absentia, was chugging along in low gear. The federal case was in discovery, a pretrial stage in every criminal case when the government discloses to the defense relevant evidence and potentially exculpatory material about the accused. The defense then studies the material, primarily to prepare for trial but even before that to see if it can gut the government's case by finding legal fault with the way the evidence was developed. If defense lawyers can persuade the judge that all or part of the evidence was somehow obtained wrongly, the judge might throw it out. Depending on how much evidence goes, the case against the accused either shrinks or, better, evaporates.

Salemme and DeLuca huddled over a Sony tape recorder. They'd been given a homework assignment by their Boston attorney, Anthony M. Cardinale. Listen to the tapes, the lawyer had instructed—listen carefully. The lawyer had brought to the prison handfuls of tiny cassette tapes that were copies of recordings the FBI had made during covert electronic surveillances—from 98 Prince Street, Vanessa's, Heller's Café, a meeting of two mafiosi at a Hilton Hotel at Logan International Airport, the Mafia induction ceremony in 1989, and others.

Tony Cardinale was listening to the tapes himself, but he wanted Salemme and DeLuca listening too. Their ears were better trained for the Mafia talk. The voices belonged to their guys. All three were looking for a way to challenge the tapes' admissibility, a way to knock them out of the ring so they could not be used in court. Listen, Cardinale instructed, for anything irregular.

Of particular interest to the lawyer were the tapes the FBI had made by using a "roving bug." Unlike any other bug, this bug was not fixed in a ceiling or wall or beneath a lamp. Instead, this powerful and portable hand-held microphone could move, inside a dish that FBI agents aimed at people to pick up their conversation, even if they were inside a car or house. The FBI turned to a roving bug when it did not know in advance the location of a meeting, or when it otherwise lacked the time necessary to install a fixed bug or a telephone wiretap. By its mobility, the roving bug was a highly effective brand of electronic surveillance that sent chills down the spines of both guardians of privacy rights and criminal defense attorneys. Cardinale, for one, was no fan. "The roving bug is probably the most dangerous government intrusion," he said. "In a sense, they've thrown out the Fourth Amendment protections. Because if you're the target, then the government can go anywhere you go. To your house. To your mother's house. To a church. Anywhere you are, the government has probable cause, a walking search warrant. It's a vast expansion of electronic surveillance, and it's a nasty little tool that should not be misused."

Cardinale had a hunch about the Boston FBI's use of roving bugs—namely, that the FBI was misusing them. He was convinced that the FBI, contrary to what agents swore under oath to judges, did know far enough in advance where certain meetings were going to take place. The agents knew this, he believed, because they had one or more of their confidential informants attending the meetings. If this were true—if federal judges had been misled—the defense might be able to get all or some of the tapes suppressed.

Salemme and DeLuca took their assignment seriously. Behind the hard green steel doors of their cells, seated on the thin mattresses of their metal bunk beds or at the tiny metal desks attached to their walls, the men played the tapes. There were hundreds of tapes, and the work was mind-numbing, as they played and replayed the conversations, straining to hear the dialogue.

Bobby DeLuca especially took to the task at hand, and one day, while concentrating on the Hilton-Logan tape, he detected something in the background. He stopped, replayed the passage, and the more he listened the more he became convinced he could hear other voices besides the two targeted wiseguys. DeLuca summoned Salemme, who listened to the tape. Salemme heard the extra voices too. DeLuca wasn't crazy. Two voices in the background were whispering. It had to be the FBI agents overseeing the taping. Somehow the roving bug they were using from the next hotel room had also captured their voices, and one agent was whispering to the other agent that they should have gotten "the Saint" to give one of the wiseguys "a list of questions."

Eureka.

DeLuca and Salemme stopped the tape and eagerly placed a telephone call to Cardinale in Boston.

■ ■ ■

THE MAFIA had been calling on Tony Cardinale for years, and at forty-five, he possessed the seasoning, ego, and stamina to go deep into any contest with the government. By the time of the 1995 indictment of Salemme, Bulger, Flemmi, and the others, he was Boston's leading mob lawyer. Fond of Hermes silk ties, fine cigars, and scotch, Cardinale relished the combat of the courtroom. He was a lawyer who was best on his feet, seemingly restless behind a desk. It had always been this way for the litigator who'd grown up in Hell's Kitchen in New York City, the son of a boxer and restaurateur. Cardinale's father and four uncles ran Delsomma's

Restaurant on Forty-seventh Street between Eighth Avenue and Broadway, popular with the theater crowd, the old Madison Square Garden folks, and the wiseguys from the West Side. His father also trained boxers, and Tony Cardinale grew up under his father's careful eye, taught to bob and weave, jab-jab, a right, *bam!* a left hook, *bam!* Boxing dominated the talk at the restaurant and at home, a railroad-style flat on the third floor of a tenement on Forty-sixth Street, right next to a fish market. Two uncles and their families lived across the street; his grandmother and another uncle lived around the corner. Tony Cardinale ran with the Forty-sixth Street Guys, a gritty, true-life version of the street gangs glamorized in the musical *West Side Story*. The teen Cardinale wore the late 1950s getup of blue jeans, white T-shirt, sneakers, and garrison belt, a thick, big-buckled belt that could double as a weapon.

Young Tony Cardinale grew up watching the city pass through the doors of his family's restaurant—fighters, gangsters, high rollers, businessmen—and this was the spot where he first picked up the notion of someday becoming a lawyer. "If my dad met a guy at the door who was a lawyer or a doctor, he would be really impressed," said Cardinale. "He would be very solicitous, very respectful.

"Something happened, something special about seeing that, because I'd think, as I saw how my father treated people who were lawyers, I'd say, 'You know, that's what I want to be, Dad,' and he'd say, 'God, if you ever do that, that would be great, that would be wonderful.'"

On a football scholarship, Cardinale attended Wilkes College in Pennsylvania. He wanted to go to law school in New York City, but NYU, Columbia, and Fordham all rejected him, so Cardinale traveled to Boston, newly married, to attend the only school that would take him, Suffolk Law School. He never left the city. Indefatigable, he made law review. In his second year he and classmate Kenneth J. Fishman began working for famed defense lawyer F. Lee Bailey. Cardinale and Fishman became life-long friends. Bailey called the two "the Gold Dust twins" because they came into the office at the same time and were attending law school together. The mentor thought of Fishman as "the law guy" for his acumen in legal analysis and Cardinale as "the fact guy" for his ability to investigate a case and track down flaws in the opponent's reasoning. "He had a good measure of self-confidence," Bailey said later, remembering a young Cardinale. "He's got good-sized balls."

Cardinale stayed with Bailey for five years, then struck out on his own in the early 1980s, working the trenches, building on the fast start he'd gotten with Bailey by piling up courtroom experience. Then in late 1983 he took on his first Mafia client—Gennaro Angiulo, of all people. The underboss's original attorney, in line for a judgeship, had dropped out of the case, and Cardinale got the call one night after Christmas: "How would you like to represent Jerry Angiulo?" It was the big break, and Cardinale was eager. "This was a major league, major league case," he said. "I want to get in the game, you know. That's the athlete part of me coming out— if this is the biggest game in town, then I want to be in it." Just thirty-three years old, Cardinale was the lead attorney in the biggest organized crime case in Boston's history.

Cardinale went to war. He relentlessly attacked the devastating 98 Prince Street tapes, their quality, their accuracy, all in an attempt to knock them out of court. The trial lasted nine grueling months, and each day Cardinale was on his feet trading blows with the government team led by Jeremiah T. O'Sullivan.

In the end the House of Angiulo had fallen, but Cardinale had made it, even if his hair turned gray during the trial. Just like that he had become the up-and-coming practitioner for the mob. During the 1980s he represented other Angiulos and Vinnie Ferrara, and he commuted to New York to represent "Fat Tony" Salerno. In the early 1990s he joined the defense team of John Gotti, representing Gotti sidekick Frank "Frankie Locs" Locascio. In the 1995 indictment of Cadillac Frank Salemme, Tony Cardinale was again the Mafia's go-to guy. Flemmi, meanwhile, tapped another leading defense attorney, Cardinale's law school friend Ken Fishman.

Cardinale was ecstatic to hear from Salemme about their cellblock discovery. He had turned his own office into a quasi-electronics center, with high-quality tape recorders and enhancers, and when he listened to the tape himself, he too heard the whispering that Salemme and DeLuca had detected. Each time he replayed the passage, he felt more certain that he now had a legal smoking gun, something he could use to land a counterpunch against the government. He had technicians enhance the tape, and the background FBI voices were less faint. The two agents operating the roving bug were complaining about the rambling, unfocused conversation under way in the next room between a local wiseguy named Kenny Guarino and a visiting mobster from Las Vegas named Natale Richichi. One agent seemed to tell the other that beforehand they should have had "the Saint" make up "a list of questions of shit . . . for Kenny to ask him . . . we could, you know, narrow the different categories."

To Cardinale this was proof that the FBI had at least one—and maybe two—informants participating in the meeting with the visiting Mafia figure from Las Vegas. Cardinale figured that either Kenny Guarino or "the Saint"—a nickname for Anthony St. Laurent—or both, were working as FBI informants. If either wiseguy was an informant, then the FBI had probably known beforehand the location of the meeting at the Hilton. And if that were true, the FBI had not had a valid basis for using a roving bug and had lied to a federal judge to win his permission for one.

Cardinale prepared new court papers and, tape in hand, argued to the judge sitting in the racketeering case, Mark L. Wolf, that a special hearing was warranted to look into possible FBI subterfuge. The documents related to the case were sealed, and the court sessions held to discuss Cardinale's findings were closed to the public. Cardinale argued that to get another judge's okay to use a roving bug FBI agents in 1991 had filed sworn affidavits saying they had no idea where Richichi was going to be when he came to Boston on Mafia business. Cardinale, urging the judge to listen to the tape himself to hear the background FBI voices, said, "The FBI knew a great deal more about the events of December 11, 1991, but wanted to protect their source." The Boston FBI, suggested Cardinale, was possibly "involved in illegal conduct in an effort to conceal the activities of their high-level informants."

Throughout the fall of 1996 the matter was pursued during court sessions that remained closed to the press and public. Cardinale and a team of prosecutors led by Fred Wyshak engaged in a legal shoving match, with Cardinale seeking to push the envelope while the government pushed back.

During this time Cardinale began to develop an even more ambitious game plan. He believed the subterfuge behind the FBI roving bug at the Hilton was not an isolated event. He felt that for years the FBI had bent and broken all kinds of rules to protect a coterie of informants. In particular he believed that the FBI was especially protective of Whitey Bulger. Cardinale had read the stories in the *Boston Globe,* and he'd heard all the talk on the street about Bulger and the FBI. He also believed that Bulger had escaped arrest because the FBI let him get away.

All the Bulger talk had gone on outside of court. But Bulger was a codefendant now, and to defend his client, Salemme, Cardinale was deciding to go after Whitey. He would employ the Hilton tape as a battering ram to knock down the wall of secrecy. Cardinale was going after the FBI.

■ ■ ■

"DEFENSE counsel seeks the disclosure of the identity of various individuals who may have served as government informants/operatives in connection with the investigation and/or prosecution of this case," the lawyer began a motion filed on March 27, 1997. The papers were submitted under seal, and the discussions before Judge Wolf regarding the FBI and Bulger continued to unfold in secret. Cardinale claimed that all or part of the government's evidence might be tainted by FBI misconduct, and to get to the heart of the matter the world needed to know about Bulger and the others.

In his motion Cardinale named Bulger and several other suspected informants, such as Guarino and St. Laurent, but not Stevie Flemmi. "I was just a little uncomfortable," said Cardinale later. "Keep in mind, one of the last things you want to do in a situation like this—I mean this guy is a defendant in the case, and if you believe he's been a rat essentially his whole life, one of the last things you want to do is to pull the trigger on the guy when you're not ready, and the guy gets scared and rolls, and he hurts your client. I thought if the finger was pointed at Flemmi too early and he rolled, he could not only try to hurt Salemme but any number of people. It could have been a disaster."

So for the time being Cardinale held back, partly out of caution and partly out of courtesy to his colleague, Ken Fishman, who was representing Flemmi. Besides, at the time the conventional wisdom still held that Flemmi was a stand-up guy. "The word on the street was about Bulger," noted Cardinale. The *Globe* stories a decade before had been about Bulger and the FBI, not Flemmi. Bulger was the one who had evaded arrest in 1995, not Stevie. "You know, nobody had ever really said anything about Flemmi. Even among the Italians, I mean they always said, 'Listen, Bulger is capable of anything,' but Flemmi, they considered him almost one of them."

Every step of the way Fred Wyshak and his fellow prosecutors fought Cardinale. They didn't know exactly what horrors were hidden inside the FBI's files, and they wanted Judge Wolf to keep his eye solely on the prosecution at hand. Wyshak had gone so far as to share with the judge—but not with the defense—an "extremely confidential" affidavit by Paul Coffey, the chief of the Organized Crime and Racketeering Section of the Justice Department. In it Coffey reported that as informants Bulger and Flemmi were never given specific authorization to commit crimes and that both were given periodic warnings that they were "not authorized to commit any criminal act absent specific authorization." Ironically, Wyshak was forced to defend the FBI deal with Bulger for the sake of stopping Cardinale. The government, Wyshak insisted, did not have any formal but undisclosed deals with Bulger or Flemmi that would bar the present prosecution. The judge, argued Wyshak, should therefore ignore Cardinale's "sweeping and nonspecific allegations." Bulger and his relationship with the FBI was irrelevant, a distraction. Just as important, the court should not put the FBI in the harmful position of having to confirm or deny in public the names of the confidential informants so crucial to the bureau's work.

But Wolf did not agree.

To the government's dismay, on April 14, 1997, the judge decided that he wanted to learn more about Cardinale's claims, at another closed hearing to start in two days. "The court has reviewed the defendant's Motion to Disclose Confidential Informants and Suppress Electronic Surveillance conducted in this case," wrote Wolf in a quick three-page ruling. "In this case, in which the defendants are charged, among other things with . . . conducting a racketeering enterprise, the fact that a codefendant was during the relevant period a confidential informant for the FBI would, if true, constitute exculpatory information to which his codefendants are entitled." Wolf even ordered the government to bring along Paul Coffey and said that Coffey should be ready to talk about informants.

Between the lines in the ruling, Cardinale thought he detected a hint that his aggressive inquiry should not stop at Bulger but embrace Flemmi as well. "He says he wants the government to be prepared to answer questions as to whether 'a' defendant in the case—what impact that has if 'a' defendant is an informant. Now what happens is, I read from that that the judge, he was indicating that it is a defendant who is actually presently in the courtroom, not one who is on the lam, as Bulger was."

The night before the hearing the lawyer shared this latest theory with his colleagues in a meeting at Ken Fishman's office. There was John Mitchell, a New York City attorney who had joined Cardinale in representing Salemme and DeLuca, along with attorneys representing John and James Martorano. The half-dozen men and women were gathered around a conference table in the office on Long Wharf in a building that was rustic waterfront—restored red brick and exposed wood beams—next door to the New England Aquarium. Cardinale couldn't even get through explaining his hunch when the other attorneys nearly hooted him out of the room. Mitchell looked at his pal and told him, quit being an asshole. Ken Fishman rolled a piece of paper up into a ball and tossed it at his former partner. No one had ever really talked about Flemmi as being part of the rat pack.

"Everybody had this sense that this guy was different than Bulger. He had been caught, and he was sitting in jail, and he was part of this 'all for one and one for all' defense effort," said Cardinale. "I was convinced otherwise."

During the meeting Cardinale did not even know if Fishman and his client had ever discussed Flemmi's secret double life with the FBI. In fact Fishman was flummoxed hearing Cardinale say he was planning to go after Flemmi. "I don't know that I have reacted so dramatically to anything Tony has ever said in the last twenty years," Fishman said. The other lawyers insisted that Cardinale was misreading the judge and was way out of line.

But Cardinale wanted to prepare them for the possibility he was correct. He told the lawyers he'd already explained his plan to his clients, going over the underlying risk to this roll of the dice: if true, Flemmi might flip and turn against the other defendants in the case. For his own client, Frank Salemme, the potential exposure was limited. "Frank had been in jail for most of the Bulger-Flemmi reign, so Flemmi couldn't give up much as far as Frank was concerned." For the others, however, the risk was real.

The next morning the defense lawyers, their clients, and the prosecuting team led by Wyshak and Paul Coffey of the Justice Department all assembled behind the closed doors of Judge Wolf's courtroom number 5 in the federal courthouse in Post Office Square. "We're here pursuant to my April 14 order, which is under seal," said Wolf from the bench, getting right into it. "I will say that I've closed the courtroom to the public because the matters that we will be discussing will relate to the disclosure to defendants and possible public disclosure of confidential informants."

The judge reviewed Cardinale's motion, mentioning the names Cardinale had included—Bulger, Kenny Guarino, Anthony St. Laurent, and two other underworld figures. The judge paused and looked up from the paperwork.

Then came the question Cardinale had been waiting for.

"Are the defendants interested in knowing about other individuals who might be similarly situated, if those people are indeed confidential informants? Or is it just those five?"

There was silence; all the dark matter that defined the world of Bulger and Flemmi as FBI informants was about to begin to ooze out, like toxic waste that had finally eaten its way through containers meant to seal the poison forever.

"It was a weird moment," recalled Cardinale. The judge, he said, had "a kind of smile on his face. I knew then that my hunch was not just a hunch." Cardinale walked over to his clients, Salemme and DeLuca. The lawyer knew there was no turning back. "I said, 'Listen, we're taking this step now. It could have some very negative impact. This guy could roll.' But their position was, 'Hey, Flemmi can't say anything about me. He'd have to lie, so go on. Do it.'"

Cardinale turned and faced the front of the courtroom. The judge's question was pending: is it just those five?

"As the old saying goes," Cardinale said, "in for a penny, in for a pound, Judge. If there's more, so be it."

"That means you want it?" the judge asked.

"Yes."

■ ■ ■

MINUTES after Cardinale's reply, Wolf retired to his chambers. He ordered Paul Coffey of the Justice Department to come along with him. During the brief recess the judge and the Justice Department official discussed the crossroads the case had reached. Coffey told the judge that "our relationship," meaning the FBI's, was not just with Bulger but included Flemmi too. That was the point, the judge replied. If the judge was going to allow the defense to explore whether any of the evidence was poisoned by the FBI's ties to Bulger, then Flemmi had to be part of that. It made no sense otherwise. (Wolf would later write that the two were "virtual Siamese twins.") Both acknowledged that Flemmi, seated in court, did not seem to realize what was about to occur.

The judge left his chambers and returned to the courtroom, where the lawyers and the defendants had simply sat, waiting. Wyshak and his team tried again to stop Wolf from going any further, insisting that the informant angle Cardinale was pushing was no more than a red herring. Cardinale protested. Wolf called a halt to the debate. "Unless the government objects, I'd like to see Mr. Fishman and Mr. Flemmi in the lobby," the judge decided.

"There's something that's come to my attention that's negative about you," Wolf said to Flemmi as soon as he, Flemmi, and Fishman had sat down in the private chambers. "I'm going to encourage you to think about it."

"That's fine," said the ever-casual Flemmi. No sweat.

Judge Wolf asked Fishman to leave the room. Then he told Flemmi he would have preferred to have Fishman present for their chat, but he didn't know how much information Flemmi had shared with his attorney about his past. Out of caution, the judge said, it was better to talk alone first.

"I just want you to listen to this," Wolf said.

The judge reviewed Cardinale's motion to Flemmi—how Cardinale wanted certain FBI informants identified as part of an effort to challenge the admissibility of the prosecution's case against Frank Salemme and the others. Wolf told Flemmi that, as part of that process, he'd received documents informing him that Bulger—and Flemmi—were indeed informants. Wolf said he was inclined to rule in Cardinale's favor and permit discovery of FBI informant names. In short, the judge was going to require that the FBI disclose publicly its work with Bulger and Flemmi.

"Do you feel comfortable about what we're going to do with this?" Wolf asked after he'd finished his lecture. "Do you feel fear or anything?"

"No. I'm comfortable about my safety," said Flemmi. "I'm not concerned about it at all." But inside Flemmi had to be churning, bewildered by this turn of events. Ever since his arrest in early 1995, he'd kept quiet about his secret life with the FBI. He'd viewed his arrest as a mistake, or maybe somehow necessary as a cover to conceal his ties to the FBI, but a charade that would eventually be resolved quickly by Bulger and their friends at the FBI. "I believed that James Bulger would contact the people that would be able to help us because we were involved with the FBI for so many years," Flemmi said later. He was quietly biding his time, remembering that years before, in the 1960s, it had taken Paul Rico and the FBI nearly four years to clean up the murder and bombing charges against him and pave the way for his return from Canada.

Flemmi also realized that the real reason Wyshak was fighting Cardinale about the disclosure of informant identities was not out of any love for him. Wyshak was trying to keep the case clean and straightforward and prevent Cardinale from knocking out *any* evidence. But now the judge was telling him that the fact he was an FBI informant was likely to come out; after all the history between him and Bulger and the FBI, Flemmi felt betrayed. He wasn't alone. Bulger sidekick Kevin Weeks had been serving as a messenger between Flemmi and Connolly, paying Flemmi regular visits in prison. "The information I received from Kevin Weeks from John Connolly was that he was very upset about the situation that Jim Bulger and I were in," Flemmi said.

What about Ken Fishman, Wolf asked. Does your lawyer know about any of this?

"I'll tell him right now," Flemmi answered. "I don't have a problem with that."

"Can I bring him in and do that?"

"Absolutely."

Flemmi, seeming to grow bouncy, complimented Wolf, offering the judge a wiseguy pat on the back. "Your honor, you're getting to the core of the matter. There's no doubt about that. You're right there. If you go a little further, you could get the whole complete story."

Fishman returned, and the judge summarized Flemmi's past, explaining that he'd been given government materials saying Flemmi had been an informant "for many, many years." Paul Coffey of the Justice Department soon returned, saying, "If the court will let me, I'd like to talk to him."

Coffey turned to Flemmi and Fishman. "I'd like an opportunity to sit down with both of you someplace and tell you what I think needs to be done."

"Great," Fishman replied sarcastically. The lawyer was doing his best to keep up appearances. The disclosure was like a sharp jab that had left him stunned, and even though he'd been around long enough not to reveal how shaken he was, his head was swimming. "After twenty-two years as a criminal defense attorney, you have a visceral reaction, a certain inherent distaste for an individual who has chosen to serve as an informant," he said.

The lawyer also knew exactly what angle Coffey was working—exploit the shock of the moment, quickly persuade a "back on his heels" Flemmi to enter the witness protection program, and testify on behalf of the government against the others.

Coffey went ahead and made his pitch. Flemmi curtly said no. "If I was so valuable to you, what am I doing here?" Fishman was trying to shake loose of his own confused feelings. He wanted time alone with his client. He needed to figure out what to do, and he was soon already thinking about a plan that would turn the "negative information" into a positive. Because the government, Fishman could argue, had "authorized" Flemmi and Bulger to commit crimes in a trade for their underworld intelligence, the mobsters could not now stand trial for crimes they were given permission to commit.

It would become known as the "informant defense," and to support his claim Flemmi soon began filing sworn affidavits describing his life with the FBI and the promises he said FBI agents had made to never prosecute him and Bulger.

. . .

ON May 22, culminating the months of closed hearings and the legal papers filed under seal, Judge Wolf granted Cardinale's wish for an open, evidentiary hearing. In a forty-nine-page ruling, Wolf said the purpose of the discovery hearing would be to allow Cardinale and other defense attorneys to question FBI agents and officials about the bureau's relationship with Bulger and Flemmi so that he could decide whether tapes and other evidence should be suppressed. To that end, the judge said he had decided he had to order the Justice Department to disclose publicly whether Bulger, Flemmi, and the other names included in Cardinale's original motion had been in fact "secretly providing information to the government."

The government, noted Wolf, did have other options if it did not want to comply with his order. He acknowledged that his ruling undercut the "generally recognized interest of the government in maximizing the confidentiality of its informants in order to encourage the flow of information from informants." He said that at times the government "elects to dismiss a case rather than confirm or deny the existence of a cooperating individual." But, concluded Wolf, if the government wanted to continue against the Mafia and the Bulger gang, it would have to share its secrets.

Wyshak urged Wolf to reconsider, but the judge said no.

Despite the ruling, this team of prosecutors was not about to drop the case. There was no turning back. The Justice Department therefore decided to go ahead and do what no federal official in Boston had ever done: on June 3, 1997, more than two decades after John Connolly first approached Whitey, it confirmed for the court Bulger's role as a longtime FBI informant.

Paul Coffey uttered the magic words: "I, Paul E. Coffey, being duly sworn, depose and say, that pursuant to this Court's Order of May 22,

1997, I hereby confirm that James J. Bulger was an informant for the Boston Division of the Federal Bureau of Investigation (FBI)." For now, wrote Coffey, the government was only going to name Bulger, and he explained why, in Bulger's instance, the decision was made to break from the strict practice of protecting the confidentiality of informants. Bulger, he wrote, "is accused of leading a criminal enterprise which committed serious violent crimes continuously over many years." It was a crime spree, wrote Coffey, that overlapped with his work as an FBI informant. Moreover, Bulger, as a fugitive, was now trying to escape responsibility for his many alleged crimes. These factors combined to create "unique and rare circumstances," wrote Coffey, which allowed for outing Bulger in order to put him behind bars. "Bulger has forfeited any reasonable expectation that his previous informant status will remain confidential."

The Justice Department obeyed the court order knowing full well that to do so meant allowing Judge Wolf to enter a no-man's-land. The FBI's Bulger files were a place where no independent body—such as a federal court—had ever gone before. None of the prosecutors—nor, for that matter, the defense attorneys—knew the extent of that corruption, but they all had a strong sense that opening up the FBI files would get ugly. Paul Coffey had said as much to the judge as the two men were discussing Cardinale's demands about Bulger and Flemmi: "We see this as a time bomb."

That bomb, after so many years, was about to go off.

CHAPTER TWENTY

The Party's Over

On a rainy winter morning in Boston, January 6, 1998, the judicial excavation into the FBI's ties to Bulger and Flemmi finally began. "We're here today," the judge announced formally in courtroom number 5 in U.S. District Court, to begin "hearings on the motions to suppress certain electronic surveillance and Mr. Flemmi's motion to dismiss based on alleged promises that were made to him."

The lawyers, standing, introduced themselves: Fred Wyshak, Brian Kelly, and Jamie Herbert for the government; Tony Cardinale, Ken Fishman, Martin Weinberg, and Randolph Gioia for the four mobsters. Off to the left side, under the watchful eye of federal marshals, sat the accused: first Frank Salemme, dressed in a gray, double-breasted suit and red tie; then Bobby DeLuca; Stevie Flemmi; and finally, to the left of Flemmi, hitman Johnny Martorano. They sat in silence. No one—not the mobsters, not the lawyers, not the judge, and none of the television, radio, and newspaper reporters who filled the benches in back—had any idea what was to

come. Never before had the matter of the Boston FBI, Whitey Bulger, and
Stevie Flemmi been the grist of open federal court proceedings.

It was now seven months since the government had obeyed the court's
order in June to identify Bulger as an FBI informant. But since that pivotal
moment, weeks and months had come and gone as the judge and the
lawyers prepared for the hearings and argued over their scope and ground
rules. The racketeering case was already almost three years old and still
stuck in its pretrial phase. But by now all the parties had realized that nothing about the case would ever move quickly, as the judge moved ponder-
ously into unknown legal terrain: the backstage, inner workings of the FBI.

In the months leading up to this moment, the Justice Department had
been downloading to defense attorneys hundreds of pages of previously
secret FBI files covering the FBI's history with Bulger and Flemmi.
Cardinale, Fishman, and the others devoured the documents. "We started
to realize there were all kinds of new motions, including government misconduct," said Cardinale. "We began to ask, 'If Flemmi was an informant
for that many years, how in the world can this indictment be any good?'"

For his part, Flemmi, having decided he had nothing more to lose,
began filing sworn affidavits describing juicy details of his double life. It
was the legal equivalent of flirting, revealing selective and sensational examples of FBI protection he claimed went to the heart of "informant defense." In one, Flemmi said that Morris had promised him and Bulger they
could commit any crime "short of murder"; in another, that the FBI regularly tipped them off to other investigations, including the timing of the
1995 racketeering indictment that he was now fighting to get booted out
of court. By year's end Fishman had refined the Flemmi defense, arguing
that Flemmi had been "authorized," mainly by Morris and Connolly, to
commit many of the crimes for which he stood accused. Because the FBI
had promised Flemmi "immunity," he could not now be prosecuted for
those crimes.

Wyshak, meanwhile, had staked out the government's response to the
various disclosures by Flemmi that now regularly made front-page headlines in the city's newspapers. The actions of "rogue agents," Morris and
Connolly, Wyshak argued, should not undermine the racketeering case;
any promises of protection they may have given Bulger and Flemmi were

illegal and therefore could not possibly constitute anything close to legal "authorization." Wrote Wyshak: "Extensive reviews of [FBI informant] files by the parties as well as by the Court have failed to unearth a single shred of objective evidence that Bulger and Flemmi were authorized to commit the crimes alleged in the indictment."

It was a high-wire argument of sorts, as prosecutors sought to protect the evidence against the mobsters but, at the same time, acknowledge the stomach-turning corruption of FBI agents. Then, late in the year, Morris was granted immunity in return for testimony that would buttress the government's point of view; he would confess, on the one hand, to crimes and FBI misconduct, but also testify that Bulger and Flemmi had never been given any formal immunity.

The two positions were reflected in the opening remarks that winter morning when the Wolf hearings finally began.

"The focus here is on the promises made to my client, Stephen Flemmi, by the FBI," Fishman told the court. "In exchange for his very unique and special cooperation, he would be protected, he would not be prosecuted."

Hogwash, replied Wyshak when his turn came. Bulger and Flemmi had never had any official deal guaranteeing they would not be prosecuted for their crimes. The defense attorneys, said Wyshak, were portraying Flemmi as if he were some kind of "Junior G-man with a license to kill.

"Isn't that preposterous?" mocked Wyshak.

■ ■ ■

BUT of course it wasn't so preposterous after all.

In the months to come Fishman and Cardinale may not have been able to uncover a paper trail showing a formal promise of immunity, but they showed that the Boston FBI was a House of Horrors when it came to Bulger and Flemmi—that agents coddled, conspired, and protected the mobsters in a way that for all practical purposes had given them a license to kill.

Right from the start, Wyshak and Wolf tangled, and the tension between the prosecutor and the judge erupted regularly as Wyshak fought

Wolf on the range of the questions put to government officials and the growing pile of government files that were being unsealed. It wasn't as if Wyshak was trying to cover up FBI corruption—by now he was oversee-ing an active investigation of Connolly and others—but he opposed Wolf's approach to staging a court inquiry that, to Wyshak, seemed with-out limits and restraints.

"You might as well put the whole file in!" Wyshak barked at the judge just two days into the hearings, on January 8. "Why don't you just put the whole file in?"

"Why don't you just sit down, Mr. Wyshak?" Wolf said.

Wyshak would not, and he continued arguing against allowing a new batch of FBI files to be made public.

"Have a seat," Wolf interrupted.

"What is the relevance?"

"Have a seat."

Wyshak remained standing.

"Do you want to be held in contempt? Sit down!"

The hearings lasted most of 1998. The testimony of the 46 witnesses filled 17,000 pages of transcripts, and 276 exhibits—mostly lengthy internal FBI documents—were admitted into evidence. Taking the stand and swearing to tell the whole truth were a former Massachusetts governor and U.S. attorney (William Weld); a sitting Superior Court judge and for-mer protégé of prosecutor Jeremiah T. O'Sullivan (Diane Kottmyer); the three FBI supervisors who ran the Boston office during the Bulger years (Lawrence Sarhatt, James Greenleaf, and James Ahearn); and a long line of federal drug agents, other FBI supervisors, and many of the FBI agents who'd worked alongside Connolly (Nick Gianturco, Ed Quinn, and John Newton). It was a who's who of the federal law enforcement establish-ment, and there was a touch of the surreal as former FBI agents on the witness stand sometimes seemed to mimic tactics usually displayed in court by the gangsters they pursued.

The godfather of the FBI's Organized Crime Squad, Dennis Condon, the retired supervisor who had first matched Connolly, Bulger, and Flemmi together back in the mid-1970s, took the stand in early May and eluded tough scrutiny. The lawyers were hoping he would shed light on the early years of the FBI and Bulger, but Condon pleaded a blank memory. He set the standard for responding, "I don't recall." Even when an attorney showed him an FBI document he'd prepared, Condon would shrug, say he didn't recall writing it, and was therefore unable to elaborate further. Cardinale and the other attorneys were left rolling their eyes, exasperated.

Jeremiah T. O'Sullivan eluded scrutiny altogether. In late February the fifty-six-year-old former prosecutor suffered a heart attack, was hospitalized, and had an adverse reaction to medication. Facing a lengthy rehabilitation, he was spared sharp questioning about removing Bulger and Flemmi from the horse race–fixing case in 1979. O'Sullivan would also have been grilled on claims he'd made publicly and to government investigators that his hands were clean because he'd never even known Bulger and Flemmi were FBI informants. The evidence to the contrary was substantial, and defense attorneys had been eager to put O'Sullivan on the hot seat.

The missing prosecutor quickly became a target of dark courthouse humor. Lawyers and commentators couldn't resist suggesting that the heart attack enabled O'Sullivan to assert a claim many mafiosi had tried to pull off—too ill to testify. In fact a fiery O'Sullivan, back in the mid-1980s, had aggressively fought Mafia enforcer Larry Zannino's medical claim that he was too sick to come to court. The prosecutor forced Zannino to appear, even though he was in full medical regalia, strapped into a wheelchair and breathing from an oxygen tank. Now people began to joke that O'Sullivan had "pulled a Zannino." Though by the end of the hearings O'Sullivan would recover and resume his private law practice at one of the city's prestigious, old-line firms, Choate Hall and Stewart, the man who for sixteen years had fought the Boston Mafia never once took the stand.

Theresa Stanley was granted immunity and compelled to testify about her life with Whitey Bulger—and his getaway when the 1995 indictment came down. In a soft voice, the blue-eyed fifty-seven-year-old, with snow-white hair and dressed in an orange floral top and black slacks, described how she and Whitey had been an item for nearly three decades. She'd cooked dinner for Bulger at her South Boston home nearly every night, and he'd spent most holidays with her family. Stanley spoke about mysterious trips to Europe. She didn't ask Bulger why they were just moving about, because such questions always ended in an argument. She recalled their hasty drive around the country—to Long Island, to New Orleans, where they spent New Year's Eve, to Graceland in Memphis, and to the Grand Canyon. Bulger made lots of calls from pay phones, but she didn't ask who he was talking to or what the calls were about. Stanley also testified that Bulger ultimately abandoned her for the much younger Catherine Greig, who he'd been seeing secretly for twenty years.

"He was leading a double life with me," a spurned Stanley concluded, "and a double life with the FBI."

Unsealed in court were FBI reports revealing that Flemmi had ratted on Salemme for three decades. Flemmi was quoted in one FBI report as calling Frank Salemme "a jerk." After hearing this, Frank Salemme moved, making sure DeLuca sat between himself and Flemmi. Cadillac Frank's affection for Stevie evaporated; indeed, Salemme became "just sickened by the sight of him," Cardinale concluded. The FBI files also clearly showed that Bulger and Flemmi had informed on Howie Winter and other Winter Hill gangsters, including Johnny Martorano, who, like Salemme, began pulling away from Flemmi in the courtroom.

Throughout, Flemmi tried to keep up his game face, coached that his only hope for freedom was to have all this surface to prove the FBI had promised not to prosecute him.

"To be in court every day with a smile on his face," Cardinale remembered, "it's crazy. I mean, one day I just got through telling the judge what a murderous piece of crap I thought he was, and he called me over. I thought he was going to say something to me, like, you know, 'Don't you ever say things like that about me again.' He calls me over and he says, 'Jesus, you're doing a great job.' It's like, whoa! That's all I can think: I-yi-yi-yi-yi. I mean, it's not even registering here. I had just literally gotten through saying he'd killed, you know, Halloran, that he'd done all kinds of horrendous, diabolical, murderous things, and I thought, Ohmygod, I went too far, he's going to say something, and he says, 'Look, you're doing a good job.'"

■ ■ ■

THE unfolding debacle for the FBI hit rock bottom when John Morris walked into court and began testifying on April 21. In the months leading up to the hearings, Morris had negotiated immunity with the prosecutors for the crimes he'd committed. During the private debriefing with FBI agents and prosecutors that accompanied those negotiations, he wept. He'd thrown his career away by getting too close to Bulger, and he knew it. Now on the witness stand for eight grueling days, a wasted Morris sought to project the composed manner of an aging monsignor as he matter-of-factly described his descent from agent to liar and criminal, confessing to taking Bulger's money and obstructing justice by warning Bulger about investigations.

Going back to the 1970s, when the unholy alliance was forged, Morris recalled a "time frame" of "intense pressure on agents to have informants" against the Mafia. "There was a lot of pressure," he testified. He talked about how he teamed up with John Connolly and, together, they rode Bulger and Flemmi to stardom in the Boston FBI office as the master agents in the war against the Mafia, even if, in truth, the ride was a free fall into hell. Morris rued the day he hitched his star to Bulger, Flemmi, and Connolly and ended his professional life in Boston in fear of both Bulger and Connolly—Whitey because of his hold on him through the $7,000 in bribes he'd taken, and Connolly because of his network of political allies, most notably Billy Bulger.

Despite a relentless effort by defense attorneys to get Morris to concede that he'd promised Bulger and Flemmi immunity from prosecution, Morris disagreed. He admitted he'd leaked investigations, but that hardly constituted a grant of immunity. He testified he didn't have the authority as a supervisor to confer immunity on the mobsters. "Immunity was a very formal process, and there's actual documentation," he said. There was none for Bulger.

Toward the end Morris began to wobble. Following questions about yet another instance where his shady work with Bulger may have cost a man his life, one of the defense attorneys suddenly departed from the set sequence of questions. Turning to Morris, the lawyer catapulted to a higher meaning, demanding to know what Morris could have been thinking all these years: did the FBI's crusade against the Mafia justify the Bulger evil? "Do you agree that your conduct as an FBI agent in connection with Mr. Bulger and Mr. Flemmi was consistent with that concept, that the end justifies the means?" Brought up short, Morris sagged noticeably, and he struggled to regain his monsignor's placid demeanor. He sighed and looked sadly off to the side.

"I'm not certain of that," he testified softly.

By the end there was nothing left except for Morris to acknowledge the part he'd played in all that had gone wrong. Urged by defense attorneys to explain "more fully for us" how he was compromised, Morris said that he "had violated standards, integrity, rules, regulations." Was John Connolly part of that process of compromise?

"I felt that he participated in it," Morris replied, "but I accept responsibility for my own actions."

■ ■ ■

THE shocking confessions made headlines, and about this same time John Connolly began to speak out—not in court but outside of court to reporters. From the sidelines the retired agent, now fifty-seven and still working as a lobbyist for Boston Edison, began offering sound bites to rebut the testimony given under oath before Judge Wolf. Each time a retired agent or government official took the stand and provided testimony that in any way criticized him, Connolly would sound off and call the witness a liar. So, for example, when retired FBI supervisor Robert Fitzpatrick testified that agents complained about Connolly "rifling" their files to find out what they had on Bulger, Connolly reacted, "That's ludicrous." Connolly angrily told reporters that Fitzpatrick's testimony was nothing more than "unmitigated nonsense."

The list of "liars" grew and grew. But Connolly saved his best lines for Morris, whom he began calling "the most corrupt agent in the history of the FBI." Each day after Morris finished testifying, Connolly would condemn his former friend and supervisor. Morris may have only met with Connolly, Bulger, and Flemmi a dozen times over the years—while Connolly saw the mobsters hundreds of times—but Connolly insisted that he himself was a model FBI agent who'd never broken a single rule. All of Morris's wrongs, said Connolly, "he did that on his own."

Talking about the difficulty of the job he'd performed so well, Connolly said that handling informants was "kind of like a circus," and "if the circus is going to work you need to have a guy in there with the lions and tigers.

"That was me. I was no John Morris, back in the office with a number 2 lead pencil. My job was to get in there with the lions and tigers. And I am no liar like Morris."

Near the end of Morris's testimony Connolly even made a brief court appearance. Having teamed up with a prominent defense attorney, R. Robert Popeo, Connolly strode into the courthouse in an expensively tailored suit and brushed past throngs of TV cameras and reporters saying he wanted to clear his name. He was a hero, not a villain, and now this band of prosecutors led by Fred Wyshak was out to bust him. He'd become the government's scapegoat, a victim of runaway prosecutorial rage, when the truth of the matter was that he was a highly decorated FBI agent who'd done nothing wrong. "The proof is in the pudding," Connolly said, defending the Bulger deal. "Look at the decimated New England Mafia."

Then, standing in court on April 30 before Judge Wolf, the lawyer Popeo explained that unless Connolly was granted immunity from prosecution—like John Morris—he would not let his client testify. He would not allow Connolly to be "blindsided" when the government had made it known that Connolly was under investigation. Connolly then asserted his Fifth Amendment privilege against self-incrimination, walked outside, and resumed a tirade against Morris, who was still inside waiting to wrap up his eight days of testimony.

"I made him look away," Connolly said of Morris. "He couldn't even look me in the face."

The Connolly sideshow continued into the summer, and a pattern developed: an affronted Connolly would issue heated public denials to any witness's incriminating words. He disputed most of former supervisor Jim Ring's testimony, particularly Ring's account of the concerns he'd had for the "stupid" way Connolly met Bulger and Flemmi for dinner. Connolly wasn't the only one in denial. Billy Bulger, now retired from politics and the president of the University of Massachusetts, joined the Connolly chorus after Ring in court told about Billy Bulger dropping in on one meeting. "I never met the man," Billy Bulger said about Ring. "It never took place, but the business of denying such things is to make it appear as if something sinister had happened."

By midsummer Massachusetts representative Martin T. Meehan announced plans to hold congressional hearings into the FBI's long affair with Bulger, saying the revelations tumbling out in the federal courthouse in Boston raised concerns about "establishing, maintaining, and monitoring relationships between agents and informants." But like much of the nation's business during late 1998, the inquiry was soon pushed aside by President Clinton's impeachment.

Eventually the Wolf hearings even changed locations, from the building in Post Office Square, which had housed the federal court for sixty-five years, to a new $220 million facility overlooking Boston Harbor, an area known as Fan Pier, right in South Boston.

The hearings were shut down for a recess in July, and by the time they resumed in early August a key participant was absent. Frank Salemme took his seat next to Bobby DeLuca, and next to DeLuca sat Stevie Flemmi. But Johnny Martorano was gone. He'd heard more than he could take. He'd sat grim-faced as agents, cops, and officials testified about Bulger's deal. He'd listened to how the FBI protected Bulger and Flemmi from the 1979 horse race–fixing case while the rest of the gang, including Martorano, were indicted. He'd learned that after fleeing to avoid arrest and living on the lam in Florida for more than a decade, he'd been found by the FBI because Bulger and Flemmi told the agency where he was. Disgusted, Martorano agreed to cooperate with prosecutors against Bulger and Flemmi. Quietly, he was moved out of cellblock H-3 in the Plymouth County Correctional Facility on Thursday, July 20, 1998, where he'd been kept along with the others, and was ushered to a secret "safe house" for a debriefing. Martorano was busy telling investigators about the murders that he, Bulger, and Flemmi had committed that had long gone unsolved. The defection shook up Flemmi.

Nevertheless, even after months of the FBI testimony, the colorful

Connolly sideshow, and the sharp reversal by Martorano, only when Stevie Flemmi took the witness stand did the lengthy hearings finally reach a climax. His back against the wall, he'd launched the "informant defense," and he had to persuade Judge Wolf that the government had promised not to prosecute him. It was tricky business whenever a criminal defendant took the witness stand, and in these pretrial hearings Flemmi and Fishman wanted Flemmi to go into deep detail about his deal with the FBI while avoiding admissions to any crimes—except crimes he insisted were approved by the FBI.

■ ■ ■

FLEMMI usually wore a black-and-white nylon jogging suit to court. But on the day he took the stand, August 20, 1998, the bespectacled crime boss wore a crisp white shirt and maroon tie under a gray, herringbone sport jacket.

"Mr. Flemmi, it may be easier if you pick that microphone up a little," the judge instructed a few minutes after Flemmi had begun his testimony.

Flemmi adjusted the mike. "How's that, Judge?"

"And pull the seat a little closer."

Ken Fishman, handling Flemmi carefully, opened right where it mattered most to the defense—at the dinner at John Morris's house in the spring of 1985, during which, Flemmi said, Morris had promised that the gangsters could freely commit any crime "short of murder." Fishman walked Flemmi through his history of the work he and then Bulger did with Paul Rico, John Connolly, John Morris, and Jim Ring. Throughout, Flemmi, at Fishman's encouragement, emphasized the protection the FBI promised—a central tenet to the deal from day one.

"It was one of our themes: how much protection do we have? We've always stressed that, and they've always answered that in the affirmative, that we were protected, we wouldn't be prosecuted," Flemmi said just minutes into his first day on the witness stand. "We insisted on it. We wouldn't be involved if we weren't protected. It's common sense. I wasn't proud of it, and I wanted assurances. And with that I can speak for Mr. Bulger."

There were times when Flemmi even waxed patriotic. "I believe I was performing a service for the United States government in my role as an informant," he told Fred Wyshak once the prosecution's turn came to ask the questions. Flemmi said he and Bulger had helped the FBI "to destroy the LCN, and I believed whatever I was doing I was doing in the interest of the United States government."

The government's chief prosecutor winced.

"Do you think it was in the interest of the United States government to control the flow of drugs into South Boston?" he asked. "Is that what you think, Mr. Flemmi?"

"I'll assert the Fifth on that."

Wyshak was no friend of Flemmi's. The two sparred for hours over Flemmi's "public service" as an informant.

"You had a good deal going," chided Wyshak, pushing Flemmi to cut the phony high-minded spin. "You were committing crimes at will, putting money in your pockets, and, in your view, being protected from prosecution?"

FLEMMI: You're forgetting one thing, Mr. Wyshak. The LCN was taken down. That was their [FBI's] main goal. They were completely satisfied with that. We fulfilled our bargain.

WYSHAK: Did you think, Mr. Flemmi, that you and Mr. Bulger single-handedly took the LCN down?

FLEMMI: I'll tell you something, Mr. Wyshak, we did a hell of a job.

WYSHAK: That's what you think?

FLEMMI: I think we did. The FBI thought we did.

WYSHAK: And when the FBI did that, you and Mr. Bulger were top dog in town, weren't you?

FLEMMI: I'll assert the Fifth on that.

WYSHAK: And that was really your goal throughout this entire period, was to gain control of criminal activities in Boston? Isn't that true, Mr. Flemmi?

FLEMMI: We had formed a partnership, the FBI and I. How we benefited from it with their assistance or with their okay—yes, we did all right.

There were even times when Flemmi got mixed up—especially about whether he was supposed to view the leaks he'd gotten from FBI agents as either legal or illegal acts. The leaks, he argued, were proof of his claim of

FBI protection. But would it matter to Judge Wolf if the leaking were illegal? Flemmi more than once wasn't sure what position to stake out. At one point Wyshak was pushing Flemmi on the range of services Connolly provided Bulger and Flemmi—from warning the crime bosses about wiretaps to burying complaints against them, such as the extortion of Stephen and Julie Rakes—when the prosecutor suddenly asked: "You knew Mr. Connolly was breaking the law in his relationship with you, didn't you?"

FLEMMI: Yes.

WYSHAK: In fact, do you know Stephen Rakes—Stippo?

FLEMMI: I'll assert the Fifth on that.

WYSHAK: Well, you told us that—

FLEMMI: Excuse me, Mr. Wyshak. I just wanted to clarify one thing, when you asked me a question about did I know he was breaking the law. As far as I'm concerned, everything he was doing was legal—illegal—excuse me, legal.

WYSHAK: Now you're saying you didn't know he was breaking the law?

FLEMMI: No. I'm saying that everything that I believe he did, he as far as —it was consistent with his job. He was protecting us.

WYSHAK: Did you think it was consistent with his job to violate the law, yes or no?

FLEMMI: Whatever he was doing was legal.

WYSHAK: It was legal to tip you off on investigations?

FLEMMI: That's correct.

Most of the time Flemmi had kind words for John Connolly, but he did express disappointment that Connolly had neither gotten him out of the current fix immediately following his arrest nor taken the witness stand during the hearings to defend their deal.

FLEMMI: He should be up here testifying on our behalf.

WYSHAK: So .... he's committed the cowardly act?

FLEMMI: Obviously—that he's not here. I feel he should be here.

WYSHAK: So you feel he's betrayed you also?

FLEMMI: I feel that we've been abandoned.

WYSHAK: Because if what you're saying is true, he would have been knocking on the U.S. attorney's door on day one, isn't that true, Mr. Flemmi?

FLEMMI: He should be.

WYSHAK: Should have been knocking on my door and saying: "Hey, Fred, you made a mistake; this guy has immunity?"

The prosecutor's near-constant mockery notwithstanding, the bottom line of Flemmi's ten days of testimony, covering the career criminal's murky collusion with the FBI, was that an FBI promise to protect was a covenant in perpetuity. Flemmi felt that he "would be protected for crimes past, present, and future." If nothing on FBI paper existed to codify the deal, no matter. "We had a gentleman's agreement," he said about the arrangement he and Bulger had with Connolly, Morris, and the other agents.

"We shook hands. To me, that was an agreement."

Perhaps the most dramatic moment came when Flemmi was asked if he'd been tipped to flee just before his indictment in 1995. With a sly smile, Flemmi replied, "That's the big question, I guess." Despite the torrent of evidence that pointed to John Connolly, Flemmi tried to convince the judge that John Morris was the one who obstructed justice by leaking a grand jury indictment. Flemmi apparently hoped this feeble scenario might lure Connolly to the witness stand to back his claim to an immunity defense. But many in the courtroom rolled their eyes. The most visible disbelief came from codefendant Frank Salemme. Until then, despite the close quarters in court and in prison, Salemme had managed to keep his deepening disdain for Flemmi in check during his week on the stand. Salemme had even weathered Flemmi's denial that he was the one who ratted to the FBI Salemme's New York location when he was arrested back in 1972.

But the Morris story was too much to bear. Salemme viewed it not only as a farce but as a threat to the immunity defense that could benefit all the defendants, not just Flemmi. In a game within a game, Flemmi looked to be currying favor with Connolly by protecting him. It put Salemme over the edge. During a break Salemme's suppressed ire flared in the court's holding cell. He went after the smaller Flemmi, lifting him up and screaming in his face. "You piece of shit," he shouted. "You've fucked me all my life, and now you're screwing everyone around you. You're scum, and you're gonna die." Bobby DeLuca jumped in between the former partners in crime and broke it up. Salemme abruptly walked away from Flemmi and never spoke to him again.

■ ■ ■

THE hearings seemed to lose steam once the drama of Flemmi's testimony ended. More FBI agents were among the remaining witnesses, including experts testifying about the FBI's guidelines for handling informants. Debbie Noseworthy—who was now Debbie Morris—appeared briefly to corroborate John Morris's account of the day John Connolly gave her $1,000 of Bulger's money for plane fare. But the remaining witnesses were anticlimactic compared to the sight of a mob boss of Flemmi's stature testifying in federal court. By October the months of testimony were winding down, and everyone had pretty much had their say.

Except John Connolly.

Thinking Judge Wolf was done, he launched a media blitz to rehabilitate a reputation that for months had taken a beating. Though he had been talking sporadically to reporters during the hearings, Connolly wanted the last word. He appeared on talk radio, on television, and as a centerpiece in magazines he'd selected to grant interviews. Each interview and article was friendly and supportive, a chance for Connolly to sound off virtually unchallenged. The headline on the cover story of the October 27 issue of the *Boston Tab* boldly announced: "Connolly Speaks Out," and the cover featured a large photograph of John Connolly, dressed in his trademark tailored suit and wearing sunglasses, standing outside 98 Prince Street, the former Mafia headquarters. The meaning of the photo was clear: here was the G-man who took out the Mafia. "I'm Proud of What I Did," screamed another headline, in bold print. But no interview was more fawning than the one Connolly had on WRKO-AM during the afternoon of Saturday, October 24, 1998. The host, Andy Moes, announced at the start that Connolly was an old friend, "a fine son of South Boston," and "a man I know to be an honorable and decent man." Then came Moes's breathless ode to Connolly.

MOES: Man, oh man. What has happened? Last time your name came up it was hero John Connolly. I've only heard your name referred to as, like, Prince of the City. Every supervisor, everybody I know who knows you in the FBI talks about what an incredibly smart, streetwise agent John Connolly was. John Connolly did the impossible. He was able to break through and literally bring down La Cosa Nostra to their knees in Boston, something the bureau was very proud of. And happy to take credit for. Those were the last stories I heard about John Connolly. All of a sudden, I'm hearing whispers, and they are whispers, that are done in back rooms, quietly: "He's a rogue agent, you know. He was a rogue agent." You a little tired of hearing that? You a little sick and tired of having people assassinate your character?

CONNOLLY: It's wearing a little thin.

Like a politician, Connolly had certain "talking" points he seemed to want to get across each time he was interviewed: that he'd never done anything wrong in handling Bulger and Flemmi; that the crime bosses were merely a "gang of two" who helped the FBI take out the Boston branch of an international criminal organization; that Bulger and Flemmi did have permission from the FBI to commit certain crimes—gambling and loan-sharking—while gathering intelligence; that John Morris was "an evil guy"; and that prosecutors Wyshak, Kelly, and Herbert had no business indicting the FBI's informants back in 1995. Connolly called the prosecutors "cowards" who violated the FBI's promise—and most important, Connolly's promise—not to go after Bulger and Flemmi. "I never would have given my word to anyone had I ever thought there was a chance that the government would break it," Connolly told Moes, his voice slowing to a crawl to put extra emphasis on his words. "They broke their word," he growled. "Shame on them, the prosecutors here. But they had no right to break *my* word."

By this time John Connolly had emerged as the kind of quintessential public figure for the 1990s, a decade increasingly obsessed with style and celebrity. It was as if Connolly had decided that if he self-assuredly proclaimed himself the true hero in the story—and he made this swaggering claim unabashedly, even tenaciously—then it would be true. Forget about the mountain of evidence before Judge Wolf and the hours of incriminating testimony. And for the most part Connolly did have his way during his media blitz. Just about the only bump in the road he encountered, albeit briefly, was a question posed by Peter Meade of WBZ-AM, who stopped Connolly to ask about an FBI actually condoning violence.

MEADE: Isn't violence an inherent part of loan-sharking?

CONNOLLY: Well, uh. Not really. I mean, loan-sharking? Yeah, I mean, you know, violence is an explicit part of loan-sharking. Uhh. If someone doesn't pay you, people hurt them. But, um, they, the deal with these two individuals and anyone else was—no violence. No murders. No violence.

During the blizzard of interviews Connolly piled up public relations points. He even turned up his rhetoric about the ongoing hearings before Judge Wolf. During most of the year he'd taken the position that, as much as he wanted to tell his side, he couldn't testify without immunity, not when the prosecutors had him under investigation. But now that the hearings seemed to be over, Connolly was saying, immunity be damned—he didn't want it, he didn't need it. "I do not need immunity for corrupt acts," he told the *Boston Tab*. "I did not commit corrupt acts. I would refuse immunity for those reasons. I don't need it.

"They can stick it," he added.

The overheated talk proved to be a misstep.

Both the defense attorneys and the prosecutors suddenly asked Judge Wolf to summon Connolly back to court, now that he was repeatedly saying that he no longer wanted immunity. It was one of those rare instances when Cardinale and Wyshak agreed. "It's time to put Mr. Connolly's feet to the fire on this issue," Cardinale told the judge. Wyshak's colleague Jamie Herbert noted that during the media interviews Connolly "has lied about what takes place in this courtroom and outside this courtroom."

The lawyers had called Connolly's bluff, and on the morning before Halloween, October 30, John Connolly returned to federal court, his lawyer Robert Popeo at his side. The broad-shouldered Connolly cut a striking pose on the witness stand. He wore a dark, fitted suit, a smart-looking yellow silk tie, and a white handkerchief was neatly arranged in his breast pocket. His hair appeared recently cut and styled.

Tony Cardinale cut right to the chase.

"Mr. Connolly, in 1982, did you give any cash to an FBI secretary named Debbie Noseworthy, now Debbie Morris?"

Cardinale was looking to provoke Connolly. "I was hoping his arrogance would get the better of him," he said later. He wanted an angered Connolly to blurt out a denial—no, he had not delivered Bulger's money to Morris! "Then *boom*—there would have been an instant indictment for perjury," said Cardinale. "It would have made my day, after what he's done to my client and to so many other people in his so-called role as a defender of the law."

The two men locked eyes, and the question that Cardinale had asked in his baritone voice echoed in the courtroom. Then Connolly shifted in his seat and removed a card from the pocket of his suit. He held the card in his right hand, delicately between the tips of his index and middle fingers.

"Upon advice of counsel, I respectfully decline to answer at this time and rely upon my rights under the United States Constitution not to give testimony against myself."

CARDINALE: On April 30 of 1998, as the Court has pointed out, Mr. Connolly, you appeared before the Court and refused to answer questions, asserting your Fifth Amendment privilege, is that correct?

CONNOLLY: That's correct.

CARDINALE: Since that time, you've been interviewed by a number of media representatives . . . have you not?

CONNOLLY: Upon advice of counsel, I repeat. . . .

Cardinale did not let up, firing off a string of questions: have you personally committed any criminal offenses with regard to any promise made to Mr. Bulger and Mr. Flemmi? Did you at any time give Mr. Morris around Christmas a box of wine containing $1,000? Did you warn Mr. Bulger and Mr. Flemmi of any existing investigative efforts that were targeting them? Did you know an individual by the name of Brian Halloran?

Each time, Connolly took the Fifth.

Then prosecutor Jamie Herbert had a turn.

HERBERT: Good morning, Mr. Connolly.

CONNOLLY: Good morning.

HERBERT: Mr. Connolly, you know what the term "bribery" means?

CONNOLLY: I assert my Fifth Amendment rights.

HERBERT: Mr. Connolly, you have told at least three different versions of this supposed deal that you had with Mr. Bulger and Mr. Flemmi, isn't that correct?

CONNOLLY: I assert my Fifth Amendment rights.

HERBERT: Mr. Connolly, in all your years with the FBI working with Mr. Bulger and Mr. Flemmi, did you ever once document this supposed deal anywhere in the FBI files?

CONNOLLY: I assert my Fifth Amendment rights.

Inside of twenty minutes, Connolly took the Fifth nearly thirty times to the questions posed by Cardinale and Herbert. The judge broke off the give-and-take, ruling that the exercise was fruitless, that Connolly had not changed his mind and decided to testify without immunity. Robert Popeo told the judge his client was asserting the Fifth at his insistence, particularly "in light of the fact that there are two separate grand juries sitting in which we have been advised by prosecutors that Mr. Connolly is a target." Even if Connolly was speaking boldly outside of court and proclaiming his innocence—a right of free speech under the First Amendment—he was not waiving his rights under the Fifth Amendment against self-incrimination.

"To each and every substantive question put to the witness," said Popeo, "he has been advised to invoke his privilege under the United States Constitution."

The judge excused Connolly. "Mr. Connolly, you may go."

Minutes later Connolly could be found outside the new courthouse on Fan Pier, holding forth to a circle of television cameras and reporters, resuming his bellicose stance toward prosecutors Wyshak, Herbert, and Kelly. He called them "character assassins" hell-bent on singling him out as their scapegoat. But even a renewed attack could not remove the lasting impression of a lackluster John Connolly reading from the Fifth Amendment card he'd just spent weeks telling the world he no longer needed.

■ ■ ■

THEN came the waiting game. In chambers, with the aid of his clerks, Wolf began the task of preparing a ruling, studying the testimony, the exhibits, and the applicable case law. Months passed, and by early 1999 the case had mostly fallen from public view. Occasionally, in other contexts, it popped up. The former U.S. attorney and ex-governor Bill Weld appeared on a radio show in 1998 to promote his first novel and ran into a host who wanted to ask about the Bulger affair with the FBI. Christopher Lydon of WBUR's *The Connection* was incredulous that Weld hadn't done more to dig out the Bulger mess. "Why aren't you more outraged?" challenged Lydon. "Did your friend William Bulger know about it? Did you ever ask him about it?"

The usually garrulous Weld went mum. He replied no, a trace of annoyance in his voice. Lydon kept going, but mostly in monologue. Rather than join in, Weld allowed seconds of silence to fill the radio space. Of particular concern to Lydon was the recent suicide of Billy Johnson, the state trooper who had gotten tough with Whitey Bulger at Logan Airport over smuggled cash and later believed the encounter had cost him his career. "He killed himself!" said Lydon. "A miserable man at the end of a life that he thought had honorably been devoted to law enforcement.

"Where's the outrage?" Lydon asked again.

The tense encounter ended finally, and the two got to talking about Weld's novel. But Weld's reluctance to get into it with Lydon seemed to capture symbolically the reluctance of Weld's generation of Boston law enforcement leaders to ever seriously tackle the Bulger scandal.

By the end of the summer of 1999 word began spreading around town that Wolf, after ten months of rumination and writing, was applying the finishing touches to his ruling. In early August, FBI director Louis Freeh arrived in Boston and, at a press conference, acknowledged publicly that the FBI "made significant mistakes" during the Boston FBI's twenty-year run with Bulger and Flemmi. The admissions were seen as an effort by a publicity-obsessed FBI to take some of the sting out of the upcoming federal court ruling. "We have a lot of mistakes to account for," said Freeh. He promised that corrupt FBI agents from Boston would be brought to justice.

Two weeks later the FBI announced that the fugitive Whitey Bulger was finally being added to its Ten Most Wanted List. The move—more than four years after Bulger fled his 1995 indictment—was seen as long overdue. In the public's mind in Boston, the perception had taken root that the FBI was never really interested in tracking down its former informant.

But now Bulger joined the likes of fugitives Eric Robert Rudolph, a suspect in abortion clinic bombings, and Osama bin Laden, the Saudi terrorism suspect. And he held a distinction all his own: he was believed to be the first FBI informant to ever make the famous top ten list, which had posted 458 fugitives since its inception in 1950. His face would now appear across the country in post offices and federal buildings, on the FBI's web site, and even in a Dick Tracy cartoon as part of an FBI Most Wanted promotion.

In cellblock H-3 three celebrated inmates were also eagerly awaiting the ruling—Frank Salemme, Bobby DeLuca, and Stevie Flemmi. Their high hopes were that the judge would find the evidence so compromised he would throw out the racketeering charges against the group—that Wolf would rule that the FBI had indeed promised blanket immunity for Flemmi and Bulger, and therefore the government could not now violate that immunity and prosecute them.

Ever since their arrest in 1995 the three mobsters had been kept at the Plymouth prison, a modern facility that opened in 1994 and was located forty-eight miles south of Boston. The new facility had been built atop an old landfill in an isolated, unwanted area of the historic community. It was also right off of route 3, a highway connecting Boston to Cape Cod, and Flemmi, from his cell, could hear the hum of freedom in the distance, the cars carrying commuters and vacationers along a route he and Bulger and John Connolly all used to take on their way to the Cape.

The cellblock could hold 140 inmates in 70 cells. It was a large rectangular space constructed as a self-contained "mini-prison," meaning that the inmates spent virtually all of their time on the block and did almost everything there. Meals arrived on wheels from a central prison kitchen, and inmates ate at the tables in the unit's common area. The cellblock had its own showers along one end, its own televisions, and its own pay phones. It was smoke-free. The unit had a "rec deck," a small, outdoor recreation area that opened up off the far end of the unit. The area was essentially a fenced-in cage, but inmates could escape the stale air of the cellblock and get some exercise by going out there. The chin-up bar attached underneath a set of stairs was jokingly called "the gym," and the cart of books positioned against one wall was "the library." Two decks of cells, on a ground floor and a mezzanine level, lined the long walls of the cellblock.

Salemme and DeLuca lived side by side in cells at the far end of one mezzanine level, near the entrance to the rec deck. Flemmi was on his own.

Over time Salemme had emerged as a model inmate and cellblock leader. The guards relied on him. He was given the top cellblock job, a position previously occupied by, of all people, Howie Winter, until Winter was moved out of the unit. Frank was the "meal server": three times a day, while all the other inmates were locked down, he set up the common area for meals. He put ice in the juice pitchers, wiped down the tables, arranged the chairs. No job on the unit carried more responsibility—not cleaning the rec deck, emptying the trash bins, cleaning the showers, or sweeping the tiled floors and the mezzanine walkway. The guards wanted the unit as shiny and clean as a hospital ward, and Frank was the key inmate making that happen. It was a far cry from his old life as a high-rolling gangster, but the job, a way to help pass the days, kept the mobster busy.

DeLuca was not as motivated a worker. His job was sweeping the mezzanine. But like Salemme, he worked out and wanted to stay in shape. He regularly performed chin-ups to keep his upper body hard and muscular. Both watched their diet, especially Salemme, who avoided the high-fat prison offerings and preferred salads and fruits. Salemme also read a lot— boating magazines, Tom Clancy, and Dean Koontz.

Flemmi was another story. During the course of the hearings in court, as the extent of his FBI deal was exposed, Flemmi was pushed further and further to the margins of cellblock life. Inmates did not want to have anything to do with him. He was ostracized—a rat, the lowest form of underworld life. Salemme would not talk to him, would not even look at him. Flemmi sometimes approached DeLuca, but the encounters were curt and brief.

The alienation that came with being a career informant was bad enough, but Flemmi withdrew further into himself the day Johnny Martorano was whisked away to commence cooperating with the prosecutors. The prison guards surely weren't going to miss the hitman. Martorano gave them the creeps—a surly, cold-blooded troublemaker who strutted around the cellblock as if to say: Get out of my way, I'm John Martorano, and I kill people. But Martorano's departure was devastating to Stevie Flemmi. It meant that Martorano was implicating Flemmi and

Bulger in murder—particularly the 1981 assassination of Roger Wheeler. It meant that even if Flemmi's lawyer Ken Fishman succeeded in persuading Judge Wolf to throw out pending racketeering charges, the prosecutors were preparing to come back with a new indictment for murder.

In early September, as everyone was waiting on Judge Wolf, the news broke that Martorano and the government had completed negotiating the terms of a plea bargain for Martorano's testimony. In exchange for a sentence of twelve and a half to fifteen years, Martorano had agreed to plead guilty to twenty murders spanning three decades and three states, including the murder of Roger Wheeler, a killing he claimed was committed on orders from Bulger and Flemmi. "The people he's giving up are people who have enjoyed the protection of the FBI for many years while committing heinous crimes," said David Wheeler, son of the slain Jai Alai executive, voicing support for the hitman's deal.

Flemmi retreated to his prison cell. In cellblock H-3 the former crime boss was shunned, and he spent most of his time alone, seated on his bunk. "Just there," said one guard. "He's like the bag of golf clubs sitting in my closet." Flemmi didn't have a cellblock job to keep him busy. He didn't have anyone to talk to. "He's about as despondent as you can get without going insane," one officer noted. Flemmi rarely, if ever, went out on the rec deck for the fresh air or the sun. It was the eve of one of the most eagerly awaited court rulings in the biggest organized crime case in Boston's history, and Flemmi's face had turned pallid, almost translucent. His skin had turned the color of the prison walls, one guard observed—a ghostly "popcorn white."

■ ■ ■

TONY CARDINALE, the lawyer who had kicked open the Pandora's box hiding the FBI's affair with Bulger and Flemmi, began the day the ruling finally came out with a workout at the Boston Athletic Club. Then he picked up his associate John Mitchell, who'd flown in from New York City, at his hotel. They swung by the courthouse, where a clerk handed the lawyers a box containing seven copies of the ruling. Immediately Cardinale dispatched a messenger to take a copy down to the Plymouth prison for Frank Salemme. Then, huddled in shirtsleeves in Cardinale's office, the Dunkin Donuts coffee and donuts spread out on the desk, the two lawyers opened up the thick ruling and began reading.

Boston Herald columnist Howie Carr would later wisecrack that Mark Wolf must have fashioned himself the Edward Gibbon of New England organized crime, penning *The Rise and Fall of the Bulger Empire:* it ran 661 pages. Cardinale and Mitchell both enjoyed the way Wolf opened his treatise, quoting from Lord Acton. "In 1861," the judge began, "Lord Acton wrote that 'every thing secret degenerates, even the administration of justice.'" To that the judge added: "This case demonstrates that he was right."

The donuts sat uneaten. The lawyers couldn't put the ruling down. The legal part—the immediate impact on the status of the racketeering case—was inconclusive. For example, the judge refused to find that all of the protection the FBI had provided Bulger and Flemmi—much of it illegal—amounted to blanket immunity from prosecution. But he had decided that some of the wiretap evidence was tainted by past FBI promises to Bulger and Flemmi and that those tapes would never be used against them. The judge said he was going to suppress that evidence, and possibly more. With that, the racketeering case seemed to be hanging by a thread. But to reach a final decision on the disputed evidence the judge had decided he would need still more information, drawn from even more pretrial hearings. "In essence," concluded Wolf, "the record for deciding Flemmi's motions to dismiss and suppress is incomplete. Therefore, the court will hold the hearings necessary to determine whether this case must be dismissed and, if not, the scope of the evidence to be excluded at trial." It meant that, for now, the case would go on.

But the legal part of the judge's ruling was not the story of the day. The hard news was the judge's "findings of facts" about the FBI and Bulger and Flemmi. More than half of the text—368 pages—was devoted to factual findings about all that had gone wrong in the FBI's deal with Bulger, judicial findings resulting from sworn testimony and the mountains of FBI documents and files.

The judge acknowledged that Bulger and Flemmi were "very valuable and valued confidential informants" for the FBI, but then proceeded to describe in minute detail the corruption, rule-breaking, and misconduct that

defined the deal, almost from its start three decades earlier. The leaks—
from the Lancaster Street garage to the DEA's car bug to the Baharoian
wire—were all there, along with the long list of tips the crime bosses got
about other wiseguys who posed a threat to them. "In an effort to protect
Bulger and Flemmi, Morris and Connolly also identified for them at least
a dozen other individuals who were either FBI informants or sources for
other law enforcement agencies." The judge cited the Brian Halloran leak
and the fact that, a few weeks after he had talked to the FBI, "Halloran
was killed."

The judge concluded that, to protect Bulger and Flemmi, agents essentially fictionalized the FBI's internal records on a regular basis, both to
overstate their value and to minimize the extent of their criminal activities. The FBI's files showed "recurring irregularities with regard to the
preparation, maintenance, and production in this case of documents damaging to Bulger and Flemmi." And despite Connolly's claims to the contrary, Wolf ruled that the handler did indeed handle Morris's bribe money.
"Morris solicited and received through Connolly $1,000 from Bulger and
Flemmi."

The judge also cleared up some of the smaller details of the sordid saga.
Despite Billy Bulger's public comments to the contrary, the judge ruled that
the powerful politician had in fact made a cameo appearance. "William,
who was the President of the Massachusetts Senate and lived next door to
the Flemmis, came to visit while Ring and Connolly were there."

"Man-o-manischevitz!" Cardinale exclaimed. He and John Mitchell
began a duel of sort, reading passages aloud, each one trying to top the
other with a juicier factual finding.

In all, Wolf identified eighteen FBI supervisors and agents as having
broken either the law or FBI regulations and Justice Department guidelines. Paul Rico, John Connolly, and John Morris were at the hub of the
wrongdoing, and the list included supervisors Jim Greenleaf, Jim Ring,
Ed Quinn, Bob Fitzpatrick, Larry Potts, Jim Ahearn, Ed Clark, and Bruce
Ellavsky, and agents Nick Gianturco, Tom Daly, Mike Buckley, John
Newton, Rod Kennedy, James Blackburn, and James Lavin.

"John Connolly is fucked," said Cardinale, shaking his head, pausing at
the section in Wolf's ruling where he addressed a central question: how

Whitey got away in early 1995. Even though Flemmi had testified that the leak came from Morris, the judge found that Flemmi, while generally truthful in his testimony, was not always "candid" and "at times attributed information received from John Connolly to other agents of the FBI in an evident effort to protect Connolly." Despite Connolly's strident public statements, Wolf had ruled that Connolly was the culprit.

"The court concludes that in early January 1995, Connolly, who remained close to Flemmi and, particularly, Bulger, had been monitoring the grand jury investigation in part through his contacts in the FBI, and was in constant communication with Bulger and Flemmi about the investigation, was the source of the tip to Bulger."

Finally, despite Jeremiah T. O'Sullivan's public comments to the contrary, as well his statement to federal investigators in 1997, the judge ruled that O'Sullivan had known Bulger and Flemmi were informants since 1979.

The ruling exposed the ugly addiction the Boston FBI had for Bulger, and it was not a pretty picture. By sheer coincidence the ruling came out just twelve days after a personal milestone for Whitey Bulger: he turned seventy years old on September 3, 1999. But the 661-page treatise was hardly the sort of birthday greeting he would have wished for. James J. "Whitey" Bulger may still have had his freedom, but there was little else to celebrate.

"Judge Blasts FBI for Deal with Bulger and Flemmi" was the front-page headline in the next day's tabloid *Boston Herald*. "Judge Says Hub FBI Broke All the Rules."

The headlines had captured the moment, and they were headlines that no doubt reached Whitey Bulger himself—out there, somewhere, still on the run, riding the back roads of rural America with a bleached blonde by his side, false papers in his wallet, and packets of $100 bills stashed in safety deposit boxes around the country.

Epilogue

Hi there. So many tough questions for John Connolly, but so little time. Number one, I think there's a number of people lined up to testify that Whitey and Stevie controlled all the cocaine and marijuana in South Boston, and shame on you ... for not going after them on that.

JACK FROM SOUTH BOSTON,
WBZ-AM RADIO, OCTOBER 27, 1998

First, I would like to say to John Connolly, I think you have a lot of courage for standing up to the U.S. Attorney's Office in this case. It's nice to know there's at least one FBI agent out there who will keep his word.

CHRISTINE FROM SOUTH BOSTON,
WBZ-AM RADIO, OCTOBER 27, 1998

Predictably, John Connolly was not happy with Judge Mark L. Wolf's factual findings issued on September 15, 1999. Previously, Connolly had been complimentary toward the judge, as if he were wooing him. On one radio talk show Connolly had referred to Wolf as a jurist "who I believe is a guy who seeks the truth."

But after a ruling that put Connolly in the middle of nearly every instance of FBI wrongdoing, Connolly changed his tune. The former agent was particularly angry that Wolf had pinned on him the 1995 leak of the racketeering indictment.

"I did not tip Bulger, Flemmi, or anyone with respect to the indictment returned by the grand jury in 1995," he said in a prepared statement he issued the night of Wolf's ruling. He said, "Judge Wolf has engaged in irresponsible speculation on a matter involving my integrity."

The rest of the reaction was vintage Connolly: attack the critic personally. The federal judge, Connolly claimed, was retaliating for an old informant report he'd written containing rumors that Wolf once leaked information that ended up in the Mafia's hands when Wolf was a federal prosecutor in the early 1980s. (The report had surfaced during the 1998 hearings and was discredited.) Connolly reached for that small moment in time to explain Wolf's findings: it was payback.

The Wolf findings notwithstanding, Connolly continued to assert his innocence, though more selectively than during his media blitz of 1998. During the fall of 1999 he even sat for a *Dateline NBC* interview, spinning and bragging about all the good he'd done.

But Connolly had more than the judge's findings of fact to worry about. For more than a year he and other former agents (such as Paul Rico) had been targets of a federal grand jury probe into FBI corruption. Then, three days before Christmas, John Connolly was busted. FBI agents showed up at his home in Lynnfield, a suburb north of the city, early in the afternoon. Connolly had stayed home that day with the flu. He was arrested, handcuffed, and taken to the federal courthouse in Boston. He appeared in the courthouse, after dark had fallen, not in a fancy suit but wearing a gray sweatshirt, black jeans, and sneakers. His hair, usually coiffed to perfection, was tussled. It had been a long journey into night, and in some ways, after so much, it ended here. Once upon a time John J. Connolly, Jr. had taken an oath to uphold the law. What happened was closer to a holdup.

In a five-count indictment, Connolly, Bulger, and Flemmi were charged with racketeering, racketeering conspiracy, conspiracy to obstruct justice, and obstruction of justice. In the government's seventeen-page filing, Connolly was charged with acting as the middle man for the $7,000 in bribes to John Morris, with regularly falsifying reports to cover up Bulger's crimes, and with illegally leaking to Bulger and Flemmi confidential information about grand jury probes and wiretaps. Included in the leak charges was Connolly's tip-off to Whitey about the 1995 indictment so that Bulger could flee and start a fugitive life.

In court Connolly pleaded innocent and was released on $200,000 bail. Prosecutors mentioned that the investigation was continuing, and it was widely reported that the focus of the ongoing probe was the role that FBI agents might have played in the murder of those men, like Brian Halloran and John McIntyre, who had posed a risk to Bulger and Flemmi's hege-mony. In launching the probe, Attorney General Janet Reno had gone out-side the incestuous Boston law enforcement community. Overseeing the corruption case was veteran Connecticut federal prosecutor John Durham. Durham had assembled a team of investigators from around the country, and they began the process of trying to figure out how every-thing had gone so wrong.

■ ■ ■

MEANWHILE, a number of major developments during the autumn of 1999 contributed to the great undoing of the Bulger years.

The John Martorano deal went public in late September when Martorano walked into court and calmly admitted to killing ten people as the key hitman for Bulger's gang. In exchange for his confession—and his testimony against Bulger, Flemmi, and FBI agents—prosecutors recom-mended he receive a fifteen-year prison sentence. The plea bargain proved controversial, with some appalled at the apparently light sentence for a cold-blooded killer. U.S. attorney Donald Stern conceded that cutting deals with killers was "distasteful" but argued that it would have been even more distasteful *not* to have made the deal to get more evidence against bosses Bulger and Flemmi. Martorano implicated Bulger in three of the murders and Flemmi in half a dozen.

Then, in early December, Cadillac Frank Salemme bailed. He pled guilty to racketeering charges that he'd run a joint venture with the Bulger gang to control the Boston underworld. In return, prosecutors agreed to drop murder charges against him. The deal did not require Salemme to testify, but Salemme voluntarily appeared before the Connolly grand jury to testify against the former agent. Wyshak and Cardinale jointly filed a sentencing recommendation that Salemme serve from ten to thirteen years. It meant that Salemme would be free in about six years, since he got credit for the five years he'd spent behind bars since his arrest in 1995. Judge Wolf accepted the plea bargain on February 23, 2000. "He's tired of fighting," Cardinale said afterward, adding that his client also wanted to get away from Flemmi. "Frank doesn't want to be next to Flemmi for another second, never mind another two years." Flemmi's attorney Ken Fishman sought to put the best face on the plea: "As far as we're concerned, we're happy to have the courtroom to ourselves."

. . .

BULGER'S in absentia foothold on the city continued its rapid erosion with the indictment of two key lieutenants. The "two Kevins," forty-three-year-old Kevin Weeks and fifty-one-year-old Kevin O'Neil, were charged with racketeering and shaking down drug dealers and bookies for more than two decades. The indictment also put both men alongside Bulger and Flemmi in the takeover of the Rakeses' liquor store and the extortion of Raymond Slinger. It cited O'Neil as the longtime operator of Triple O's, which one columnist had nicknamed the "Bucket of Blood." It accused Weeks of carrying out Bulger's commands in the daily operation of the gang's criminal activities as Bulger found ways to keep in touch by using calling cards to reach Weeks at the businesses and homes of friends.

Initially, Kevin Weeks kept up the bounce and bluster he'd displayed publicly as a supreme Bulger loyalist. He'd been a man about the neighborhood, even appearing in a tuxedo for the Oscar party in 1998 to honor the nomination of the set-in-Southie film *Good Will Hunting* at the L Street Tavern. Standing by him at his arraignment on November 18 was lawyer Tom Finnerty, Billy Bulger's old friend and former law partner. Weeks pleaded not guilty, and on his way out of the courtroom he turned to columnist Howie Carr of the *Boston Herald*. "Be kind, Howie. Be gentle."

In a matter of days Weeks was a different man. He'd never in his life faced serious criminal charges like this—racketeering, extortion, loansharking, drug trafficking, with murder charges probably in the offing. Finnerty was soon gone, replaced by another lawyer. Then word spread that Weeks was talking.

The morning of January 14, 2000, the city awoke to news reports that state police had spent one of the coldest nights of the winter digging up the remains of two men and a woman stacked in a makeshift grave in Dorchester. Kevin Weeks, looking now to cut a deal for leniency but first having to demonstrate his bona fides, had pinpointed the burial site in the gully across from a popular meeting hall, down an embankment from the Southeast Expressway. By daylight, TV camera crews and reporters circled the troopers' big dig about eight feet under to recover the remains. The site was once a mostly marshy area, located conveniently right off the routes that Bulger and Flemmi drove between Southie and Quincy.

Based on dental records, one of the bodies was soon identified as John McIntyre. The parking lot where McIntyre's abandoned truck and wallet had been found the day he disappeared in 1984 was less than a mile from the burial ground. Though not positively identified, the other bodies were believed to be Deborah Hussey, missing since the fall of 1984, and Arthur "Bucky" Barrett, the safecracker who disappeared in 1983.

For the victims' families, the discovery brought some relief. For investigators, having Weeks turn on Bulger was like holding a stake to drive into the gang's heart. Negotiations continued in secret regarding Weeks's deal; in the street Whitey's surrogate son acquired a nickname to play off how long it had taken him to fold: "Two Weeks."

■ ■ ■

BY early 2000 John Morris had moved on to Florida after losing his job with an insurance company in Tennessee. He occasionally flew to Boston to appear before the ongoing grand jury. Jeremiah T. O'Sullivan and Jim Ring continued working together at the Boston law firm of Choate Hall and Stewart. Bill Bulger continued in his second career as president of the University of Massachusetts. Though his appointment by then-governor Weld was at first controversial, Bulger generally has won passing grades for his stewardship of the state university.

The Boston FBI office had become the most heavily investigated field office in the bureau's history. Retired and current FBI agents grew defensive and weary, wondering, who's next? Paul Rico? Dennis Condon? Both were under the intense scrutiny of the ongoing grand jury overseen by prosecutor Durham, along with a number of other agents, such as Mike Buckley and Nick Gianturco. Connolly's pal John Newton was notified that he was going to be fired for allegedly lying to protect Connolly during court hearings in 1998 before Judge Wolf. Newton pledged through his lawyer to fight the move.

Beyond the bureau, the city continued to assess the damage and to ask what went wrong. Was it two guys from the projects—Connolly and Bulger—whose loyalty to one another outweighed everything else? Deeply flawed government oversight? Man's capacity for evil and self-deception? Probably all of the above. The Bulger harm had certainly been felt in ways immeasurable and difficult to quantify. There were some who felt that the corruption had seeped not only into the heart of Southie and the FBI, but into almost everything—the State House, law enforcement, and public life.

The writer James Carroll, winner of the National Book Award and a regular columnist for the *Boston Globe,* identified a "moral blindness" at work when it came to the Bulger brothers in a column written in late 1999.

For many years, large parts of the Massachusetts political establishment willingly winked at the savage behavior of James Bulger, and that succession of winks eventually became a pervasive moral blindness. The explicitly expressed tolerance for James Bulger polluted not only law enforcement but government itself, fueling public cynicism, spreading fear, and turning the public sector into a murderer's accomplice.

Obviously all of this is tied to the role of James Bulger's brother William Bulger, the former Senate president. No one can lay the crimes of James Bulger at his brother's feet, and no one can fault William Bulger for his expressions of brotherly love despite everything. But the former Senate president went much further than that. It was his winking at the exploits of James Bulger that sponsored everyone else's.

"In the magical curl of William Bulger's wit," wrote Carroll, "James Bulger emerged as a figure of fun."

Carroll singled out the annual St. Patrick's Day breakfasts that Billy hosted, in particular the one in 1995—just two months after Whitey got an FBI tip and hit the road—when then-governor Weld sang a "ditty" he had

composed to the gathering of public leaders that included both U.S. senators from Massachusetts and the city's mayor. "Weld's song was to the
tune of 'Charlie on the MTA,'" Carroll reported, "and once again it was
about the killer. 'Will he ever return?' Weld sang. 'No, he'll never return.
No, he'll never come back this way. I just got a call from the Kendall
Square Station. He's with Charlie on the MTA!' The gang loved it, but
imagine how pleased James Bulger's tipster must have been."

> Weld, in these instances, provides a measure of the depth of this corrup-
> tion. He had served, after all, as a U.S. attorney, with direct knowledge of
> James Bulger's crimes. A wink from him could make even the most com-
> promised FBI agent relax, and it could enable so many others to stifle their
> misgivings and sign on to this deadly arrangement.
>
> James Bulger, still at large, is an embarrassment to the FBI. He is a dan-
> ger to the public. And in the way in which his fate became entangled with
> his brother's and in the way they then used each other to advance their sep-
> arate agendas, the entire story remains a mark on the soul of the
> Commonwealth.

■ ■ ■

STEVIE FLEMMI, meanwhile, continued to keep his own counsel in cellblock H-3 of the Plymouth County Correctional Facility. Over time the
crime boss had developed a twitch in one eye. There were times when his
arm would jerk involuntarily. He seemed to fidget. The facial tic and
spasms had not gone unnoticed.

"It's the Devil eating his body," Salemme told others.

Flemmi was moved out the cellblock early in the new year amid growing concerns for his safety.

Whitey continues to elude investigators. Since his indictment in 1995,
he's been spotted in New York, Louisiana, Wyoming, Mississippi, even in
his old neighborhood, Southie. He's been added to the FBI's Ten Most
Wanted List and featured on the television show of the same name.
But no amount of FBI talk about how hard it was trying to capture

Bulger could overcome the public's impression that the FBI didn't really want to.

New Orleans? Dublin? Southie?

By the end of 1999 the dark history of the FBI and Bulger may have been revealed. It was all there in 17,000 pages of sworn testimony, Judge Mark L. Wolf's 661-page ruling, and a fresh round of sensational criminal indictments. But none of those historic records contained the one answer a bedeviled city was still dying to know:

Where's Whitey?

Sources

Since 1987 we have written a number of in-depth articles for the *Boston Globe* about the Mafia, the Bulgers, John Connolly, and the FBI in Boston. This book is based on the more than 180 interviews conducted over the years in connection with those articles—interviews with officials from all levels of law enforcement and government, with Bill Bulger, with many residents of South Boston, and with a number of underworld figures.

In addition, we have relied on the official record—most notably the sworn testimony of forty-six witnesses during pretrial hearings in 1998 before U.S. District Court Judge Mark L. Wolf in the racketeering case *United States v Francis P. Salemme, James J. Bulger, Stephen Flemmi, et al.*, U.S. District Court, District of Massachusetts, criminal docket 94–10287. On September 19, 1999, Wolf released a 661-page memorandum and order (hereafter Wolf, "Memorandum and Order,"), more than half of which was devoted to "findings of fact" about the FBI's relationship with Bulger and Flemmi.

The witnesses at the Wolf hearings included present and past FBI agents, federal prosecutors, Justice Department officials, and Stephen Flemmi. The testimony took about 115 days, spread out over nine months, and produced 17,000 pages of transcripts. The Wolf hearings were nothing short of a judicial excavation into the history of the FBI and Bulger.

The use of unattributed quotations is an exception; we almost always use names.

The book is also based on thousands of pages of once-secret government records, mostly from the FBI, that were unsealed as part of the hearings before Judge Wolf. In addition, we drew on hundreds of pages of other records and documents regarding the Bulgers, the Mafia, and the FBI that we have accumulated during our own reporting.

Through interviews, government records, and sworn testimony, we had ample material from which to reconstruct the history of the Boston FBI's ties to Bulger and Flemmi. Even so, we attempted during the writing of this book to conduct further interviews with several key persons. Many who have figured in this story were willing to talk to us. Unfortunately, John Connolly, John Morris, Jeremiah O'Sullivan, and Bill Bulger were not, despite our effort to seek their comment about particular events.

We have also relied on a number of other criminal and civil cases. Many of these cases included court-approved taped conversations that became the basis for the dialogue that is reconstructed in the book. The main cases are:

- *United States v Patrick McGonigle et al.*, U.S. District Court, District of Massachusetts, criminal dockets 79–111-MA; 79–112-MA; 79–113-MA.
- *United States v Howard T. Winter, James Martorano, et al.*, U.S. District Court, District of Massachusetts, criminal docket 79–42-MA.
- *United States v Gennaro Angiulo et al.*, U.S. District Court, District of Massachusetts, criminal docket 83–235.
- *Thomas E. Finnerty v Harold Brown*, Suffolk County Superior Court, Massachusetts, civil action 87–2479, along with a counterclaim by Brown against Finnerty.
- *United States v Paul E. Moore et al.*, U.S. District Court, District of Massachusetts, criminal docket 90–10203.
- *United States v Edward J. MacKenzie et al.*, U.S. District Court, District of Massachusetts, criminal docket 90–10204.
- *United States v Nicholas L. Bianco et al.*, U.S. District Court, District of Connecticut, criminal docket H-90–18.
- *United States v Howard T. Winter*, U.S. District Court, District of Massachusetts, criminal docket 92–10008.
- *United States v Stephen M. Rakes*, U.S. District Court, District of Massachusetts, criminal docket 96–10131.
- *United States v Kevin P. Weeks and Kevin P. O'Neil*, U.S. District Court, District of Massachusetts, criminal docket 99–10371.

- *United States v John J. Connolly Jr., James Bulger aka "Whitey," and Stephen Flemmi*, U.S. District Court, District of Massachusetts, criminal docket 99–10428.

We have also relied on a number of books and articles for information about the Mafia, the FBI, the history of South Boston, the history of Boston, and the use of informants.

BOOKS

Beatty, Jack. *The Rascal King*. Reading, Mass.: Addison-Wesley, 1992.

Bulger, William M. *While the Music Lasts: My Life in Politics*. Boston: Houghton Mifflin, 1996.

Charns, Alexander. *Cloak and Gavel: FBI Wiretaps, Bugs, Informers, and the Supreme Court*. Urbana: University of Illinois Press, 1992.

Gillespie, C. Bancroft. *Illustrated History of South Boston*. South Boston: Inquirer Publishing Co., 1901.

Goodwin, Doris Kearns. *The Fitzgeralds and the Kennedys: An American Saga*. New York: Simon & Schuster, 1987.

Halberstam, David. *The Fifties*. New York: Ballantine Books, 1993.

Kee, Robert. *Ireland: A History*. Boston: Little, Brown & Co., 1982.

Kessler, Ronald. *The FBI*. New York: Pocket Books, 1993.

Lukas, J. Anthony. *Common Ground: A Turbulent Decade in the Lives of Three American Families*. New York: Alfred A. Knopf, 1985.

Maas, Peter. *The Valachi Papers*. New York: Putnam's, 1968.

MacDonald, Michael Patrick. *All Souls: A Family Story from Southie*. 1999. Boston: Beacon Press, 1999.

Marx, Gary T. *Undercover: Police Surveillance in America*. Berkeley, Calif.: Twentieth Century Fund, 1988.

Neff, James. *Mobbed Up: Jackie Presser's High-Wire Life in the Teamsters, the Mafia, and the FBI*. Boston: Atlantic Monthly Press, 1989.

O'Connor, Thomas H. *South Boston: My Home Town*. Boston: Quinlan Press, 1988.

———. *Bible, Brahmins, and Bosses: A Short History of Boston*. Boston: Trustees of the Public Library of the City of Boston, 1991.

———. *Boston Catholics: A History of the Church and Its People*. Boston: Northeastern University Press, 1998.

O'Neill, Gerard, and Dick Lehr. *The Underboss: The Rise and Fall of a Mafia Family*. New York: St. Martin's Press, 1989.

Pileggi, Nicholas. *Wiseguy*. New York: Pocket Books, 1987.

Sammarco, Anthony Mitchell. *Images of America: South Boston*. Dover, N.H.: Aradia Publishing, 1996.

Shannon, William V. *The American Irish: A Political and Social Portrait*. 2nd ed. Amherst: University of Massachusetts Press, 1989. First published in 1963.

Sherrill, Robert, et al. *Investigating the FBI*. Edited by Pat Watters and Stephen Gillers. Garden City, N.Y.: Doubleday & Co., 1973.

Sullivan, William C., with Bill Brown. *The Bureau: My Thirty Years in Hoover's FBI*. New York: W. W. Norton, 1979.

Ungar, Sanford J. *FBI: An Uncensored Look Behind the Walls*. Boston: Atlantic Monthly Press/Little, Brown & Co., 1975.

ARTICLES

Kleinman, David Marc. "Out of the Shadows and into the Files: Who Should Control Informants?" *Police* 3, no. 6 (November 1980).

Lee, Gregory D. (FBI special agent). "Drug Informants." *FBI Law Enforcement Bulletin* 62, no. 9 (September 1993).

Mount, Harry A., Jr. (FBI special agent). "Criminal Informants: An Administrator's Dream or Nightmare." *FBI Law Enforcement Bulletin* 59, no. 12 (December 1990).

Reese, James T. (FBI special agent, Behavioral Sciences Unit, FBI Academy, Quantico, Va.). "Motivations of Criminal Informants." *FBI Law Enforcement Bulletin* 49, no. 5 (May 1980).

"Symposium: Perspectives on Organized Crime." *Rutgers Law Journal* 16, nos. 3 and 4 (Spring-Summer 1985).

Finally, we would like to point out that a number of myths about Whitey Bulger and the Boston FBI have been in circulation locally for a long time; many of them are examined in this book. These stories were sometimes promoted by a few local writers—perhaps owing to personal relationships, perhaps because it was easier to see the FBI deal in simplified and elementary terms. The reality is far more complex than any gilded version. Fortunately, most Boston journalists and writers who have covered this story did not opt for the easy way out. Most have struggled with the voluminous record now available for public scrutiny. For our part, we have tried our best to be guided by the weight of the evidence—that is, our own interviews and reporting, the sworn testimony, the government records, and the court rulings. If, after all that, we have still erred on occasion in nuance or shading, it was not from any lack of effort to get the story right.

Notes

INTRODUCTION

Nearly all of the material came from our own firsthand experiences reporting the initial story in the *Boston Globe* in 1988 disclosing Whitey Bulger's ties to the FBI and John Connolly. Other material was drawn from Billy Bulger's memoir *While the Music Lasts: My Life in Politics* and from wiretapped conversations as part of the 1990 indictment of nearly fifty people in a South Boston drug case.

CHAPTER 1: 1975

Main sources: The sworn testimony at the Wolf hearings of Stephen Flemmi, August 20, 21, 24, 25, 26, 27, and 28, and September 1, 2, and 15, 1998; retired FBI agent H. Paul Rico, January 9, 13, and 14, 1998; retired FBI agent Dennis Condon, May 1, 4, and 5, 1998; on-the-record interviews between retired FBI agent John Connolly and the *Boston Globe* (1998), WBZ-AM Radio (October 27, 1998), WRKO-AM Radio (October 24, 1998), *Boston* magazine (November 1998), and the *Boston Tab* (October 27, 1998).

For other parts of this chapter, particularly for the historical context of the city, busing, and law enforcement, we drew on our own book *The Underboss: The Rise and Fall of a Mafia Family* and historian Thomas O'Connor's *South Boston: My Home Town.*

For biographical information on Bulger, we relied on our prior reporting and articles in the *Boston Globe*, published in September 1988 and July 1998. *Globe* columnist Jeff Jacoby's two columns titled "Busing's Legacy" (January 6 and 7, 1999) provided a sharp analysis and summary of busing. Information regarding the killing of Tommy King came from the superseding indictment unsealed on September 28, 2000, in *United States v Kevin P. Weeks and Kevin P. O'Neil*, U.S. District Court, District of Massachusetts, criminal docket 99–10371 and from newspaper articles in the *Boston Globe* and *Herald* on September 22, 2000.

We also drew on government documents and FBI reports either in our possession or released as part of the Wolf hearings. In particular, we drew on FBI reports about meetings with Bulger in the early 1970s and with Flemmi during the 1960s, including but not limited to reports released during the Wolf hearings as exhibits 20, 21, 24, 25, 28, 95, 97, 215, 217, 219, and 220.

The FBI's *Manual of Investigative Operations Guidelines* (MIOG) and *The Attorney General's Informant Guidelines* address the rules and regulations regarding the appropriate handling of criminal informants by government agents.

Judge Mark L. Wolf's ruling of September 15, 1999, pinned down a number of facts about the FBI's early alliance with Flemmi and Bulger. In particular, it is interesting to note that, under oath, Paul Rico denied calling Flemmi to tip him off to his indictment. But the judge ruled that, based on all the "credible evidence," Rico's denial was "not persuasive" ("Memorandum and Order," p. 95). "Flemmi received a call from Rico," the judge ruled. Wolf also found that Rico "aided and abetted the unlawful flight of a fugitive, in violation of 18 USC, sects. 1073 and 2" (p. 94).

CHAPTER 2: SOUTH BOSTON

Interviews: John Connolly's 1998 interviews with WBZ-AM Radio and WRKO-AM Radio and with the *Boston Globe* (see main sources for chapter 1).

The biographical sections on William and James Bulger used dozens of background and on-the-record interviews for *Boston Globe* articles on the brothers in 1988 and 1998.

For the history section, we relied on: Michael Patrick MacDonald, *All Souls: A Family Story from Southie;* William V. Shannon, *The American Irish: A Political and Social Portrait;* Thomas H. O'Connor, *Bible, Brahmins, and Bosses: A Short History of Boston, Boston Catholics: A History of the Church and Its People,* and *South Boston: My Home Town;* J. Anthony Lukas, *Common Ground: A Turbulent Decade in the Lives of Three American Families;* Doris Kearns Goodwin, *The Fitzgeralds and the Kennedys: An American Saga;* Robert Kee, *Ireland: A History;* Jack Beatty, *The Rascal King;* Gerard O'Neill and Dick Lehr, *The Underboss: The Rise and Fall of a Mafia Family;* and *Boston Globe* and *Boston Herald* articles about the murder of Donald Killeen, the arrest of Thomas Nee, and William Bulger's unsuccessful attempt to amend the Massachusetts constitution to allow aid to parochial schools.

FBI records: Dennis Condon's reports on unsuccessful efforts to recruit James Bulger as an informant in 1972; John Connolly's reports on meetings with James Bulger from 1975 to 1980.

Court records: The sworn testimony at the Wolf hearings of Dennis Condon, May 1 and 5, 1998; Wolf, "Memorandum and Order."

Judge Wolf addressed the issue of Stephen Flemmi telling the FBI where Frank Salemme could be found in New York City.

Both Flemmi and [Dennis] Condon deny that Flemmi provided the FBI with information that led to Salemme's arrest. In the context of all of the credible evidence in this case, it appears that this claim is not correct. In any event, Salemme's arrest and subsequent prosecution for the Fitzgerald bombing proved to be beneficial to Flemmi. In 1970, Hugh Shields, a codefendant in the Bennett murder case, had been tried and acquitted. In 1973, Salemme was tried on the Fitzgerald bombing charge. Robert Daddeico, who was being protected by the government, was an important witness. Daddeico testified that Salemme had participated in the Fitzgerald bombing. Daddeico claimed, however, that he had lied previously when he had said that Flemmi was also involved. Salemme was convicted and, as a result, spent the next fifteen years in prison ("Memorandum and Order," pp. 100–101).

CHAPTER 3: HARD BALL

Interviews: Former Norfolk County district attorney William Delahunt, former Norfolk County prosecutor John Kivlan, former Norfolk County prosecutor Matthew Connolly, and a brief interview with former loan company executive Rita Tobias.

Police records: Written reports of Quincy Police Department detectives on interviews with a waitress on April 22, 1983, about media calls concerning Delahunt, and on May 9, 1983, about a visit she had from Stephen Flemmi. Another Quincy Police Department report on a May 14, 1983, interview with a restaurant chef who was visited by FBI agents.

FBI records: Several reports in 1976 and 1977 concerning Francis Green's account of an extortion attempt by James Bulger and others at Green's restaurant.

News articles: Several *Boston Globe* and *Boston Herald* accounts of the murder trials of Thomas Sperrazza and Myles J. Connor, Jr. from 1979 to 1985.

CHAPTER 4: BOB 'N' WEAVE

Main sources: The sworn testimony at the Wolf hearings of Stephen Flemmi, August 20, 21, 24, 25, 26, 27, and 28, and September 1, 2, and 15, 1998; retired FBI agent John Morris, April 21, 1998; Paul Rico, January 13, 1998; and FBI agent James P. Darcy, Jr., September 28 and 29, 1998; Wolf, "Memorandum and Order."

For information on the history of the Mafia in the Boston area, we relied on our book *The Underboss*. For information on the handling of criminal informants, we drew mainly on the FBI's *MIOG;* background interviews with Justice Department officials; David Marc Kleinman, "Out of the Shadows and into the Files: Who Should Control Informants?"; 1998 interviews with retired FBI agent Robert Fitzpatrick; and Gary Marx, *Undercover: Police Surveillance in America.* Sanford J. Ungar, *FBI: An Uncensored Look Behind the Walls,* provides a useful overview of FBI history and was the source for examples of agents' dirty tricks. Also helpful was Robert Sherrill et al., *Investigating the FBI.*

We also drew on John Connolly's 1998 interviews with WBZ-AM Radio and WRKO-AM Radio. On February 12, 1999, we sent a letter to Jack Kerner of Melotone Vending Inc. requesting an interview. He neither answered the letter nor returned several telephone calls we made.

We drew on FBI reports about meetings with Bulger and Flemmi during the 1970s, including but not limited to reports we obtained and records released during the Wolf hearings as exhibits 30, 40, 41, and 68.

It is interesting to note that even though the reporting of crimes by informants is regarded as a central principle of the informant guidelines, Boston was not alone in construing that provision narrowly. In practice, FBI field offices interpreted the requirement as covering only actual arrests or indictments of an informant; the field offices rarely, if ever, notified headquarters about an informant's "suspected" criminal activity.

Judge Wolf emphasized the FBI's autonomy in deciding to authorize criminal activity by an informant: "In 1977, the Levi Memorandum expressly treated the issue of authorization as solely within the province of the FBI" ("Memorandum and Order," p. 124). Wolf also stressed that reporting an informant's unauthorized crime was of paramount importance, but that in Boston this requirement was "regularly ignored with regard to Bulger and Flemmi" (p. 125). In Boston, ruled Wolf, "the *Guidelines* were ignored at the outset" (p. 128). Overall, ruled Wolf, "with regard to Flemmi and Bulger, the requirements of the *Guidelines* were either ignored or treated as a bureaucratic nuisance. . . . The evidence also indicates that FBI Headquarters did not effectively supervise the implementation of the *Guidelines*" (pp. 129–30).

In his factual findings, Wolf ruled that Rico had leaked to Flemmi the pending indictments against him, a fact that Flemmi himself had admitted in his own sworn testimony.

Of the Melotone incident, Judge Wolf ruled that "Connolly intimidated executives of National Melotone from pursuing their complaint that Bulger and Flemmi were extorting the vending machine company's customers" (p. 17). Wolf wrote in his findings of fact:

Several officials of National Melotone, a vending machine company, tried to prompt an FBI investigation of Flemmi, Bulger and their associates for using threats of violence to have National Melotone's vending machines replaced with machines from Flemmi and Bulger's National Vending Company. Rather than pursue this information, report it to local law enforcement, or advise anyone other than perhaps Morris . . . Connolly successfully sought to protect Flemmi and Bulger. More specifically, Connolly claimed that if an investigation of their allegations was conducted the executives of National Melotone and their families would be in great danger, requiring participation in the federal Witness Protection Program and relocation. . . . It dissuaded the representatives of National Melotone from pursuing their charges. Connolly did, however, tell Bulger and Flemmi about the problem. (pp. 134–35)

CHAPTER 5: WIN, PLACE, AND SHOW

Main sources: The sworn testimony at the Wolf hearings of Stephen Flemmi, August 20, 25, and 28, and September 1 and 2, 1998; John Morris, April 21, 22, and 24, 1998; retired FBI agent Nicholas Gianturco, January 15 and April 20, 1998; Wolf, "Memorandum and Order."

Interviews: Anthony P. Ciulla, January 2000; a number of background interviews conducted in connection with our *Boston Globe* articles about Bulger in 1988 and 1998; transcripts of conversations recorded by the FBI in 1981 at 98 Prince Street, Boston.

We drew on FBI reports about meetings with Bulger and Flemmi during the late 1970s, including but not limited to reports we obtained and records released during the Wolf hearings as exhibits 5, 30, 35, 41, 60, 65–68, 70, 71, and 78. For information on the bookmaker Chico Krantz, we relied on government filings and *Globe* articles.

We also drew on our 1988 interview with Jeremiah T. O'Sullivan and O'Sullivan's 1997 statement to the Justice Department's Office of Professional Responsibility that he had not known Bulger and Flemmi were informants for the FBI during the race-fixing investigation. It is interesting to note that Judge Wolf found that O'Sullivan's position was false: "Morris and Connolly told O'Sullivan that Flemmi and Bulger were FBI informants" ("Memorandum and Order," p. 140). Wolf also noted that the meeting between the agents and O'Sullivan "violated FBI policy" (p. 141). Moreover, the judge ruled that Morris's subsequent report to headquarters explaining why Bulger had not been indicted—that no prosecutable case had been developed—"was not true. Rather, Bulger and Flemmi were not prosecuted in the race-fix case because Connolly, Morris and O'Sullivan decided that their value as informants outweighed the importance of prosecuting them" (pp. 142–43).

CHAPTER 6: GANG OF TWO?

Main sources: The sworn testimony at the Wolf hearings of Stephen Flemmi, August 20, 25, and 26, 1998; and John Morris, April 21, 22, 23, 27, 29, and 30, 1998; a March 1981 affidavit filed by Massachusetts State Police trooper Rick Fraelick to obtain court permission for electronic surveillance; the surveillance logs prepared by state police troopers observing the Lancaster Street garage in the spring of 1980; John Connolly's 1998 interviews with WBZ-AM Radio, WRKO-AM Radio, and the *Boston Globe.*

We drew on FBI reports about meetings with Bulger and Flemmi during the early 1980s, including but not limited to reports we obtained and records released during the Wolf hearings as exhibits 1–10, 50, 51, 63, 64, 69, 72–74, 78, 82, 87–89, 223, and 231.

We also drew on interviews with retired Massachusetts State Police Lieutenant Colonel John O'Donovan and retired detective Robert Long, as well as a number of our own background interviews conducted in connection with our 1988 and 1998 articles about Bulger and the FBI.

CHAPTER 7: BETRAYAL

Court records: The sworn testimony at the Wolf hearing of John Morris, April 21, 22, 23, 27, and 30, 1998; Stephen Flemmi, August 20, 25, and 26, 1998; and retired FBI agent Lawrence Sarhatt, January 7, 1998.

Interviews: On the Lancaster Street garage investigation and dealings with the FBI, retired Massachusetts State Police detective Robert Long, retired Massachusetts State Police Lieutenant Colonel John O'Donovan, and a brief interview with Sarhatt; extensive background interviews with Massachusetts State Police detectives and a Suffolk County prosecutor for *Boston Globe* articles in 1988 on the Bulger brothers.

FBI records: Documents from the Wolf hearings included exhibits 1–10, 50, 51, 62–64, 69, 72–74, 82, 87, 88, and 231.

News articles: Globe articles in July 1981 about a senate budget amendment affecting the Criminal Intelligence Division of the Massachusetts State Police.

Police records: 1981 affidavit submitted by the Massachusetts State Police to get court approval for electronic bugging of James Bulger and Stephen Flemmi.

CHAPTER 8: PRINCE STREET HITMAN

Court records: Transcripts from the daily log of conversations inside Mafia headquarters at 98 Prince Street from January to May 1981; 1995 court affidavit by FBI agent Edward Quinn on 98 Prince Street tapes about the activities of James Bulger and Stephen Flemmi; the sworn testimony at the Wolf hearings of Stephen Flemmi, August 20, 25, and 27, 1998.

News articles: Several *Boston Globe* and *Boston Herald* articles about the Bennett brothers murders in 1967, 1968, and 1985; *Globe* articles in 1986 about challenges by defendant Gennaro Angiulo to the racketeering statute.

Books: O'Neill and Lehr, *The Underboss.*

FBI records: Documents released at the Wolf hearings as exhibits 50, 51, and 73 about John Connolly's reports on dealings by James Bulger and Stephen Flemmi with Mafia leaders at 98 Prince Street.

Police records: 1981 affidavit submitted by the Massachusetts State Police to get court approval for electronic bugging of James Bulger and Stephen Flemmi.

CHAPTER 9: FINE FOOD, FINE WINE, DIRTY MONEY

Main sources: The sworn testimony at the Wolf hearings of Stephen Flemmi, August 20, 25, and 26, 1998; John Morris, April 21, 22, 23, 27, 29, and 30, 1998; retired FBI agent Jim Ring, June 5, 8, 9, 10, 11, 15, and 22, and September 18 and 22, 1998; FBI agent John Newton, May 22, June 2, 1998; Nick Gianturco, January 15 and 20, and April 20, 1998; Theresa Stanley, September 16, 1998; Debbie Morris, September 22, 1998; John Connolly's 1998 interviews with WBZ-AM Radio, WRKO-AM Radio, the *Boston Globe,* and the *Boston Tab;* Wolf, "Memorandum and Order."

We also drew on FBI reports about meetings with Bulger and Flemmi from 1980 through the spring of 1983; John Connolly's divorce records, Norfolk County Probate Court, 82MO351-DI; 1998 interview by the Justice Department's Office of Professional Responsibility with Rebecca Morris; interviews with retired FBI supervisor Robert Fitzpatrick; and numerous background interviews we conducted in connection with our 1988 and 1998 stories about Bulger and the FBI.

Regarding the payoff Morris sought from Bulger, it is interesting to note that John Connolly, in 1998 media interviews, denied that he'd delivered any cash to Debbie Noseworthy. Judge Wolf ruled, however, that

> Morris solicited and received through Connolly $1,000 from Bulger and Flemmi . . . Recalling the offer communicated through Connolly, he [Morris] asked Connolly if Bulger and Flemmi would provide funds necessary to buy his secretary a plane ticket. Connolly subsequently gave Morris's secretary an envelope containing $1,000 cash, which Morris understood had come from Bulger and Flemmi. . . . The court finds that Morris's understanding was correct. (pp. 19, 166–67)

Regarding the dinner parties, Wolf ruled:

> The timing of these dinners suggests that they were often arranged to celebrate milestones in the FBI's relationship with Bulger and Flemmi. . . . At these dinners, the agents, Bulger and Flemmi at times exchanged gifts. Although FBI procedures required that all contacts with informants be documented, there is only one, a 1979 report, reflecting matters discussed at these dinners. There is no record of the gifts exchanged. (pp. 5–6)

Regarding the FBI's failure to look at reports of Bulger and Flemmi's criminality, Wolf ruled: "In 1979 and early 1980, the FBI received information from informants that Bulger and Flemmi were involved in other criminal activity, including illegal gambling and trafficking in cocaine. These allegations too were not investigated" (p. 144). Earlier the judge had noted that "the FBI neither investigated nor disclosed such information to any other law enforcement agency because Connolly and Morris were 'very anxious' to continue to receive the 'valuable' assistance of Bulger and Flemmi in the investigation of the Mafia to which Morris had by then dedicated every member of his Organized Crime Squad" (p. 143).

The judge also mentioned Connolly's growing influence in the FBI office. He found that when other FBI agents "received reliable information about criminal activity in which Bulger and Flemmi were engaged, they regularly consulted Connolly and then did not pursue any investigation" (p. 194).

It is also worth noting that in his "justification memos" of late 1980 and early 1981, John Connolly cited a second instance of Bulger putatively saving the life of an FBI agent. The dynamic at work in the second example reflects the dynamic of the first episode involving agent Nick Gianturco. Once again, Connolly seems to take a nugget of information and polish it into Bulger hype. In the 1980 memo that Connolly was ordered to write to justify keeping Bulger as an FBI informant, Connolly recalled that in 1977 Bulger had told him of a plan to kill agent Billy Butchka. Butchka at the time was posing as a buyer of stolen paintings and jewelry from a burglary ring. Connolly wrote that Bulger, "on his own, was successful in preventing the prospective hit men from taking any action against Butchka."

Just like Gianturco, Butchka today supports Connolly's version of events up to a point. In a 1998 telephone interview, Butchka told us: "I will verify I was working undercover and that I did receive a call that someone was going to hit me, and later I was told it was attributed to one of John Connolly's informants. This was basically all I knew about it." Butchka said he was no longer able to recall the name of the agent who warned him or the names of the thieves he was told were after him.

But just as in the Gianturco example, the life-saving scenario Connolly described is contradicted by other key officials who participated in the stolen art probe. The purported threat to Butchka's life did not come up in the case proceedings in court, either as an issue at bail hearings or in the eventual dispositions. "I don't remember him [Butchka] ever being threatened," said Michael Collora in a 1998 telephone interview. Collora, now in private practice, was the federal prosecutor who oversaw prosecution of the burglary ring infiltrated by Butchka. (During 1998 he actually had John Morris as a client.) Said Collora: "I would have known about any threat because we would've had to make a decision whether to pull him off, and that was never done."

CHAPTER 10: MURDER, INC.

Court records: The sworn testimony at the Wolf hearings of John Morris, April 22, 24, 27, and 29, 1998; Stephen Flemmi, August 26 and 28, and September 1, 1998; former Massachusetts U.S. attorney William Weld, May 26 and 27, 1998; retired FBI agent Robert Fitzpatrick, August 17 and 18, 1998; James Ring, June 10 and 11.

Interviews: Tulsa homicide detective Michael Huff; retired FBI agents Robert Fitzpatrick, James Ring, and Gerald Montanari; an anonymous prosecutor about the decision by former assistant U.S. attorney Jeremiah O'Sullivan to not give Brian Halloran witness protection program status; Brian Halloran family cousin Maureen Caton; an anonymous former police investigator on the murders of Louis Litif and George Pappas; an anonymous Massachusetts State Police detective on the Roger Wheeler murder (1988 background interview); an anonymous 1998 interview with a Boston Edison executive about the company's 1990 hiring of John Connolly.

News articles: Articles about the 1981 murder of Roger Wheeler in the *New York Times, Wall Street Journal,* and *Boston Globe;* stories in the *Globe* and the *Boston Herald* on the murders of George Pappas, Brian Halloran, and John Callahan and the murder trial of James Flynn; an extensive 1997 article in the *Hartford Courant* on the World Jai Alai murders and the Boston FBI office.

FBI documents: An extensive February 23, 1982, report of the six-week debriefing by agents of Brian Halloran and other documents released at the Wolf hearings as exhibits 47, 52–55, 83, 91, 155, 157, 225, and 226; John Connolly's reports in October and December 1981 and April and May 1982 from Bulger and Flemmi on the danger to Halloran posed by the Boston Mafia.

Judge Wolf addressed the FBI's role in the World Jai Alai murders.

> Morris caused Connolly to tell Flemmi and Bulger that Brian Halloran was providing the FBI information that implicated them in the murder of Roger Wheeler. Halloran was murdered soon after. Morris believed Bulger and Flemmi were responsible. When Halloran was murdered, Connolly prepared a 209 stating that Flemmi reported that "the wise guys in Charlestown" had heard that Halloran was cooperating with the Massachusetts State Police and, therefore, had a motive to murder him. Similarly, shortly before John Callahan, another associate of Bulger and Flemmi implicated in the Wheeler investigation, was murdered in Miami in 1983 [*sic*], Connolly prepared a 209 stating that Flemmi had reported that Callahan was trying to avoid a "very bad" Cuban group. Flemmi and Bulger remain suspects in the still open Wheeler, Halloran, and Callahan murder investigations. ("Memorandum and Order," p. 84)

Although John Connolly denied informing James Bulger about Halloran's attempt to become a FBI informant, Wolf held otherwise: "In addition, when Brian

Halloran became a potential witness against Bulger and Flemmi in the Wheeler homicide investigation, Morris told Connolly. As Morris anticipated, Connolly told Bulger and Flemmi. Several weeks later Halloran was murdered" (p. 163).

Wolf also addressed the FBI indexing issue.

> With one exception, however, the many reports containing Halloran's charges against Bulger and Flemmi were not properly indexed with a reference to their names. Thus, these documents were not found or considered by the Department of Justice officials who were assigned in July 1997 as a result of this case to review allegations that had been made by informants and witnesses against Bulger and Flemmi. (p. 173)

In the case of *United States v Kevin P. Weeks and Kevin P. O'Neil,* the November 1999 affidavit of Thomas B. Duffy in support of pretrial detention of the defendants Kevin J. Weeks and Kevin P. O'Neil addressed the murder of Brian Halloran. About a year after the murder of Roger Wheeler, "Bulger and Flemmi learned that a Boston resident, Brian Halloran, was providing information to the FBI regarding the murder of Wheeler. Bulger, Flemmi, and others shot and killed Halloran on the South Boston waterfront" (p. 12).

CHAPTER 11: BULGERTOWN, USA

Main sources: The 1998 sworn testimony of Julie Rakes, Joseph Lundbohm, Jean Miskel, Jamie Flannery, and Richard Bergeron at the perjury and obstruction of justice trial of Stephen M. Rakes, *United States v Stephen M. Rakes;* the sworn testimony at the Wolf hearings of Stephen Flemmi, August 26, 1998; Jim Ring, September 22, 1998; and Theresa Stanley, September 16, 1998; John Connolly's 1998 interviews with the *Boston Globe* and *Boston Herald* during the Rakes trial; Wolf, "Memorandum and Order"; *United States v Kevin P. Weeks and Kevin P. O'Neil; United States v John J. Connolly Jr., James Bulger aka "Whitey," and Stephen Flemmi;* FBI reports on meetings with Bulger and Flemmi from 1981 through early 1984; interviews conducted in connection with articles about Bulger and the FBI published in the *Boston Globe* in 1990 and 1998.

It is interesting to note that John Connolly, in media interviews in 1998, denied ever talking to Bulger about the Rakeses. In sworn testimony, Stephen Flemmi said he believed Connolly had tipped off Bulger, giving them a "heads-up" so that Bulger could issue Rakes a warning.

In his 1999 ruling, Judge Wolf found:

> Connolly received very reliable information concerning an ongoing extortion by Bulger and Flemmi. In violation of FBI policy and practice, Connolly did not record the information or disclose it to his Supervisor as

required by the FBI Guidelines. Nor did he try to obtain the testimony of the victims or conduct any other investigation. Instead, he told Bulger of the charges. ("Memorandum and Order," p. 181)

Following his 1998 perjury conviction, Stephen Rakes decided to cooperate with federal prosecutors. During late 1998 and 1999 he testified before the federal grand jury that indicted Bulger associates Kevin Weeks and Kevin O'Neil in November 1999. The racketeering charges against the two included the takeover of the Rakeses' liquor store. In exchange for his cooperation, Rakes was spared prison when he was sentenced on November 22, 1999. Rakes told the judge he had "great remorse" for lying twice to earlier grand juries. He was placed on probation for two years.

Several other points are worth noting about the Rakes affair. The first is that Boston police detective Joseph Lundbohm eventually ran afoul of the law himself; he was convicted in 1990 of taking bribes to protect Mafia gambling operations. Also, the FBI's apparent "hands-off" policy regarding Whitey Bulger covered small matters too. After the liquor store was taken over, FBI agent James J. Lavin III was notified by a *Boston Globe* photographer, Joe Runci, about unusual improvements under way on the store's property. Runci provided the FBI with photographs showing city workers installing guard rails on the private property. During the Wolf hearings, Lavin testified that the construction work by city employees represented a possible case of public corruption. Lavin testified that he told John Morris about the photographs and that Morris told him to "run it by John Connolly."

Lavin testified that he then sought out Connolly and explained the situation; Connolly asked him: "What are you going to do with that?" Lavin testified that Connolly then told him that Bulger had provided "valuable information to the office." Lavin testified that one could infer from Connolly's response that Connolly was suggesting to him to drop the matter. Lavin did just that. He testified that he stuck the photographs in his desk drawer at the Boston office of the FBI and never even wrote up a report. "I didn't do anything with it," he testified on May 6, 1998. The photographs sat in his desk until the 1998 Wolf hearings. During his testimony Lavin admitted it was unusual—a breach of standard procedure—to leave the photos in his desk and to fail to write a report. "In hindsight, I should have put [the photos] in the file." Furthermore, Lavin said that shortly after his meeting with Connolly he got word that the guard rails had been taken down. It was an end-of-story twist mirroring the Rakeses' experience—all roads seemed to lead to Bulger.

Lavin testified that he was surprised to hear the guard rails were removed so quickly. "It was a possibility that someone called Mr. Bulger, or it could have been a coincidence. I thought it was very odd." He said he did not know if Connolly had alerted Bulger. "You know, it could have been. I just don't know."

Finally, there is Stephen Flemmi. Usually talkative on the stand during the Wolf hearings, particularly about the protection the FBI had provided him over the years,

Flemmi turned remarkably mute when the questions turned to Stephen and Julie Rakes. On August 26, 1998, federal prosecutor Fred Wyshak and Flemmi had the following exchange:

> WYSHAK: Let's talk a little bit about . . . Stephen Rakes.
>
> FLEMMI: I'll assert the Fifth on that.
>
> WYSHAK: He and his wife Julie opened up a liquor store; did you know that?
>
> FLEMMI: Assert the Fifth on that.
>
> WYSHAK: And you took the store from them, didn't you, you and Mr. Bulger?
>
> FLEMMI: I'll assert the Fifth on that.
>
> WYSHAK: And they complained, didn't they, to Joe Lundbohm?
>
> FLEMMI: I'll assert the Fifth on that.
>
> WYSHAK: Didn't you have a conversation with John Connolly where he told you that Joe Lundbohm had reported to him that you and Mr. Bulger had extorted the liquor store away from the Rakes[es]?
>
> FLEMMI: I'll assert the Fifth on that.

CHAPTER 12: THE BULGER MYTH

Main sources: The sworn testimony at the Wolf hearings of Stephen Flemmi, August 20, 24, 26, 27, and 28, and September 2, 1998; John Morris, April 21, 22, 23, 27, 29, and 30, 1998; Jim Ring, June 10 and September 22, 1998; FBI agent James R. Blackburn, Jr., May 7 and 22, 1998; retired FBI agent Roderick Kennedy, April 14, 1998; DEA agent Stephen Boeri, May 14, 15, 18, and 19, 1998; DEA agent Al Reilly, May 20, 1998; former assistant U.S. attorney Gary Crossen, May 11 and 12, 1998; former U.S. attorney for Massachusetts William Weld, May 26 and 27, 1998; former Quincy police detective Richard Bergeron, June 3 and 4, 1998; former Boston DEA agent in charge Robert Stutman, April 15, 1998; former Boston FBI agent in charge James Greenleaf, January 8, 1998; Theresa Stanley, September 16, 1998; Wolf, "Memorandum and Order."

In addition, we relied on John Connolly's 1998 interviews with WBZ-AM Radio, WRKO-AM Radio, the *Boston Globe,* and the *Boston Tab.* For background on Operation Beans, we relied on a number of internal investigative reports, particularly the surveillance logs kept by the Quincy Police Department for 1983 through 1985 and the DEA affidavits in support of the agency's bid to obtain court permission to attempt electronic surveillance of Bulger and Flemmi. For information about John McIntyre's cooperation, we relied on a forty-eight-page transcript of his debriefing with Quincy police and the DEA on October 14, 1984. For information on the burial of three bodies in the basement of a South Boston home, we relied on the superseding indictment unsealed on September 28, 2000, in *United States v Kevin P. Weeks and Kevin P. O'Neil*, U.S. District Court, District of Massachusetts, criminal docket 99–10371. For information about the anti-drug poster in Bulger's store and the perception of Bulger in South Boston, we drew on Michael Patrick McDonald's 1999 memoir *All Souls.*

We drew on extensive FBI internal reports, including reports about Bulger's drug activities. The FBI documents include but are not limited to those released at the Wolf hearings as exhibits 11, 12, 14, 19, 45, 48, 63, 88, 89, 91, 102, 104–107, 133, 135, 136, 138, 139, 141, 142, 145, 146, 164, 173, 175, 176, 178, 179, 233, 237, 254, 255, 257, and 258.

We also drew on numerous interviews conducted in connection with articles in the *Boston Globe* about Bulger and the FBI published in 1988 and 1998. A number of other *Globe* stories were helpful regarding drugs in Southie—specifically, articles by Brian MacQuarrie published March 5 and April 16, 1997, and December 27, 1999, and an article by Charles Stein published in the *Globe's* Sunday magazine on December 13, 1998.

It is interesting to note that during the 1998 Wolf hearings Flemmi testified that FBI supervisor Jim Ring was the one who called to tip Bulger and Flemmi to the telephone wiretap on George Kaufman's telephone. "I heard from him in December of 1984," Flemmi testified about Ring. "It was a telephone call to my mother's home. Very, very brief conversation. It was Jim Ring telling me that there was going to be a wiretap coming down on George Kaufman's phone as well as my own, and they advised me of that." For his part, Ring testified that Flemmi's "absolutely false" accusation was a bid to spread the corruption at the FBI from Connolly and Morris to himself. In his findings of fact, Judge Wolf ruled

> that this is a matter on which the court finds that Flemmi's testimony is in part accurate and in part false. More specifically, the credible direct and circumstantial evidence proves that Bulger and Flemmi were told of the investigation generally and of the electronic surveillance particularly. It was, however, Connolly not Ring who gave them this information. ("Memorandum and Order," p. 215)

Wolf found that Connolly constantly leaked information about Operation Beans, ruling that, "armed with information provided by colleagues . . . Connolly contributed to assuring that DEA's efforts would not succeed by alerting Bulger and Flemmi to the investigation generally and to the electronic surveillance particularly" (p. 197). Regarding the *Valhalla,* investigators at the time of the incident said they did not have enough evidence to charge Bulger and Flemmi. But following a lengthy probe, Bulger associates Patrick Nee and Joseph Murray of Charlestown were convicted in the gunrunning scheme. Regarding John McIntyre's disappearance, Judge Wolf commented in his findings of fact: "The evidence raises a question of whether Connolly also told Bulger and Flemmi about John McIntyre, who was providing information about them and their associates, and who disappeared about six weeks after the FBI learned of his allegations" (p. 175). Connolly denied leaking to Bulger and Flemmi the identity of the promising informant.

CHAPTER 13: BLACK MASS

Main sources: The sworn testimony at the Wolf hearings of Stephen Flemmi, August 20, 26, 27, and 28, and September 2, 1998; John Morris, April 23, 27, and 29, 1998; Jim Ring, June 9, 10, and 11, 1998; Dennis Condon, May 1 and 5, 1998; and John Newton, May 22, 1998; Wolf, "Memorandum and Order."

We also relied on the statements provided by John Connolly, Dennis Condon, and Rebecca Morris to the Justice Department's Office of Professional Responsibility during the summer of 1997. In addition, we relied on Connolly's 1998 interviews with the *Boston Globe*, WBZ-AM Radio, WRKO-AM Radio, *Boston* magazine, and the *Boston Tab.*

We drew on FBI reports on meetings with Bulger and Flemmi during the mid-1980s; for background information on the case involving former FBI agent Dan Mitrione, we turned to articles in the *Miami Herald,* March 15 and 16, 1985, October 3 and 5, 1985, and November 14 and 15, 1985.

In his sworn testimony during the Wolf hearings, John Morris said he had "no recollection" of telling Bulger and Flemmi at the dinner that they could commit any crime short of murder. "I have no recollection of ever using that phraseology. I think I would recall that," he testified. "I recall asking John Connolly, 'What do these guys want from us?' And his response was, 'A head start.'" In his findings of fact, Judge Wolf ruled:

> The court finds that the statement, as related by Flemmi, was made. It is possible that Morris merely forgot a comment that he made thirteen years before his testimony. If the matter does not involve a failure of recollection, however, Morris has lied again. Morris acknowledges that he has a long history of lying to protect himself. ("Memorandum and Order," p. 255)

Regarding the $1,000 Morris took from Bulger, John Connolly denied in interviews that he played any part in delivering the case of wine with the cash in it. In his ruling, Wolf did not address Connolly's alleged role and referred only in passing to this payment: Morris "received a second $1,000 payment from them, and a case of wine... in the spring of 1984" (p. 213).

CHAPTER 14: SHADES OF WHITEY

Court records: The sworn testimony at the Wolf hearings of John Morris, April 28, 1998; South Boston realtor Raymond Slinger, September 23, 1998; John Newton, May 28,1998; Roderick Kennedy, May 28, 1998; and FBI agent Bruce Ellavsky, June 1, 1998.

Interviews: Several with Senate President William Bulger for a 1988 series of articles on the Bulger brothers; with William Bulger on 75 State Street on November 27, 1988; several in 1988 with Old Harbor housing project residents; several with a state investigator on 75 State Street and with a former federal prosecutor on 75 State Street and Harold Brown's indictment and conviction on bribery of a City of Boston inspector.

Miscellaneous records: William Bulger's financial disclosure forms for state legislators for 1984 to 1987.

News articles: Boston Globe articles on William Bulger and Thomas Finnerty's role in the 75 State Street controversy, December 8, 1988; several subsequent *Globe* articles, most of them by Brian C. Mooney; *Globe* and *Boston Herald* articles in 1985 and 1986 about Harold Brown's indictment and conviction on bribery; *Globe* and *Herald* articles on Jeremiah O'Sullivan's 1989 press conference ending the 75 State Street investigation; *Globe* and *Herald* articles on a 1992 announcement by Massachusetts attorney general Scott Harshbarger that he would bring no charges against William Bulger on 75 State Street.

Books: William M. Bulger, *While the Music Lasts: My Life in Politics.*

Court records: Several filings in 1987 and 1988 by litigants Thomas Finnerty and Harold Brown; Wolf, "Memorandum and Order."

Wolf addressed the issue of the FBI ignoring its own rules in handling Slinger's extortion account:

> Slinger's allegations and willingness to testify provided, under the Attorney General's Guidelines, a quintessential case for either referring Slinger's allegations to state or local law enforcement, or reporting the desire not to do so to FBI headquarters and the Assistant Attorney General. The guidelines, however, were utterly ignored. Instead, [Lawrence] Potts and [Bruce] Ellavsky evidently decided that no further investigation would be conducted. The FBI did not speak with Slinger again. ("Memorandum and Order," p. 280)

Wolf also addressed John Connolly's involvement in the Slinger case:

> Slinger testified that in an effort to protect himself, he promptly told O'Neil that he had been visited by the FBI. If this occurred, it would not alone have been enough to deter Bulger, who had for many years been consistently protected by the FBI. Rather, the court infers that Bulger was advised by Con-

nolly to desist. The day after the FBI interview of Slinger, O'Neil told him that he would not have to pay the remaining $25,000 that he owed. (p. 281)

Federal and state investigative records: We relied on the September 5, 1991, report to Attorney General Scott Harshbarger and related documents, including William Bulger's December 19, 1988, affidavit and a February 28, 1989, statement by William Bulger to the FBI. The 1991 state report and the 1989 FBI interview are reproduced here in their entirety.

MEMORANDUM TO MASSACHUSETTS ATTORNEY GENERAL SCOTT HARSHBARGER ON THE STATUS OF THE AGENCY'S INVESTIGATION OF 75 STATE STREET, SEPTEMBER 5, 1991

I. BACKGROUND

During the past several months we have been reviewing information and documents pertaining to allegations made by Harold Brown that in connection with his development of 75 State Street he paid monies to Thomas Finnerty because of official acts or official influence which Finnerty could provide through his relationship with Senate President William Bulger. Our inquiry has focused upon the prior investigation conducted by the U.S. Attorney's office in Boston and a more limited review conducted by the State Ethics Commission.

As you know, we have encountered substantial delays in obtaining access to information and documents gathered during the federal investigation as a result of Department of Justice policies and the restrictions of Federal Rule of Criminal Procedure 6(e). In addition, we have been informed that a cooperation agreement entered into between Harold Brown and federal prosecutors expressly prohibited disclosure of any information, testimony or documents provided by Brown or derived from his cooperation without his prior express approval. Federal authorities have further informed us that Brown has declined to allow us access to testimony, information or documents in connection with our review. We have been provided with copies of transcripts of grand jury testimony of persons having knowledge of certain aspects of 75 State Street transactions. In particular, we have received and reviewed transcripts of the testimony of Graham Gund, Bruce Quirk, Richard McDonough, and accountants for Thomas Finnerty and William Bulger together with records and documents furnished by those individuals in connection with their grand jury appearances. In addition, selected bank accounts [*sic*] records and other financial documents of Thomas Finnerty's law firm, his personal accounts and certain accounts in the name of William Bulger have been furnished to us by the U.S. Attorney's office with prior court approval.

We have also obtained and reviewed the investigative files of the State Ethics Commission which conducted an initial screening of the allegations to determine whether preliminary inquiry was warranted regarding possible violations of the Conflict of Interest or Financial Disclosure Laws. Based on those files, it appears that the full Ethics Commission declined to authorize a preliminary inquiry into those allegations and also allowed Mr. Bulger to file amendments to his annual statements of financial interests for calendar years 1985 thru [sic] 1988 without initiating enforcement proceedings for omissions in those prior filings. Files have also been obtained from the State Police State Office of Investigations pertaining to Finnerty's divorce filings and the Middlesex District Attorney's Office pertaining to Robert and Bruce Quirk. It should be noted that no investigative or other files of this office concerning 75 State Street have been found in the records of the prior Shannon administration.

We have also conducted interviews of Robert and Bruce Quirk, Attorney Robert Frank, Graham Gund and Attorney James McDonough. Counsel for Richard McDonough (Earl Cooley) has thus far failed to reply to our requests to interview Richard McDonough.

II. INVESTIGATIVE FINDINGS

Based on the foregoing it has been established that Brown paid a total of $500,000 dollars to Thomas Finnerty in July of 1985 as a partial payment for Finnerty's partnership interest in the 75 State Street development. (In 1988, Brown agreed to pay Finnerty an additional sum of $200,000.00 in settlement of a civil suit initiated by Finnerty for the balance of his partnership interest in 75 State Street.) Checks issued by Brown were made payable to the Saint Botolph Realty Trust which Finnerty had recently established and opened an account in the name of that trust at the Bank of Boston. Those funds remained in that account for approximately 1 month at which time Finnerty issued two checks, each in the amount of $225,000.00 dollars, payable to himself and William Bulger which were issued to open separate investment accounts with Fidelity Investments in Boston in each of their names. Two additional $15,000.00 dollar checks were issued to Thomas Finnerty and William Bulger in October, 1985. Bulger's check was also deposited into his Fidelity Investment account. In November, 1985 a superceeding [sic] indictment was issued by the Federal Grand Jury in Boston that Harold Brown had made illegal payments to an official in the city of Boston building department and further alleging that other public officials had received monies from Brown. That superceeding [sic] indictment was the first public indication that federal prosecutors were focusing upon Brown's dealings with other government officials beyond the city of Boston building department. Within three (3) days of that indictment being made public, Bulger repaid the Saint Botolph Realty Trust $215,000 dollars via a check drawn against that same Fidelity Investment Trust account. Two weeks later, Bulger made an additional repayment of approximately $39,0000.00 dollars to the Saint Botolph Realty Trust account.

Three years later, in 1988, when Brown's allegations were made public in Boston media articles in connection with a civil suit between Brown and Finnerty over the balance of the partnership fee reportedly due Finnerty, Bulger publicly stated and filed an affidavit in Suffolk Superior Court claiming that the monies he received from Finnerty via the Saint Botolph Realty Trust in 1985 was [sic] a "loan in anticipation of a legal fee" due to Bulger from Robert and Bruce Quirk in connection with civil litigation between the Quirk's [sic] and a firm known as Data Terminal Systems of Maynard. Bulger stated that no promissory note or other written memoranda concerning that loan, the interest rate or terms were executed. According to Bulger, his repayment of approximately $254,000.00 dollars to the trust represented the principal borrowed ($240,000.00) plus interest computed by his accountants for the period of time (approximately 3 months) during which he had use of those monies.

Bulger also has stated publicly and, in that affidavit, he has maintained an "of counsel" relationship with the Finnerty law firm and that he has continued a limited private legal practice while a member of the Massachusetts Senate. He utilized Finnerty's law office facilities and office staff to handle his billings and collect his fees. In addition, Bulger claimed that through the years he and Finnerty made a number of joint "investments" in various enterprises such as real estate properties, stocks and other business ventures. A copy of Bulger's affidavit and prior interview report by the FBI is attached to this memorandum.

Review and analysis of the bank accounts [sic] records of the Saint Botolph Realty Trust together with account records of the Finnerty law firm and other related Finnerty accounts have confirmed that notwithstanding Bulger's assertion that he repaid in full with interest all monies he received from Thomas Finnerty in 1985 which he learned were derived from Harold Brown, substantially all of those funds were later returned from that trust to Bulger over the next twelve months. During that time period, monies from the Saint Botolph Realty Trust were periodically deposited into another Finnerty law firm account also at the Bank of Boston before they were then distributed by checks payable to Bulger. By first depositing the Saint Botolph monies into a Finnerty law firm account and then issuing checks drawn on the law firm account to Bulger, approximately half of the $500,000.00 paid by Brown was funnelled [sic] to Bulger without creating a direct link on paper by means of a check drawn on the Saint Botolph Realty Trust payable directly to William Bulger. As an example of these transactions, on June 6, 1986 a check drawn on the Saint Botolph account in the total amount of $61,000.00 was issued by Finnerty payable to "Thomas Finnerty, P.C." That check was immediately deposited into the Thomas Finnerty law firm account at the same bank. Three (3) days later, a check drawn on that account in the same amount ($61,000.00) was issued and made payable to "William Bulger." Bulger deposited all of those funds back into the same

Fidelity Investment account in his name which ten months earlier, had been used to accept the original Saint Botolph checks which Bulger later repaid. Of particular interest is that the source of those monies ($61,000.00) from the Saint Botolph account in 1986 remained the original Harold Brown checks. Based on Bulger's prior public statements in the tenor of his previous affidavit, it can be assumed that his and Finnerty's explanation for those transactions will be that the monies paid to Bulger in the succeeding twelve months were either legal fees or other "loans" in anticipation of legal fees for which Bulger had no knowledge that the indirect source of those funds was the Saint Botolph Realty Trust or Harold Brown.

Review and analysis of Finnerty and Bulger account records obtained thus far also establishes [sic] a number of other transactions involving Bulger and Finnerty. In particular are transactions involving one Richard McDonough, a former employee of the Mass[achusetts] Department of Commerce who is now a registered lobbyist in Massachusetts. Richard McDonough received $70,000.00 dollars of a $280,000.00 dollar legal fee apparently charged to Robert and Bruce Quirk by Finnerty and Bulger in late 1985 for Bulger's efforts settling a civil suit and obtaining a $2.8 million dollar mortgage loan from the South Boston Savings Bank for the Quirk's [sic] in connection with the settlement of that suit. When asked what role Richard McDonough had in connection with those services, neither the Quirks, Bulger nor McDonough could offer any specific information regarding Richard McDonough's services for which he earned a $70,000.00 "consulting" fee. McDonough was immunized by the U.S. Attorney's office in Boston and testified before the Federal Grand Jury concerning his relationship with Bulger, Finnerty and the Quirks. A copy of the transcript of his testimony is attached to this memorandum.

In addition to the Quirk fee, Richard McDonough and William Bulger each received over $50,000.00 dollars from a firm in California known as Herbalife reportedly for out of state "consulting" activities by McDonough and Bulger on behalf of that firm.

During 1985 and 1986, Finnerty and Bulger also purchased real estate located in South Boston via the Mount Vernon Realty Trust and appear to have made a number of joint investments in cable television companies and other investment firms.

III. ISSUES

Our efforts to ascertain the underlying facts gathered during the prior Federal investigation of Brown's allegation that he paid Finnerty $500,000.00 dollars for or because of official acts or official influence which Finnerty could provide through William Bulger has been severely limited by the prior cooperation agreement between the Federal authorities and Brown which gives Brown the right to refuse access to his statements and documents. Without having access to Brown's testimony and information regarding any communications he had with Finnerty, Bulger or their representatives concerning the true purpose of that $500,000.00 payment, it is impossible for us to evaluate whether Brown's allegations could be successfully prosecuted.

With the information and documents that are available to us, it appears that Finnerty provided little or no substantive input, advice or services in return for his partnership interest in a multi-million dollar commercial real estate venture. In addition, the limited records and documents furnished to us pertaining to Finnerty's law practice and his relationship with Bulger reveals [sic] a curious relationship in which Bulger appears to provide little or no substantive services in return for approximately one half of all fees generated by the Finnerty law firm. For example, during the last four months of 1985 the Finnerty law firm bank account records indicates [sic] that Bulger was paid over $50,000.00. In 1986 over $350,000.00 in checks payable directly to William Bulger were issued from law firm accounts. Copies of those checks payable to Bulger are attached to this memorandum. Of those monies paid in 1986 from the Finnerty law firm account, contrary to Bulger's public statements, it appears that Bulger actually received less than half of the total legal fee paid by the Quirks ($280,000.00 dollars) in connection with the Data Terminal Systems and the South Boston Savings Bank mortgage. Analysis of the deposit of the Quirk legal fees into the Finnerty law firm account and subsequent withdrawals indicates that Bulger received approximately $110,000.00 dollars of the total Quirk fee while Finnerty received approximately $100,000.00 of that fee with the balance ($80,000.00) being split between Richard McDonough ($70,000.00 "consulting fee") and approximately $10,000.00 going to attorney James McDonough, an associate in Finnerty's law firm who appears to have performed the bulk of the work relating to the litigation and the real estate closing. Besides those checks payable directly from the Finnerty law firm account to William Bulger, a series of other checks totaling in excess of $100,000.00 dollars during 1986 have been identified which appear to be paid to various investment firms which may also be for the benefit of William Bulger as well. In addition, at least $50,000.00 dollars in funds from the Finnerty law firm account were utilized to pay William Bulger's one half share in the purchase of commercial property located adjacent to the Columbia Point project formerly owned by Mary Teebagy.

As noted in the grand jury testimony of Richard McDonough, an example of Bulger's apparent ability to obtain lucrative fees for little or no substantive service can be seen in the transactions with Herbalife of California during 1985. McDonough's grand jury testimony and other materials provided by Federal authorities indicates [sic] that McDonough and Bulger were retained "consultants" by that firm to advise them on unspecified legislative and other governmental affairs issues outside of Massachusetts during 1985. In return, Bulger and McDonough were each paid approximately $50,000.00 dollars by that firm.

IV. RECOMMENDATION

A. 75 State Street

To [*sic*] respect to Brown's allegations concerning his payments to Finnerty concerning the 75 State Street project, it is recommended that counsel for Harold Brown, William Bulger and Thomas Finnerty be contacted and a request to interview their client be made regarding their respective roles in that project and the payments and ultimate disposition of $500,000.00 paid by Brown. Richard McDonough's counsel (Earl Cooley) has thus far failed to reply to our prior requests to interview his client.

A further recommendation regarding the appropriate follow-up action will be made after they have been contacted and responded.

B. Other Aspects of the Finnerty/Bulger Relationship

Further investigation is warranted regarding the payments made to Bulger through the Finnerty law firm accounts. In particular, the original sources of those funds should be identified and the true purpose through those payments should be ascertained including the precise nature of services provided in return for those payments. Identifying the source of those payments and ascertaining the person or persons having knowledge of those transactions will require the use of grand jury subpoenas for records and documents to trace the original source of those funds and obtain the testimony of persons having knowledge of those transactions.

FBI INTERVIEW WITH MASSACHUSETTS STATE SENATE PRESIDENT WILLIAM BULGER, FEBRUARY 28, 1989

> William M. Bulger, Senate President, Commonwealth of Massachusetts, was interviewed at the Boston law office of Mintz, Levin, Cohn, Ferris, Glovsky and Popeo, 1 Financial Center, Boston, Massachusetts. In attendance during the interview was Assistant United States Attorney (AUSA) Ralph Gants, AUSA Alexandra Leake, Attorney Robert Popeo, Attorney William Homans, and William Bulger, Jr. At the outset of the interview, Bulger was advised of the official identity of the interviewing individuals as well as to the nature of the interview. Thereafter, Bulger furnished the following information:
>
> Bulger advised that he and Thomas Finnerty grew up together in South Boston, Massachusetts. Bulger advised that he and Finnerty were close friends since early childhood. They both went to high school together and attended college together. Bulger advised that Finnerty was a 1960 graduate of the Boston College Law School and that he graduated in 1961.
>
> Bulger advised that he and Finnerty formed a law partnership in either

1962 or 1963. Bulger advised that at that time, he had been elected as a State Representative. Bulger advised that the partnership lasted for approximately thirteen years until Finnerty was elected District Attorney for the County of Plymouth. Bulger advised that there was never a partnership agreement in writing between he and Finnerty.

In regards to billings for the above law practice, Bulger advised that they split the profits during this period of the partnership. When Bulger left his partnership with Finnerty he became "of counsel" with Finnerty. Bulger advised that this required him to bring in his own law business and that Bulger would only be paid for the amount of work he generated. He advised that his arrangement with Finnerty was an oral agreement. Bulger advised that he was not salaried by Finnerty's office during that period of time. Bulger was not required to cover any of the office overhead expense incurred by Finnerty. If Bulger brought in any clients which were not represented by him, during this period of time, he would receive a percentage of the income derived from the clients. Bulger could not be any more specific regarding this agreement.

Bulger advised that he performed legal services for Robert and Bruce Quirk in their civil suit against Data Terminal Systems, Incorporated. This suit involved the ownership of property in Maynard, Massachusetts. Bulger advised that this particular client was brought to him by Richard McDonough who is an associate of Bulger's. Bulger advised that he personally dealt with the matters regarding this civil case. Bulger advised that Finnerty did assist for a short period of time regarding this case. Bulger advised that James W. McDonough Jr., an associate of Finnerty's law firm, also assisted in the work done on this case. Bulger advised that James McDonough accompanied him to all court appearances in regard to this case. Bulger advised that he does not keep records regarding the time he spent on this matter but feels that the fee that he charged the Quirk's [sic] was fair for the effort put forth on their behalf by him. Bulger advised that he billed the Quirk's [sic] on a sense of what was fair and had no documentation to support the charge.

Bulger advised that he was very instrumental in the negotiations which settled the above case. Bulger attributed most of his work in regards to this case to the negotiations that he handled. He advised that the period of time that he worked on this case was considerable and that he was entitled to receive the fee which he charged the Quirk's [sic].

Bulger advised that Thomas Finnerty was aware of the fee that Bulger would be receiving from the Quirk's [sic] in regards to this case. Bulger knew prior to his vacation to Europe in the Summer of 1985 the amount of money that Quirk's [sic] would be paying him for services rendered. Bulger

knew that he would be receiving $267,000. Bulger advised that he expected
to get the entire $267,000 and there were no objections by anyone either as-
sociated with Finnerty's firm or by Thomas Finnerty about Bulger receiving the entire amount. Bulger felt that he was providing 90% of the effort
that went into this case resolution and felt that he was entitled to the entire
amount. Bulger advised that the $267,000 was paid by the Quirk's [sic] to the
law firm of Thomas Finnerty. It was anticipated by both he and Finnerty
that this amount would be received by the end of the year, 1985. Bulger advised that there was some discussion between he and Finnerty in regards
to Bulger receiving 100% of this fee. Finnerty did not think it was fair
and Bulger did. In any event, Bulger advised that it was resolved that he
would receive the entire $267,000.

Bulger advised that sometime in 1986, Richard McDonough requested
$70,000 for his referral of the Quirk's [sic] to William Bulger. Bulger advised
that it was his feeling that McDonough did deserve some fee but this
amount was exorbitant. Bulger recalled telling Finnerty that although he
did not think it was fair to pay Richard McDonough $70,000 that he thought
the firm should in order to make McDonough go away. Bulger advised that
he and Finnerty decided to pay this amount to McDonough and that fee
would be allocated to the firm's office expenses. Bulger advised that
McDonough's claim for this $70,000 was not made until after the $267,000
in fees had been collected from the Quirk's [sic]. Bulger advised that he certainly absorbed some of the $70,000 paid to McDonough because the
McDonough charge was partially taken from incoming fees he expected
from other clients during 1986.

Bulger advised that he had many shared investments with Thomas
Finnerty. He advised Thomas Finnerty was not his financial advisor but that
he followed Thomas Finnerty's lead on many investment opportunities. In
regards to investments jointly made by Thomas Finnerty, Bulger advised
that his first investment was in land purchased in the 1960s at the Fort Banks
area of Winthrop, Massachusetts.

Bulger recalled a second investment that Finnerty involved him in with
the purchase of a share in a limited partnership in American Cable Systems
Midwest in 1985. Bulger thought that Finnerty made this investment on his
behalf while Bulger was vacationing. Bulger advised that Finnerty had
Bulger's permission to invest on Bulger's behalf if any investment opportunity looked promising and Bulger was not available to authorize it. Bulger
could not recall ever objecting to any investment made by Thomas Finnerty
on his behalf. Bulger stated that it was common for Finnerty to put up the
initial investment funds and then to be repaid later by Bulger. Bulger advised that he had a "sense" there were other investments with which he was

involved with Thomas Finnerty around this same period of time. Bulger could not be more specific regarding these investments.

Bulger advised that Finnerty brought to him the investment opportunity of purchasing a building on Mount Vernon Street in the Columbia Point area of Boston. Bulger's recollection was that Finnerty brought this deal to him just prior to the actual closing date on the property in June, 1986. Finnerty put all the required money down on the purchase of this property and Bulger eventually repaid Finnerty with money Bulger and Finnerty had borrowed jointly from the South Boston Savings Bank (SBSB). Bulger and Finnerty borrowed $100,000 from the SBSB with the intention of using the proceeds to invest or purchase stock in Boston Telecommunications Group, Inc. Bulger eventually changed his mind regarding the above investment and decided to put the loan proceeds towards the joint purchase of the Mount Vernon Street property.

Bulger advised that he does not possess a great deal of knowledge regarding the Mount Vernon Realty Trust (MVRT). Bulger explained that Finnerty established the MVRT and Bulger does not even know if he (Bulger) is a beneficiary of this trust. Bulger advised that he has never seen any trust documents regarding the MVRT. Bulger only knows that he is a 50% owner of the property located on Mount Vernon Street.

Bulger advised that the purchase price on the Mount Vernon property was $190,000. $90,000 of the $190,000 was back taxes due to the City of Boston. Bulger did not participate in negotiating the purchase price of this property. Bulger did recall being told by Finnerty that the back taxes could be paid in installments to the City of Boston. Bulger advised that he is still confused on how he paid for his share of ownership in this property but that he paid Finnerty $50,000 within thirty days of the closing date on the above property. Bulger also recalls that he has made installment payments to Finnerty and the St. Botolph Realty Trust regarding the back taxes owed on the above property. Bulger assumes Finnerty paid the real estate taxes from this account.

Bulger reiterated that he depended on Thomas Finnerty to involve him in the above investments and that it was not unusual for Bulger to repay Finnerty for the investment at a later time after the purchase had been made. Bulger cannot recall ever extending any loans to Thomas Finnerty or receiving any loans from Thomas Finnerty other than for the short period of times [sic] for investment purposes.

In regards to Harold Brown, Bulger advised that he has no recollection of ever meeting Harold Brown and has had no financial dealings with him.

Bulger recalled that the first time Thomas Finnerty ever mentioned Harold Brown to him was when Finnerty mentioned he was having a business disagreement with Brown. Bulger believes that Finnerty mentioned this in late 1984 or early 1985. Finnerty also mentioned that the disagreement was over the Kilby Street Development [another name for 75 State Street]. At the time of Finnerty's first mention of Harold Brown, Finnerty never disclosed to Bulger his business relationship with Brown or any terms of any agreement between Finnerty and Brown. The only knowledge that Bulger had of Harold Brown at that time was that Brown had a bad reputation as a large landlord in the City of Boston.

Bulger recalled being told by Finnerty at a later time that Finnerty was having some dealings with the Beacon Companies in regards to the Kilby Street Development. It is Bulger's recollection that at some point Finnerty said he had worked out his disagreement with Brown and that Finnerty was currently attempting to define his ownership interest in the Kilby Street Development. Finnerty also mentioned that he would be selling his interest to the Beacon Companies. Finnerty described this interest as an asset.

Sometime during the Summer of 1985, Finnerty mentioned to Bulger that he had received $500,000 from Beacon Companies as a buy out of Finnerty's interest in the Kilby Street Development. Bulger said he was told this by Finnerty because Finnerty was just sharing his good news.

Subsequent to Finnerty receiving this $500,000, Finnerty told Bulger that he had ideas about how both of them could benefit through various investments. Bulger recalled that it was Finnerty's suggestion that the both of them invest in tax free bonds through the Fidelity Fund. Bulger surmised that Finnerty's suggestion regarding these investments were [sic] made in light of Finnerty just receiving the $500,000 and Finnerty's knowledge that Bulger would be receiving $267,000 for his legal work regarding the Quirk case. Sometime after this discussion, Bulger borrowed money from Finnerty in order to place it in the Fidelity Tax Free Bond Account. Bulger borrowed $225,000 from Finnerty in August, 1985, in the form of a check drawn on Finnerty's St. Botolph Realty Trust Account at the Bank of Boston. Bulger said there was no written documentation regarding this loan and Bulger borrowed it with the understanding that it would be repaid after Bulger received the Quirk legal fee. At the time that Bulger received the $225,000, he did not know the source from which the funds originated other than it came from Finnerty's account. Bulger said that the St. Botolph Realty Trust was Finnerty's account and he had no knowledge at that time regarding the details of the trust including who the beneficiaries were.

Bulger advised that in October, 1985, he borrowed another $15,000 from Finnerty for an investment opportunity. Bulger could not recall what investment the $15,000 was used for by him. He believes that it might possibly have been used to purchase stock in the South Boston Saving[s] Bank.

Bulger advised that his real reason for taking the loans from Finnerty was to insure that he got the money in hand that he expected the Quirk's [sic] to remit to the law firm of Thomas Finnerty. Bulger said that his logic for taking the advance was the fact that he would be in Europe and if anything ever happened to him this money would already have been put in his accounts and not retrievable by Finnerty or anyone else. He assumed that Finnerty would use the Quirk fee as repayment of Bulger's loan if anything ever happened to Bulger.

Bulger advised that sometime around this period of time and after he had learned that Harold Brown had been indicted by the Federal Grand Jury in Boston, Massachusetts, Finnerty disclosed to him that the source of the St. Botolph Realty Trust Funds, which Bulger had borrowed from Finnerty, was from Harold Brown. Finnerty did not go into any great detail regarding Finnerty's association with Brown but it was clear that the $500,000 had come from Brown in some indirect fashion. Bulger did not think he should be anywhere near or associated with Brown because of Brown's reputation and in order to disassociate himself from Brown, Bulger decided to repay Finnerty the money he had borrowed. Bulger advised that he repaid the loans by issuing checks to the St. Botolph Realty Trust from his Fidelity Account. This repayment was done out of the principal borrowed plus interest after Bulger conferred with his Certified Public Accountant, Lee Hyler, who was responsible for calculating Bulger's debt on the loan. Hyler assisted Bulger in determining the means Bulger would use to repay the loan and what assets of Bulger's would have to be liquidated in order to make repayment. Bulger reiterated that he never received much in the way of detail from Finnerty regarding Finnerty's interest or Finnerty's receipt of money from the Kilby Street Development. Bulger could not recall specifics as to what Finnerty's role was in the development.

Bulger's only knowledge regarding Edward McCormack and McCormack's involvement with the Kilby Street Development was that McCormack represented Finnerty as his lawyer. This representation was needed by Finnerty in order to insure that he received his payment from Brown for the Kilby Street Development.

Bulger advised that he is familiar with name [sic] Graham Gund because of Gund's architectural work. Bulger does not recall ever speaking with Gund and has had no business dealings with Gund. Bulger advised that Finnerty has mentioned Gund by name but Bulger had no specifics as to why his name was mentioned by Finnerty. Bulger had no information or knowledge regarding Gund's role in the Kilby Street Development.

Bulger advised that Thomas Finnerty has sworn to him that Finnerty has never used Bulger's name in order to influence individuals who were dealing with Finnerty. Bulger advised that the first time that he ever heard that his name was used by Finnerty was in documentation filed by Harold Brown in his civil suit with Finnerty on October 27, 1988. Again, Bulger advised that Finnerty has denied he ever used Bulger's name to influence anyone.

Bulger advised that in regards to the St. Botolph Realty Trust, that he has never been a beneficiary of that trust. He advised that he has never seen any documentation regarding the realty trust. Finnerty has told him that Finnerty is the sole beneficiary of the trust and Finnerty has never disclosed who was on the Schedule of Beneficiaries regarding the trust. Bulger reiterated that the St. Botolph Realty Trust was a separate trust owned by Finnerty and used solely by Finnerty.

The 1991 law enforcement memorandum, prepared by then Massachusetts Assistant Attorney General David Burns, became the basis for a March 2000 story in the *Boston Globe*. The article examined discrepancies in William Bulger's public account of his share of money from 75 State Street. It was disputed by Bulger and by his lawyer, R. Robert Popeo, who also represents FBI agent John Connolly. Neither addressed the story's content but rather criticized the authors and the *Globe*. Popeo asserted: "What you have here is a recycled old news story by two *Globe* reporters who are hyping a book." A statement issued by the University of Massachusetts for president Bulger stated in part: "Periodically, the *Globe* likes to reconvene its Star Chamber regarding this matter. We may have entered a new century but some things never change at Morrissey Boulevard."

CHAPTER 15: CONNOLLY TALK

For the sections about the Vanessa's bugging operation, we relied on the sworn testimony at the Wolf hearings of Stephen Flemmi, August 20, 1998; Jim Ring, June 6, 9, 11, and 15, 1998; and FBI agent Rick Carter, August 17, 1998; government documents and FBI reports either in the authors' possession or released as part of the Wolf hearings as exhibits 15–18, 61, 116–120, 123, 128–130, 153, 165, 175, 207, and 237; a firsthand encounter between John Connolly and the *Boston Globe*'s Dick Lehr on February 8, 1988; a *Globe* article by Lehr and Kevin Cullen, April 17, 1988; numerous articles in the *Globe* archives reporting on Harry "Doc" Sagansky's life and the content of the taped exchange between Sagansky and the Mafia; Connolly's 1998 interviews with the *Globe*, WBZ-AM Radio, WRKO-AM Radio, *Boston* magazine, and the *Boston Tab*; Wolf, "Memorandum and Order."

For the section on the FBI bugging of the Mafia induction ceremony on October 29, 1989, we relied on the sworn testimony at the Wolf hearings of Stephen Flemmi, September 1, 1998; government documents and FBI reports released as part of the Wolf hearings as exhibits 190–194; and a case that included extensive transcripts of the taped ceremony, *United States v Nicholas L. Bianco et al.*

For the section on the meeting between Connolly and Brendan Bradley of the Boston Police Department about the murder of Tim Baldwin, we relied on internal government reports prepared between 1992 and 1998 as part of an inquiry into possible misconduct by Connolly; these reports covered FBI and DEA interviews with Bradley, Boston police officer Frank Dewan, and attorneys James Hamrock and John Kiernan.

For the section on John Morris leaking the Baharoian wiretap to Flemmi and Bulger, we relied on the sworn testimony at the Wolf hearings of John Morris, April 22, 23, 28, 29, and 30, 1998; Stephen Flemmi, August 20, 1998; government documents and FBI reports released as part of the Wolf hearings as exhibits 93 and 229; and *Globe* articles about Baharoian and Puleo.

It is interesting to note that Judge Wolf found that at the time Bulger and Flemmi gave the FBI information about Vanessa's "the LCN in Boston was diminished and in disarray. This created a vacuum which, according to their plan, Flemmi and Bulger sought to fill by expanding their own criminal activities." The FBI's focus on prosecuting the Boston Mafia, the judge ruled, "provided an opportunity for Bulger and Flemmi to take over criminal activities in Boston that had previously been controlled by the LCN. With the protection of the FBI, Bulger and Flemmi could operate very profitably" ("Memorandum and Order," p. 260).

In the month following the 1989 FBI bugging of the Mafia initiation ceremony in Medford, Massachusetts, a number of Mafia figures were arrested on charges of extorting Sagansky, including Ferrara, Russo, and Carrozza. Mercurio was charged but fled and avoided arrest. Eventually the mafiosi were convicted of this and other charges in federal court and sent to prison.

It is also worth noting that no known action resulted from the internal inquiry the Boston FBI conducted in 1992 into John Connolly's meeting in 1986 with Brendan Bradley of the Boston Police Department. In February 1992 the special agent in charge of the Boston office, Tom Hughes, notified the investigating agent, John Gamel, that he was concerned that the inquiry into possible misconduct was against a retired agent (Connolly retired in December 1990) and that the "statute of limitations may have run." After conducting the interviews, Gamel submitted his report to Hughes on February 24, 1992, and that was the apparent end of the matter. In July 1997 FBI agents questioned Bradley again as part of an Office of Professional Responsibility inquiry into Connolly's activities. Bradley was scheduled to testify at the Wolf hearing during 1998, but he was one of a number of witnesses who were dropped after the judge urged both sides to trim the witness list. In an interview with a DEA agent in May 1998, in anticipation of his court appearance, Bradley apparently pulled back from what he'd reportedly told investigators originally in 1992 and 1997. In 1998 Bradley told the agent that he thought Connolly was just trying to put in a "good word" for a family friend, not trying to squash a subpoena. This change occurred just when Bradley was embroiled in a dispute with his own department. He was facing departmental charges after he was picked up during a department sting involving prostitution in Boston. Bradley said he had done nothing wrong; he resigned from the police department before his case was ever adjudicated. Finally, Mark Estes, the man whom police believed murdered Tim Baldwin outside Triple O's in 1986, was himself fatally shot early in the morning of June 12, 1995, on a South Boston street.

During a brief interview in January 2000, Connolly denied ever meeting Bradley for coffee to discuss the O'Neil subpoena. "That's an abject lie, like so many of the other nonsensical fabrications in this whole matter."

It is also worth noting that earlier in the FBI investigation of bookmaker John Baharoian and Boston police corruption—well before Morris leaked news of a wiretap in early 1988—the FBI had already done Bulger and Flemmi a big favor. A Boston police lieutenant, cooperating with federal investigators, was wearing a wire to obtain incriminating statements by Baharoian and others. Flemmi was also a target. The FBI tipped off Bulger about the body wire, and Bulger warned Flemmi. "He [Bulger] told me that I was targeted by Lieutenant Cox," Flemmi testified on August 20, 1998, "and he was going to be approaching me at some point." Flemmi testified that the tip to Bulger came from either Morris or Jim Ring. (Ring strongly denied leaking the information.) Flemmi testified that Bulger and Connolly talked about the wire and that he also later discussed the situation with John Connolly. On September 5, 1986, the police lieutenant taped a conversation he had with Flemmi, but Flemmi knew not to say anything beyond small talk. "We was pre-warned, forewarned." Flemmi testified that later Connolly happily told him that he'd heard at the office that the tape was "unproductive." (In an example of how many of these events overlapped, Flemmi was tipped off about the wired-up police lieutenant around the same time that Connolly was calling Bradley of the Boston police to meet about the subpoena to Kevin O'Neil and just as Flemmi was giving information about Vanessa's.)

In his September 1999 findings of fact, Judge Wolf ruled that Connolly—not Ring or Morris—was the agent leaking information about the Cox wire to Bulger and Flemmi. "Connolly had asked Morris, and perhaps others, whether Cox was 'wired.' The court infers that Connolly is the person who told Bulger and Flemmi that Cox was cooperating with the FBI" (p. 297).

Furthermore, the judge ruled, Connolly then tried to cover his tracks by filing false paperwork. At the time Connolly filed an informant "insert" reporting that Flemmi had learned about the Cox wire from a leak at the Boston Police Department. "The court concludes that this insert is another document containing false information in an effort to make it more difficult to discern and demonstrate improper conduct by Connolly" (p. 298).

CHAPTER 16: SECRETS EXPOSED

For the section on the souring relations between Morris and Connolly, we relied on the sworn testimony at the Wolf hearings of John Morris, April 27, 1998; 1998 media interviews by John Connolly; Wolf, "Memorandum and Order."

For the section on the *Globe*'s September 1988 article about Bulger and the FBI, *Globe* interviews with Dennis Condon, Jeremiah T. O'Sullivan, Tom Daly, and Jim Ahearn. During the Wolf hearings, Morris testified extensively about his role in the story (April 27, 28, and 29, 1998). In 1998 Robert Fitzpatrick granted the authors permission to identify him as the second FBI source for the story. We also relied on government documents and FBI reports released during the Wolf hearings as exhibits 42, 85, and 159. The exchange between an undercover DEA agent and dealer Tom Cahill came from a DEA sworn affidavit by DEA agent Bonnie Alexander dated January 17, 1990, and from another sworn Boston police affidavit in February 1989.

For the section on Sue and Joe Murray and the FBI, we relied on the sworn testimony at the Wolf hearings of William Weld, May 22, 1998; and FBI agent Ed Clark, June 3, 1998; government documents and FBI reports released during the Wolf hearings as exhibits 147–152, 156, 157, 159, 160.

For the section on Bulger's trouble at Logan Airport, we relied on the document released during the Wolf hearings as exhibit 154; a *Globe* interview with trooper William Johnson on July 27, 1988; and numerous *Globe* and *Herald* articles about Johnson. Regarding the attendance of two retired New York FBI agents at a dinner at Gianturco's house, we relied on the sworn testimony at the Wolf hearings of Nick Gianturco, January 15 and April 20, 1998; and reports by the Office of Professional Responsibility of July 1997 interviews with Pistone and Bonavolonta. Regarding the Boston FBI office purchase of Christmas party liquor at Bulger's liquor mart, we relied on our own interviews and reporting for a *Globe* article on that subject published in October 1990.

Jim Ahearn's attack on the DEA and defense of Connolly and Bulger were contained in a letter he wrote to FBI director William Sessions on February 10, 1989 (released during the Wolf hearings as exhibit 126).

In his September 1999 findings of fact, Judge Wolf noted that the Boston FBI office essentially swept Joe Murray's information under the rug. Murray's information "implicating Bulger and Flemmi in the Halloran and Barrett murders was not provided to any agents responsible for investigating those matters or indexed so that it could be accessed by such agents. . . . Accordingly, Murray was effectively eliminated as a threat to the symbiotic relationship between the FBI and Bulger and Flemmi" (p. 296). The judge said that even though the FBI characterized Murray's charge that Connolly and John Newton leaked information as "unsubstantiated . . . [t]he evidence presented in the instant case, however, demonstrates that Murray's claim was correct" (p. 292).

Trooper Billy Johnson's career and life spiraled downward in the years following his run-in at Logan Airport with Whitey Bulger. In interviews Johnson blamed Bulger and his politician brother Billy for many of his troubles. Billy Bulger declined comment in articles written about Johnson. But following the incident, airport officials were out to get Johnson's report, which Johnson viewed as political meddling and payback. Johnson, a Green Beret veteran of Vietnam and decorated state trooper who twice was awarded the Medal of Merit and the Trooper of the Year Award, spoke his mind. Eventually he was reassigned from his plainclothes, anti-drug work inside the terminals to cruising the airport parking lots. Johnson had run-ins with superiors, and he was court-martialed, suspended, and then transferred from Logan. He retired early, a broken man. In the woods of southern New Hampshire, at the age of fifty, he shot and killed himself on September 25, 1998. "Exactly 11 years ago, Billy Johnson's sense of purpose became entangled in the political riptide of the state police," wrote columnist Peter Gelzinis in the *Boston Herald* on September 29, 1988, referring to the Logan run-in with Bulger as the beginning of the end of Johnson's distinguished career. "Outside the Delta terminal, he encountered the foul-mouthed czar of all local thugs, James J. 'Whitey' Bulger."

The book that retired New York FBI agent Jules Bonavolonta eventually wrote, with Brian Duffy, is entitled *The Good Guys: How We Turned the FBI 'Round and Finally Broke the Mob* (New York: Simon & Schuster, 1996).

It is worth noting that although Jim Ahearn was shocked and angered about being formally notified of a DEA drug probe of Bulger that had been under way since 1987, the investigation was old news to Connolly, Bulger, and Flemmi. Flemmi testified that the three had been trading notes and information for some time—just as they did in a number of other investigations targeting the gangsters. In testimony Flemmi gave on August 20, 1998, he was asked, "Do you remember having a conversation with Mr. Connolly that related to the DEA investigation?"

FLEMMI: Jim Bulger and I were both present when we discussed that.

QUESTIONER: What was the discussion that you had?

FLEMMI: The ongoing DEA investigation.

QUESTIONER: Did he confirm that there was an investigation?

FLEMMI: No doubt about that.

QUESTIONER: What did Mr. Connolly say?

FLEMMI: He said the investigation was ongoing, Your Honor.

CHAPTER 17: FRED WYSHAK

Interviews: Several federal and state prosecutors and Massachusetts State Police officials about assistant U.S. attorneys Fred Wyshak and Brian Kelly; former U.S. attorney A. John Pappalardo about his handling of FBI informant Timothy Connolly; former head of the Massachusetts State Police Charles Henderson on the strategy for targeting James Bulger and Stephen Flemmi.

Court records: A 1995 court affidavit by FBI agent Edward Quinn on 98 Prince Street tapes concerning the activities of James Bulger and Stephen Flemmi; the government's post-hearing brief in opposition to defendant's motion to dismiss indictments and to suppress electronic surveillance evidence, January 29, 1999; *United States v Kevin P. Weeks and Kevin P. O'Neil;* affidavit of Thomas B. Duffy in support of pretrial detention of the defendants Kevin P. Weeks and Kevin P. O'Neil, submitted in November 1999 (see pp. 44–48 for details on the secretly recorded conversation between Weeks and Timothy Connolly about his prospective testimony before a federal grand jury); Suffolk County Registry of Deeds, mortgages on Thomas Cahill's South Boston property from 1986 to 1994, and the trusts and transactions involved in Stephen Flemmi's 1992 acquisition of $1.5 million in property; Wolf, "Memorandum and Order."

Judge Wolf addressed the warning given to James Bulger about Timothy Connolly: "[I]n 1988 or 1989, [John] Connolly told Bulger that Timothy Connolly, who is alleged to have been a victim of extortion in the instant case, was cooperating with the FBI and would attempt to record conversations with Bulger and Flemmi. Bulger shared this warning with Flemmi" ("Memorandum and Order," p. 310).

News articles: Boston Globe and *Boston Herald* articles in 1991 and 1995 on Bulger's share of a $14.3 million lottery ticket; *Globe* and *Herald* articles in 1991, 1992, 1997, and 1998 on the 1989 induction of new Mafia members that was secretly recorded by the FBI; *Globe* and *Herald* articles in 1990 about the arrest of fifty-one men in South Boston on drug charges; a 1993 *Globe* article on Flemmi's purchase of residential property in and around Boston; *Globe* and *Herald* articles in 1993 and 1994 on Howie Winter's conviction on cocaine charges; *Newark Star Ledger* articles in 1990 on the successful prosecution of Mafia boss John Riggi.

CHAPTER 18: HELLER'S CAFÉ
Interviews: Former federal prosecutor Michael Kendall about the Michael London case; former Massachusetts State Police detective Joseph Saccardo about the surveillance and investigation of Heller's Café; former head of the Massachusetts State Police Charles Henderson on strategy and cases against Burton "Chico" Krantz; criminal defense attorney Robert Sheketoff on the use of money-laundering charges against bookmakers; several background interviews with Massachusetts State Police and DEA investigators and FBI agents for a 1995 *Boston Globe* article about the arrest of Stephen Flemmi; federal courthouse sources about the split between Stephen Flemmi and Frank Salemme.

News articles: A 1995 *Boston Globe* article on how the Bulger and Flemmi investigation came together from 1991 to 1995 and how it came to focus on the extortion of bookmakers; *Globe* and *Herald* articles in 1993, 1994, and 1995 on the indictment, arrest, and conviction of Joseph Yerardi; *Globe* and *Herald* articles in 1991, 1992, 1993, and 1994 on the state and federal prosecutions of Burton Krantz, James Katz, and George Kaufman; *Globe* and *Herald* articles in 1993 and 1994 in which FBI officials and unnamed officials gave updates on the case building against James Bulger; *Globe* and *Herald* articles on the indictment, escape, and arrest of Frank Salemme.

Court records: The sworn testimony at the Wolf hearings of Stephen Flemmi, August 20, 21, 24, 25, and 28, and September 1, 1998 (including his account of how Paul Rico arranged for attempted murder charges to be dropped when Flemmi returned from hiding in 1974); John Morris, April, 28, 29, and 30, 1998; and Theresa Stanley, September 17 and 18, 1998; the federal indictments in 1994, 1995, and 1996 against Robert DeLuca, James Bulger, Stephen Flemmi, and Frank Salemme; the court filings in the 1993 federal conviction of Michael London; the 1992 conviction of Vincent Ferrara and others; the 1991 Massachusetts and 1993 federal prosecution of Burton Krantz, James Katz, Vincent Roberto, and others; the 1992 federal indictment of Krantz and Katz and others on money-laundering charges; the 1994 testimony in federal court by state police sergeant Thomas Foley as part of the government's opposition to having Krantz's lawyer, Richard Egbert, represent other defendants in the same and related cases; Wolf, "Memorandum and Order."

Judge Wolf addressed John Connolly's reliance on FBI contacts for information about the grand jury investigation of Bulger and Flemmi.

> Finally, as indicated earlier, members of the Organized Crime Squad kept Connolly advised of at least some developments in the investigation of Flemmi and Bulger that was initiated after Connolly retired. Connolly used that information to honor his promise to protect Bulger and Flemmi. . . . While the United States Attorney could not obtain information that he was seeking from the FBI, Connolly, who was no longer employed by the Bureau, was able to monitor the progress of the grand jury investigation and keep Bulger and Flemmi advised concerning it. . . . Connolly's enduring relationship with members of the Organized Crime squad gave him access to some information concerning the ongoing investigation of Bulger and Flemmi. As explained below, that information was at times not complete or fully reliable. However, Connolly used the information that he received to honor his promise to protect the sources who had contributed so much to his success. (pp. 26–27, 392–93)

We also relied on Massachusetts criminal offender records for bookmakers

Burton Krantz, James Katz, Joseph Yerardi, Richard Brown, Howard Levenson, Edward Lewis, and Mitchell Zuckoff; and the Plymouth County Registry of Deeds on mortgage and foreclosure documents from 1991 to 1994 on property owned by Paul E. and Donna Moore at 1722 State Rd., Plymouth.

CHAPTER 19: IN FOR A PENNY, IN FOR A POUND

Main sources: The sworn testimony at the Wolf hearings of Stephen Flemmi, August 21 and 24, 1998; interviews with Anthony M. Cardinale in 1997 and 1999; interviews with Kenneth M. Fishman in 1998 and 1999; tour and 1999 interviews at the Plymouth County Correctional Facility; Wolf, "Memorandum and Order"; defense and government motions, memorandums of law, and affidavits filed in *United States v Frank Salemme et al.* on March 27, April 9 and 10, and June 3 and 25, 1997; and orders and rulings made by Judge Mark L. Wolf on April 14, 21, and 24, and May 22, 1997. It should be noted that the early 1997 motions and rulings were sealed from public view at the time of their filing, but Judge Wolf eventually ordered them unsealed.

It is an interesting coincidence that on the same day Cardinale filed his motions, March 21, 1997, two agents of the Boston FBI office interviewed John Connolly about Bulger and his possible whereabouts. The agents were Connolly's old friend Nick Gianturco and Walter Steffens. Connolly told the agents the story of Bulger buying him an ice cream cone when he was a boy. He said he hoped that "Bulger was never caught." He mentioned the infamous party at Morris's house in April 1985 at which Morris told Bulger and Flemmi they could commit any crime short of murder. Connolly also told the agents he knew about Bulger's telephone threat to John Morris, a fact that was not public.

One of the agents, Steffens, was shocked by Connolly's remark about hoping Bulger was never caught. He was further shocked by the omission of that telling quote by Connolly from the report that Gianturco prepared about the interview. Gianturco's report—which he did not file until May 7, 1997, or more than a month later—was flawed in other ways as well. He failed to include Connolly quoting Morris's remark at the dinner party but did include the false statement that Connolly "has not seen or heard from Bulger since December of 1989."

CHAPTER 20: THE PARTY'S OVER

Main sources: The sworn testimony at the Wolf hearings of Stephen Flemmi, August 20, 21, 25, 26, 27, and 28, and September 2, 1998; John Morris, April 28, 29, and 30, 1998; Jim Ring, June 5, 1998; Dennis Condon, May 1, 4, and 5, 1998; Robert Fitzpatrick, April 16 and 17, 1998; Theresa Stanley, September 16, 1998; Debbie Morris, September 22, 1998; and John Connolly, October 30, 1998; exchanges during court sessions between Judge Wolf and prosecutor Fred Wyshak, January 8, April

23, June 5, August 24, and September 15, 1998; interviews with Anthony M. Cardinale in 1997, 1998, and 1999; interviews with Kenneth M. Fishman in 1998 and 1999; tour and 1999 interviews at the Plymouth County Correctional Facility; Wolf, "Memorandum and Order."

News articles: Boston Globe articles and columns about Bulger, the FBI, and the hearings, December 30, 1997, January 4, 6, 7, and 8, April 23, May 1 and 3, June 11 and 14, and July 18 and 19, 1998; a five-part series by the *Globe's* Spotlight Team, July 19–23 and 24, August 4, September 7 and 29, and October 28 and 31, 1998, August 20, September 9, 10, and 16, 1999; *Boston Herald* articles and columns about the hearings, December 30, 1997, January 6, 7, and 8, March 25, April 17, May 1, and October 31, 1998, August 5, and September 16, 1999; Christopher Lydon, interview with William Weld, *The Connection*, WBUR-FM, October 7, 1998; John Connolly 1998 interviews with the *Globe*, the *Boston Tab*, *Boston* magazine; WBZ-AM Radio, and WRKO-AM Radio.

EPILOGUE

Main sources: Wolf, "Memorandum and Order"; *United States v John J. Connolly Jr., James Bulger aka "Whitey," and Stephen Flemmi; United States v Kevin P. Weeks and Kevin P. O'Neil.*

News articles: on John Martorano's plea, Frank Salemme's plea and the indictment of Kevin Weeks and Kevin O'Neil, and the recovery of three bodies, we relied on articles in the *Boston Globe*, September 9, October 10, November 18, 19, and 22, and December 10, 1999, January 16, and February 23, 2000; and in *the Boston Herald,* November 19, 1999.

Acknowledgments

The *Boston Globe* gave us a leave of absence to write *Black Mass: The Irish Mob, the FBI, and a Devil's Deal,* and we want to thank a number of *Globe* publishers, editors, and colleagues who, along the way, extended a helping hand.

Publishers William O. Taylor and Ben Taylor and editors Tom Winship, Jack Driscoll, and Matt Storin have all been supportive of our coverage of the Bulger-FBI story, reporting that now dates back more than a decade. Kevin Cullen helped get us started in 1988, and we teamed up afterward on a number of Bulger-FBI stories. It's always a pleasure to work with him. Christine Chinlund played a crucial role in the 1988 series that first reported Whitey Bulger was an informant for the FBI. Researcher Mary Beth Knox was helpful in the early work, as well.

We'd also like to thank Mitch Zuckoff. He worked with us on a 1998 *Globe* series probing deeper into Bulger's ties to the FBI, and then provided invaluable assistance throughout the writing of this book in 1999. He found the time to listen to our ideas as we developed the book's outline and themes, and most important, he read the first drafts of our chapters as we wrote them. His suggestions were always helpful.

Ben Bradlee, Jr., the *Globe*'s deputy managing editor for projects, edited the 1998

Globe series on Bulger and the FBI. It turns out that a member of the Bradlee family has had a hand in this story on two fronts—first at the newspaper and now at our publishing house. PublicAffairs was founded by Peter Osnos in tribute to Benjamin C. Bradlee and two other leading figures in American publishing and journalism, Robert L. Bernstein, the longtime chief executive of Random House and founder of Human Rights Watch, and the journalist I. F. Stone. Stone, for one, had plenty to say about agencies such as the FBI. During a 1971 academic conference held at Princeton University—the basis for the book *Investigating the FBI*—Stone warned that the FBI's deeply rooted obsession with its public image has led it to resist tough outside scrutiny. The FBI, he noted, has "been engaging in brainwashing and self-glorification and this makes it difficult to control." The bureau's job, he added during a panel discussion, "is the investigation of crime, not indoctrination of the public."

We'd also like to acknowledge Brant Houston at Investigative Reporters and Editors (IRE) and Peg Lotito at the Fund for Investigative Journalism (FIJ). The FIJ supported us with a research grant that was essential in the writing of the book.

Mary C. Velasquez read the early chapters of this book as they were written, providing a jump-start that helped us get some momentum going. Reading the final draft, she found ways to improve the narrrative. She helped in many other ways too, and having her hand in all of this was indispensable.

A number of colleagues at the *Globe* deserve mention. Al Larkin was always supportive. Steve Kurkjian and Tim Leland are friends who got investigative reporting underway at the *Globe*. Tom Mulvoy and Mike Larkin are friends and fine editors who expedited and improved our work. We appreciate the reporting work about the Bulger case done by Shelley Murphy, Bill Doherty, and Patricia Nealon. Matt Carroll, Bob Yeager, and Sean Mullin provided guidance in managing our databases and software. John Tlumacki's knack for capturing photographs of Bulger was uncanny.

David Butler created a fine map of Boston. Stan Grossfeld advised us about the book cover. David Warsh showed us where the key to the writers' room at the *Globe* was hidden. Columnist David Nyhan has always been supportive and made it fun. Joan Anderman gave us some music. Linda Hunt helped us navigate the *Globe*'s bureaucracy, and Barbara McDonough and her colleagues at the *Globe*'s message center kept us in touch.

Head librarian Lisa Tuite was invaluable in organizing *Globe* and *Herald* news stories that frequently reached back two and three decades. The rest of the *Globe* library staff was always helpful in running down information. They are Wanda Joseph-Rollins, Jimmy Cawley, Richard Pennington, Kathleen Hennrikus, Donna Ritchie, Bill Boles, Betty Grillo, Charlie Smiley, Marc Shechtman, Christine Quarembo, and Rosemarie McDonald. If we have left someone out, we apologize.

There a number of people who, as friends or writing mentors, have shared their encouragement and wise counsel, either now or way back when: the late Richard T. O'Neill, who loved to talk about writing with his son, the late George V. Higgins, Harry Goldgar, the late Bill Alfred, John L'Heureux, Dominick Dunne, Howard O'Brien, Phil Bennett, Larry Tye, Wil Haygood, Jack Thomas, Maureen Dezell, Brian C. Mooney, Nick King, Bruce Butterfield, Jon Albano of Bingham Dana & Gould, Jonathan Tisch, Dave Holahan, Kyn Tolson, Mark Melady, Joel Lang, Donna DiNovelli, Dennie Williams, Andy Kreig, Tom Condon, Lincoln Millstein, Irene Driscoll, John F. and Kellie Lehr, Jr., and John and Nancy Lehr.

The late Bernadette Rossi Lehr cherished the written word and always urged patience so the work would turn out right.

A number of other journalists have for years pursued this story aggressively, each in his own style: namely, Christopher Lydon, first at WGBH-TV's *The 10 O'Clock News* and today at WBUR-FM's syndicated radio show *The Connection;* Howie Carr, Peter Gelzinis, Ralph Ranalli, and Jonathan Wells of the *Boston Herald;* and Edmund Mahony of the *Hartford Courant.* They all made significant contributions to the public's understanding of the involvement between the Boston FBI and the Bulgers.

We'd like to thank Esmond Harmsworth, Lane Zachary, and Todd Shuster of the Zachary Shuster Literary Agency for their representation and solid support, and we'd like to thank our editor and publisher at PublicAffairs, Geoff Shandler and Peter Osnos, for their strong backing. Shandler is a special editor with a keen eye. Gene Taft, PublicAffairs' director of publicity, who is originally from Boston, was the one who first read our series as it ran in the *Globe* in 1998 and brought it to his colleagues saying they should get us to write a book.

In many ways, without U.S. District Court Judge Mark L. Wolf, we wouldn't have had access to the material needed to flesh out a history of Bulger and the Boston FBI. The judge was responsible for holding court hearings that generated for public scrutiny FBI files that the bureau had expected to remain secret forever. Moreover, many participants who still refuse to be interviewed about this story were forced by court subpoena to answer questions under oath. Over time we already had accumulated many files, documents, records, and interviews on our own, but that testimony and the FBI files were vital in giving the story the scope, depth, and drama it warrants. The work of all the lawyers involved in the case before Judge Wolf also deserves acknowledgment. They have been at it for nearly a decade now, and their collective abilities in court and in their legal filings always impress: U.S. attorney Donald Stern and assistants Fred Wyshak, Brian Kelly, and James Herbert; and Anthony M. Cardinale, Kenneth J. Fishman, Martin G. Weinberg, Randolph Gioia, Kimberly Homan, and John Mitchell for the defense.

Finally, we want to acknowledge some of the state troopers, local police, and federal drug agents, most now in retirement, who were trying to do their jobs not knowing that the playing field had been fixed by the Boston FBI. We probably have missed a few people, and for that we apologize, but they include Robert Long, Rick Fraelick, Jack O'Malley, Charles Henderson, John O'Donovan, Joe Saccardo, Thomas Duffy, John Tutungian, and Tom Foley of the Massachusetts State Police; Jim Carr, Frank Dewan, and Ken Beers of the Boston Police Department; Richard Bergeron and the late Dave Rowell of the Quincy Police Department; Mike Huff of the Tulsa Police Department; and Al Reilly, Steve Boeri, and Daniel Doherty of the Drug Enforcement Administration.

Index